A FORK IN THE ROAD

Also by André Brink

The Ambassador
Looking on Darkness
An Instant in the Wind
Rumours of Rain
A Dry White Season
A Chain of Voices
The Wall of the Plague
States of Emergency
An Act of Terror
The First Life of Adamastor
On the Contrary
Imaginings of Sand
Devil's Valley
The Rights of Desire
The Other Side of Silence
Before I Forget
Praying Mantis
The Blue Door

Mapmakers (*essays*)
A Land Apart (*A South African Reader, with J. M. Coetzee*)
Reinventing a Continent (*essays*)

André Brink

A FORK IN THE ROAD

A Memoir

Harvill *Secker*

LONDON

Published by Harvill Secker 2009

2 4 6 8 10 9 7 5 3 1

First published in Great Britain in 2009 by
HARVILL SECKER
Random House, 20 Vauxhall Bridge Road
London SW1V 2SA

www.rbooks.co.uk

Addresses for companies within The Random House Group Limited
can be found at: www.randomhouse.co.uk/offices.htm

The Random House Group Limited Reg. No. 954009

A CIP catalogue record for this book
is available from the British Library

ISBN 9781846552441 (hardback)
ISBN 9781846552458 (trade paperback)

The Random House Group Limited supports
The Forest Stewardship Council (FSC), the leading international
forest certification organisation. All our titles that are printed on
Greenpeace approved FSC certified paper carry the FSC logo.
Our paper procurement policy can be found at www.rbooks.co.uk/environment

Typeset in Minion by Palimpsest Book Production Limited,
Grangemouth, Stirlingshire

Printed and bound in Great Britain by Clays Ltd, St Ives plc

To my wife Karina, with love

What I have done is yours; what I have to do is yours; being part in all I have, devoted yours

William Shakespeare

When you come to a fork in the road, take it

Yogi Berra

Even a heretic must believe in something, if nothing
more than the truth of his own doubt

Barack Obama

Grateful acknowledgment is made to the following for permission to reproduce the extracts listed below. The publishers have endeavoured to seek permission from all appropriate parties and will be happy to rectify any oversights for future editions of this work.

p. vii: from *Dreams From My Father* by Barack Obama, first published in Great Britain by Canongate Books Ltd, 14 High Street, Edinburgh, EH1 1TE

pp. 1–2: from an interview published in *William Kentridge: Flute*, edited by Bronwyn Law-Viljoen, published by David Krut Publishing, Johannesburg

p. 83: permission granted by Peter Louw for the author to quote and translate from 'Julle is die oorheersers' from the collection *Versamelde gedigte* by N.P. van Wyk Louw, co-published by Human & Rousseau and Tafelberg, Cape Town

p. 273: permission granted by Mrs E.H. Gili to quote from the essay 'The theory and function of the duende' from *Lorca: Selected Poems* by Federico García Lorca, translated and edited by J.L. Gili, published by Penguin, London

p. 330: from 'The Ninth Elegy' of *Duino Elegies* by Rainer Maria Rilke, translated by J.B. Leishman, published by Hogarth Press. Reprinted by permission of The Random House Group Ltd., London and Insel, Suhrkamp Verlag GmbH & Co., Frankfurt

p. 323: from 'Every day you play' translated by W.S. Merwin and p. 372 and p. 378: from 'I'm explaining a few things' translated by Nathaniel Tarn, both from *Selected Poetry* by Pablo Neruda, published by Jonathan Cape. Reprinted by permission of The Random House Group Ltd., London

p. 379: permission granted by Albie Sachs to reproduce an extract from his speech 'Preparing Ourselves for Freedom', quoted in *Exchanges*, edited by Duncan Brown and Bruno Van Dyk, published by University of Natal Press, Pietermaritzburg

p. 435: from *Soul on Ice* (first edition, 1969) by Eldridge Cleaver, published by McGraw-Hill, New York

CONTENTS

Foreword   1

Violent Villages   4

Words, Words, Words   28

Awakening to Black and White   41

The Play's the Thing   49

Ingrid   90

My Father's Cupboard   113

Political Stirrings   122

France   129

Cape of Storms and Good Hope   171

Black and White in Crisis   189

Sestigers, Censors and Security Police   207

Happy Returns   253

Back to France   256

Power in the Streets   275

Home Sweet Home   307

Option Clause   315

Writing the Deep Blue   321

The Pink Shoe   326

The Undiscover'd Country   331

Black and White After the Fall   345

The Ruins of Sarajevo   383

Salzburg: A State of Mind   390

Still Black and White   401

Postscript: A Letter to Karina   432

FOREWORD

CONVENTIONAL WISDOM HAS IT THAT EVERY CHOICE ONE MAKES IMPLIES THE elimination of others: at a given moment in the development of a painting the artist may have the choice of using, say, red, or blue, or green in a given spot. If he chooses to make it red, this choice eliminates the two other colours. One solution, often demonstrated by Picasso, may be, at this juncture, to make a series of paintings – one red, one blue, one green, and so on – and follow the unfolding of each of those options until the next moment of choice arrives, at which stage a new series opens: one exploring a round shape, the second a square, the third something else, once more following each possibility until the road forks again. But even if this leads to, say, 128, or 256 paintings, the choice is still finite. One cannot follow *every* possibility *all the way*. It is, after all, not a matter of following numerous choices, but leaving the whole notion of choice altogether open: to imagine *all* choices as coexisting, forever.

I am reminded of an interview with the artist William Kentridge at the time of his international production of Mozart's *Die Zauberflöte*:

Thought may follow one particular path, but there are all the other paths not taken, and all the other paths still being thought through, or not yet thought of, that language can latch on to at different stages as it goes.

1

He talks about:

> 'a highway of consciousness' where you have a channel but many different lanes and different things moving in different lanes, overtaking, stopping, leaving the highway.

This idea suggests something about the texture of this memoir. For me, in the writing of it over the last two or three years, each of the components has become a kind of cluster surrounding a set of possibilities, each of which may be thought of as a road or a path. At any moment new thoughts may split off from the one at present under consideration, and invite me to follow them; I know that in due course I will return to the path – but for the moment the other, or further possibilities prompted by any new turn, may lead to the exploration of other directions. And even if it seems bewildering at times, the path – or the paths – are there; and they exist for, and derive their meaning from, the forks that pose new challenges along the way.

What intrigues me is that one need not even choose between the two modes: the path that forks, and the possibility of endless forkings. One choice does *not* eliminate the others: all the others may well continue to exist, as possibilities, even *after* an initial decision has apparently been made. I may follow Frost in choosing the path less travelled by, but all the other, travelled, paths continue to exist around and behind the chosen one. Nothing is ever really eliminated. The choices *not* made continue to exist as surely as do the few that in fact can be said to have been 'chosen' – just as the unsaid word persists within the said. It may well be this coexistence that ultimately (inasmuch as there ever is an 'ultimate') defines the *texture* of a life.

And this texture can be further enriched if one brings to it the notion of the *heretic*, in the original meaning of the word: *someone who chooses*. As the writer Monique Zerder-Chardovoire explains it:

> Heresy comes from the Greek word meaning *choice*: for heresy to exist, there should be an ideology, a faith, to which a community adheres, and inside this community there must also be people who distance

themselves, no longer accepting the received truths, in order to choose for themselves.

Against this background, our fork in the road, the traditional *either/or* is replaced with an incomparably more complex notion of *both/and*. It simply leaves no room for straight or conclusive answers. *This* or *that* may be true, but *at the same time* many other things may be just as true. And whenever there's a fork in the road: take it. What the hell.

VIOLENT VILLAGES

IF I CLOSE MY EYES AND SILENTLY MOUTH THE WORD *DORP*, WHAT I CONJURE up, even now, sixty or more years later, is an image of wide dusty streets, the pavements overgrown with thorns (which we called, with good reason, *duwweltjies*, little devils), in a predictable grid around the tall spire of the Dutch Reformed Church, that sat brooding over the surrounding houses like a large and somewhat unwieldy hen with outstretched wings protecting her chickens. Twice on Sundays, and on Wednesday evenings for prayer meetings, the congregation would be summoned by the booming of the church bell, and men, women and children would respond – not so much out of conviction as because an empty place would undoubtedly invite ever-expanding circles of gossip rippling through town and district, possibly for weeks on end. After the Sunday service, having reviewed all the most recent news and scandals and secrets of the town, everybody would hurry back to the gargantuan meals prepared by black women on Aga or Dover stoves in kitchens as hot as the furnace of Nebuchadnezzar: roasted leg of lamb, and *frikkadelle* or meatballs, a joint of venison in winter, or chicken, perhaps a tomato stew on the side, and potatoes and sweet potatoes, yellow rice with raisins, beans and peas and carrots, stewed prunes and peaches, and quinces, pumpkin with cinnamon and sugar, gem squashes, possibly rhubarb, beetroot with sugar and vinegar, bean salad, followed by blancmange and yellow and green and red jelly, and a banana foam, maybe trifle or a vinegar or brandy pudding or roly-poly, or the custardy dessert our family knew as 'My mad aunt's sister', with or without green fig preserve or quince jelly or the

4

grape syrup called *moskonfyt*, all of it washed down with sweet wine, preferably muscadel or jerepigo. Afterwards, as grown-ups snored in a stupor of overindulgence, and giggling, viciously inventive children went about their arcane business while they were supposed to 'rest' on their beds or read edifying books, the same women would clear the tables and wash and stack the dishes, before carrying off the scraps to their own kids waiting in the 'location' (but only after the most tasty morsels had been scraped off for the chickens, the dogs and cats, and sometimes a pig wallowing in the backyard).

Near the church would be two or three streets of shops with wide stoeps: a pharmacy, two or three grocers recognisable by large posters advertising Big Ben or C-to-C cigarettes, Lyle's Golden Syrup, Marmite, Elastoplast, Black Cat peanut butter, shoes, khaki overalls; butcher, baker, a café or two, an undertaker who might also sell books and newspapers and cover his customary suit of solemn black with a soiled white dustcoat to double as hairdresser, a Pegasus garage with handpumps, the bank, and some offices, one or two lawyers. And a hotel – Royal or Masonic or Commercial – with an off-sales where even before the official advent of apartheid separate entrances kept white and black decently segregated. And of course the magistrate's office, red brick or sandstone, seldom more than a stone's throw from the police station with its blue lamp and pepper trees, or a couple of scraggly palms, and a long low prison ineffectually camouflaged behind aloes or sisal plants, or even reckless bougainvillea or lantana covered with a layer of dust.

The school would usually be set apart, in a backstreet on the outskirts, the red paint flaking from its steep roof, patches of face-brick, and rickety gutters, surrounded by an interminable expanse of gravelled playground, with separate rows of outside latrines for boys and girls. At the back of each cubicle was a hatch that could be opened to remove and replace the buckets. One night a week Mr Venter's mule-wagon – later replaced by a tractor pulling a trailer – did the rounds through all the streets of the town. By choosing the right moment, some of the more intrepid boys occasionally managed to lift a hatch behind the girls' block to trap someone in the act. But if you were caught, it could result in a near-fatal beating and a house visit by the principal, which inevitably invited further action, no less murderous, by the parents of the offender.

The houses, most of them, except for the dingy hovels of the poor-whites below the railway line, were large and sprawling, and set in spacious gardens. If 'garden' is the right word for a stretch of largely unspoilt veld in which a few unconvincing vegetable beds had been courageously staked out, dug up, manured, and heartbreakingly coaxed into producing something akin to vegetables; there might also be a patch of mealies, a few straggling pumpkins, or an attempt at flowers: zinnias, hardy orange and yellow marigolds which we called 'smelly Afrikaners', perhaps some phlox, even the odd dahlia. But mostly these plots were overgrown with weeds, or more or less abandoned as naked patches of red earth where chickens scratched or somnolent dogs licked their balls. One or two of the plots sported wind pumps, usually with several missing vanes, and making the eeriest of ghostly sounds when an unexpected gust of wind came up in the night. But the majority of the inhabitants relied on round tanks of corrugated iron for watering the gardens. Which was fine for a few months after it had rained. But then they would go dry and succumb to the cancer of rust. In the Free State and Griqualand West rain was a rare phenomenon. I remember how my little sister Marita nearly went mad when she saw rain for the first time. She was then three years old. She danced like a dervish on the dining table and then rushed outside and started rolling in the puddles until even her customary halo of white hair was covered in red mud.

Such events, and family illnesses, letters received or sent off during the week, radio news about the distant war, and various items of spicy gossip, were discussed on the wide red stoeps where families gathered before or after supper, in a leisurely review of current or remote events. One of them I still recall, not because it was in any way exceptional but precisely because it was so typical of a hundred others. Our family are lounged on the front stoep, taking the breeze as holidaymakers would 'take the waters' after a ferociously hot day, with a few friends or neighbours who have ambled past in the street and were invited to come in, or had invited themselves. A young barefoot girl with long blonde braids in a recklessly short floral dress comes past in the deepening dusk. She may be the very girl who was seen skipping on a street corner a month or so earlier, revealing her skinny bare bottom every time the brief skirt flared up, hopping her way right into my

Rumours of Rain, closely watched by Oom Koot, the Sunday school superintendent who leads our singing in a curiously clipped, staccato manner – the only way to keep his dentures from falling out. And at some stage his wife, Aunt Saar, unexpectedly came out on the stoep and demanded to know in a most intimidating voice what he was looking at. 'I'm not looking at anything,' he growled. 'That thing is like God's lightning: you needn't look at it, you just *see* it.'

On this particular evening, the girl is called over to the front gate by one of the more voluminous aunts.

'What's your name, girl?'

'Nellie, Auntie.'

'You Aunt Meisie's daughter?'

'Yes, Auntie.'

'And how is she? I didn't see her at the prayer meeting last night.'

'She was sick, Auntie.'

'What was the matter?'

'It's her chest, Auntie.'

'Still that bronchitis thing she had?'

'Yes, Auntie. But it's better now, Auntie.'

'So she's up and about again?'

'Yes, Auntie. But the headache is still there, Auntie.'

'Tell her I'll send some Grandpa powders over in the morning.'

'Yes, Auntie. But then there's her throat too, Auntie.'

'That woman must take better care of herself.'

'Yes, Auntie. And then she says her left shoulder is also very painful, Auntie.'

'Zambok ointment will help.'

'Yes, Auntie. And the corns on her little toes also hurt all night.'

More sounds of commiseration.

'And she said her back teeth were bad too, Auntie.'

'That's the wages of sin.'

'Yes, Auntie. And her left knee is still terribly swollen with the water, Auntie. And she thinks her right hip is out of joint, Auntie.'

And so it goes on, an unbelievable catalogue of the innumerable shocks that flesh is heir to. Only when the girl runs out of ailments and the aunties on the stoep out of remedies, everybody says goodnight and with a last fluttering of the skimpy dress the girl is gone in the gathering dark.

The grown-ups are still discussing the information gleaned and comparing it to their own experience of suffering and recovery and disaster, when the girl reappears at the garden gate, out of breath with running.

'Excuse me, Auntie,' she says, 'my mother says to tell you that her back is also giving her trouble, Auntie. She thinks it's her kidneys, Auntie.'

The conversation flows on, like water irrigating a garden of many beds and patches, making little swirls and eddies along the gossip and the small scandals of the day – what the principal and the school secretary are up to after school hours; what business the sixty-year-old Mr Yanasch, the richest farmer in the district, can possibly have in the hotel after the bar has closed, when the curtains are drawn in front of the windows of my vivacious piano teacher, Marie Jordaan; how come that Katie Venter, the precocious fourteen-year-old daughter of the night-soil wagon driver, has suddenly been blessed with a new baby sister when everybody knows that her mother already started having hot flushes two years ago; how, and by whom, the South African Party candidate at the last elections was tarred and feathered; how two unmarked graves have appeared overnight on the farm of Gert Greyling following an altercation with some of his workers after he allegedly held back their wages; what a coincidence it is that old Oom Hennerik Hanekom, the chief elder, should have died when his car left the road on the very night he spent hours in prayer and Scripture reading with the young Lettie van Wyk while her husband, the mechanic at the Pegasus garage, was in Bloemfontein to find spare parts for his Chev. Small fragments of news and rumour in the larger jigsaw puzzle of the place. Even if there is nothing obvious to link them on the surface, somewhere in the background there always lurks something vaguely sinister or overtly menacing, something violent, something inexplicable. A sense of sin and menace without which no village could survive.

And then another day is gathered into another night. In a few hours the village's generators at the power station will be cut and medieval darkness will take over while stars the size of huge white flowers descend almost

8

within reach, so close that by turning your head at the right angle, it is said, you can hear them. In the houses lanterns and paraffin lamps will be lit, the smell of wax candles will invade the bedrooms. In those nights it isn't difficult to imagine ghosts and spectres and poltergeists and revenants; and to risk going to the graveyard after dark, as some of us boys may do in response to a dare or to prove our mettle to ourselves, means risking one's life in the very portals of hell.

That this was still another age was evident, too, in the shops, where open bags of flour or mealies, sugar beans, coffee beans and sugar and dried fruit were arranged in tidy rows, beside rolls of wire and wire mesh, boxes of tea, glass containers filled with sweets – jube-jubes and acid drops and sticky Wilson's toffees and strips of liquorice and twirls of barley sugar and Nestlé chocolates and the special treat universally and offensively known as 'nigger balls'. It was evident also on Sundays, when scores of farmers, as unwieldy as bales of hay in their Sunday best, would come in to church on their horse-drawn buggies and 'spiders' or on decoratively painted mule-wagons or donkey-carts.

The church. Some of these villages might have a synagogue or an Anglican or even a Catholic church; but the heart of all the communal activities was Dutch Reformed, ruled over by the undisputed trinity of dominee, sexton, and organist. They were the immediate representatives of God Almighty on earth, and the legend painted on the whitewashed wall behind the pulpit, proclaimed that *God is Love* with the same flourish of conviction as the *Mené Mené Tekél Ufarsin* on Balthazar's wall. The only flaw in the presentation was that, over the years, irreverent dampness had created an unsightly rust-coloured stain that nearly obliterated the *Love*. A sign of the times, no doubt.

This did not prevent me from seriously considering, at an early stage of my life, following my parents' fondest wish by taking the cloth. But the closest I ever came to the seat of power – after having finally disappointed them by deciding not to become a dominee after all – was by being allowed to play the straight-backed little harmonium for the children's weekly prayer meeting on Tuesday afternoons; which I did with great devotion and so much embellishment that most of the hymns were stretched to double their

9

original length. This was where sin was defined – and at least to some extent had its origin – and where much of my youthful notion of evil was conceived.

Even more than the stories of the brothers Grimm, the Bible had all of us in its thrall with its litany of violence and cruelty, much of it thrillingly mixed with sex and intimations of sex. It started with God's totally unfair expulsion of Adam and Eve from the Garden of Eden where they only did what he should have foreseen from the beginning. And then Cain clobbering the namby-pamby Abel over the head. And all those violent sons of God taking to wife the comely daughters of men. And Lot offering to throw his own daughters to the mob baying outside his house in Sodom for the two strangers inside whom they want to fuck, or to 'know' as the Bible primly phrases it. And after the destruction of the town, these same daughters making their poor old father drunk so that, as the Bible once again phrases it, they can 'lie' with him for the sake of allegedly preserving his seed. And God ordering Abraham to cut the throat of his son Isaac just to tempt him. And Joseph's brothers throwing him into a well to rid themselves of his discomfiting dreams. And the rape of Dinah, and the bloody revenge of Simeon and Levi. And Moses ordering the slaughter of all the Midianite women except the virgins who are reserved to satisfy the lust of his soldiers. And Tamar, disguising herself as a prostitute, cheating her own father-in-law into fucking her. And God-fearing Jephthah killing his own daughter to fulfil a vow to a bloodthirsty God. And Aholah and Aholibah lusting after the young paramours 'whose flesh is as the flesh of asses, and whose issue is like the issue of horses'. The New Testament has its own litany of atrocities, although most of these are committed by the enemies of Israel. But even Jesus is suspect: not so much because of violence as of more subtle cruelties – once when he refuses to speak to his own mother and brothers (*But he answered and said unto him that told him, Who is my mother? And who are my brethren? And he stretched forth his hand towards his disciples, and said, Behold my mother and my brethren!*); once when his mother asks him for wine at a wedding and he chides her: 'Woman, what have I to do with thee?' I have heard numerous dominees offering very abstruse explanations of these episodes; but they all sounded too much like whitewashing. It could not efface – even if it did manage to suppress, for years – the impression that just below the surface of the words in the Bible lurked the same kind of menacing darkness that I could sense in the small villages of my youth.

Even acts of charity and good deeds depended on violence. I had no compunction about the slaughtering of poultry and could laugh my own head off at the mad flutterings of headless chickens in the backyard in preparation for a good Sunday meal, although they tended to return to me at night in terrifying dreams. I never attempted a decapitation myself, even when offered the knife my father had sharpened with consummate skill. But there was something more morbid about cutting the throat of a sheep – stretching the neck back to tauten it to the utmost, the eyes turning white, then the single deft stroke of the long, sharpened blade, and the last smothered bleat subsiding into a liquid gurgle as a fountain of bright red blood gushed from the slash. This ritual used to be performed by my father and some helpers just before Christmas every year, when generous food parcels were prepared in our backyard and kitchen by the Women's Auxiliary, to be distributed, accompanied by colourful tracts about the mercy of God and the healing powers vested in the sacrifice of his Lamb, among the poor and the needy. And there lingered some atavistic lust in hearing, at *nagmaal*, the dominee intone: 'Eat, drink, this is my body and my blood.'

This was, it seems to me more and more, the clue to all those little villages of my youth, strung like dusty pearls along the endless dirt roads of the interior. And the impact of that awareness was heightened by the loneliness that encompassed each of them, the space of eternity itself that surrounded them under the vast resonant hollow of the sky.

A hundred miles away might lie another town to which, once every three or six months, one's mother might drive with a car full of friends, for a day's shopping, to return with a small orange-brown suitcase crammed with spoils from another world. Apart from Christmas or birthdays these were the only occasions for presents. Even if one's father were a magistrate there was never enough money to spoil children. Until I was well into high school I never received more than two pennies a week pocket money; which meant that when I saw a little red car in a grocery shop, at the mind-boggling price of ninepence, I had to arrange with the daunting shopkeeper, Mr Levin, to keep it for me for five weeks until I could pay the full amount. I still remember the long, exciting, fearful walk to the shop, with my pennies safely stowed in a buff envelope and pinned into my shirt pocket, and how I kept looking round every few yards to make sure I was not followed by a gang of robbers. Even the knowledge that if I was in fact attacked, the miscreants were bound to be sent to jail by my father, did not altogether make me feel any safer.

There might be other dangers lurking along the way. I might be confronted by Ria, the ever-smiling hunchback daughter of friends of my parents, who was known without any warning to fall down in the dust where she would writhe and kick and utter terrible sounds and foam at the mouth like something from the Bible. Or Agnes with the harelip, cleft by the Devil himself to visit on her, as we all knew, some unspeakable sin committed by someone in her family, three or four generations back. Or the young giant Neels who after the lingering, painful death of his father was known to beat up his fat mother every Saturday. Or Mrs Oberholzer who had been buried in a shoebox when she'd allegedly died as a baby, and then somehow was salvaged when at the funeral someone heard a whimpering sound in the box, and grew into a woman of over seven feet tall. Or old Uncle Rohloff, who was a German and therefore under house arrest all through the war, a puny bow-legged old man with a shock of Einstein-like white hair and watery eyes that peered myopically through very thick, and very dusty, glasses. He had in a showcase a most amazing collection of teeth – of sharks and whales and warthogs and a lion. Towards the end of the war it was rumoured that in a hidden chest he also kept the teeth of seven Jews. I once tried to blackmail him into selling the collection to me for sixpence; when he refused I staged a robbery to steal the teeth, but it was foiled by his beautiful daughter Christa who gave me piano lessons. I only desisted after Uncle Rohloff attempted in vain to teach me, with reference to photographs of Toscanini, to conduct the school percussion band. Or I might run into Robert, the black policeman who ate cats. Once, when for some reason never explained to us children, my parents had to get rid of a stray tomcat, my father offered it to Robert, who duly came the next day to thank him and to assure him what a great meal the tom had made; which did not, however, prevent the cat from returning home to us a week later. Or I might be waylaid by any of the ghosts from the delightful horror stories old bearded uncles or moustached aunts used to tell us on weekend visits to farms near the town.

But in the end I safely reached the shop and got my red car; and then hardly ever played with it.

I was more interested in playing with my sister Elbie's dolls. I had one of my own, a boy rag doll called Jannie, with an imbecile painted face, for whom I once tried to knit a tie; but never having been taught how to end off a piece of knitting I gave up when the tie just grew and grew until it started creeping out of the front door. After that I confined myself to Elbie's dolls, not only because of that tie but because unlike Jannie, her dolls were all girls and it was much more fun undressing them. I also made sure – little shit that I was – that I always claimed for myself whichever one, at any given moment, was her own favourite.

Only one of her dolls I couldn't stand. A real spoilt brat, with rosebud lips and blue eyes that opened and closed, and a silly simpering smile. Elbie loved Tootsie. But Tootsie, with her hard, painted head and arms and legs that hypocritically pretended to deny her stuffed torso, gave me no peace of mind. Even at night she would stalk my dreams. I hated her. So passionately that I decided to kill her. Which I did one afternoon by driving an iron stake through her painted throat. Afterwards I buried Tootsie in a shallow grave. Instead of restoring my sleep, guilt made me wake up in cold shivers at night. Only religion could save me. On the vacant plot behind our home I stacked an altar on which I intended to sacrifice my most prized possession to atone for my guilt. For some reason I believed that it had to consist of twelve stones. But the only stones a weak and skinny little fellow like me could handle resulted in a most unimpressive altar barely a foot tall. So I cheated, adding about ten more. On top I placed the little red car. But at the last moment, fearful that it might really be consumed by the fire from heaven I would be praying for, I substituted a nicely shaped soapstone. It took some time to persuade myself that this stone was really my most prized possession. Nothing less, I knew, would find favour in the eyes of the Almighty. I prayed and prayed until I was sure that God was convinced of my utter sincerity. But it was like the priests of Baäl trying to milk rain from their heathen god. No one up there would hearken unto me. And in the end, when my mother called me home for supper, I had to give God up for a bad job. Another sleepless night.

The next day I confessed to the murder. First I tried to fob it off on the Devil, as the South African cricket captain Hansie Cronjé tried many years later; but long before him I found that the story didn't wash. I wasn't killed in a plane accident for it, but my backside burned for days afterwards. At least I am still alive, and no longer plagued by God.

The murder of the doll was set in a context of pervasive violence. In my readings over many years in the many histories of South Africa, most particularly the eighteenth century, it has always struck me how excessively violent encounters between racial or national groups, or even individuals from the same group, have been. Violent encounters occur in all societies: but in South Africa there almost invariably appears to have been an added edge to it, a fortuitous *surplus* of violence. A friend at university once told me about a trip he had made with a posse of police in search of some cattle rustlers who had wreaked devastation on his father's farm. After a day and a night of futile tracking they found a young black man walking along a farm road carrying a bundle on a stick. There was nothing to connect him with the crime. But he was black, and they met him at the height of their rage and frustration; so they jumped out of the police car and started shooting wildly. The youngster, scared out of his wits, started running. A sure proof of guilt. He was shot in both legs, and fell down. At point blank range he was then given a shot in the back, which shattered his spine. Then came the *supplement*, as they fell on him and kicked and beat him to a pulp before the broken body was flung into the back of the van and taken to the station, where he was kept in a cell overnight. At irregular intervals policemen would come in to beat him up some more. Only the next morning was he taken to hospital. Quite miraculously, he survived. Months later he was taken to court. My father found him not guilty.

And this goes back for centuries: white violence perpetrated on blacks, black violence on whites, white on white, black on black. As if something in the very geographical make-up of the country stimulated a kind of desperation for which excessive violence became the only manageable expression.

14

Violence as a kind of language in its own right, an articulation which is either preverbal or which begins where language stops. And those people who now flee the country because it has become 'too violent', or foreigners who fear to visit South Africa for the same reason, lack perspective on the long, long history of excess that has led to the current situation.

In the villages of my childhood violence was not necessarily always excessive; much of it, in fact, was muted or obscure, domestic in scope, restricted in pain or effect. But it was always there. And it manifested itself as a mark of the ordinary and the everyday. There was the dominee with his ruddy, fleshy face, who beamed goodwill and the radiant love of God from the pulpit twice every Sunday, and whose thin pretty wife one day, after we'd moved to another town, pitifully confessed to my mother in a long letter about how he slept around among the wives of deacons and stalwarts of the congregation, and how he would beat her if she dared to confront him with it. Once he actually threw a Bible at her, and a hard corner left a purple bruise on her cheek. My friend Katkop whose father, the butcher, a massive man with biceps like hams, ritually rounded up his family – wife and five children, boys and girls – after family prayers on Saturday nights and thrashed the hell out of all of them. Often the mother was unable to take her place behind the counter on Mondays and Tuesdays; Katkop himself would regularly, with a curious show of pride, stagger to school on Mondays to show us his bruised back: sometimes it was so badly scarred that his shirt stuck to it and had to be cut loose. And of course, there were canings at school – girls on their hands or legs, but in serious cases on their buttocks as well, boys on their backsides. Ritual demanded that after such a thrashing the culprits would parade in front of their classmates behind the toilets to remove their shorts and show the damage. Anything less than blood was scoffed at.

And I remember Elise. She was a year older than I, the daughter of the police sergeant, an attractive blonde girl with long plaits down her back, blue-eyed, with the face of an innocent angel. She taught me the rudiments of stamp collecting. She also introduced me to some of the discoveries she had made through her father's job. She knew in advance when boys – some of them eighteen or nineteen, others as young as fourteen, or even twelve – had been sentenced to be caned. (My father would have done the sentencing, but he never spoke about this.) The boy would then be brought to the police station, which was built on a corner of our large plot, and taken into a corrugated iron shed depressingly covered in faded, peeling red paint. Inside, the boy would be stripped naked. There was a long narrow table on which he would be forced to lie face down, and his wrists and ankles were held by four policemen. There was a district surgeon in attendance. And of course the man who had to inflict the punishment, usually the burliest cop on the premises.

We could not see what was happening inside, of course. But Elise knew exactly where to crouch to listen to the blows and screams from inside. For her, the *pièce de résistance* came when the door was flung open and to the accompaniment of bellowing laughter from the assembled cops, all clustered in the doorway, the caned boy would stagger out and start running frantically this way and that through the gravelled backyard, like a decapitated chicken. How she laughed – even though I think, in retrospect, that there was hysteria in that laughter, a touch of madness – and how she would revisit, in our conversations afterwards, every horrifying little detail of the event: the bleeding stripes on his back and pale buttocks, the streaks of blood and piss and shit down his legs, the pathetic dangling of his prick. On one occasion she was so worked up that she actually lifted her blue dress, her eyes unnaturally and feverishly bright, to show me that she'd peed herself. Once was enough for me. After that I always concocted reasons for missing the show. But Elise never missed one, and afterwards she would seek me out with a glowing account of everything that had happened.

In that very same gravelled yard a young policeman, Grobler, committed suicide one Wednesday afternoon by shooting himself, but slightly botched it and took quite a while to die. I don't know why the doctor wasn't called immediately. The body was taken to one of a row of outdoor privies where it was left to be collected; and once again it was Elise who came running to tell me about it. But all we could see from our vantage point behind the barbed-wire fence that separated the police station from our yard, was one bare bluish-white foot sticking out from the open privy door, and a wide circle of blackened blood on the gravel. I remember his dirty toenails. Remember, too, my resolve to make sure I washed my feet every evening before going to bed, just in case I died in the night.

It was Elise's recklessness that captivated me. When she and her best friend, the dominee's elder daughter Maritha knew that there were visitors in the parsonage, the two girls would strip themselves naked and climb up the huge pepper tree beside the garden path that ran from the front door to the gate; there they would sit and wait until the people emerged from the parsonage, and at the crucial moment they would take careful aim and pee on the heads of the visitors.

Not all of the memories from those days are quite so dramatic, even if they remain vivid. Like the occasion when a rickety little mule-cart came past in front of our house, with a large brown family piled on it. The driver was, presumably, the father, a small wiry man wearing an old floppy hat at a precarious angle and swearing and shouting at the top of his voice as he mercilessly flogged the solitary wretched grey mule straining to drag the impossible load along the dusty street. At a given moment the animal could not take it any more. He stopped, and tried to lie down in his harness. The father jumped off the cart. Wielding his heavy whip he started belabouring the whimpering little beast. It was unbearable. I remember the small puffs of dust that rose from the mule's bony back with every blow. With an almost unbelievable effort the animal slowly began to move again, moaning like a human being.

'You can't do that!' I said from the pavement, scared to shout too loudly, but unable to contain my fear and rage any longer. 'I'll call my father.'

'Ha!' shouted the man. With a show of glee the driver gave the mule a last series of blows, folding double under the effort, and then put his foot on the step to hoist him back on the cart. But looking over his shoulder to cast a final look of triumph at me, he missed his foothold, and fell down in a fierce cloud of dust, and the nearest wheel of the cart went right over him.

Call my father . . . That was always the last resort – even though I knew he would generally refer the problem back to me, at least he would provide the perspective to understand it better. He was the magistrate. He was second only to God. He knew all about Right and Wrong, about Good and Evil. From the time I was about nine, I would often slip into the courtroom through a side door while he was hearing a case, and slide into the very back bench, to listen to the proceedings. The crimes were usually pretty nondescript. Invariably some miserable black man in threadbare clothes would be accused of petty theft, or being drunk and disorderly, or brawling and fighting, or trespassing, or being found on the streets after the evening curfew that was announced by the tolling of the church bell. More rarely a white man might be accused of having dealt too severely with one of his black labourers, or beating his wife, or failing to pay maintenance for a child born out of wedlock. I would listen transfixed, trying to sift the evidence for and against, or making sense of the interpreter's version of what had been said. There was no court secretary or stenographer around: my father had to write everything down in his small, immaculate handwriting, with ever-widening margins on feint foolscap paper. As the last page was filled, he would tap the pile of papers into position and proceed immediately to deliver the verdict. Only in rare cases was the court adjourned for an hour, or until the next day. And every time, without fail, I would be stunned by the precision with which he summarised all the evidence and went straight for the kernel of truth hidden within so much verbiage. Years later, I once asked a friend who had become an advocate and who had occasionally pleaded in cases in my father's court, for his opinion; and he said, 'With old Brink on the bench, one always knew that what counted in that courtroom was the simple truth, no matter what the applicable law might say. He couldn't care less about the legal prescriptions. But he had an unfailing instinct for what was truth, and what a lie.'

It made me feel rather proud. With God in his heaven and my father on his bench, justice would prevail in the world.

But then came the Saturday afternoon when the strange black man turned up in our backyard. He wasn't wearing anything remotely resembling clothes: they were mere tatters, and he was reeling and staggering as if drunk, but he wasn't. He was in pain. His face looked as if it had been battered completely out of shape and then put through a mincer. Blood was streaming from a gash in his head, and his eyes were almost invisible. I was practising tennis against the back wall of the house when he came through the gate. He hobbled towards the back door, flopped down on the gravel, propping his back up against the wall.

Numb with shock I edged towards him and asked what he wanted. For a long time he just moaned and mumbled. When at last he tried to articulate through his grotesquely swollen lips all I could make out was that he wanted to speak to the *baas*. But my father was out, playing tennis, as was his wont on a Saturday.

It seemed like ages before I dared to ask, 'What happened to you? Was there an accident?'

He shook his head and mumbled incoherently. At long last he managed to explain. His *baas* had beaten him. I couldn't make out why. And I couldn't believe that a beating could be so severe as to result in *this*. I wanted to talk to him, to find out more, but I was too shocked to speak. In the end I simply squatted down beside the man and sat in silence. Waiting for my father, who would no doubt know the answers and offer a solution.

But when he came home, he went straight from the garage in his tennis clothes, barely glanced at the battered man, and walked into the house. I gazed after him, unable to understand, then got up and scurried after him.

'You must come and help,' I gasped. 'Something terrible has happened.'

'It is Saturday,' my father said. 'I'm tired, I'm going to have a shower.'

'But that man was nearly killed,' I said, feeling my voice break. 'Please, Pappie.'

'He can come back on Monday.'

'Please!' By now I was sobbing openly.

'Well, at least give me time to shower.'

I stood there, shaking my head. And waited outside the bathroom. Until at last he emerged. He seemed to head for the lounge, where my mother would be waiting with the tea, but I waylaid him. With a sigh of impatience he resigned himself and followed me outside.

Once again the man mumbled his story, even less intelligibly than the first time.

Before he could finish, my father said, 'You must go to the police. There is nothing I can do for you. It is not my work.'

'I been to the police first time,' said the black and bleeding man. 'They beat me some more. So now I come to you.'

'They are the only ones who can help you,' said my father. 'I must go now.'

In at least two of my books I have written about this episode, hoping to exorcise the memory. But it is no use. It still haunts me. I still see that head, those hands, that blood-streaked face before me. And I don't think it is an exaggeration to say that the world has never been quite the same place as before. My father not quite the same man. Something shifted. The centre no longer held.

There were other occasions too, when violence came very close to engulfing me. There is no need to wallow in this darkness. Only one more memory, not involving my father this time, but a particularly jocular and generous man whose family, old friends of my parents, offered me a room during my first few years at university. A farmer and a businessman, Oom John was one of the funniest people I had ever met. With a heart of gold, everybody said. And even in this episode he would have been under the impression that he was acting in a particularly humane and magnanimous way.

It concerned a young black boy of about sixteen or seventeen, whom Oom John had brought from one of his several farms in the Northern Cape to become his houseboy in my university town, Potchefstroom. In those days – and regrettably, in spite of everything that has happened in the country in recent years, things have still not changed all that much – an ancient feudal system still operated on farms, where land would be bought and sold together with the livestock, labourers included; and while the farm was yours, you could dispose of any man, or woman, or child on it in any way you wished. So when Oom John needed an extra pair of hands in town, a few hundred miles away from the farm, young Adam was brought there without considering even for a moment that it might not suit him. As it was, Adam was a rather frail boy, and very attached to his mother, who happened to be seriously ill at the time, and who died soon after the day in question.

Within a month of being transplanted to the small outroom in the back-yard of the sprawling house in Potchefstroom, Adam ran away. He was caught on the outskirts of Potchefstroom and brought back. He'd wanted to go and see his mother, he explained. He was generously let off with a warning and a few slaps around the ears. And assured that he could go to the farm for Christmas. Oom John was indeed a generous man. The problem was that it was only April then, and the boy's mother might not last that long.

But there are matters more serious than the life or death of a labourer's mother on a distant farm.

The second time Adam ran away, Oom John still treated it as a joke and didn't beat the boy too badly. After three days he was ready for work again, his rebellious spirit seemingly subdued.

The third time it was serious. Oom John took Adam to the police station to discuss the matter. There he was roughed up a bit just to make him understand that there were ways to behave oneself properly. The sergeant on duty suggested to Oom John that they could either take care of Adam in their own time-honoured way, or he could take the boy home and flog him himself.

No, no, said Oom John, he didn't want to see the boy maimed or killed; he'd prefer just to deal with it on his own. If they could assure him that he had their permission.

They were happy to give their permission.

'But don't let the little bugger off too lightly,' the sergeant called jokingly as Oom John prepared to leave. He, too, was a man of humorous bent.

And so the next morning at about ten o'clock Oom John brought two of his neighbours over, and Adam was taken to the coal shed. Each of the men had a length of hosepipe in his hand. With a few lengths to spare, should the need arise. Even then Oom John demonstrated his considerate nature. To prevent the boy soiling himself or spoiling his clothes he was stripped naked. And then the door of the shed was closed behind them.

Oom John's wife and the ladies she had invited to tea ensured that every door and window in the house was tightly closed. Yet it could not shut out the regular sound of the blows. At eleven o' clock I went out, preferring to continue my studies in the university library.

When I returned just after two, the wailing sound, to the steady, unflinching accompaniment of the dull thuds, could still be heard from the back of the property. I turned on my heel and went back to the library.

At five o' clock they were still beating the boy. Even though by that time one could no longer hear him wailing.

I went to lie on my bed and covered my head with both my pillows.

Shortly before suppertime the men came in, streaming with sweat and exhausted, in dire need of some refreshment after their strenuous day.

I did not sleep that night. One stupid sentence kept on careering through my head. *I was lying on my bed and covered my head with two pillows.* As if the whole of my life, perhaps the whole of white civilisation in South Africa, could be crammed into those few words. I knew then that Adam's voice, and the dull smacking sound of those blows would remain an accompaniment to the rest of my life. It would never let go of me again. Not ever. The stark, simple fact of violence would never leave me. It was there, and would be there, wherever I went, whatever I did, for ever and ever, amen.

My own acts of violence never amounted to much, although they were cruel enough. To my disgrace I must admit that I enjoyed shooting birds; but more often than not they were too quick for me. Then I started trapping them. My most successful contraption was a mesh-covered cage with a large opening shaped like a funnel, through which birds would enter, lured by crumbs inside. Most days the cage remained empty. But one day, quite unexpectedly, there were no fewer than fourteen birds trapped inside, fluttering about wildly and hurling themselves against the mesh. I waited for my father's return to ask his advice. 'Wring their necks,' he said laconically. I eagerly poked my hand in through the funnel, managed to grab a bird – a very tiny little thing, with shiny green feathers and white-rimmed bright beady eyes. Suddenly it no longer seemed like so much fun. But I grasped the little head between forefinger and thumb, turned away, and started twisting. No luck. I began twisting more and more furiously, like turning a crank-handle. When after thirty or forty spins I put the bird down, it uttered a faint cheep, dizzily flopped a few steps this way and that, then remained hunched up. But its eyes were still open. I vomited.

Back to my father.

'Why don't you just let them go?' he said.

'But it took me days to build that trap.'

'Well, you caught them, so it's up to you to deal with them.'

I went over to the neighbours to borrow their airgun. One by one I shot the remaining thirteen birds. Soon I was sobbing. It took thirty or forty shots to kill them all, and the inside of the cage was spattered with small green feathers and blood.

In due course, my father introduced me to the more worthy world of hunting. First he led me through target practice, at which I became quite adept. Then I graduated to the real thing. How proud I was to be taken with him when he was invited to farms to bag springbok, or – more rarely – blesbok. He had a formidable .303, I had to make do with a .22. I must have been thirteen or fourteen when I bagged my first springbok. Quite a good shot, too, on the left shoulder. He had taught me well. There is a photo of me with that first victim of my hunting prowess, which in a way reveals much of what that childhood world was about. On the surface, innocence. The casual innocence of a young, smiling boy wearing what may well have been his first long pants and bursting with pride about his achievement, standing astride his dead springbok which looks uncannily lifelike, holding it by the horns in an attitude of easy domination. But behind the charm of the scene – *Look what a good boy am I!* – lurks a very real and very bloody truth: something beautiful that has had to be killed to satisfy an instinct for maiming and death the boy has never even been aware of in his eagerness to be accepted into the world of his people.

The killing itself was something of a fluke: I lacked the temperament indispensable to a successful hunter. Generally, whenever a group of buck approached, I simply pressed the butt of the gun to my shoulder and started firing blindly – quite literally, as I tended to shut my eyes. Not even the sight of a wounded animal scampering off on three legs with the shattered fourth swinging dizzily alongside, until it flopped down with a bleat of agony, could deter me: it was part of the game, part of being a man.

It was only many years later, when I was directing a play in Windhoek, Namibia, then South-West Africa, and a group of us went camping on a game farm, that I made a deliberate choice to give up hunting. On that late afternoon we were on the back of a small pickup when someone spotted a small herd of gemsbok among a sprinkling of camel-thorns, about a hundred yards to the right. I took aim very carefully. When I pulled the trigger, I knew I'd got it. But the herd cantered off, and mine was nowhere to be seen. I had a sick feeling in my stomach. The farmer had sternly warned us not to wound anything. We gave up the search when night fell. In the morning some Bushman trackers found it, in a thicket not twenty yards from where I'd hit the gemsbok. A shot in the heart. Only then I learned that after such a shot the quarry would often run off at full speed for some distance before dropping in its tracks. By the time the Bushmen brought us to the dead gemsbok, the vultures and jackals had already got to him. Most of the carcass was gone, leaving the obscenely white crescents of the ribs sticking up from the red-black mess of the chest cavity. The head was relatively unharmed, except that the eyes had been torn out. The beautiful horns formed a stark heraldic V against the sky. They were offered to me as a trophy, but I did not want them. I never hunted again.

My most significant personal involvement in violence remained largely imaginary, and that was incomparably more terrifying than anything I could have experienced physically. These images came mainly from reading, erupting in vivid dreams when I was least prepared to face them. Sometimes they were based on stories my father had told – about dying children in the concentration camps of the Anglo-Boer War, or about cases that had come before his court. Once, friends of my father who were visiting passed round a set of forensic photographs from a murder inquiry in which he had been involved. When I entered the room on some innocuous mission, the photos were hurriedly put away and I was not allowed to look. But after school the next day, while my father was still at work, I came across the small pile of photographs on the oval dining table. Of course I rifled through them, after making quite sure that there was no one around. I wished immediately that I had never looked. They were stark and graphic: the bodies of a man and a woman attacked on their farm and hacked to pieces with hatchets. The man's skull was bashed in. The body of the woman, spread awkwardly across a sofa, wearing only one shoe and with her head on the floor, was covered in huge gashes and black with blood. Before that day I had always assumed that one day I would follow in my father's footsteps and become a magistrate. Or possibly a lawyer. But after gazing at those photographs I knew that I would have to think of something entirely different.

The event did turn me into a murderer, though. Not only in my six-year-old dreams at night, from which I would wake up screaming, but in the games I devised in the afternoons or over weekends when I was by myself. I would take my father's small hand-axe from the shed where he kept the firewood for the geyser, and set upon some of the thorn trees in the expanse of veld surrounding our house. On other days I would wander among the trees and rehearse my lessons to them, or preach to them from the Bible; but on these afternoons I was bent on killing them. And the bright amber-like gum that tended to cover the wounds in the course of time, gave me a peculiar sense of accomplishment. Often, of course, I would be an investigating policeman discovering a criminal lurking in the shape of the tree, in which case I would perform my noble civic duty. But quite often I indeed assumed the role of the murderer. Until my father discovered some of the mutilated trees and ordered me, by way of punishment, to chop them off properly and cut the branches into firewood.

There were other incidents that might have ended badly. Quite recently my sister Marita reminded me of how, when she was five and I fourteen, I'd unscrewed a light bulb from its socket in the dining room – one of those lamps that worked with a pulley and a counterweight so you could easily raise or lower it – and then ordered her to climb on a chair and put her finger in the socket, whereupon I flicked on the switch. She could have been electrocuted. But she assures me that her recollection of the event was wrapped in a feeling of glee and accomplishment, as she knew that my mother would give me hell for it.

One particular act of violence was a consequence of falling in love. I must have been about thirteen at the time. There was a pretty girl in my sister Elbie's class, the dominee's younger daughter, whose name was Driekie. Like Orlando in the Forest of Arden I started carving her name on thorn-tree trunks previously disfigured in my murderous frenzies. Or I would climb up to my perch among the fragrant branches of the pepper tree beside the house, where I could weep about the bitterness of unrequited love, as I tried to conjure up the image of her sweet, impish face, her dark blue eyes, her long thick plaits. I would of course never, ever consider making any direct overture or even sending a tentative note hinting at my feelings. That had no place in my notion of true and

25

everlasting love. I would simply pine away and, maybe, one day, her name might mysteriously figure on my tombstone. Unless . . .

It is possible that I might have hinted at my suffering in a confession to the only person I could trust, my sister Elbie, and that she was the one who had the idea of playing school in our garage. All that matters is that one Saturday a number of children drawn from Elbie's class and my own gathered in our garage, which I had fitted out as a classroom. Elbie, Driekie and a few others were the pupils. I was, of course, the teacher. My friend Stephen would be the principal. Although I enjoyed the prospect of running the lessons and imparting wisdom to my young charges, the whole morning was actually conceived around the notion of punishment. Corporal punishment. Which was the only way I could think of, to get close to Driekie.

The pupils were all subjected to some rigorous and vigorous teaching, and classwork was organised in such a way that mistakes and transgressions could in no way be avoided. Initially it was regarded as great fun, and amid much giggling and sniggering the first culprits had to approach the teacher's desk to be caned. It was only then that they discovered there was nothing playful or funny about the caning. Elbie was the first to receive the order to offer her hand for three whacks with the sturdy but supple green switch I had cut from a pepper tree. I'm sure it took all the defiance she could muster not to cry, but she was tough.

After that the pupils became recalcitrant. Driekie refused to put out a hand and was adamant that she would absolutely not bend over. So she had to receive her stripes on her bare legs. At the first blow she started crying, a thin reedy wail. I was horrified. Somehow the reality of her pain shocked me out of the imaginings that had gone before. At the same time I could not give up and suffer the humiliation of being insulted as a teacher. I aimed another serious stroke at her thigh, but she avoided it, kicked over the chair she had been sitting on, and scurried to the far side of my teacher's table. An undignified scuffle followed. Most of the children were laughing boisterously, but a few of the girls were shouting at me in outrage.

The only way to salvage my dignity was to order Driekie to the principal's office for some severe chastisement. And then it all fell flat. Stephen confronted me with a broad smile and said that he didn't think a silly little offence in the classroom deserved more than a light-hearted reprimand. As I tried to get past him to take the matter in hand myself, Driekie deftly side-stepped me and ran home. No one was in a mood for lessons any more.

I pleaded with a very reluctant Elbie to placate and beg Driekie not to report the matter to her dominee father, which might unleash the full wrath of God on me; and so I was spared the consequences. It was the end of my first attempts at teaching; it was also, as far as I can remember, the end of my sullied love. What the whole experience brought home to me about the nature of violence, and perhaps of love, I am not quite sure. All I can recall, and the memory still unsettles me, is the amount of unresolved violence there must have been in me at the time; and the relation between this dark, smouldering rage inside me and the angry world that surrounded me. And it seems to me that the excessive energy of my reactions was directly related, not to any masochistic or sadistic urge, but to the simple fact that I have always been *terrified* by violence.

I can remember only one fight I was involved in as a schoolboy, with my best friend, Danie Pretorius. For some long-forgotten reason he drove me mad during one playtime, and after school I waited for him beside the tennis court and fell on him with flailing fists until he ran off crying, and then he told his big brother Kokka about it, and Kokka beat *me* up, and I told my father to take up the matter with their widowed mother, and my father told me to fight my own battles, and then Danie and I were friends again.

These were the issues that rippled along the surface of our lives: personal upheavals that arrived quietly, or with spectacular suddenness, and then subsided into the even tenor of a small-town existence. There was a benign equanimity over it all; but often something else became visible, a narrow-ness, something threatening, a sense of danger, of darker forces moving like muscles under the skin of the everyday. Things we either tried to ignore or suppress, or which remained like a lump in the stomach or a clot in the blood, something we knew that ultimately we could not control and which one day, one night, might rise up like a freak wave to engulf us and the little world in which we had, in vain, tried to shelter or to hide for too long.

WORDS, WORDS, WORDS

A LONG, LONG TIME AGO, BEHIND THE SEVEN MOUNTAINS, BEHIND THE SEVEN woods, behind the seven rivers, there lived a man who had three daughters. For my wife Karina, this was the beginning of writing: the formula with which all stories in Polish began.

For me, language began on the day we started learning English in school. I must have been six. In Jagersfontein, the small village in which we were living then, English was a foreign language. To us, to me, everything happened only in Afrikaans. For the black people in the 'location' at a safe distance from our white enclave in the vast dust bowl of the southern Free State, where you could see forever in every direction, another language, Sotho, also existed, but it was never consciously absorbed by our white-tuned minds. Except – but I shall get to this later. I knew that my parents occasionally spoke English to visitors from other planets; and my mother, who had grown up in the Eastern Cape among the descendants of the 1820 British Settlers, had always cherished delusions of grandeur intimately linked to that language. But to me, as part of a captive audience suddenly addressed in English by our beloved teacher, Miss Gouws, who was small and wide and the guardian of knowledge that spanned the globe three times, this was something wholly new.

Some of the children – certainly the foul-mouthed Thys, and most certainly the beautiful dark-plaited Louisa, but perhaps not Fanie, whose father had joined the army to go to war for the English – giggled and elbowed each other; some were stunned into silence. I could feel my scalp shrink and start to itch, could feel shivers like spiders running up and down my spine, could feel my small balls contract and my throat go dry. The lesson itself, read from a bright blue book, must have been unspeakably drab. Something about a boy called Sam and a girl called Pam who lived in a caravan and had a ridiculous little dog called Bob. (*See Bob wag his tail.*) To me it was like discovering a new hemisphere to the known world. And I remember how, that afternoon after school, I wandered among the pungent lavender bushes and the dry blue smell of the bluegums, reading aloud to myself about Sam and Pam and the caravan and Bob of the perennially wagging tail, and later abandoning the blue book on the gleaming red stoep, to continue my wanderings without help or hindrance, faster and faster, enfolded in a whorl of red dust as I recited from memory the lines I had learned in school. When that was no longer enough, I started improvising, addressing in an English of my own invention the shrubs and diehard zinnias and my father's beds of beetroot and carrots and peas and beans. I would intone the word *caravan* and listen to the sound dying in the trembling white heat. Or pronounce, trippingly upon the tongue, the line *See Bob wag his tail.* Or invent English-sounding words to hurl among the thorn trees and the stunted peach and apricot trees, entranced by their mere sound. There was, soon, no more meaning inhering in the words. It was only sound: rhythms, cadences, vowels, consonants. *Language.*

It was my first conscious discovery of words. Suddenly, language was no longer something that happened by itself, a give-and-take that required no effort or concentration, but a material thing that could be shaped and manipulated, a thing that could, in turn, manipulate *me.*

I know now that there had been another, comparable discovery of language, years earlier, but this had happened subliminally.

It had occurred when I must have been two or three years old. At that time my mother had suffered from a long illness, so that I was mostly brought up by my old back nanny, a Sotho woman, who used to carry me in a tightly wrapped bundle on her back, my first intimation of safety and security; and as she went about her chores in the house, she would tell me or sing to me the stories of her people. In our family she didn't even have a name: she was simply known by the generic name of 'old Aia', borrowed from early

29

Malay slaves. Long before I could understand a word, the cadences of her stories were insinuated into me. And there they were to lie dormant for years until in some of my later novels – *Devil's Valley*, *Praying Mantis* and perhaps one or two others – I found myself almost instinctively groping back for those impulses I had long regarded as lost, and began to recover in the arcane processes of my own storytelling.

After those early discoveries the thrill was repeated every time I tried to learn a new language. I would stroll in some more or less deserted place and haltingly, fumblingly, talk aloud to myself, in Dutch, in German or French, in Spanish or Italian or Portuguese, tuning my ear and my tongue in to the syllables and rhythms of the new words, as if learning their meanings for the first time. In a way the most challenging of the languages was the Latin my father started teaching me when I was thirteen. We never went beyond *Fabulae Faciles* and an early primer, but this certainly came from a space beyond anything else I'd ever come across. In this case the issue was, perhaps, less language than the fact that it was something to be shared with my father. We never had very much contact; and particularly in later years we seldom went beyond ferociously beaming goodwill at one another from a great distance. But it did teach me something very vital about language anyway: not the meaning of *laudo/laudas/laudat*, or of *agricola/agricola/agricolam*, but of the innumerable things language can communicate *behind*, and even *divorced from*, the words on the page. Together with those very first discoveries about the materiality of language, this was where, for me, writing began. Not in the thoughts or ideas one can convey through words, but in the very means through which one tries to communicate those thoughts and ideas – that is, in the language itself.

So if, today, people presume that it was something like apartheid that brought me to writing, they are very far off the mark. It started with language – the language without which a word like *apartheid* could not even have existed.

Almost inevitably my first excursions into writing were in poetry. And when my first piece of doggerel was published in a children's magazine at the age of nine and I received the princely sum of half a crown for it, at a time when my weekly pocket money amounted to twopence, my future was settled. I knew then that whatever else I might choose to do for a living – painting houses, or growing vegetables, or driving a train – writing would form part of it.

Soon, once I'd followed in the footsteps of Molière's Monsieur Jourdain and discovered prose, I moved to fiction. At the age of twelve I wrote my first 'novel', all of seventy-seven pages long, recounting the blood-curdling adventures of four children on holiday among cannibals and wild animals in Nigeria; my father, with infinite patience, typed it out for me, sagely editing a few of the luridly sadistic scenes. The next novel ran to a full 315 pages, this time typed out by myself. This one dealt with the discovery of what remained of the lost civilisation of Atlantis in the jungles of the Congo, with some Cro-Magnons thrown in for good measure. It was duly returned by the luckless publisher to whom I had sent it, with the comment that, among other things, it was too erotic – notably in the embraces between Arno, the leader of the South African expedition into the jungle, and Menore, queen of Atlantis, who was not in the habit of wearing too many clothes.

After the rejection letter, I prayed to God for guidance in my hour of dire need, then cried myself to sleep, and when I woke up, swore that one day I would be vindicated. The following morning I started on my next novel, *Rajah, Lord of the Highlands*, inspired by Tarzan, King of the Jungle; and to my unmitigated anguish at the time and my unspeakable relief afterwards, this one, too, died an untimely if richly deserved death.

For several years I continued to write feverishly, but unsuccessfully. However, if there was nothing measurable to show for all this activity on the surface, a steady, invisible, subterranean growth was taking place – not through writing but through reading. Both my parents were voracious readers and all four of us children were infected by them. Ever since my paternal grandfather's involvement in the Boer War, my father had brought with him all the Anglophobia of the stereotypical Afrikaner: although the two great passions of his life were rugby and religion, he would unfailingly turn off the radio whenever a match or a church service was broadcast in English; yet he spoke an impeccable English with an astounding vocabulary – fired no doubt by a belief in knowing thine enemy. And, with the exception of English newspapers, he read anything he could lay his hands on, from

Shakespeare to whodunits. My mother, with her Eastern Cape background, had none of his reservations. Her light reading focused on writers like Georgette Heyer, but she loved Dickens and the Brontës and, like my father, worshipped Shakespeare. Even today strangers stop me in the street to tell me how my mother had turned them into lifelong acolytes of the Bard. Every week my parents would make a trip to the library and return, hours later, with armloads of books. And this habit – more than a habit: an addiction, a passion – was inculcated in us too. My whole childhood was awash with books; and it was amazing to see what unexpected treasures could be teased out of the shelves of libraries under the iron-fisted rule of wizened, ancient little ladies in the dusty villages that provided my early years with a local habitation and a name.

I became so enamoured of libraries that by the time I was about twelve I established my own version among my classmates at school, which had no library of its own. I invented an elaborate system of cataloguing for the twenty or thirty books on my own shelves and began to circulate them, at a rather exorbitant fee, among my friends. But in this case I'm afraid my motivation was less the urge to share knowledge than a venal urge to profiteer: never in my youth did I pass up an opportunity to make a quick penny.

Still, the village library continued to form the centre of my most vital enquiries and excursions, the starting point of all the imaginary travels I undertook around the circumference and into the core of the earth. In a very real sense, long before I'd ever heard the name of Ludwig Wittgenstein, I discovered, at first hand, the truth of that great line from his *Tractatus*, that 'the limits of my language are the limits of my world'. There was nothing those books could not explain or illuminate, except, perhaps, the domain of the erotic.

But the immersion in language, in the magic of words and sounds and invocations, did not come only through books and reading. In unexpected ways the speech of ordinary people brought its own intimation of other words and spaces. It was through my association with two boys from the neighbours' property, Archie and Thys, that I made the startling discovery that some words were much more equal than others. Archie and Thys introduced me to words like *cunt* and *shit*, which I soon found out in a very distressing way could land one in the deepest sulphurous pit of hell. That a combination of some sounds into a word could be harmless or even commendable, whereas other sounds, or the same sounds in a different combination, could be offensive or shocking to others and in fact damning to oneself, was a mystery and a kind of black magic that took me years to figure out. At the time, I had to take my parents' word for it that there was a direct and immediate connection between the utterance of one of 'those' words and the pain inflicted on my backside, or the taste of vile blue soap in my mouth.

In one case a word led to less predictable consequences. Like all children of my generation I was familiar with the word *vry*, which is the Afrikaans equivalent of *petting*. That is, I knew the sound of the word but not its meaning. And no one would tell me. True, my parents were not shocked by it in the way they had been by the vocabulary of Archie and Thys. But they were not to be drawn into explanations. My peers were simply dismissive, or started giggling, convincing me that they all knew something I did not. The lovely Louisa was more willing to help, but all she could tell me, blushing a fiery red and chewing the ends of her black hair, was that to *vry* meant to *kiss*. And that I found most unsatisfactory. If the two words meant the same, why did they *look* different? Like Pantagruel in search of a definition of marriage, I set out to discover the meaning of *vry*. No go. All the grown-ups I approached branded me as precocious and asking for trouble; the kids of my own age treated me as a dimwit.

Until at long last a girl younger than myself (I must have been ten or so, she nine), provided the answer. She was a friend of my sister Elbie. Her name was Maureen. Her father was the bank manager. Impeccable credentials. During a game of hide and seek Maureen and I were behind a sofa in a bay window in the house of her parents while our mothers were outside on the stoep and all the other children were scouting about in the garden. I put the Question. And without blushing or fidgeting or looking at all uncomfortable – for which I shall remain beholden to her until my dying day – she said: 'Yes, of course I know.'

'Well? What's it mean?'

'It's not so easy to explain,' she said, quite frankly. 'But if you want to, I'll show you.'

'Okay, then show me.'

'I can't really show you here,' she said. 'We don't want the others to catch us.'

I could sense that I was on the verge of a momentous discovery.

'Then where shall we go?'

'Can we go to your house?'

And so we went the few blocks up the road. I knew that my mother and sister were still at Maureen's and that my father would not come home from his office until much later.

In the bedroom I shared with Elbie we solemnly faced each other.

'You sure you know about *vry*?' I asked in some trepidation. The moment was almost too much to handle.

She nodded.

'*How* do you know?' I croaked.

'Because my sister Daphne told me. And one evening after last Christmas she *showed* me. We went down the passage to my parents' bedroom and the door wasn't quite closed and we *looked*. And I *saw*.'

Proof doesn't come much more convincingly than this.

And so I meekly followed her example in taking off my clothes. Nothing remarkable in itself. My sister and I had grown up together and shared all our baths. But at the same time it was amazingly, and delightfully, different: it was like that day in the garden when I'd first discovered the texture, the very differentness of words. The world had just been reinvented.

But that was only the beginning. For Maureen proceeded dutifully, and very meticulously, to *show* me, as she had promised. Not an altogether successful exercise, I'm afraid, as I was so overwhelmed by the discovery that I did not exactly rise to the occasion. But I certainly knew at least one meaning of *vry* after that.

There was one more aspect to this event and this discovery. The end of our exploration is hidden in a cloud. For the life of me I cannot remember whether my father came home from the office earlier than expected, or whether we were so carried away by our explorations that we became oblivious of time passing. So I simply do not know whether he caught us in the act if act it was. But I cannot help thinking that the terrible feelings of guilt concerning all things sexual that obscured my whole youth cannot be explained simply by the devastations and corruptions of Calvinism but must have been caused by something very specific and traumatic that turned the unmitigated joy and wonder of that summer's afternoon into a shameful memory. Whatever it was, it remained forever entangled with language, with the never-ending search for the meaning of words.

Those times, that day, remain in a secret place in my mind. A discovery of the magic of sex. And, through the telling, the magic of words.

Of course not all the discoveries of words through other people were traumatic. One of them concerned the Dwarf. And it happened during my school years at Douglas, in the arid north-west of the Cape Province, in Griqualand West, near Kimberley. This was between my eleventh and my sixteenth year, when I spent many weekends and holidays on the farms of friends. My favourite farm belonged to the parents of my friend Theuns. One of the reasons for the hold the place had on me was the pretty girl from the neighbouring farm. Her cheekiness. And the attempts by Theuns's two big brothers, both already in matric, to persuade her to pull down her panties for them. And how she refused and put out her wet little red tongue and left them high and dry. Another reason for the fascination of the farm was the signs of early peoples in the veld: the cairns erected by long-disappeared Khoi – or 'Hottentot' – tribes who had marked the graves of the hunter-god Heitsi-Eibib whose many deaths had been followed by as many resurrections, incomparably more wondrous, I secretly thought, than the biblical rebirth of Jesus. There were also flat stones marking the more ordinary graves of Griqua and Koranna tribesmen. And one afternoon Theuns led me, without prior warning, across several of those flat rocks. Only afterwards, brimming with malicious glee, he told me that I should watch out as the dead who lay buried in those graves had the unsettling habit of coming in the night to take revenge on whoever had desecrated their resting places.

'Well,' I retorted with some bravado which came easily in the hot after-noon sun, 'then they'll be coming for you too. We walked over the graves together.'

'Oh no,' he said. 'I took great care not to *step* on the graves. Only you did.'

I felt a sudden contraction in my throat. But in the excitement of the rest of the afternoon the incident was soon forgotten; we found a *geelslang*, or Cape cobra, slipping into a hole and quite impulsively Theuns grabbed it by the tail and pulled it out. What followed was a terrifying comedy which involved dashing across the veld in large circles, clutching the snake by the tail, and taking turns to duck through boundary fences and handing the furiously wriggling creature from one to the other while keeping up such a pace that the snake couldn't bend over to bite the hand that held it. In the end, reaching the farmyard where his father and some labourers were stacking a stone wall, Theuns managed to pass the *geelslang* on to one of them and the latest incarnation of the Devil was duly stoned to death.

In all this activity the ominous trespassing on the graves was forgotten, until Theuns brought it up at supper. The whole family joined in with dire predictions about the wrath of the ancestors, so I felt none too easy by the time we took our candle and went to bed. We spent some time with a perfunctory brushing of teeth and reminiscing about the day before we prepared to turn in. I had just blown out the candle and was on the point of restoring the chamber pot to its rightful place, when a devilish commotion under the bed scared me witless. With the most unearthly yelling and screaming some apparition came dashing out from under the bed and tried to grab me. As it happened, I emptied the chamber pot on the apparition's head, which mercifully subdued it on the spot. Theuns managed to light a match, and the impostor turned out to be none other than Theuns's older sister, who had been making my life a misery over the past few days with constant teasing, and cornering me in dark places in the sprawling farmhouse to grab me between the legs, which seemed to amuse her hugely.

This put an end to her exuberance, but for several nights I had the most awful nightmares. It was in these circumstances that Theuns's father told me about the Dwarf who lived in a hole on the farm. It seemed that for long periods he would mysteriously disappear, only to resurface at unexpected moments. This was one of those moments, and I was invited to visit the little creature. I didn't know what to expect, but to some extent my image of the Dwarf must have been shaped by Walt Disney, whose *Snow White and the Seven Dwarfs* was the first movie I had ever seen.

Nothing could have been farther off the mark. The Dwarf on Theuns's farm was indeed very small, barely a metre tall, but he was very black. One of the last remnants, I was told, of the nearly extinct Koranna tribe. Only recently it occurred to me that my memory of the Dwarf must have prefigured Cupido Cockroach in my mind when I came across his story almost half a century later and started plotting *Praying Mantis*.

At first I was scared of the little man. He was unspeakably filthy, and smelled of death and dead things. The hole in which he lived, and which he used to cover with an old sheet of corrugated iron, was littered with bones and peels and dirty tufts of sheep's wool and patches of snake skin and little pouches stuffed with god knows what. The black labourers on the farm gave him a wide berth and were, I learned, horribly cruel to him. The whites also treated him with suspicion, and Theuns approvingly told me that at irregular intervals, without any particular reason, his father would go into the veld and thrash the little man with a sjambok more violently than the occasion could possibly have warranted.

But there was something about the Dwarf – whose name I never learned – that fascinated me no end. I could not stay away from that filthy hole. At least once a day I would find an excuse to wander from the farmyard, pretending to go off in a completely different direction, and then follow a long circular route to the hole. It was always covered with the iron sheet when I approached. But he seemed uncannily to sense my approach, and as soon as I came within a few metres, the sheet would be pushed away by a small, gnarled black hand with long, yellow, horny nails. With a hideous smile of welcome, and without any preamble or warning, he would plunge into the telling of a story that I could barely follow – because not only did he tell it in a frightful mix of Afrikaans and, I suppose, the Koranna language, but he also suffered from some speech impediment. Perhaps for that very reason, I could not tear myself away. Story would follow story, and I would remain sitting on my haunches until just as suddenly as he'd started he would pull the iron sheet over his shrivelled grey head again and stop talking.

All I could recall of those stories was a hotchpotch of half-sentences, images, obscenities, funny flashes, cackles of laughter, short bouts of crying. But what made it impossible to stay away, was the impression of a whole other world, existing perhaps parallel to the one I knew, but magically different, a strange subterranean world presumably linked to the deep jagged hole in which he lived. Some of the stories I recognised, many years later, from old Khoisan myths – about the great snake that lives in a fountain wearing a diamond on its forehead, or of a first man and a first woman emerging from the bole of a big tree, or of the Devil assuming the form of a whirlwind to track down sinners who had something to hide . . . But many of them I could not trace; and, of course, at the time I didn't think of writing them down. They were just stories. Part of the vast net of stories that covered the whole world like a web, and to which some individuals who knew where to look, and how to reach for them, and how to prepare themselves for the encounter, would have constant access.

When I went to the farm again, some months or a year later, the Dwarf was no longer there. Nobody was sure what had happened. Perhaps he'd just died. Perhaps he'd gone off on one of his journeys and didn't bother to come back. Perhaps he had permanently returned to his own secret story world. Perhaps Theuns's father had killed him.

The intimation of that world persisted inside me. But for many years it was to remain dormant. Other stories, other forms and conventions of story-telling took over. Like too many other white people of my own tribe, I came to undervalue, if not to despise, whatever intimations I had gleaned in childhood of the black world. And only later, but thank God not too late, did I rediscover those wellsprings of storytelling to which I'd had access as a boy.

By the time, towards the end of my adolescence, I really became serious about writing, a rather broad foundation had been laid. The trigger, towards the end of my school years and the beginning of university, was my sister Elbie's breakthrough into publishing her stories in grown-up magazines. This was unbearable. She was, after all, three years younger than myself: there was something unfair about a universe that allowed such an inversion in the natural order. But for the time being all I could do was to gnash my teeth, and pray to God, and put in more hours of writing. Until, towards the end of my first year, the Almighty hearkened unto me and restored justice to his world.

A few hundred magazine stories saw me through university. But I knew the process would only begin to make sense once I had seen my name on the cover of a book. Several attempts – much more ambitious now than the heart of darkness in Nigeria and the Congo – had to be abandoned, after five or eight or twelve rewritings. Then, in my sixth year, in some desperation, I sent off to a popular magazine a novella I'd written in a day. It soon came back. But this time it wasn't branded 'too erotic': what the editor found was that it was 'too literary'. Which it certainly was, and not in the best sense of the word. Titled *Die Meul Teen die Hang* (*The Mill on the Slope*) it was the rather heavy-handed account of a cripple arriving in a small village in the Eastern Transvaal, who is ostracised by the community, befriends a little girl who comes to his sawmill every day and then is killed by an electric blade. At the inquest he is found not guilty, but the whole white community turns against him. There is serious racial strife in the area and one night violence breaks out among the black labourers at the mill. The sawyer hobbles into town to warn the inhabitants, but no one is prepared to listen to him. On his way home he sees his mill going up in flames.

Not much of a literary event. But it was a beginning. And in retrospect it was perhaps significant that racial tensions lay at the heart of the story; and that a very subdued kind of eroticism once again stirred under the surface. I was still very much the conventional Afrikaner boy; but even without being really conscious of it, I may have been beginning to turn to writing, no longer as escape or diversion, but as a way of coming to grips, however limply and tentatively, with some of the real tensions underlying my seemingly placid, untroubled, terribly conventional world.

But there was so much more to learn. What I had begun to acquire at the time of that first book was an awareness of language and of its specific functioning in storytelling. The marvel of Hamlet's words, words, words. But there was another major step ahead. It was one signalled by a philosopher friend in a discussion about truth – truth in fiction, truth in general. 'As I see it,' he said, 'you can approach truth from two opposite directions. You can see it as something that has been said so many times that it crystallises into a final and definite shape. For this, language is indispensable. But you can also see truth as only that which can *not* be said. Not ever. In no word. That which eternally eludes the word.'

Today it seems to me that truth – at least the truth of fiction, of writing – does not lie in either of these extremes, but in their interaction. Neither in the word nor in silence, but in the tension *between* them. It was Calvino who showed me that what is said, ultimately, can only be said by virtue of what remains forever unsayable.

AWAKENING TO BLACK AND WHITE

HOW COULD ANYONE, I OFTEN WONDER, HOW COULD *I*, NOT SEE WHAT WAS happening in the country, what was going to happen? I grew up among black people. The small white villages of my childhood were always enclaves surrounded by blacks. I *must* have seen. I must have *known*! There must have been an unbearable tension, all the time, day after day, day and night.

But perhaps tension itself becomes normal after a while. It is the benchmark by which one judges everything. And at the core of it all was the simple – *simple*?! – fact of black and white.

Black and white, black and white, all the time. Shorthand for the full complexity and all the problems it poses to South Africa.

Yet we did not face it as a problem, not *then*, not when I was a child. It was simply the way we lived, the way God had ordained it. Or was it?

Nowadays, particularly at times of near despair about the uncertainty that lies just under the skin of the new South Africa, I reach for the kind of faith that informs a small incident which happened a few years ago to a good friend in Cape Town. At the age of five, his son had just started preschool. And much to the delight of my friend, who is white, his son very quickly became close friends with a black boy. It was no ordinary friendship. The two were quite inseparable. Then, after a few months, one afternoon, the white boy was present when his black friend was picked up from school by his father. The little white boy gawked in amazement. And very early the next morning he was at school to await the arrival of his friend. The moment

41

he saw him, the white boy ran to the gate, breathless with excitement. 'You never told me,' he cried, 'that your daddy was black!'

There is much that is still not working in our new system of education. But if this is what it does to perceptions of race, we must be doing something right. It is an anecdote which I trot out time and time again, whenever I encounter sceptics about the significance of the changes that have been happening in South Africa. And obviously one such tiny swallow cannot make a summer. But something *is* happening! And it is enough to make one want to weep for all the lost chances of the past. How different, how devastatingly different, the world was when *I* went to school, when black and white moved in completely different orbits.

We had contact, naturally. But in the home, at work, at school, everywhere we met on the most superficial level imaginable, emerging from our alien, different worlds, and returning to them after every fleeting encounter.

There was even, in our youth, something that might pass for friendship. During the weekends and holidays I spent on the farms of friends, we experienced a natural, unquestioned and unquestioning affinity among all the boys, black and white. We would spend whole days playing together, fashioning clay oxen at the river, hunting birds with catapults, staging wars with *kleilatte* – long switches, usually cut from quince trees, with small balls of wet clay affixed to the tips, a hit from which could sting like a wasp. We would scour the veld for tortoises, or the sloughed papery skins of snakes, the whitened skulls of long-dead cattle, or duikers, or meerkats, or hares. We would brag about our biceps, and some of the boys would compare the size and shape of their pricks, we would hide behind the outdoor privy to raise the flap covering the bucket to spy, with fiercely suppressed giggles, on whoever came to squat on the grainy seat inside, or invent jokes or postures that would send us into fits and howls of laughter. But as the daylight faded, we would disperse and go to our different homes: we, the white boys, to the sprawling homestead of the farmer, the black boys to their huts and hovels. This was never discussed. It didn't even occur to us to do so. It was how the world functioned, according to the same immutable laws that governed the rising or setting of sun and moon, the slow reeling of the constellations of stars overhead at night, the way poultry and dogs and cattle and sheep followed the habits of their kind. God was in his heaven, and all was right with the world.

This lasted more or less until puberty, when the black boys were drawn into the patterns of the lives of their elders, with their appointed chores and their subservience, and the white boys into the lives of the bosses; and if, previously, they might have called us 'Theuns' or 'André' or 'Gert', this would, almost unperceived, change to 'Kleinbaas Theuns', 'Kleinbaas André', 'Kleinbaas Gert', just as our sisters would become 'Kleinnooi' or 'Kleinmies'. And there was reassurance in this. Life had its patterns and rites and fixed commandments.

Fear? Yes, there was fear. It surfaced mainly in small, real – and often preposterous – pockets of experience. For instance: some mornings when Elbie and I woke up in the room we were sharing at the time, there would be a black man sleeping under the bed. We never saw him. We just knew he *was* there. He had a long, sharp knife. And sometime he was going to get us. He would carve us up into little bits and devour us. The fact that it never happened, did not make it any less real.

Where did the image come from? Our parents were gentle, decent, Christian people. But ah, what darkness and terrors lurked under that harmless appearance! We knew, by then, some of the lurid or scary passages tucked away between the black leather covers of the Bible. But we had no secure knowledge – only ominous intimations – about the hidden, threatening corners and recesses behind the most everyday occurrences of our lives.

I believe that a whole history lay submerged behind the black man under the bed. That version of South African history that had been prepared, and sanctioned as an extension of biblical truth, through 300 years of colonialism – a racist and patriarchal version devised by white men (and in this equation both 'white' and 'men' were determinants). Year after year at school we were brainwashed by holier-than-thou accounts of the 'Kaffir Wars' on the eastern frontier of the Cape colony in which wave upon wave of murderous attacks by black, heathen savages on the small bastion of white civilisation between Table Bay and the Great Fish River to the east, and Table Bay and the Gariep River in the north were repelled by steadfast Christians fighting with God on their side. Scattered through this unfolding scroll were small, specific incidents of black brutality: the families of free burghers or intrepid colonists in remote wattle-and-daub homes in the deep interior attacked and wiped out; Voortrekkers who fled British domination to found free republics of their own in Natal and Transvaal, set upon by murderous hordes and treacherously slaughtered, small children lured into the veld to have their limbs hacked off and their throats slit, unprotected laagers of women and children left behind at the Blaauwkrantz River while the men were at the kraal of the Zulu king Dingane to negotiate a peaceful settlement, over-whelmed in the night and exterminated – the women butchered with assegais, the children's brains dashed out against the wagon wheels. Later, in the Anglo-Boer War, blacks – in this sanctioned version of Afrikaner history – were enlisted by British soldiers to rape Boer women, burn down their home-steads, and transport them on open wagons to concentration camps where they were fed on ground glass.

Rare indeed were narratives about friendly blacks – of the motherly woman Amakeia who rescued a white baby in the Amatola range of the Xhosa territory during a time of war and sheltered him against her own people; or of Xhosa warriors during the frontier wars killing white men in combat but refraining from raising a hand against white women or chil-dren; or of an old black man saving the lives of two white boys on a remote farm and then getting killed for it by warriors from his own tribe. Such incidents occurred, in history or poem or story, but they caused amazement and wonder precisely because of their extraordinary and exceptional quality. Deep in the national consciousness slumbered the darker and more violent memories, conditioning a whole people to see their survival in the African wilderness as a re-enactment of the Old Testament and a direct consequence of divine intervention.

All of this found expression in the local literature. Silence itself was a form of articulation. Even in the early work of a much admired Afrikaans writer like Karel Schoeman blacks are often simply absent. The farms and villages of the country are represented as if only whites live there. In the novels of other writers black and brown characters feature sometimes as comic relief, or as a kind of descant to 'white' themes. When they do move to the centre of the stage, as in some work of the forties and fifties by Mikro,

44

the attitude is paternalist and patronising. In the wake of Alan Paton's *Cry, the Beloved Country*, the hugely popular F. A. Venter produced a strongly derivative novel, *Swart Pelgrim (Black Pilgrim)* that closely followed the stereotyped recipe of *Jim-comes-to-Joburg*. It was not without merit, but the message was laid on with a heavy hand: only in their own demarcated areas could black people find some measure of fulfilment. One of my own early short stories, written in the fifties, but mercifully never published in book form, recounts the via dolorosa of a black man from a 'homeland' who loses contact with his roots in the white man's city, and then returns to his place of origin, only to find that he can no longer be at home there either. Depressingly moralising. But perhaps it was, at least, an attempt – failed, but well meant – to express something of an inner unrest about the racial situation in the country.

From my own childhood I remember a serial in a children's newspaper recounting the life of a little slave girl, Fytjie, in the early days of the Cape, and its haunting account of the cruelties she suffered at the hands of her owners, and of how she was stripped naked and flogged in front of the castle for some minor infringement. A story of another kind, by the author Jan Scannell, from the time I was about fourteen, narrated the remarkable – and ultimately tragic – life of a black child reared by a white family and his vain attempts at being accepted by their community. The moral was obvious: races can only lead successful lives if kept apart. But there was something about the human waste involved that kept nagging my thoughts for years, just as little Fytjie's suffering came to lodge like a live coal in a sensitive spot of my memory, waiting to be resuscitated in some of my own later writings.

Those readings were an indispensable part of my growing up: in a large measure I can say today that every watershed in my life, every moment of true discovery, has been marked by a book, or books. This holds true for discoveries of an emotional, intellectual or moral kind through writers such as Camus, Dostoevsky, Fitzgerald, Faulkner, Undset and others, but inevitably also for a gradual progress in thinking about race.

Apart from these glowing exceptions, the reading matter we were raised on, and the history transmitted to us in church and school and home, fixed indelibly in my young mind the image of the dark Other, the dangerous black man lurking under the bed. It was that basic fear which made it possible to excuse almost any outrage committed upon black people around me in my youth. That – and the absence of sufficiently strong images to the contrary.

I remember that in my fourth or fifth year at university somebody invited a black academic to address us. He was, as I recall, the renowned Professor Z. K. Matthews, known as a man of very moderate and accommodating views and therefore condemned and rejected by many black leaders: but to us he was a stranger. For the first and only time in my youth I encountered a black man who was *not* a servant or a labourer of some kind. The mere fact of a black person in the role of a teacher, or a doctor, or a lawyer, had never even entered my consciousness. And Matthews was too unique, his appearance on our campus too fleeting, to unsettle the thought patterns of my first twenty years.

What did set me thinking, because it must have occurred at almost the same time as the performance by Professor Z. K. Matthews, was one of the most remarkable lectures I have ever heard. It was in our final undergraduate year in history, and it was delivered by Professor D. W. Kruger, an academic famous for his pro-apartheid convictions. But he was also a true historian who assiduously went in search of historical truth. And in this lecture, in preparation for a course on the French Revolution, he compared the situation in South Africa at the time, the late fifties, with that in France on the eve of the Revolution. It was a tour de force. And because of Kruger's reputation as a historian, it did prepare a small space in my mind for what was to happen.

Many years later, at the end of 1989, on the eve of the political changeover in South Africa (although very few people in South Africa could actually foresee it at that time), a small group of mainly Afrikaans intellectuals were invited to Paris to meet members of the ANC in exile. It was a follow-up encounter after the watershed meeting in Dakar in 1987. One morning we were scheduled to meet French politicians in the Assemblée Nationale. Thabo Mbeki was scheduled to speak on behalf of the South Africans. But on that morning Thabo was reported to be unavailable. The term used was 'indisposed'. And on the bus on the way to the Assemblée Pallo Jordan (now minister of arts and culture) was asked to stand in. There was no time at all to prepare. Yet minutes later he went to the podium in the Assemblée and stunned everybody with his analysis of the French Revolution. In a way a circle was completed, bringing together a Nationalist professor of history at the University of Potchefstroom and a black activist in the French National Assembly.

Racism, in its vicious and destructive forms, was never overtly preached in our home. Yet it was omnipresent. The subtly pernicious way in which it manifested itself was evident from my father's attitude to music. He was never what one could call a musical man, but there were songs he loved – none as much as that aria from *Samson and Delilah*, 'Softly awakes my heart', sung by Marion Anderson. He would drop whatever he might be doing to come and listen to that magnificent voice. If ever he could be moved to tears by a piece of music, this was it. And then, when I started university, I made a discovery which I couldn't wait to share with the parents. 'Did you know,' I asked them at the lunch table, 'that Marion Anderson is black?'

My father never listened to that aria again. And when it did come on the radio, he would turn it off or leave the house. I remained bewitched by her voice.

Indirectly, events like these paved the way for an incident which happened near the end of my studies at Potchefstroom. The government had just announced a series of severe new restrictions on access to university studies for blacks. The measure went under the name of The Extension of University Education Act, an appellation typical of the convoluted thinking of the Nationalist government: there were no extensions involved, only restrictions, which severely limited the opportunities of black students wishing to study at white universities. Our Students' Representative Council arranged a debate with the liberal, English-speaking University of the Witwatersrand (Wits) and the whole event was staged as a showdown between Afrikaner and English universities, and on the evening the hall was packed.

The debate, regrettably, was predictable. All our students spoke in

Afrikaans and supported the apartheid line; the Wits students vehemently rejected it, in English. In a surge of bravado I also joined in. I spoke in English and aligned myself with the opponents. There was surprise and glee among the visitors, outrage among my fellow Afrikaners. The matter was regarded as so serious that I was summoned by the rector. But after that everything simmered down. In the larger context it was a non-event. It made no difference whatsoever to the course of the bill through parliament or the debates in the country. But on our campus I was now irrevocably branded as a renegade, a *kafferboetie*. Even that did not make much of a dent: in the safe, comfortable context of our student body everybody knew everybody, everybody had a preassigned role. Mine was that of the rebel, the heretic. It didn't warrant more than a shrug or a wry smile: most of my fellow students presumably saw it as a deliberate minor act of provocation. A gesture in Sartre's terminology; not an act.

But to me, secretly, it did mark some kind of a shift. The problem was that I lacked the guts to go beyond the gesture; I could not really step outside the laager. It was much too dark and unpredictable out there. And deep down I still clung to the values I had been brought up with. It would take more than a student debate to make a difference, either to others or myself. That black man was still lying, and waiting, ominously, under the bed.

THE PLAY'S THE THING

IT MUST BE A NATURAL IMPULSE THAT HAS ALWAYS LINKED THE TWO EXPERIENCES of theatre and religion in my mind. And it came back to me through my wife Karina's account of her early experience of religion in Poland, when she must have been about seven and became intrigued by her friend Gosia's habit of 'going somewhere' every Sunday morning. Having grown up in an almost non-religious home it meant nothing to Karina when in reply to her inevitable question Gosia said, 'Church.'

'What is church?' she asked.

Gosia tried to explain, but that didn't really clarify the matter; so the following Sunday she took Karina with her. Almost immediately she was hooked. It might have been inspired, at least partly, by the fact that little Gosia also happened to be the first girl that introduced her to sex. In a way church was the next step, and might turn out to be just as pleasurable and adventurous. The first real problem arose when Karina turned nine and learned that she could not take her first Communion with her friends as she had not been christened. Serious family deliberations. Then, a lasting credit to their understanding, her parents agreed to what must have been something of a traumatic weekend: first, they had to consent to getting married in church (her father undoubtedly tongue in cheek), followed by Karina's and her brother Krystian's christenings. At last she was ready to become a little bride of Jesus. But there was a final ritual to go through: blessing her splendid new rosary with a sprinkling of holy water. Unfortunately, she was playing soccer with the boys that afternoon and forgot all about Mass. The only remedy was to slip into church early the next morning, dipping her small hand into the holy water, and liberally sprinkling her own rosary, before drying off the excess holiness on her dress.

From there, everything went smoothly. Except that she began to have misgivings about confession. For a while she handled the challenge by inventing wild and weird sins for every session with the priest, but in the long run it became too taxing for the imagination. She reached an understanding with God that she would privately keep him informed of all her transgressions, imagined or real, without the intervention of a third party, and for some time religion became more or less manageable. Most of the time her devotions were confined to the construction of endless small shrines, mostly underground. But even that became boring. In due course the upheavals in her family life became too much for faith: fleeing to Austria when she was ten; and then emigrating to the United States for a year when she was twelve. The idea of confessing one's sins, not only to a total stranger, but in a completely foreign language, English, became too much for religion to bear and in due course she happily settled into atheism.

There was so much intrinsic theatricality in the whole story that my own youthful infatuation with religion faded by comparison. It made me realise that one of the main reasons why in the long run (and it did indeed take a long time for me to make the break) religion failed me, was that it simply could not fulfil the need for spectacle and drama I had brought to it.

That is why, whenever I think about that long and unrequited affair with religion, the theatre inevitably becomes part of it.

In my own life, it is not easy to decide which of the two came first. If exposure as such must determine the answer, religion would win, beginning I presume with my christening, when the dominee, the pastor, a well-meaning old man known for the rather irresponsible vigour with which he sprinkled the holy water on the foreheads of the infants at the font, became so carried away by the actions he performed on that cold but bright Sunday morning that according to the reports of my parents I was all but drowned. But it need not have been an altogether traumatic experience. I can remember when at the age of five or so my youngest son, Danie, came swooshing down a slide and splashed into the deep end of a swimming pool at a resort where we were on holiday. It happened right in front of me, but it was so unexpected that for a while I couldn't believe my eyes. Only when after about a minute he still hadn't reappeared I dived in, got hold of his long blond hair and plucked him to the surface. He spluttered and belched and choked. But as soon as he caught his breath again he gasped, 'Can I go again?' That may well have been my own reaction to my watery introduction to organised religion.

But after that early moment of drama church remained, for many years, a rather uninspiring business. The only visual feature in the stark Protestant interior of our church on which one's eyes could profitably dwell, was the legend proclaiming, in Gothic script so unreadable that we used to believe it must have been written by God himself: *God is Love*. It was disfigured by the large water stain on the whitewashed wall above the dominee's head, on which I have dwelled before, in which one could conjure up all kinds of fantastic shapes: a dying Jesus, a rampant Devil, the monsters Brolloks and Bittergal from the wonderful, scary Afrikaans stories by C. J. Langenhoven, naked fairies, a camel, a weasel, something very like a whale. In Sunday school in Jagersfontein there was the entertainment provided by Oom Koot, who led the singing. In Douglas there was Ouma Sielie who took a peppermint to church to bribe her granddaughter Santie into silence; but the process of biting the sweet in half by positioning it between the only two teeth she had in her mouth, one top left, the other bottom right, was so laborious that it kept me oblivious of any divine message. Sermons, I must confess, never held much interest for me and served mainly as occasions for daydreaming, making up stories, or cherishing all manner of thoughts, not all of them pious. It was only well into my university years that for the first time it dawned on me that sermons were actually meant to be listened to.

The Bible was different. Most of its stories I came to know by heart. It became, as Peter Ackroyd described its influence on Shakespeare's youth, 'an echo chamber of the imagination'. For me, as for most other Afrikaner children, it provided the only coherent mythology we could consistently draw on. It underpinned the ubiquitous violence of the world we grew up in. We were spellbound by the stories of Cain and Abel or of Esau and Jacob – what a perverse old man their God was – the exploits of Samson with his bare hands or with the jawbone of an ass, Jephthah sacrificing his only daughter and Abraham preparing to slaughter his son Isaac and to drive Hagar off into the desert with his firstborn son Ishmael, the Israelites dancing around the golden calf, the destruction of Jericho, David mourning the loss of Jonathan and later of Absalom, the death of Jezebel, Jonah in the belly of the whale or Daniel in the den of the lions, the passion of Christ, the terrifying visions of Saint John. And there were the darker, more troubling undertones in the stories of Lot and his daughters, of Samson and Delilah, of Onan, of David and Abigail, and David and Tamar, and David and Bathshebah.

Indeed, religion meant primarily the enthralment of stories, all the more so because of the booming organ tones of the language of the Bible. In many of the families with whom I spent weekends and holidays on their farms, the Bible was still the old seventeenth-century state version in Dutch; but even the much more recently translated Afrikaans version had a grand, archaic ring to it. This, more than any doctrine or liturgy, determined the hold of religion on my youthful mind. And a stranglehold it certainly was, induced primarily, as it now seems to me, by fear of any alternative. Hell was such a dire reality that one really had no choice but to cling to God.

There was also a theatrical element to it: not just in the tones of the dominee's voice as he summoned us to salvation or (most gorily and spectacularly, with weeping and gnashing of teeth) to perdition, but also in the games I could devise in our garden. With my sister Elbie I could play Adam and Eve, naturally without clothes, until my father put a stop to it. On my own I could walk in the furnace of Nebuchadnezzar or in the Garden of Gethsemane, I could wrestle with Jacob's angel or climb up the steep slope of Mount Zion to receive the Tables of the Law, or look on Canaan from the distant summit of Mount Nebo, or test, with Gideon and his kneeling band, the syllables of *shibboleth* on a host of enemies, or climb in a barren fig tree to watch the passing Jesus, or be resurrected from death with the smelly Lazarus, or preach with the apostle Paul in the Areopagus in Athens, or become a stuttering Moses turning a walking stick into a snake or a snake into a walking stick, or try to suspend myself from a pepper tree branch to die with the crucified Jesus. Those were not just re-enactments, not roles I played: I *knew* what it was to see the smoke of my burnt offering rejected by God and to be driven to the Land of Nod, I *knew* what it meant to be thrown into a well by my own brothers and sold as a slave and carried off on the back of a camel to a distant Egypt, even, so help me God, *knew* what it was – especially after my tryst with the smooth little Maureen – to have the wife of Potiphar groping at me, *knew* how to kill the giant Goliath, or how to duck when King Saul hurled his sword at me and tried to pin me to the wall. Religion in those days could be dangerously real.

It was not enough to be a member of a congregation. I had to play an active role. I needed a congregation of my own. After entertaining for some time the notion of running away to what was then Nyasaland, now Malawi, or to China, and devote my life to preaching to the heathen, I decided to avoid the unpleasant risk of becoming a martyr. And it occurred to me that there might be enough souls in my immediate surroundings who were in danger of being condemned to everlasting flames. And so, once a week our garage was converted into a church, with a number of upturned boxes as pews, two big crates precariously balanced as a pulpit; and thither I would summon, with my mother's small dining bell, all the domestics of the neighbourhood for an hour of blood-curdling preaching, boisterous singing, and passionate prayers. A particularly painful memory is of transposing directly into one of my most fervent sermons a message I had heard in church and at prayers in school: this was based on the sad scene following the Deluge, when the drunken Noah lay naked, in a stupor, in his tent. His dutiful sons Shem and Japheth walked backwards into the tent, to cover their father with a blanket; but poor Ham, who had the misfortune of first discovering the snoring roisterer, and the temerity to laugh his head off, was cursed for all eternity to have his descendants serve as the water carriers and the hewers of wood for the offspring of his brothers. And very conscientiously I transmitted to my congregation the message I had heard in church and school, to the effect that, being black, *they* were the fruit of the cursed loins of Ham, which meant that it was the will of God that they should be the servants of us whites. In quiet dignity and serene humility they took in every word.

If I were still a believer today I often think that a well-aimed bolt from heaven might not have been entirely amiss.

As a sign that I was truly the messenger of God, I performed a miracle. Before the service I had placed a saucer filled with methylated spirits inside the top crate of my pulpit. Entering the church at the beginning of the service, with a striped towel over my shoulders as a cassock, I brought with me a second saucer filled to the brim with clean water. After my sermon I sipped from it, then passed it round for the congregation to do likewise. Once everybody had tasted it and pronounced the water to be indeed water, I placed this saucer inside the crate, then invoked the power of God to descend upon us all, removed the *first* saucer from inside the crate and lit a match to set it alight. After that, no one dared to suspect me of not being the anointed of our Heavenly Father, and my congregation grew at a most satisfactory pace.

In one of my never-ending attempts at making money, I performed the same trick during a more secular show of magic for a group of school friends. But this time it ended in spectacular failure when my best friend, suddenly turned traitor, came rushing up to the table which I used as the main prop of my performance, grabbed the flaming receptacle from my hands, took a sniff at it, and promptly denounced the chicanery. In my attempts to retrieve the saucer, the meths spilled on the table, setting alight the sheet that served as a cloth, and causing a fire that nearly burnt down the garage. It brought an untimely end to my show – which I'm sure was just as well as it prevented me from proceeding to the next item, in which I'd planned to stuff my sister Elbie into a box and saw her in half. In the larger scheme of things, as they say, it also brought an end to the earliest phase in my theatrical career as well as to my ambition of becoming a man of the cloth, since my parents denied me the future use of their premises for the mounting of any kind of performance whatsoever, including services aimed at the saving of souls and the perpetuation of white domination.

But they could not diminish the lure of the theatre. I was already near the end of my high-school studies before I saw my first live performance – an Afrikaans version of Molière's *Malade Imaginaire* in Lydenburg, a town rather larger than Douglas, where performances by theatrical companies must have been nearly as rare as rain. I was about fourteen or thereabouts when the only show deemed suitable by my parents came our way; but at the last moment the leading actor fell ill (an occurrence interpreted by many members of our congregation as an intervention from heaven) and the performance was cancelled, and that was that. Television was still unimaginable. There was a cinema, though, but my parents were very strict about what I was allowed to see. *Lassie*, yes; and oh, *Tarzan*. And the occasional Walt Disney and Shirley Temple. But nothing else. What occasions those were. The projector would invariably break down four or five times during a show, and it could take anything between five and forty-five minutes to repair, but we kids had a royal time during the breaks, with cold drinks and ice creams and chewing gum that could be turned into pellets with which to pepper unsuspecting grown-ups in the dark. The menu leading up to the main attraction was utterly predictable, starting with the advertisements, most of them handwritten, each one energetically applauded. Then came the news – *African Mirror* – always weeks after the event, followed by a cartoon that caused howls and screams of laughter. Next came the weekly instalment of a cowboys-and-crooks serial, in which every appearance of the villain was booed, every move of the hero wildly cheered. Then an interval. And only then the lights came down to a hush of anticipation. Even today, when a cinema grows dark, I feel something of the same tingle in the spine. But in those days it was magnified into almost unbearable expectation. Nothing could disappoint us or let us down. Every moment was climactic. And for days afterwards, with my friends on the playground, or on my own in the garden, those stories would be repeated, reinvented, blown up, appropriated, assimilated into a heightened awareness of a magic at the heart of the everyday world.

There was magic, too, in the shows of a conjuror and hypnotist called Craill who visited the villages of the north-west once every two years or so. This probably meant that he couldn't make it in the cities. But for us, for me, he was a true magician. On stage, in his black cloak spangled with silver moons and stars, and wearing a top hat from which white pigeons, rabbits or metres and metres of coloured silk scarves could be produced at the flick of a wrist, he was like a messenger from God, or from the Devil, as the case might be. The memories he left behind were intimations of another kind of world altogether. His acts of hypnotism stirred up unruly dreams about the feats I could perform should I ever gain access to that source of demonic power. For several years he was the hero of my dreams. Then something unexpected happened. For weeks every available space in town was plastered with multicoloured posters to advertise The Great Craill's forthcoming show. It took days of pleading before my parents caved in: as it was on a Saturday, and I'd be accompanied by my best friend, Louis Wessels, they could not very well refuse.

During the afternoon I went to the café next to the hall where the performance was to take place. As I emerged, eagerly stripping the first bar of chocolate of its wrapping, I became aware of outlandish sounds coming from the hall. With constricted throat and bouncing heart I crept to the door and peeped inside. In the dark foyer, sprawled across an easy chair, was a rather dishevelled old man in loose shirtsleeves and dirty trousers with open flies, snoring like a sawmill in need of repair, an empty White Horse bottle in one hand. He looked more like a tramp than the posters of the great magician with the massive silver mane and aristocratic mien overexposed in the blinding sun outside. Yet somehow I knew it could only be him. I just stood and stared. At some stage I must have made a sound of some kind, for he started in mid-snore and sat up, dropping his bottle, and uttering the kind of imprecation which would have earned me a mouthwash with blue soap. Such an encounter might have stripped him of all his magic forever. But it turned into an unforgettable afternoon. His tongue loosened, perhaps, by the White Horse, he talked in a long rambling monologue that washed over me like a river in flood. For all I know, he was stringing together most of Shakespeare's soliloquies, with some sonnets thrown in for free. I couldn't make out very much. But the language, the language alone, was like a torrent in which one could willingly drown. He was a man possessed. *This* was theatre. *This* was real magic.

As his possession wore off, his speech became more intelligible, if less spellbinding. I even dared to start asking some questions about his art. And he answered! He became more and more affable. He even offered to show me a few of his tricks: the less exotic ones, with cards, or producing a scarf from an eggshell, or making a magic wand disappear. Some of these I subsequently repeated, with great effect, to my school friends. But then I pushed my luck. What I really wanted to know, was how to make a girl float in the air, or to put someone in a box, pierce it with swords and daggers, and cause the person to reappear unscathed. He just smiled and shook his shaggy grey head. I pleaded more passionately. That was when he proposed a deal. He would show me if I . . . The terms of the deal were whispered very fast and wetly in my ear. I did not understand what he meant. He winked and brought his face closer. I could smell his breath. Like a meerkat mesmerised by a snake I just stared at him. He was salivating.

'I shall make you the greatest boy magician in the world,' he promised. 'You can ask me anything you want.'

I swallowed, unable to utter a word or make a move.

Then I became aware of his hand. An unusually large hand, moving slowly down my back like an enormous spider.

'Would you like that?' he asked, his face still very close to mine.

'My – my mother is waiting for me,' I mumbled, and fled.

That evening I went to his performance nevertheless.

For years I thought I must have imagined it. But I know I didn't. The strange thing is that even when that tawdry reality came between the great magician and me, I could not rid myself of my reverence for his greatness. And I still believe in magic.

Only once in all the years we lived in Douglas, from my eleventh to my sixteenth year, an Afrikaans film came to town, a tear-jerking, chauvinistic melodrama that extolled the virtues of rural life and decried the sins and horrors of the city, played by actors who mouthed their words with grotesque exaggeration and struck poses borrowed from the starkest of Greek tragedy. The experience was unforgettable. Old bearded men and their wives like loaves of bread that had risen outrageously overnight, bedecked in their Sunday best, the men in three-piece suits with watch chains across their ample bellies, the women in floral full-length dresses and broad-brimmed hats and black shoes with buttoned straps, arrived from outlying farms on horse-drawn spiders or donkey-carts, some of the more affluent in straight-backed Fords or heavily chromed Buicks and Hudson Terraplanes and Studebakers, each family lugging a large basket of *padkos* or food-for-the-road: hams and sausages, blue-boiled eggs, massive sandwiches, fried chickens, sliced legs of lamb, flasks of coffee, even the occasional camou-flaged bottle of Mellow-Wood or Collison's brandy. On the market square they mingled with the townsfolk with their own provisions and accoutre-ments. And during the interval there was a massive orgy of eating and drinking that spilled from the seats into the aisles and the foyer and right across the market square, which meant that many members of the audience returned late for the main film, missing their seats in the dark or finding the seats occupied by chancers who had slipped in during the interval; which caused such an uproar that the film had to be stopped so that the mayor, the more than life-size Oom Boy Cilliers, wearing his chain of office, could first confer with the projectionist until agreement was reached to start again. But by then the rolls of film had become mixed up, so that the story started in the middle; and it was nearly midnight before the show was over and the crowd, many of them with staggering or swaggering gait, could break out into the streets, women weeping, men singing patriotic songs. It was worse than any New Year's Eve.

In the absence of live theatre there was something even better: the circus. It never came to Jagersfontein, but it did pay the odd visit to Fauresmith, which was only seven miles away. Usually my parents found good reasons for not allowing us to go. But once, only once, when there was a perform-ance on a Saturday night and friends of the family offered to take me along, they gave their permission. That night came closer to magic than anything I had ever experienced before. It began from the moment we entered when the legendary Mrs Pagel, wife of the circus owner, dressed in a lion's skin, sat poised on a multicoloured drum at the entrance to survey the crowd and occasionally, with a huge roar, pounced on a few terrified black chil-dren as they tried to slide in under the tent. The trapeze artists, the clowns, the dogs and horses and ponies, the camels and zebras, the lions and striped Bengal tigers, the huge brown bear, were quite literally from another world. The scene of the bear chasing a terrified little clown who finally dived into a doll's house which promptly collapsed on him, haunted me for years. Later Charlie Chaplin became the only person with whom I could identify as unreservedly as with that hysterical little man; and in the bear was concentrated all the dark, louring, unresolved energies that haunt the night side of the world and the deepest recesses of dreams.

The blaring music and blazing lights, the ringmaster with his articulate whip, the wild and beautiful and unbelievable creatures parading before us, stunned me so overwhelmingly that on the way home, afterwards, I couldn't utter a single word. Tiptoeing into the dark house after I had been dropped at the gate, I was terrified at what might be following me: I would have walked backwards if I hadn't been even more scared of what might jump on me from inside the house. I don't think I slept a wink all night. But I might have slept throughout the following day, if I hadn't been dragged out of bed the next morning to go to church, where in front of my eyes the gesticulating, bellowing dominee kept on changing shape: one moment he was a ringmaster, then a clown, then a lion, then an almost naked girl in a dazzling silver costume, then a bear rearing on its hind legs and preparing to jump on me. I came round with a scream that must have woken up half the congregation, and only my mother's face, red with shock and shame, made me realise where I was.

For weeks after that I performed the circus on our back stoep and in the garden. Elbie and our housekeeper, Mina, had to play all the minor roles, from dog to camel to gymnast to Mrs Pagel to lion. For one whole Saturday Elbie had to squat on the ground tied to a tree, while I was, of course, the ringmaster, the lord of magic. I knew then that I would either acquire my own circus one day, or become a lion tamer. My future was secure.

Shortly afterwards I made my own debut on stage. Once again it was in Fauresmith, this time in a school concert. All I had to do was to recite a poem. It was short and humorous, and I practised for weeks to make sure I would make a lasting impression on my audience. But none of that could prepare me for the reception I got. The poem brought the house down. I was hugely satisfied, having practically made up my mind that if something went wrong with my designs on a circus career, I might settle for a future on the stage. But when I arrived backstage, the audience still yelling and laughing and cheering in their seats, my father was there, waiting. And I could see that something was very wrong. It turned out that I had gone on stage with an open fly and that a thin tail of the brand new, stark white shirt I was wearing, had found its way through the gap in my navy blue shorts. Not such a propitious beginning. In fact, my career as a public performer might have ended before it had properly begun. For a while I considered a career in the church after all.

What held me in thrall to the church was not only the stories and their magic, but – even in those arid Calvinist services, in those whitewashed interiors – the sense of ritual. And, undoubtedly, an awareness of authority, of power, pointing ultimately to God Almighty.

Ritual pervaded everything. Although it had neither the colour nor the variety of Catholicism, the unwavering, predictable order of a service provided a feeling of security, suggesting the presence of immutable laws. Even to lighter moments it lent a gravity, a deeply satisfying sense of coherence. To my writing, over the years, ritual has always been important: Mozart or Chopin in the background and Beethoven's Third whenever I really get stuck, a pair of scissors within reach to snip at my hair in moments of doubt, the *Don Quixote* on the shelf above my left shoulder. And although for many years now there has been no religious dimension to it, I believe that the origins of these little rituals lie in the churches of my youth – in Miss Libby's overambitious skirmishes with Bach and the surprising movements of her floral hat behind the organ, in the way the dominee led his row of elders and deacons in black, my father always among them, from the vestry to their pews before he ascended the pulpit, in his way of opening the big Bible, in the alternation of singing and reading and praying, in the cadences of his preaching voice. Even in the rhythmic swinging of Driekie's pretty legs opposite our appointed seats there was the gravity and reassurance of ritual: it was the one occasion in the week when I could stare and stare at her to my heart's content and feel the blessed closeness of the Lord. The fact that it was her father up on the pulpit, so much closer to God than the rest of us in our pews, added an awareness of danger to her presence.

And week after week the service was repeated, in the same order, with the same portentous weightiness. Whatever else in our lives might change, those Sunday mornings kept their shape, and held us in check. Because behind the ritual loomed the authority of God the Father, the Son, and the Holy Ghost, on whom everything depended. It was raw fear, it was awe, that circumscribed my world. Until . . .

I don't know how or when the shift came, and it was only much later that I acknowledged what should have been obvious: that it is the very *presence* of authority, the *fact* of power that evokes rebellion and makes it possible. Without the threat of power the heretic – the one who chooses – cannot exist.

I must have been at least fourteen when I broke the ritual for the first time. There was no particular reason: I simply 'did not feel' like going to church that morning. And said so, firmly expecting all hell to break loose. But it did not. My father had already left for the church council meeting that always preceded the morning service. My mother merely looked quizzically at me and asked, 'Are you sure?'

With a parched throat I said, 'Yes. I'm not going.'

'All right then,' she said calmly. 'You can stay here and think of God.'

She left with Elbie and little Marita. I remained behind. I couldn't wait for them to be gone. A whole glorious morning all to myself . . . !

It was the dreariest Sunday morning of my childhood. There was nothing to do. Not even cafés were open on a Sunday. On the radio there was only a church service to tune in to. I opened a book, became bored after a single page, and put it away again. I had always thought that the Sunday afternoons of the summer holidays we spent on the farm of my mother's sister, Auntie Dolly, were the worst imaginable: for there we would be confined to our beds in the steaming heat, instructed to read 'edifying literature' on which we were required to report later, dazedly aware of the green and deep blue farm stretching out to all sides around the house, redolent of summer – heavy bunches of black grapes, bees buzzing among yellow peaches and purple plums, the amber water of the farm dam lapping against the banks with their smell of bruised grass. But this Sunday was worse. There was nothing to drag me through the hour of the church service, no relief to hope for, no diversion at all from the utter blankness of just sitting there, waiting and waiting and waiting for the time to pass. The emptiness of God was unbearable.

And there was another perception of God waiting to break like a huge pomegranate spilling its seeds. After we had moved on to the small Transvaal town of Sabie, my mother started corresponding with the wife of the dominee who had stayed behind, the successor of Driekie's father: a kindly, thickset man who resembled a large pink pig, with a perennial smile incised on his fleshy face. My mother usually never minded if I read the letters she received from the many friends and aunts and cousins with whom she corresponded. But that particular letter from Mrs Dominee was forbidden territory. For that very reason, of course, I couldn't wait to read it behind my mother's back. That was the letter in which I learned about the disillusioning marriage of the couple who represented God the Father in our congregation, about the violent abuse by which it was marked, how Dominee would kick and beat his wife if she dared to confront him with his affairs. I wanted to get rid of the letter, but in morbid fascination I had to read it to the end before I stuffed it back into its blue envelope. I felt sick. This was the man of God who week after week had invoked the flames of hell to scare us on to the straight and narrow, who would hover over us with tear-streaked chubby cheeks as he spoke of the infinite love and mercy of the Lord. There was no reason at all to believe that what I had discovered about him inside that blue envelope was true of all dominees. Certainly, Driekie's father must have been very different. But this could not redeem the fat one. For a couple of years he had been not only the representative of God but, in a disquieting way, God himself, just like the bread and wine of Holy Communion that turned into the body and blood of Christ. So if our dominee was contaminated, God himself was at risk. At great risk. All of a sudden both the religious and the theatrical became extended endlessly. Good and evil could no longer be readily distinguished. Even without realising it then, something inside me was being prepared for more dangerous and more significant future choices.

In the meantime another preoccupation, which may be viewed as theatre of a different kind, had begun to claim my interest. It was sport, which even today is one of my deepest passions. My own involvement, inherited from my father, was tennis. From the age of about eight, when I could barely handle a racket, he made sure that I spent a fair deal of my time on the red clay courts of the villages we lived in. Wherever we went, he was the number one player of the local team. My mother played an indifferent game, mainly for the enjoyment, but to him it was serious. It was a pleasaure to watch him, and something of an ordeal to be coached by him. Even though he had infinite patience, his restrained way of showing displeasure was enough to make me shrivel up inside.

From the beginning he made it clear that he expected only the best from me, in tennis as in everything else; and he imposed a somewhat one-sided pact with me: if ever I became good enough to beat him, he would retire from the game. For many years this possibility never even entered my thoughts; but as I grew more proficient it became a kind of threat at the back of my mind. I *wanted* him to be invincible, he just *had* to be the best. And in later years I have begun to wonder whether it wasn't this mindset that literally paralysed me to make me incapable of beating him. A theme for a story, perhaps? Certainly, one of the most traumatic moments of my life, when I was about seventeen, was when a group of South Africa's top players visited Sabie, where we then lived, to play a series of exhibition matches against each other and our local stars. My father was chosen to play singles against Abe Segal, then – following Eric Sturgess, who once made the mixed doubles final at Wimbledon – the country's number one. Deep inside me, I had no doubt. My father would thrash Segal. Afterwards he would move on to Wimbledon to join the great names from past and present I adopted for myself whenever I was practising in the gravelled yard against the back wall of the house: Fred Perry, The Three Musketeers, Jaroslav Drobny, Ken Rosewall.

Segal beat my father 6–0, 6–0. It was like a personal humiliation, as if darkness had descended over my own future. Long before my father had his first heart attack, which forced him to abandon tennis, this match stamped him as mortal. Things between us were never quite the same as before. My father dutifully continued to encourage me, but I never even made the second team either at school or at university, although I continued to love the game;

and one of my unforgettable experiences was to go to Wimbledon with my friend Naas in 1961, and watch the great final between Rod Laver and Chuck McKinley.

I continued to play, on and off, while I lectured at Rhodes University, and later at UCT; but I never cherished any secret hopes of grandeur any more. Which did not prevent me from living intensely through every Grand Slam played by Bjorn Borg. Later on, I transferred my enthusiasm to Sampras. Today I watch Federer with admiration, but not with the passion I reserve for Nadal – for the same reason that I adore Beethoven more than Bach, or Dostoevsky more than Tolstoy.

Rugby is a different matter. I never played, except in a single disastrous practice when I scored under the wrong posts when I was nine; but I have been an aficionado all my life. At university, I regret to say, I often took a book with me to the stadium for an intervarsity match, to do some reading during the interval or when the game became boring. But I certainly went to much trouble to attend the great international games against the Wallabies or British Lions, even if it meant hitch-hiking for most of a day to and from Ellis Park in Johannesburg.

What had first turned my interest into fanatic enthusiasm, was the All Blacks tour of South Africa in 1949. Our school travelled in a rickety bus from Douglas to Kimberley, where Fred Allen's team took on, and demolished, Griqualand West, and I cheered for the lanky local full back, Jack van der Schyff, even when he wasn't on the field. Not long afterwards, Hennie Muller's Springboks toured the British Isles – the most unforgettable match being the Test against Scotland at Murrayfield; and the final score, 44–0, remains etched into the mind of any rugby-loving South African. I loved the blood and gore, the crunching, death-defying scrums and tackles, of those games, the sheer power of the forwards, while the skill of the successful backline movements – from Fonnie du Toit to Hansie Brewis, to Lategan and van Schoor, and then to a wing like Tom van Vollenhoven – enthralled me like chess, or ballet, or the elegance of a solved mathematical problem. If a bad game can be an insult to the emotions and the intelligence, a good and fluid game may indeed resemble a concerto or a symphony, a tone poem or a ballet.

In the late eighties, my very good friend Gerrit Geertsema, then director of the Performing Arts Council of the Transvaal, made a trip to Paris to meet Nureyev and attempt to secure the rights for his company to produce the ballet of *Don Quixote*, for which Nureyev had devised the choreography. This seemed like a totally impossible idea at the time, at the height of the international cultural boycott of South Africa, but Gerrit is not a person to be thwarted lightly. In Paris he went to the Opéra, where Nureyev was said to be rehearsing; there was some kind of strike going, but he managed to get through the barriers. Inside, he told the receptionist that he had an appointment with Monsieur Nureyev. She much regretted the inconvenience, but said that Nureyev was not available. Gerrit pointed out that he had travelled 10,000 kilometres to keep the appointment. *Tant pis*, she commiserated. Don't worry, he assured her. He would just wait here until Nureyev was free. You don't understand, she said. Oh, but I do, I do, he assured her. A battle of wits began. After about eight hours, the receptionist told Gerrit that she was going to lock up. Don't worry about me, he said. If necessary, he would just wait there until the next day.

In a state of near-consternation, she disappeared through a door behind the counter, marked *Privé*. After ten minutes, she returned, somewhat the worse for wear.

Monsieur Nureyev was on the point of going into a rehearsal, she said with clipped syllables. But he was prepared to see his South African visitor provided he would not take up more than five minutes.

Mumbling something unintelligible, Gerrit followed her.

Nureyev expressed his regret for not being able to have a proper discussion. It would have been a pleasure to spend a few minutes with someone from the country of the Springboks.

You know about the Springboks? asked Gerrit.

I never miss any of their games on TV, Nureyev assured him. Unfortunately we do not often have the chance.

It is not easy at the moment, with the sanctions, said Gerrit. But they are a rather formidable team right now. I saw them a week ago and—

You saw them a week ago?

And right there everything changed. For an hour, like two excited schoolboys, they eagerly discussed the Springbok game; and then Gerrit was invited to accompany Nureyev to his rehearsal. In the late evening, exhausted but radiant, Gerrit was reluctantly allowed to go. As a little aside to their eager discussions, Nureyev mentioned that if he really wanted the rights to the choreography of *Don Quixote*, they were his.

There is indeed music and poetry in rugby, of a kind I learned years later to admire in a good *corrida* in Spain: although the beauty of a successful encounter is derived largely from its rarity; as a truly good game of rugby is more often than not achieved only against the background of innumerable wretched and messy failures. Perhaps this is what keeps one hooked to Springbok rugby, which is so often the most brutally awful in the world, allowing the rare gems of perfection to shine with a brilliance seldom encountered anywhere else. But even more pertinently than music, it is drama that has always lured me to rugby. Because I was a timid and scrawny kid, my bloodlust had to be projected elsewhere; and rugby was the ideal theatre of vicarious adventure and drama. Not only did it present the classical struggle between a protagonist and an antagonist, and lots of action, but over the years – throughout apartheid, and ever since – it has served as a spectacular barometer for political and moral issues in the psyche of the nation. The old issue of Boer versus Brit, dating back to the Anglo-Boer War, has been in the foreground since that 1949 All Blacks tour which followed so soon after the election victory of the Nationalist Party a year earlier. By the time the Springboks went to Britain in 1951, they had become the embodiment of Afrikaner hopes. Although the tour was nominally led by a very able lock forward, Basil Kenyon, we all spoke of the group as 'Hennie Muller's Boks', and we were secretly relieved that Kenyon had to withdraw from active combat very early on because of a torn retina. If our school was anything to go by, we were simply not comfortable with an Englishman as our captain. Before that, in the battles against the Kiwis, we could accept Okey Geffin in spite of his Jewish background, because of his prowess as a goal kicker – after five penalties against zero in the first game of the 1949 series: South Africans have always been adept at avoiding problems through semantic strategies. Years later, Japanese could be treated as 'honorary whites' because the country imported vast quantities of pig iron from them; sometimes local blacks, like my dear friend Richard Rive, the writer of *Buckingham Palace, District Six*, found themselves admitted to white areas or events by pretending they were from Malawi, or Mozambique.

Whenever something went wrong in the nation, it would show up in rugby – either in the administration, or in team selections, or coaching problems, or all of these. In particular, the game would provide a key to the handling of race relations in the country, and very specifically to the state of Afrikanerdom.

This is why the Springboks' triumph in the World Cup of 1995, only a year after the first free elections, had such special meaning – comparable, in fact, to the amazing experience of voting on that first election day of 27 April, 1994. When Joel Stransky slotted his drop goal in the final seconds of extra time, the country went berserk, from the mink-and-manure white English bastions of Sandton and the sugar estates of the South Coast in KwaZulu-Natal, to the traditionally staid Afrikaner strongholds of Pretoria or Bloemfontein and the black townships of Alexandra in Gauteng or Khayelitsa in Cape Town, the Indian quarters of Cato Manor and Lenasia, the sprawling coloured areas of the Cape Flats. Everybody was in a state of near-hysterical jubilation, lasting throughout that night and spilling over into the days and even weeks to follow. The most unforgettable moment came at the end of the game, when Nelson Mandela, wearing the number 6 jersey of captain Francois Pienaar, held aloft the Webb Ellis Cup. 'You have done this,' he said, waving his arms towards the dancing, cheering crowd in the stands, 'not just for your team but for more than 50,000 around us.' And Francois responded in a line that immortalised the moment: 'No, Mr President,' he said. 'We have done this for forty million people.'

In the years after that, when disillusionment and despondency began to set in, it seemed as if the magic of that moment, and of the game that brought it about, would dissipate and slowly dissolve. But then came the World Cup of 2007 in France, when after all the infighting and backbiting – in rugby, and in the politics of the country – once again that trophy was raised, this time by John Smit and his Boks; and once again, at least for a brief moment of respite in the turbulence of the country, South Africans of all backgrounds celebrated together. This time, Thabo Mbeki was there to share in the magic. But behind all the ecstatic explosions of joy, every South African, in France where the match had been played, in South Africa, and wherever in the wide world the diaspora had flung them, felt the joyful presence of that first charismatic president, Nelson Rolihlahla Mandela. Even in his physical absence he was still triumphantly and overwhelmingly present.

But rugby also insinuated itself into the most cherished part of my personal life. At the end of 2004 I met Karina in Salzburg. And soon afterwards the seal on our relationship was provided by nothing less than rugby. In the Super-12 series of matches involving provincial teams from South Africa, Australia and New Zealand, there was one morning when I had to wake up at about four to see the match of our Stormers against the Auckland Blues; knowing about my addiction, Karina telephoned from Austria fifteen minutes before the kick-off to make sure I was awake; and then, just after the match, she sent a message: *Did we win?* At that moment there was no more doubt in my mind. I knew we would make it – in sickness or in health, for richer or poorer, till death us do part.

Recently, she awoke one morning from a dream about being reunited with a boyfriend from her early youth, a particularly happy dream that suppressed all the ordinary or unpleasant events which had eventually caused that relationship to founder. Now he suddenly reappeared in a very alluring fashion and invited her to return with him to Poland, where they had both grown up. For a moment she was tempted. Then she very firmly turned him down – because, she explained, it had occurred to her that she now lived in a country where she had learned to love biltong and where she had become addicted to rugby. She could no longer live without it. For both of us it is a form of theatre which has settled in our bones.

My true baptism of fire in the real theatre came in my second year at university, when the dramatic society tackled a Dorothy Sayers play, *Busman's Honeymoon*. The mere fact of an exclusively Afrikaans-speaking university going on tour with an English play, was not just pretentious but presumptuous. My strongly accented English was not helped at all by my total lack of stage experience, while my complete ignorance about amorous matters did not bring much conviction to Lord Peter Wimsey's wooing of his bride.

My only consolation was that the bride, Harriet, knew as little about the behaviour of a couple on honeymoon as her bridegroom; and in spite of a few clumsy private rehearsals to improve our kissing skills there was no erotic spark in the performance, and, I suspect, nothing on either side to inspire it. But through two months of hard labour under the benign but unsparing eye of the English professor, R. E. Davies, a bunch of raw young Afrikaners reached the stage where they could expose their version of English manners to a fortunately undiscriminating public.

The venture taught me little about acting, but a lot about interaction. In spite of the closeness within our family, and a fair amount of consorting with friends at school, my youth was a largely solitary voyage of discovery. But on this tour the bunch of students in the group became an inseparable unit. We had to do everything together: set up and strike our rickety decor, manage ticket sales in streets and shops, take care of the front of house, wade through parties and receptions, many of which were opened and closed with a prayer, and manage relationships, some more intimate than others, sort out our accommodation with private people in the towns we visited. In the village of Greytown in Natal two of us had to fend largely for ourselves as the lady of the house, as it turned out, had just run away with a lover, leaving her morose and hard-drinking husband and a little boy of ten in charge of catering for my friend Christie and myself.

I'd met Christie on my first day at university. He was the son of the professor of music; and on the first evening of our friendship he invited me over to their house for an evening of piano playing. I started with my only showpiece, Liszt's second Hungarian Rhapsody. He followed with Chopin's Grand Polonaise. Right there I decided that I would never touch the piano again, and I have always been indebted to Christie for saving me from endless wasted hours, and many potential audiences from boredom unto death.

It was towards the end of our run with *Busman's Honeymoon* that he committed another act of rescue. I had decided that the tour would be rounded off with a performance in the capital, Pretoria. All the others were sceptical about our chances of success. But Christie supported me. Our main argument was that we should be able to secure the attendance of a number of schools, which would readily fill the large hall we were planning to rent.

The real inspiration behind this ambitious plan was Esther. She was a junior pupil at one of the choice Afrikaans schools. If I went about it the right way her principal might be persuaded to give permission for her school to attend. She would see me perform. Our future together would be assured. Another Olivier and Vivien Leigh.

For a month I spent most of my afternoons, and all my savings, on making calls to Pretoria schools to offer them the chance of a lifetime to attend the definitive performance of *Busman's Honeymoon*. Initially, almost all of them sounded exceedingly encouraging. I was making endless sums in my tour notebook. It promised to become the single most substantial contribution the dramatic society had ever made to the coffers of the university.

But one by one the schools cancelled their promised attendance. There were clashes with their own performances, with sports meetings, swimming galas, folk dancing, political meetings, God knows what. Even Christie was becoming hesitant. But I persisted with a doggedness only a tragic hero could understand. A week before the event Esther's school withdrew. By now it was too late for us to cancel: the booking fee for the hall had been paid, Pretoria had been covered in a rash of posters, tickets had been sold, pre-publicity had started appearing in the press.

There was still a chance – a very small, but vital chance – that Esther might attend – not as part of a block booking for her school, but privately, with a friend or two. I actually dared to telephone her myself to seal this. Almost too shy to speak, and sounding more annoyed than anything else, she declined to commit herself in any way. But before she rang off she did mumble something that sounded like, 'I'll see what I can do.' Of course I took this as a promise. Christie did his utmost to make me acknowledge how slim this possibility really was. But he stood courageously by me even when all the other members of the touring party were shaking their heads.

It was a rather disconsolate group that travelled to Pretoria by bus, set up our by now very seedy little set, dwarfed by the immensity of the stage, desperately made another round of phone calls to school principals and teachers of English, and took to the streets for some last-minute personal advertising.

Ten minutes before the curtain there were about thirty people in the audience, a small scattering in that vast, lugubrious hall. And no sign of Esther.

The mood backstage was bleak. No one felt like going on. But by now it was too late to turn back.

Five minutes to go. Then three, two, one. Still no Esther.

'Here we go,' said Lood Muller, who played the murderer, with a scowl to match his role. And tugged at the rope to open the curtain. But it stuck.

'This is a sign from God,' said somebody. Quite in keeping with the Christian character of our university. But I refused to pay heed.

'Open the bloody thing!' I shouted, close to tears.

Some of the other actors came running to give Lood a hand. This time the curtain yielded. Which caused considerable confusion, as at least three characters who were not supposed to be in the opening scene now found themselves centre stage. In their haste to scuttle backstage, one of them – Jurie, who played the parson – tripped over a counterweight supporting the OP wall of the set, which collapsed to tumultuous applause from the audience. It was a total disaster. And yet, because of the uproar in the audience and the near-hysteria onstage, when the play began at last we were all fired up by the extremity in which we found ourselves; and for at least twenty minutes we turned it into one of our best performances. Until the adrenalin became exhausted and the play started sagging. By the end of Act One several members of the audience trickled out through the side doors.

Esther had still not shown up. And was very obviously not going to grace us with her presence.

Unable to face the others in the dressing room, I slinked off to a little storeroom backstage where a number of boxes and some scaffolding were stacked around a very dusty upright piano. I collapsed on the floor, too drained even to strike a tragic pose. That was how Christie found me. He didn't say a word. He came past me and sat down on the piano stool. Almost mechanically he opened the lid. He played a few random chords. The old piano was sadly out of tune. But he paid no attention. Slowly the chords began to slide into a recognisable pattern. He was playing Chopin's Third Ballad. That was the last straw. I broke down and sobbed like a baby.

Halfway through the ballad somebody came in and said something about

71

time to start. I heard Christie shooing him off. He played through to the end. Then he came to sit on the floor next to me, put an arm round my shoulders, and said, 'Let's go.'

'I can't,' I sobbed.

'You're going to get up,' he said very quietly but very firmly. 'And you're going to go out on that stage. And you're going to act like you've never acted before.'

I shook my head against his shoulder.

'Go,' he said.

I got up. There was a washbasin in the corner. I went to it and splashed cold water on my face. And then a very dishevelled Lord Peter Wimsey went to the stage, the curtain was opened, the play resumed its inexorable course. We were all playing like never before. And at the end the fifteen or so people left in the audience applauded like a full house. I was exhausted, but also felt strangely fulfilled. I had made a discovery that would need time to grasp fully: that in every performance there are at least two plays being acted out simultaneously – one to the audience, another in the mind and the emotions; one public, the other personal. Sometimes they might overlap, but at times they are in conflict. Both are indispensable. And I knew that if the theatre could undo a life it had its own way of also *making* one. And that it would never let go of me again.

In due course I also turned to playwriting. My first piece to be published, with the unpromising title of *Die Band om ons Harte* (*The Bond Around Our Hearts*), was written when I was twenty-one, and set in 1820 on the eastern frontier of the Cape Colony, soon after the arrival of the first contingent of British Settlers. It was a time when relations between Dutch/Afrikaans colonists, the newly arrived settlers, and the government at the Cape came under great pressure from the Xhosa nation who, trying to flee in their turn from the expansion of the Zulu empire in the east, were extending their boundaries into colonial territory. Strange alliances were forged in those circumstances. I'm afraid the play was rather superficial and I did not have any real grasp of the deeper complexities involved. Its only redeeming feature was, perhaps, the use of a wholly non-realistic figure, the old Boer woman

Alida Landman, who came to transcend the obvious divisions to represent, rather darkly, the brooding spirit of the land itself. But good intentions certainly did not salvage a bad play. All it did was to commit me more resolutely to the possibilities and intricacies of playwriting and stagecraft.

The years I spent in Paris, from 1959 to 1961, brought an unprecedented exposure to the theatre. During my last school year at Lydenburg, in 1952, I had attended two or three performances by the touring company of South Africa's National Theatre Organisation, which for the first time exposed me to live, professional theatre, just enough to whet my appetite. At university I became an assiduous theatregoer, but even then it was not possible to see more than four or five shows a year – mainly local plays in English or Afrikaans, or classical works translated into Afrikaans: a few Ibsens, a few Molières, the odd Shakespeare. And from time to time there was an opportunity of hitch-hiking to Johannesburg or Pretoria and seeing performances by visiting companies, most impressively a series of Flemish productions. In this case it was not just the professionalism of the work that enthralled me, but the newness, the modernity of the plays – a translation of *Look Back in Anger*, a performance in the original Flemish of Claus's *Een Bruid in de Morgen* (*A Bride in the Morning*). Theatre no longer meant just a story told on the stage, but a wholly new kind of experience, working with new ways of transforming the everyday into *play*, into *performance*. The space of the stage became charged with magic, with endless possibilities of celebration, an acting-out of both joy and despair.

It was *this* discovery of theatre that turned Paris into a decisive step in my own progress towards the stage. Whenever my then wife Estelle and I could afford it, we were in the theatre. Any number of classics, at the Comédie Française or the Palais de Chaillot or the Odéon, in lavish and spectacular productions. But there were three playwrights who changed my whole perception of theatre in the world. There was Anouilh, particularly in *Becket*, but even in a farce like *l'Hurluberlu*, where the ludic imagination soared above mere reality, mere history. Then there was Ionesco. I had never seen anything remotely like *La Cantatrice Chauve*, or *La Leçon*, or *Jacques*, or *Les Chaises*. It was as stunning as any of the shows of 'magic' from my youth. What Peter

Brook was later to call 'the concrete language of the stage' was abundantly, exuberantly, and also chillingly, demonstrated in the dizzying word games which played havoc with meaning and turned language itself into a 'thing', a character in the open space, a reality, both grotesque and sublime, in its own right.

And then there was Beckett. There was *Endgame*. There was *Krapp's Last Tape*. Many years later, at the Odéon, there was *Oh les Beaux Jours* (*Happy Days*) in which Madeleine Reynaud defined cosmic solitude in a never-to-be-forgotten solo performance. But during that first stay in Paris there was, above all, *Waiting for Godot*. Of *Godot* we saw three vastly different productions during those two years, one in the Odéon, the second in a tiny, dilapidated theatre in Montmartre, the third in Montparnasse, to be followed by countless others in many countries, in the years to come. But never enough. What I see on the stage is, every time, something strung from my own entrails. That play – in which, as one famous early review declared, 'nothing happens, twice' – still holds me in its thrall. Whenever I hear the hackneyed phrase 'the human condition', *Godot* is what I see before me, inside me.

Sadly, it is a play that broke up one of the most significant friendships of my youth. Since I was seventeen or so, I had admired the author W. A. de Klerk. He was one of the first Afrikaans novelists to break away from the stark tradition of naturalism to experiment (very safely, almost coyly, yet with a measure of courage not easy to muster in our stifling cultural world) with existentialism. In his plays he remained a staunch follower of Ibsen. However new much of this writing was in Afrikaans, it was – although I did not realise it at the time – depressingly derivative. But for several years he'd remained, for me, the Great Playwright in Afrikaans. I had spent some summer holidays on his farm in the Western Province, helping his farmhands to labour in the vineyards and orchards – in exchange for long conversations in the evenings, after the day's work, a leisurely swim in the dam, and a sumptuous supper. It was he, more than anybody else, who guided me towards foreign literature and philosophy – from Mark Twain to Goethe, from Ibsen to Dostoevsky, from Kierkegaard to Colin Wilson. It was he who encouraged me to learn German and read *Faust* in the original. He was my mentor, my guru, my philosopher-friend. When I left for Europe for the first time, he came to see me off in Cape Town harbour, with a box of grapes from the farm to wish me bon voyage.

Then, early in our second year in Paris, he wrote to ask whether he could visit us for a week. It was almost impossible to find space for him in our minuscule attic flat, but we did. It felt like a visit from an emissary of God. Estelle was more sceptical about his greatness, but for my sake she was willing to give it a go. He was a Great Man who had come to bestow upon us the magnificence of his creative presence. Even when he turned out to be more interested in being shown around Pigalle than in accompanying us to the Louvre or to the theatre, I stubbornly stuck to my adulation of him. Far be it from me to disparage the seedier attractions of Paris. When it turned out that his real interest in coming to Europe was not to drink at the fountains of wisdom and beauty but to pursue a paramour, even I began to feel a bit more apprehensive. But the breaking point came when *Waiting for Godot* came up for discussion. As it happened, it was less than a month after we'd seen it for the first time; I could not stop talking about it. Please, please, please, I begged him: it was still running, he should be able to get a ticket. To my consternation he exploded. He had read the play, he said in a tone of voice that boded no good. In his considered opinion it was an abortion. It was, he said, pausing for maximum effect before he pronounced the final word, *shit*. It was the only time I had ever heard him utter a profanity. To make absolutely sure that I had heard correctly, he repeated it. The play was shit. If this was the way drama was going in Europe – although he had reason to believe that the British and the Americans were slightly more enlightened – then the end of the theatre was nigh. *Der Untergang des Abendlandes*. Worse, a *Götterdämmerung*. (He always favoured German as the summit of European – and world – literature.)

I was flabbergasted. I tried to reason, to argue, to plead. He refused to enter into any discussion. He knew the play was shit, and that was that. Drama meant action. Action meant conflict. Conflict meant a confrontation of wills. Will demanded a demonstration of greatness, of heroism, a sense of grandeur. 'This little shit of a play,' he proceeded, 'negates everything drama has stood for in 3,000 years of civilisation. Instead of an Oedipus, instead of a Lear, instead of a Faust, instead of Brand or Hedda Gabler, here we have two fools, two idiots, two vagrants, two good-for-nothings, two *shits*. Doing what? Doing nothing. Talking. Yes, talking. I beg you. For hours on end. Talking about the state of their boots, talking about a tree sprouting a leaf, talking about talking. Talking about waiting for a man who never turns up. Talking about—

'Talking about shit?'

'Yes. Talking about shit.'

This went on – this near-endless ranting about shit – in circles and spirals and Miró-like squiggles – until I actually dropped off into an unsound sleep. This was the last straw.

'Do you realise that you actually fell asleep while I was talking?' he asked. 'I must say this is an experience that is quite new to me. I had thought for years now that you were an intelligent young man, that you had a lot of promise, that you were not untalented as a writer, that you were at least *interested* in what I could teach you. Now, here, tonight, I find that you – that you actually—'

'I'm sorry,' I mumbled. 'But I don't think Godot will ever come.'

He found this singularly unfunny. Two days later he left – for Germany, as far as I can remember; and for the middle-aged lady he was pursuing across the face of Europe.

I felt guilty for a long time. Guilt feelings came very readily to me in those days.

After our return to South Africa we tried a few times to make up, but it was all very formal, like a creaky amateur show. I had lost a treasured friend. But I had gained Godot.

During the years that followed, Paris remained, like London, New York, Edinburgh, Adelaide, a Mecca for theatre. No inventory is called for here, only the briefest mention of some productions that shifted my perception of theatre or added something to the way I experience myself in the world. There was a *Lear* in this class that I saw in 1995, with Philippe Morier-Genoud, in the Odéon, played at a dizzying tempo on an almost bare stage featuring an elliptical disk that suggested the curve of the globe suspended in open space; and because of the way in which the spectator was carried along by a kind of cosmic force against which they were helpless, it was breathtaking. There was one other *Lear* I can compare with this one: it was offered in the Maynardville open-air theatre in Cape Town, featuring the great Afrikaans actor Johann Nel, and during his ranting in the storm in Act Two a real thunderstorm broke out which truly reduced us all to *poor naked wretches*.

Where pure spectacle is concerned, I can think of few other productions that made such a total onslaught on my senses as Peter Brook's *Timon of Athens* in a half-demolished old theatre in the north of Paris. In which even the state of the building was incorporated into the 'language' of the play. Another was Jean Genet's *Les Paravents* (The Screens) in the Odéon. And undoubtedly also Jean-Louis Barrault's *Rabelais* in which all the senses were bombarded in a dense 'language of the stage' in which words were only one dimension.

At Rhodes University, where I taught for nearly thirty years from 1961, a fair deal of my time was spent in the Drama Department, where I could profit from the presence of talented and enthusiastic students to become more extensively involved in theatrical practice. Apart from mounting some productions, the most enjoyable being Lorca's *The House of Bernarda Alba*, it also provided an opportunity to try out some of my own plays on the stage before they reached a more final form.

The text that benefited most obviously from this experience was *Elders Mooiweer en Warm* (*Elsewhere Fine and Warm*) which was subsequently staged, in English, in Namibia, and in due course also in Bulgaria and some other Central European countries. Written in 1965, it was the first of my plays to be inspired by the political situation in South Africa, though on the surface there was nothing overtly political. It was based on the experience of a friend at Rhodes University, Terrence Beard, who had been placed under banning orders following his involvement in an investigation of a massive campaign of torture and persecution of black communities in the Eastern Cape and Transkei following the murder of a white family at the Bashee Bridge. My friend's banning order included the standard stipulation that, except during lectures, he could not be in the company of more than one person at a time.

Some colleagues decided to show their solidarity by inviting him to a party where he had to sit in the kitchen while everybody else gathered in the lounge: from there, one at a time, they would visit the kitchen to enjoy a glass of wine and have a chat with Terrence. In the course of the evening the mere presence of 'the man in the kitchen' cast a pall over all the assembled guests, leading to unpredictable reactions ranging from gloom to excessive hilarity and festivity. People were inspired to share confidences about very private affairs, secret grievances and hidden fears. It was like the machinations of a small Truth and Reconciliation Commission many years before such an enterprise had ever been dreamed up. In the play, which undeniably had some echoes of both Sartre's *Huis Clos* and Albee's *Who's Afraid of Virginia Woolf?*, a group of decadent partygoers are cut off from the outside world after an outbreak of the plague in the city; all they can do to while away the time is to devise endless theme parties, which under the guidance of an evil old master of ceremonies degenerate into an inquisition to dredge up the most hidden secrets of all the guests.

I had real problems with the ending. There seemed to be too many loose threads dangling. During rehearsals at Rhodes with the students, and subsequently in a production with the Performing Arts Council of the Orange Free State (PACOFS) I made cuts and changes, but nothing really seemed to work. Then in a most unexpected turn, which could only have happened in the theatre, a solution presented itself. At a performance in the Oppenheimer Theatre in the mining town of Welkom, the stage manager, the worse for wear after several stiff drinks during the interval, fell asleep in the wings. When he woke up, confused and bewildered, he took one look at the actors on the stage, thought it was the last scene of the final act, and brought down the curtain – almost ten minutes before the end.

The performance got a standing ovation, and afterwards Truida Louw, a grande dame of the theatre, who happened to have seen the play before, enthusiastically congratulated me on the judicious and most effective cut. In subsequent performances I stuck to this ending.

But the performance itself nearly ended in tragedy: the stage manager, convinced that he had fucked up the show, clambered up to the catwalk high above the stage and attempted to commit suicide by jumping. It took at least half an hour to calm him down. By then he was so thoroughly drunk that he was out of action during the entire process of striking the set.

There was another 'double performance' prompted by *Elsewhere Fine and Warm*, illustrating just how unpredictable and far-reaching the effects of theatre can be. During the year I spent in Paris in 1968 a young woman, a poet and journalist living in Pretoria, started corresponding with me; we met after my return and I discovered that she had a provocative and creative mind, a character with many facets and tantalising darknesses, and that she was unusually beautiful. Her name was Lise. I was unattached at the time, but Lise was having affairs, simultaneously, with two of my best friends in Johannesburg and it seemed to me wise to keep out of it – all the more so as she soon turned to me as a father confessor. The situation was complicated even further when both my friends, each unaware of the other, began to confide in me about their involvement with Lise. For months I toyed with the idea of persuading all three of them to write their accounts of the story, and contributing my own version of it to what might become a most entertaining novel. But for obvious reasons I refrained. And then everything changed. The reason was *Elsewhere Fine and Warm*.

In France, I'd seen from close up what a mess can result from a clash between different levels of reality. It happened during the summer festival in Carpentras where I attended a particularly dramatic performance of *Carmen*. Throughout the production there had been a peculiar electricity in the love scenes between Carmen and Don José. Then, after the last curtain, as the actors took their final bow, a young man came rushing from the raked floor of the outdoor arena, bellowing like a bull just escaped from the ring, took the stairs up to the stage three or four at a time, and tackled the handsome Don José to the floor. It transpired later that he was the real-life husband of the soprano who sang Carmen. Actors and audience all joined in the fray, until someone, presumably the stage manager, had the presence of mind to switch off all the lights and prevent a riot.

Towards September of 1969 I was working on a student production of my play at Rhodes University. There was a letter from Lise to say that she was planning to visit a friend in the Eastern Cape and wondered whether she could look me up. By all means, I responded. She would come in time for the final dress rehearsal on the Friday night, followed by the opening on Saturday. I offered her the small spare room in my flat.

Just before she arrived I decided that the spare room might be too cramped, so I prepared my own bedroom for her and transferred my belongings to the spare room. The dress rehearsal was a great success. Afterwards Lise and I retired to my flat, had a nightcap, and then she happily settled into the big double bed in my bedroom while I prepared to make myself as comfortable as possible on the narrow single bed in the spare room. But before I could bed down I heard a knock on the front door. There, when I opened, stood my good friend Francois Swart, actor and director of the Performing Arts Council of the Transvaal (PACT), who had decided to drive all the way down from Pretoria to surprise me and attend my opening night.

Excitement all round. But what about the sleeping arrangements? There really was only one solution I could think of. I tiptoed upstairs to my bedroom. There was still a chink of light under the door. Lise opened. She was clutching only a small towel against her, and looking even more irresistible than usual. I gulped, fixed my eyes on her dimpled kneecaps, and explained about Francois. More generously than I had ever expected, she agreed to my proposed solution. And so Francois was put up in the small spare room downstairs while I moved in with Lise.

Truly, the theatre has its own kind of magic.

For a full year I had attended every possible performance, including the unrehearsed and spontaneous happenings in the Sorbonne, in the Odéon and in the streets during the mind-blowing student uprising in the month of May, 1968. Now, knowing about my long-standing passion for Camus, PACT had asked me to translate *Les Justes* into Afrikaans, under the rather unfortunate title of *Die Terroriste*, which betrayed the playwright's whole purpose. I had barely delivered the text when there was a telephone call from Pretoria. They needed to see me. Personally. And urgently. I was staying with my parents in Potchefstroom at the time, less than two hours away, while my resumption of lecturing at Rhodes was still being finalised. That same afternoon I was in Pretoria.

What transpired at that meeting with Francois, his colleague Mannie Manim, and the head of PACT, Eghard van der Hoven, left me shaking. The director contracted for the production of the Camus play, I learned, had pulled out; rehearsals were scheduled to start within a few weeks. Francois was already involved with another project, and there was no one else at PACT available to take over. Would I be prepared to step in? They knew they were taking a chance. I had no professional experience. All I could offer, apart from some student productions, was a long-standing infatuation with Camus, and boundless enthusiasm. And, of course, enough chutzpah to accept.

How could I possibly turn it down? The theatre had become a passion to me. I was aware of the enormity of the risk. But I also knew I could rely on Francois as a safety net, and on the cast. At that time the PACT ensemble was quite simply the best group of actors in South Africa.

Within days I had to wind up everything else I was involved with at the time, and move to Pretoria. Lise had found lodgings for me in the converted garage of a formidable old lady whose main claim to fame was that she had published more letters in newspapers than anybody else in the country. In me she recognised a kindred soul, which meant that I was hauled in for endless discussions on literature, particularly on some of the Afrikaans doggerel perpetrated by would-be poets from the early years of the century. She watched over my life like a trained falcon. Keeping journalists at bay was her speciality. 'Don't you have any compassion with the man?' I once heard her scold a newspaperman who had dared to telephone too early in the morning. 'He is only fear and blood, you know.' This line of existen-tialist truth made even more sense in Afrikaans, since *vlees en bloed* sounds suspiciously similar to her *vrees en bloed.*

Before embarking on the four weeks of rehearsals I consulted a professor of drama in Potchefstroom for some practical tips. The sum total of his informed advice was, 'There is only one way of ensuring that you are in total control of the actors, and that is to throw a tantrum at the very first rehearsal.' I found an excuse to leave very early.

Those four weeks of working with a group of truly professional artists turned out to be pure bliss. Francois provided never-ending stimulation and inspiration. On stage, backstage, in front of the stage, in everything he did he seemed constantly to reinvent a play and redefine the theatre. His sense of humour was incomparable. I shall always remember him being cornered at a party by several well-meaning middle-aged ladies who eagerly wanted to know what he 'really' did for a living when he was not on stage. His reply could wither the blossoms in spring: 'Madam, I'm an artificial inseminator of cows.'

But the daily immersion in rehearsals was the greatest revelation. To see the play take shape from day to day was like watching a sheet of pure white photographic paper in a basin of developer rapidly and miraculously transform itself into a picture of exquisite definition and rare beauty. There was only one explosion, right towards the end, when I invited Francois to attend a rehearsal and give his comments. The only actor in the cast reputed far and wide to be 'difficult' reacted adversely to some of the notes. 'If I am on the wrong track as Francois said, then you're the only one to blame!' he stormed after Francois had left. 'How can I have any confidence in you again? You're a bloody amateur!' Francois had to be summoned back. A master of diplomacy after years in the theatre, he managed to resolve everything. At the end of the day's rehearsals the actor generously came to thank me for my 'patience'. I assured him that I had in fact been terrified and that at heart I really *was* only an amateur. From that moment our collaboration was warm and trusting.

And yet our rehearsals caused an incredible rumpus in the press. It turned out that my appointment had not been approved by the board and by the administrator of Transvaal, a notorious politician from the extreme right. Of decisive importance was the fact that the appointment was now being opposed by the most powerful member of the board, Professor Geoff Cronjé, a sociologist who had been one of the key theoreticians of apartheid and who had turned to drama mainly because it was a position from which he could wield inordinate power in cultural matters.

So this sociologist/politician-turned-drama-expert protested against my involvement and insisted that Francois take over. Given the political over-tones of the controversy it came as no surprise that it was front-page news for weeks. I had returned from France wearing my hair rather long, bedecking myself with chains, and professing my support for the French students rioting against de Gaulle – all of which was interpreted as signs, either of the Antichrist or of communism, which was worse. It was during this time that I wrote a rather audacious letter to the prime minister, John Vorster, to remind him that his own strong-arm repression of protesting students in Cape Town was reminiscent of de Gaulle, and that very soon after the 1968 riots de Gaulle had to vacate his seat of power. I ended the letter by expressing the wish that the prime minister's conscience would not stand in the way of a good night's sleep. Somewhat to my surprise His Excellency wrote back to say that my letter, coming from a pink liberalist, had not surprised him; and to wish me, in my turn, 'a good night's rest, in spite of the curlers in your hair.' Such was the stuff that prime ministers were made of.

The administrator ordered a Commission of Inquiry. Francois threatened to resign as artistic director of PACT. There were indications that Mannie would join him, and rumours that even the director, Eghard van der Hoven, might resign. Geoff Cronjé proposed a compromise: I could continue to direct the play, but my name was not to appear on the programme or anywhere on the publicity material. Francois steadfastly refused. In the end the authorities grudgingly resigned themselves to the inevitable, insisting only that Francois be placed officially in charge of the direction, which he quietly refrained from doing.

Even in compiling the programme I was given a free hand, with the result that quotes from Fidel Castro, Che Guevara and others were used. In only one instance was permission refused: it concerned a stanza by the great Afrikaans poet N. P. van Wyk Louw, from a poem written in the late thirties, ironically a period when he had briefly come under the spell of Nazism:

> *You* are the oppressors
> and *you* the ones who trample us,
> us who are strong
> but helplessly humiliated

The play opened to rave reviews. An exception was the Afrikaans Sunday paper *Rapport* which published a long article by my friend Bartho Smit, headed 'Mountain Gives Birth to Mouse'.

But even more important than the reviews was, for me, the opportunity the production offered of breaking into the real theatre. For the first time I could combine the writing of plays with stagecraft, working with professional actors. I could break out of the solitude that surrounds the writer and collaborate with others on projects that were larger than ourselves. It was an indispensable preparation for the battles of the seventies which lay ahead, when writers of all race and culture groups, threatened by the same power establishment, would learn to fuse their energies and offer a united front of resistance to a system which, otherwise, might have shattered us through the time-honoured tactic of dividing and ruling.

Other opportunities followed. It so happened that one of the actors in the cast of *Les Justes* was also drama manager of PACT, Gerrit Geertsema; and soon after my stint in Pretoria he moved to Bloemfontein as director of drama for PACOFS. It remains a standing joke between us that playing the role of the police guard in the prison scene of *Les Justes* Gerrit could not resist stealing the show with his vivid facial contortions, even when the main actors were on stage. The only remedy I could think of was to let him keep his back to the audience, persuading him that such an articulate back simply *had* to be exploited for its full theatrical value. We became very close, a friendship that has now survived and grown for nearly forty years. Once installed at PACOFS, he started contracting me as a director on a regular basis, several times for productions of my own plays. And when one of his actors, Johan Botha, moved to Windhoek, to the then South West African Performing Arts Council (SWAPAC), I was invited to do a production of a new play by the innovative Afrikaans playwright Chris Barnard for that company as well. Those years, until the mid-seventies, were the culmination of my work in the theatre, and as far as creativity was concerned, one of the most productive and satisfying periods of my life.

Among the plays I produced during that time was *Pavane*, which was not published before 1974, although it was already written in 1970 as the direct outcome of a visit to Brazil. There were two prongs to this inspiration – one a place, the other a person.

The place had a hauntingly beautiful name, Quitandinha, and it was lost in a tumble of tropical mountains, built as a casino in the thirties, later a hotel, now some kind of club. I had first heard about it from the improbably beautiful blonde-and-blue-eyed model, Claudia, who had accompanied a small group of journalists, and also including me, on an assignment to Brazil for a travel article and a fashion shoot. Claudia remembered Quitandinha as a magical dream-place from a previous visit, when she'd been high on LSD for most of the time; and now I could see it for myself in all its outrageous splendour: more like a theatre set than a building. In my play it started as a convent, before being converted into a brothel; and now it was a hideout in the mountains where the daughter of an American ambassador is abducted in South America and executed when the demands of the rebels who have kidnapped her, and with whom she comes to identify herself, are not met. It came as a shock when, soon after I'd written the play, Patty Hearst was captured in the US by the Symbionese Liberation Army and famously sided with her captors. The real trigger, however, was Claudia. An initial impression of a spoilt little rich girl, arrogant and supercilious and full of airs, was soon dissipated; and because we were the 'young ones', as well as the only two unequivocally heterosexual members of the group, we found ourselves spending more and more time together. We were not, as they say, 'romantically involved', although I predictably felt very soon that I could fall in love. She was surprisingly well read. And she had a great love of Paris, where she had also spent 1968. She had been in a relationship for the past few years, but it was now on the point of breaking up. So there was really no reason for resisting involvement. If I think back now, I believe we simply had too much to talk about to find time for more non-verbal pursuits. Except in the last minutes we shared, before she had to leave. Those minutes with her were unforgettable. It was as if both of us, our bodies and thoughts and emotions, were overwhelmed by desire. But there was, by then, no time; no time. We made all the inevitable promises, but we both knew that they were unrealistic and impossible. We still corresponded for some time after I went back to South Africa. But that was that. A door had closed.

The play, however, survived. Although it marked a turning point in my involvement with the theatre.

Since the banning of my novel *Kennis van die Aand* (*Looking on Darkness*) in 1974 I was a constant target for the state security authorities and their extension, the censors on the Publications Control Board. With books an author still had some space, however cramped, in which to manoeuvre: in the absence of pre-censorship a book had to be published before it could be banned, which at least made it possible, if one played it skilfully, to put a fair number of copies into circulation before the censors pounced. But the theatre was a most vulnerable target: a single complaint from a member of the audience might result in the cancellation of a play. Playwrights like Athol Fugard or the satirist Pieter-Dirk Uys who had their own companies and venues, could manage, more often than not, to stay one step ahead. But I had only students at my disposal at Rhodes University. In the professional theatre, subsidised by the state, there was little or no leeway. The Chris Barnard play we produced in Windhoek, was stopped before it could tour in the Cape Province, as scheduled. A planned run of *Pavane* was stopped even before rehearsals could begin. My friend Bartho Smit, arguably, with Adam Small, the best Afrikaans playwright of our generation, had an even rawer deal as play after play of his was banned. Given the costs of a production, management of subsidised theatres became less and less willing to court the risk of bans which would seriously cripple them financially.

A very painful choice had to be made: at a time when it was vital to counter the ravages of apartheid with all the means at one's disposal, including culture, I could not take the risk of spending months and months on writing or producing plays which stood a real chance of being stopped before opening night. After *Looking on Darkness* my novels might indeed be banned again: but by now I had succeeded in thwarting the censors by having my books published abroad. Plays like *Pavane*, which might be regarded as contentious, found themselves in a cul-de-sac. And so I stopped writing for the theatre, preferring from then on to direct my creative energy towards the writing of novels.

*   *   *

There were many times when the temptation to return to the theatre became almost too strong to resist. Certainly, every time I saw Athol Fugard, the lure was there, naked and strong. His *Blood Knot* was the first South African play I saw after my return from Paris in 1961 – in the Rhodes University Great Hall – and from the very first time I met him, he had a special place in my life. Partly because so much of what inspired him, revived my indebtedness to Camus – and Athol's published *Journals* meant almost as much to me as did Camus' *Carnets*. The Beckettian spareness of his plays, his strong faith in Grotowski, and in Jan Kott, not only fed into my lectures on drama at Rhodes University, but clarified and justified my passion for the theatre. How can I ever forget some of his wise, often wry, pronouncements? – on some recent plays: *There are plays that are shaped like onions: you start peeling them, and remove layer after layer, until you're left with nothing: but at least you've had a good cry.* Or on the need for storytelling: *A story is the only safe place in the world.*

The conversations we've had over the years, and the way in which his theatre practice corroborated his views on the world, have sustained me in many dark moments. Athol brought home to me – through his passionate need for seclusion, his periods of withdrawal to Skoenmakerskop outside Port Elizabeth or New Bethesda in the Karoo – the need to draw both strength and solace from solitude, which often sent me back, both in reality and symbolically, to the semi-desert landscapes of my childhood. For much of my life, landscapes, more than people, have nourished my need for understanding or for insight. Withdrawal and return have, for me, always been redefined in Athol's work and in the realities of his life, and they became keystones in my own world. And to a large extent my withdrawal from the theatre was made bearable by remaining in touch with what Athol was doing – his probing of inner landscapes in *Boesman and Lena* or *The Road to Mecca*, later in *Playland*, as he charted our way through the upheavals in South Africa, until well beyond the political change of 1994.

This absence lasted for nearly twenty years, until the late nineties. Then came an invitation from the Salzburg Seminar to offer a series of master classes in drama with Arthur Miller and Ariel Dorfman. I had been to Salzburg before, but this occasion was something extraordinary. For a week the three of us, in the atmosphere of intense creative energy unique to the theatre, worked together with people like the director Brian Herzov, the critic Benedict Nightingale, and the wonderfully inventive director David Thacker and his team of actors from the National Theatre in London, who were then engaged in rehearsals for *Death of a Salesman*. By the end of the week each of us had to mount a production. Ariel worked on a scene from his *Widows*; I presented excerpts from my plays *Elsewhere Fine and Warm* and *Pavane*. But the highlight of the week was the *Salesman*, where David's interaction with his troupe was overseen by Arthur Miller. Throughout his many interventions, each a small masterpiece in its own right, Arthur did not once issue an instruction or a direction. At most he would say, 'What about . . .', or 'Do you think we could . . .', or 'Suppose, when you enter this scene, you were to think . . .' It was a reinvention of Stanislavski's 'magic if' that had changed the course of stagecraft in the twentieth century. And once again the two-pronged nature of the theatre was brought to life: there was the play itself, after nearly half a century still as alive as an electric wire, Willie Loman's tussle with his sons Biff and Happy, and with death, and with life; and there was at the same time David's involvement with his cast, and Arthur's inter-action with all of them. I know that not one of us privileged to be in that group will ever forget that Salzburg experience. We were present at a thing of beauty coming to life in front of our eyes, drawing all of us into the act of creation itself.

That week made me acknowledge just how much I had been missing in my life during the twenty years of absence from the theatre. The feverish involvement with a group of exceptionally talented, professional actors to pool all our inventive resources and bring into being something incompa-rably more than all our separate contributions and our separate selves, added an almost forgotten dimension to the experience of creation. It took me back to the first melding of theatre and religion in my youth – restoring, to my own life, the impulses which had, just as in ancient Greece or in ancient China, led to the birth of theatre from the religious breath of music. And given that events in South Africa around the release of Nelson Mandela from prison and the first democratic elections of 1994 had restored the possibilities of a free theatre in the country, I left Salzburg knowing that I *had* to resume playwriting again.

The result was *Die Jogger*, written almost immediately after my return, and staged and published the next year. The play evolved around a retired brigadier in the security police, now in a mental institution where he is haunted by shadows from his past and the memories of a life of betrayals, both public and very private. How fortunate I was that a young director as energetic and inventive as Ilse van Hemert was placed in charge of the production; and that she invited me to be involved in the rehearsals. Her approach of free improvisation, of truly allowing all the actors to be drawn into the conception and execution of the text as a living, changing thing, brought new levels of understanding to my own view of the stage. At the beginning of every day I would rush to the office of the publisher who was already preparing the text for publication, to rewrite the section we had rehearsed the day before. This drew the printing process itself into the act of production.

Since *Die Jogger* there has not been enough time to turn to another play. But as new novels take shape, I continue making notes – on scraps of paper, or in my mind – for plots and characters that are not primarily meant for the printed page but can come to life only on the stage. And I know it is only a matter of time before this crucial dimension of my life will be restored to its rightful place in my world.

INGRID

IT IS NOW MORE THAN FORTY YEARS SINCE INGRID JONKER DIED. YET, THROUGH her poetry, there may be more people to whom she is a living presence than she was during her short lifetime. In other respects she may be more remote than ever. She was drowned in the night of 19 July, 1965 when she walked into the fiercely cold Atlantic Ocean at Three Anchor Bay in Cape Town, and moved straight into myth. The myth of the maligned, rejected, abused, misunderstood nymph of sea and sun who had foretold her death in her poetry since she'd been a teenager, finally canonised when Nelson Mandela read her poem 'The Child' at his inauguration in parliament in May 1994. How little could we, could anybody, have expected this life after death in that dark time when she opted out of the world?

Until recently, I have chosen not to be drawn into discussions or evocations of her life, notably in documentary films, some unforgivably bad. But precisely because of these I have begun to believe that perhaps I owe it to her at last to unfold, without drama or melodrama, some of the things I have kept to myself. Not the icon but the person. The woman I loved. And who nearly drove me mad. In some respects, it should be done to set the record straight; in others, simply to remember. To hold on.

There is a photo of that sad, obscene funeral, four days after her death, with family massed in a dour black bank on one side of the grave and windswept friends on the other. Her long-time lover Jack Cope tried to jump into the grave like a latter-day Laertes, and everything threatened to implode in low drama. What strikes me when I look at it today, is the realisation that almost everyone in that photo, in fact, everyone involved with Ingrid in one way or another, is now dead. Her father, the arrogant loser, followed her to the grave within a few months. Jack, who knew, as I did, the agony of being with her and constantly losing her, and who faced, long before I had to, the dread of growing old, is dead. Uys Krige, the perennial golden boy of South African letters and the one who averted the most vulgar of explosions on the day of the funeral, is dead too – unbelievable as it still seems to all of us who have heard him reciting poetry or talking non-stop in five languages. Jan Rabie, beachcomber and romantic, the first modern writer of Afrikaans fiction, is dead. So is his wife, Marjorie Wallace, who sang the joys of life in sprightly colours on canvas. So is the gloomy and suspicious sister, Anna, who was prepared to do everything she could to cherish her own narrow view of Ingrid at the cost of everybody else's. And Ingrid's husband Piet, always a lone stranger among the artists surrounding his wife. So are Bartho and Kita, the friends who so anxiously urged Ingrid and me to have a baby they could adopt to exorcise their own childlessness. So are many others from yesteryear.

So many people have claimed her for their own purposes over the years, transforming her into South Africa's own *poète maudite*, another Anne Sexton, another Sylvia Plath. Songwriters have used her poems as lyrics on which they could ride to their own easy fame. Broadcasters and cineasts and playwrights have tried to trace her light footsteps on sound-tracks and in films – sometimes, but not always, with the best of intentions. All the vultures Ingrid had scorned and feared so passion-ately during her life.

It was in the late afternoon of a blue and golden late summer's day, Thursday 18 April, 1963, that Ingrid walked into my ordered existence and turned it upside down. Until that moment I was ensconced in an ultimately predictable life as husband and father, lecturer in literature; dreaming about a future as a writer after the early surprising shock of a novel, *Lobola vir die lewe* (*Dowry for Life*) that caught the Afrikaans literary establishment unprepared, but painfully aware of the claims and the curtailments of domesticity, the threat of bourgeois complacency, of being a small fish in a small pond.

And afterwards? A world in which nothing would ever be sure and safe again, and in which everything, from the most private to the public, from love to politics, was to be exposed to risk and uncertainty and danger.

We were in the dusky, dusty front room of the rambling old house in Cheviot Place, Green Point, were Jan and Marjorie lived, perhaps the only truly bohemian artist's house in the Cape – a group of writers gathered to plan a protest against the new censorship bill which was then taking shape in parliament. Several of us had already launched individual attacks on the proposed onslaught on the arts sponsored by a prominent right-wing parliamentarian, Abraham Jonker, whose own early forays into realist fiction had failed to live up to their initial promise, and who had become notorious for proclaiming that even Shakespeare could do with some censoring. But it was now time for organised resistance on a larger scale. The discussion was energetic and passionate, but there was nothing yet to mark the day as exceptional.

And then she came in, small and quiet, but tense, her blonde curly hair unruly, her dark eyes guarded but smouldering. The daughter of the would-be chief censor, Abraham Jonker. She was wearing a white, loose man's shirt several sizes too big for her, and tight green pants, a size or two too small. She was smoking. Her bare feet were narrow and beautiful. I would never again meet a woman without looking at her feet.

In the course of the weekend that followed I saw her eyes move through an amazing range of expressions, from cool and detached to flashing with ferocity, from serene to exuberant to apathetic to disillusioned to eager, from brazenly challenging and defiant to outraged and contemptuous, from widening with childlike wonder to burning with passion, from quietly content to scathing and vicious. And her sensitive, sensuous, mouth: cynical, content, angry, vulnerable, playful, bitter, mocking, tranquil, raging, happy, generous, wild. Unpredictable and endlessly fascinating, those quicksilvery changes of mood and expression.

It was love at first sight, for both of us – even though I was married and she had been, for several years already, but unbeknown to me, in an intimate if unstable relationship with Jack Cope, twenty-odd years older than either of us.

Even in the course of that first tumultuous weekend, before I had to return to Grahamstown where I taught Afrikaans at Rhodes University, our head-over-heels conversations introduced me to the landscapes of her life – often in brief, cryptic, unsettling flashes of almost blinding intensity, sometimes in longer, sustained journeys of discovery. Landscapes, moonscapes, seascapes, bodyscapes, eyescapes.

How could I have had the faintest intimation of the ways in which this small person with her large eyes and her unkempt hair would change the course of my life, and of my writing, how my choice of female characters in my books would be affected for the next forty years, how my notions of plot and my involvement with other people would be altered? To what extent all my perceptions of relationships would, from that moment on, be defined by the awareness – the fear – of betrayal, a scepticism about permanence, a mistrust of commitment, or guilt feelings about turning my back on stability and security?

And *why*?

It was not just because Ingrid was Ingrid. But surely also because, in an uncanny and unsettling way, meeting her was like being suddenly confronted with the living incarnation of a character I'd just written in a novel: Nicolette in *The Ambassador*. There was still time before the book was published, to introduce a few small references to Ingrid: the way she had of twirling a little curl on her forehead, whenever she was upset, until she fell asleep; a small birthmark on her thigh . . . There was even more 'evidence' of Ingrid in the character of Gillian, in the tempestuous relationship with her father, her excessive raging against religion . . . But these were almost irrelevant compared to the full reality, and the full impact, of the girl-woman Ingrid. The real problem is that from the outset it was almost impossible for me to see her clearly, cleanly, *as she was*, rather than as the projection of a pre-existing fictional character.

How could I ever again keep life and fiction apart? How could I prevent myself from attempting to turn my life into a series of stories, or to project imagined stories into events in my life? Perhaps, it seems to me now, more than forty years later, my only solution was to divide my own life into innumerable compartments – each friend, each acquaintance, each woman sealed off behind locked doors of memory and imagination from all others. It was the only way in which I could remain in control of my world.

The simple backbone of facts about Ingrid is all too familiar by now; it has become the fibre of the legend, the image, the icon: the depraved innocence, the abused child, the misunderstood waif, the yearning for a father figure, the lure of death, the urge for self-destruction. All of it true. All of it just a bit too easy?

Ingrid was born in September 1933 on the farm of her maternal grandfather Fanie Cilliers, near the small North-Western Cape town of Douglas, close to the confluence of the Vaal and Orange rivers, where I myself had spent some of the most formative years of my youth. In one of her earliest photographs, she stands naked on the edge of the swirling, muddy water, a small nymph escaped from another world, scowling defiantly at the camera, clutching one of the lips of her little cleft between a thumb and a forefinger.

At that stage her mother, Beatrice, had just been abandoned by Abraham Jonker, who had accused her of carrying another man's child. In due course he remarried twice and eventually started a new family in Cape Town with a woman who couldn't stand the two 'unruly' little girls from his first marriage – Ingrid and her sister Anna, born two years before her. Beatrice remained ailing for several years: leukaemia, and a nervous condition which was to deteriorate so drastically that in the end she had to be committed to the mental institution of Valkenberg where, like Ingrid herself much later, she was confined more than once. 'I saw my mother going mad in front of my eyes,' Ingrid told me during that first weekend, and often afterwards. And then she would continue, 'I remember how she would sit at the window with a rug on her lap, picking at a frayed edge, and talking to herself: "If I pull out this one, a strange woman comes. If I pull out this one, a strange man comes. And if I pull out this third one, *Abraham Jonker comes!*" And how she would then start howling and screaming hysterically.'

After the grandfather's death Beatrice, her mother and her two daughters moved to Durbanville, near Cape Town, where they lived in 'the house with the pepper tree'; and from there to Gordon's Bay, where Ingrid was to spend most of her early childhood. The girls played on the beach and in the sea – 'like two small otters', Ingrid said – or buried themselves in the fantasy world of books, or spent hours gathering and then hiding 'secrets' in the pine forest. These hidden or buried secrets became an indispensable part of her life – not just as a treasure trove, but as a repository for memories, a self-made subconscious to the ordinary world. Many years later, she would cryptically, in her poetry, refer to a lover's sperm as 'secrets' too, as traces of a private space all her own. The sea was the background music to her verse. She was passionate about it and could swim like a fish. And yet there was often an ominous undertow. As a small girl, even before she moved to Gordon's Bay, Ingrid had two frightening experiences of nearly drowning – once in a river, once in a dam. This, in a strange but significant way, linked in her mind the forces of life and death. And over the years all of it would find expression in her writing.

The childhood world beside the sea brought the girls such bliss that they were hardly aware of the dire poverty in which their mother and grandmother had to eke out an existence. On many days there was only soup or fish-heads to eat; and when there was nothing at all, the fervent faith of the grandmother somehow saw them through. She used to preach to the coloured fishermen's families on Sundays, which provided Ingrid with an early inspiration for writing doggerel with a determined religious slant. Throughout her life the Bible remained a major frame of reference for her writing, not only in content but even more so in her choice of words, imagery, style. It provided the dark and the light, the dread and the exultation, the fear of hell and the expectation of heaven, as an answer to Ingrid's need to find a mythology of her own. And where the Bible ended, Ouma's elaborate commentaries, in the form of a Thought for the Day, took over. Often, while we were together, Ingrid would take out Ouma's *Thoughts* and read from the small blue pages covered in meticulous handwriting, collapsing in laughter as she adopted the declamatory voice of a dominee; religion became even more important to her after she had broken away from all organised forms of it. In a curious way the rejection of religion made her even more dependent on it. And as I myself was right then in the throes of breaking with the church, meeting Ingrid was probably the decisive event in my own process of 'moving out'.

Death had first invaded Ingrid's world when her grandfather passed away.

In 1944, only a year after her mother, her beloved grandmother also died. This placed a barrier between the young girl and her most precious memories of an Edenic youth. From now on death would be a dark undertone to almost everything she wrote, but often in very ambiguous terms: sometimes as a dream-state she continued to yearn for, sometimes as a fearsome, threatening presence, as lover or dreaded enemy, as darkness or ultimate light.

Abraham returned out of the blue to reclaim his daughters. He did his best to integrate them into his new family (he soon had two new children with his new wife) and sent them to good schools; but Ingrid continued to feel neglected, and in later years complained – perhaps with some exaggeration – that she'd been made to work like a Cinderella for a stern and forbidding stepmother. It was, as I now see it, part of her construction of herself as the rejected and misunderstood outsider. Whatever happened on the surface of her life, she found more and more of a refuge in writing poetry, encouraged by a sympathetic teacher; and before she turned sixteen she had written most of the poems subsequently published in *Ontvlugting* (*Escape*), in 1956.

The small volume was dedicated to Ingrid's father. But when she took the first copy to him, his tight-lipped reaction was: 'My child, I hope there's more to it than the covers. I'll look at it tonight to see how you have disgraced me.'

At the end of 1951, Ingrid had completed her schooling with a not very impressive D aggregate – but with an A in Afrikaans. She was eager to go to university, but her father would not hear of it. She could enrol for a secretarial course to qualify herself for a job, but that was that. 'If you are old enough to write, you're mature enough to fend for yourself,' said Abraham, prompted by his new wife. And so Ingrid moved out of the parental home. 'There was space in the house, but not in the heart,' she explained laconically. She moved into a flat near the city centre, where for three years she did proofreading and copy-editing for various printers and publishers.

Her life entered a new phase in 1954 when she met Piet Venter, seventeen years older than herself, with two failed marriages behind him; a businessman with ambitions to become a writer. And two years later, soon after the publication of *Ontvlugting*, they were married – which was more her decision than his. What she had always desperately desired, after the disruptions of her childhood, was the security of marriage. And one of her long-cherished dreams, to have a child, now came within reach. Still, an illogical fear of a miscarriage cast a pall over that eager expectation, as witness one of her best-known poems, 'Pregnant woman', which dates from 1957, the year of her pregnancy: it is dominated by the hallucinating, surreal image of a woman lying singing under the dark water of a sewer with her bleeding offspring. Ingrid had just moved into a cosmopolitan circle of creative artists among whom Piet, in spite of his ambitions, or perhaps because of them, felt sadly out of his depth. Among these friends were Jan Rabie, who had recently returned from a seven-year stay in Paris, and his Scottish wife Marjorie Wallace, the painter Erik Laubscher and his French wife Claude Bouscharain, and the young art student Breyten Breytenbach, with the renowned bohemian poet and world traveller Uys Krige as *primus inter pares*. Through Uys, who spent days and nights introducing her to his translations from the poetry of the French surrealists, or of Lorca, or the South Americans, she would soon meet his close friend Jack Cope, with whom Uys shared a bungalow on Second Beach at Clifton and who in due course became her lover. This circle transcended all the boundaries and taboos of the then newly established apartheid state, by including a number of coloured poets and writers as well: Piet Philander, Richard Rive, Peter Clarke, Adam Small.

The birth of Ingrid's daughter Simone was a watershed. The fulfilment of motherhood was accompanied by a discovery which she confided to me in the rather seedy lounge of the Clifton Hotel soon after we met: that at a house party on the day she returned home from the hospital, she surprised Piet with another woman. And less than eighteen months later the company he worked for transferred him to Johannesburg, which Ingrid was to describe as 'probably the most primitive city on earth', and which, moreover, meant leaving behind all the friends who had come to give sense to her world. Whether there was any direct link or not, it comes as no surprise, with hindsight, that an early attempt at suicide dates from this period. But one should bear in mind a memory evoked by Marjorie Wallace: that on the very first day she met Ingrid, the fledgling poet interrupted a carefree, happy conversation on Clifton beach by asking totally out of the blue, 'Do you think I will commit suicide one day?' This was one of the key questions she persistently asked me during our first weekend together.

'We miss the sound of the sea, and of course everything,' she wrote to Jack in her very first days in the north, '. . . I'm sorry my letter is so boring – there's nothing I can tell which I can say – I am so "robbed"!'

One of her earliest experiences in the then Transvaal was attending a cultural gathering, part of countrywide celebrations of the Afrikaans language, addressed by the infamous 'architect of apartheid', Dr Hendrik Frensch Verwoerd, whom she classified among the 'animals': 'One form of verbal violence after the other occurred without a blush, until at last the seducer of our nation smugly sat down to the applause of White Afrikanerdom.' How well I remember a cold, clear winter's night on the balcony of her flat, when we discussed Verwoerd. Ingrid had already had rather too much to drink. In the middle of the conversation she stopped to peer at me through the smoke of her cigarette, and asked, 'Do you hate Verwoerd?'

'Of course,' I said.

'I mean, do you really *hate* him?'

'Yes, I do.'

'Then go and shoot him.'

'How do you mean, "shoot him"?'

'Go out this moment and get a gun and shoot the bastard.'

'But Ingrid, one doesn't just go around shooting people!'

'If you're really serious about what you feel you would do that.'

'Now please be reasonable.' How many times during how many conversations did I use those words! And every single time she sneered: 'Stick your *reasonable* up your arse!'

'If you don't go and do it, *now*, I won't ever again believe a word you say.'

'Ingrid!'

'You're just a coward, like everybody else! You haven't got the guts of your own convictions! I despise you!'

It turned into a raging argument that lasted through most of the night. Until she was too tired to know what she was saying, and I had to take her to the bedroom and put her to bed, where she slept until the morning, without any recollection of what had happened.

In most respects the sojourn in Johannesburg was disastrous. Within three months Ingrid fled back to the Cape, leaving her clothes and Simone behind. Despite her fierce, possessive, demonstrative love of Simone she could also be disquietingly negligent of the little one. When she had visitors she would readily pack the child off to Piet's parents, or her sister Anna, or friends.

Behind her decision to return lurked also the fact that she had developed a crush on Jan Rabie. They had become close friends earlier, while Marjorie was still in Scotland following their years together in Paris; and Jan, with characteristic frankness, had written to tell Marjorie that unless she came to join him very soon he would have an affair with Ingrid. But now, with Marjorie back at his side, there was no chance of a relationship: Jan was much too set on the fierce loyalty prescribed by the Calvinism of his father. Marjorie's reaction to Ingrid's return was just as characteristically forthright: Let Ingrid come and stay with them, she said: that would soon cure her.

Piet Venter soon followed to take her 'home' again, but for all practical purposes the marriage was over; and from this time, Jan being out of bounds, the relationship with Jack Cope became serious – even though at first he tried to keep her at a distance by warning her that he was 'just like an old broken reed'. In a letter to Uys Krige, written at about the same time, Ingrid manipulates the exchange by telling her father-mentor-friend that what Jack had actually written to her was: 'Uys thinks you're a broken reed.' Whatever the correct version, it found its way into the poignant poem, 'The Song of the Broken Reeds', a lyrical lament about death and loneliness.

Moving into the more lively, cosmopolitan Johannesburg suburb of Hillbrow made life more bearable for Ingrid; but not for long. Early in 1960 she finally left Piet and returned to Cape Town, this time taking Simone with her. The divorce was finalised in early 1962. It was, of course, a critical moment in the country's history, precipitated by the massacre at Sharpeville on 21 March, 1960. Violence erupted all over South Africa. In Cape Town, among other shocking incidents, a black baby was shot dead in his mother's arms by police in the black township of Nyanga. Driven by outrage and morbid fascination, Ingrid went to the police station at Philippi to see the small body. And in a single burst of inspiration she wrote what many readers still revere as one of the very best poems in South African literature, 'The Child Shot Dead by Soldiers at Nyanga'. Although many friends voiced fears about possibly dangerous repercussions from the poem, she refused to change a word, and like the baby she addressed in it, the poem has since travelled the world in many languages. 'I am surprised when people call it political,' Ingrid wrote in an article in *Drum* soon after we met. 'It grew out of my own experiences and sense of bereavement. It rests on a foundation of all philosophy, a certain belief in "life eternal", a belief that nothing is ever wholly lost.'

In other respects, too, those years were difficult for Ingrid. The relationship with Jack offered her a sense of security, although its open-endedness, and Jack's persistent refusal to get married – inspired, perhaps, by the way he continued to be haunted by his first failed experience of matrimony – was a source of frustration and friction; a nadir was reached when she discovered, in the middle of 1961, that she was pregnant. She postponed telling Jack for two months; when she finally mustered the courage to do so, his only reaction, as she told me two years later, was to ask, 'What are you going to do about it?'

As to what she did, accounts differ. Her sister Anna, always keen to cover up, reported that Ingrid had checked herself into a hospital. Ingrid herself maintained, in gory detail, that it was a backstreet affair, performed by an old coloured woman armed with a knitting needle. The brush with death intrinsic to the experience found expression in another of her best-known poems, 'Little Grain of Sand', in which an unborn child cries from his mother's womb about futility and nothingness. It was one of the most traumatic moments of her life, which continued to haunt her till the end. And although the relationship with Jack resumed, it could never be the same again.

What particularly distressed Ingrid about the abortion was remembering her mother who, when abandoned thirty years earlier by Abraham Jonker during her pregnancy, had chosen, nevertheless, in dire circumstances, to keep her baby. That Beatrice, who had had much more reason than Ingrid herself for getting rid of a child, had rejected this option, caused Ingrid guilt feelings of which she could never absolve herself. Often, in moments of high tension, she would confuse herself, the child who had survived, with the foetus *she* had aborted. No wonder that in the period following the abortion she had to be hospitalised more than once in the Valkenberg mental institution, where among other forms of treatment she submitted to electric shock therapy. And her fixation with suicide became near-pathological.

These dark years – the final months in Johannesburg, the return to the Cape – resulted in heightened poetic activity. Much of the verse in *Ontvlugting* had been written in rhymed couplets, which persisted in her work for a long time; but gradually, notably under the influence of Uys Krige and his magnificent translations of Éluard, Lorca, Neruda, Andrade and others, she turned to free verse. And soon she had the small collection of poems that was destined to become the cornerstone of her legacy, *Rook en Oker*, published in October 1963 by Bartho Smit at APB Publishers in Johannesburg. The cover was designed by a young Cape artist, Nico Hagen.

The weekend following our meeting, I spent in the small Bantry Bay apartment which Ingrid shared with a good friend, Lena Oelofse. Late on the Friday afternoon Nico unexpectedly turned up, with a nervous young woman in tow. He had come, he announced, to inform Ingrid of his wedding earlier that same day. She was speechless with shock. It transpired that she had been having an affair with Nico and that he had already proposed marriage to her.

'We would love to have you as a friend,' he beamed.

'Fuck your friendship!' Ingrid responded in rage. 'Get the hell out of here, you bloody traitor!'

She promptly withdrew into the warm amniotic water of a bath, where she sat for an hour in total silence, smoking one cigarette after the other. We had already arranged to go out for a meal, but it was almost impossible to extricate her from the bath. In the end she agreed to go with me – not to eat, but to drink. 'I want to get drunk tonight,' she said.

Outside the restaurant she collapsed in tears. When at last she became calmer, she started talking compulsively. How could Nico have hurt her in such way? And he wasn't the only one. *Everybody* took advantage of her, used and abused her. What was wrong with her? Because, surely, it was all her own fault . . .

It took a long time before we went inside. Over the meal – she did consent to eat something, in the end – she told me the whole convoluted story of her life and loves. Over and over, obsessively, she returned to Simone, who was with Piet Venter in Johannesburg at the time. 'They're going to take away my child. And the court will side with them. Because I take drugs. I drink. I sleep around. But I *want* my child!' And like so many times during that weekend, she spoke of suicide. She showed me the thin white scars on her wrists from a previous attempt. Yet when I left very early on the Monday morning to drive the nearly 1,000 kilometres to Grahamstown, there was something incredibly serene and almost happy in the smile with which she said goodbye.

We had both assumed that our weekend together would remain outside of time, outside of our ordinary lives; we never believed it could have a sequel. But within a week everything had changed. We both realised that we were too deeply in love to extricate ourselves. By coincidence I received an invitation to return to Cape Town for a series of lectures at the end of May. For Ingrid, this seemed like an unexpected new lease on life. At the same time my appearance on the scene had rekindled Jack's amorous interest which had waned in recent times while she'd had her affair with Nico. Whereas previously he had kept her at a distance, seeing her for sex when he needed it and then – literally – throwing her out of the bed when he wanted to be alone, he now assured her of his undying love and for the first time began to mention marriage as an option. This, at least, was how she represented it to me.

There was one near-farcical writers' party at Paarl where he cornered her to assure her, 'Do you realise that you're the only woman I have ever loved?' In reply, she showed him a small ring with a red stone I had given her earlier in the day. 'I'll buy you a bigger one,' he promised. Yet as soon as I had returned to Grahamstown, all promises were forgotten.

For the rest of the year, unable to stay away, I drove down to Cape Town every few weeks. Ingrid had become a fever in the blood. When we were together, the ordinary flow of life stopped; time no longer existed. We would spend the weekends in romantic hideouts: country hotels near Stellenbosch, Franschhoek, Gordon's Bay, Hout Bay. She was swept along on a new wave of writing poetry. Even I began to write poems – very bad ones, terribly derivative, but I needed the outlet. Our relationship became an extension of our writing. But very soon a fatal pattern was established: my life became a frantic pendulum oscillating between Cape Town and Grahamstown. The moment I was home, the longing for the freedom and wildness Ingrid represented, would become overwhelming and I would rush back to her in a frenzy of desire, only to find that in my absence she had been with Jack again – sometimes because *he* would not leave her in peace, just as often because *she* could not bear to be alone. This vacillation would inhibit my urge for commitment, and I would become serious about returning to Grahamstown and the security and comfort of my marriage. And of course this decision would then persuade Ingrid to turn to Jack again – by which time, back at the ranch, I would decide that my marriage had failed after all, and I would dash back to Cape Town, only to find that in my absence . . . et cetera.

Time and time again we would break up, sometimes with a whimper, often with a bang. Time and time again we would return to the love which beckoned like a dark and dangerous current. It could not possibly last. The guilt attached to both my shrinking worlds was becoming unbearable; the fire of uncertainty and doubt was devastating. It was the only time in my life – apart from a moment in Paris in 1968 after the shipwreck of another love – that I actually started thinking about suicide.

One of the most agonising moments came during my visit to Cape Town in November 1963, when Ingrid had gone to work and I found on her table a writing pad she had left open, deliberately for me to see, as she admitted afterwards. The top page was covered with an almost illegible scribble, in English, written the night before, after I had already gone to bed. That evening, during a meal in a restaurant, we had quarrelled – an argument, in fact, that followed an angry contretemps she'd had with Jack earlier in the day, when he had contemptuously called her 'a minor poet'. How ironical that Jack's own hang-up had been that, compared to Nadine Gordimer and others, *he* would be classified by history as a minor political writer from South Africa.

In tears, I copied out what she had written that previous night:

One's art which is a justification for your existence but when you have seen through that justification, is it then still possible to exist for it? One tries to compensate for something, but when there is nothing to compensate for, is it still important? Question for the minor artist. To live hereafter; to *give* to the future? No voice is wholly lost. No SMALL voice is lost – but does that really matter? When one is selfish, and minor, as your talent? No. It is not worthwhile. The small voice dies. And it deserves to die. The small-hearted selfish person deserves to die. He will not have, doesn't deserve, life eternal. I deserve to die.

The people important to my small existence:

Jack Cope: who doesn't want to be burdened (right!) with this small voice.

Simone: whom I cannot give emotional and material security. A good start. No more.

André: who has other obligations.

Sum total.

Which leaves 'left over life to kill.' 'For each man kills the thing he loves' – differently – goodbye to Jack, Simone, André

Sick sick sick

Do you understand, Jack Cope, that I am sans Jack, sans Simone, sans André

The biggest conflict

Ever, for *me*

And as I exit

– to 'free'?

Left over life to *kill*. If one has the 'organising power'

I don't I go And this is nothing else but the small 'personal' problem – '*de versmorende ik*' ['the suffocating I': this phrase was a quote from a Dutch poem] And when this 'I' these adult obligations – there is no way out. I do not say this to alarm or to hurt you – it has been thus for a long time; the *usefulness* of this life is *gone*: I can't live for myself or my ART; everything is gone – all service, which is and gives *meaning*. Blame my past, or whatever has made me, 'all is vanity, says the *prediker*' ['preacher', written in Afrikaans]; *I have failed everyone and everything, I have indeed a left-over life to kill, I will kill it. And, last dignity* (sic!), on my own terms. Even now there is an impure element, and I'll have to stop. I have failed, FAILED, which is a personal '*begrip*' ['concept', written in Afrikaans]: I cannot be cheerful, loving, giving; I am mean and turned in on to my own conscience. I do not like it. It influences my 'sanity'.

I am Ingrid. Pity, but there it is.

This was raw despair. And yet, not only in the confession itself but in her decision to leave it open on the table for me to see, I could sense – unbearably cruel as this might seem – her urge to 'act out' her anguish, to play a role she had come to appropriate for herself – the urge to be *seen* as the outcast, the despised, the rejected, the misunderstood, who soaks up the pity of others to feed her emotions and to squeeze poetry out of it. For Ingrid could be unbelievably cruel herself, inconsiderate of others (friends, lovers, family, child), wrapped up only in herself and her own needs. For those of us who lived close to her, such bouts of histrionic despair were exquisitely balanced with periods of serenity and considerateness, of loving and cherishing; and of laughter and fun. Perhaps, deep down, she was really meant to be a summer child, who loved dancing and teasing and frolicking; there were days and nights when she and her lover could laugh uncontrollably throughout a long bout of lovemaking. And this is what one tends to remember: wandering hand in hand over dunes or just inside the delicate lace of foam at the edge of the sea; or rushing out, on an impulse, at midnight or one o' clock in the night, to Clifton or Llandudno, to run naked along the beach, and into the literally breathtaking cold of the Atlantic, arctic icicles stabbing up through our veins, then darting out again to make love on the sand, or to lie on the side of a mountain staring up at the clouds drifting past and imagine distant places, magic places, worlds forever beyond our reach but worthy of being dreamt about. But somewhere in the background there was this darkness lying in wait, this constant doubt, this undirected and unresolvable rage, this urge to hurt and wound and destroy.

I am Ingrid. Pity, but there it is.

Early in 1964 Ingrid was awarded the biggest literary prize in South Africa at the time for *Rook en Oker*. She decided that she would use the money to go to Europe, where she had never been, possibly to study in Holland. The first person she telephoned with the news of the prize, offering to pay for his air ticket to the awards ceremony in Johannesburg, was Abraham Jonker. He coolly declined. We agreed that as soon as possible I would follow her to Europe. We would go to Paris, the city I loved more than any other; afterwards we would travel through Spain. Our travel plans had to be kept secret, of course: Jack was not to know; and my own marriage was still precariously surviving, even though the consciousness of failure and betrayal was becoming an almost unbearable burden.

At the end of March Ingrid left Cape Town for Southampton on the *Windsor Castle*. Almost every day she wrote letters to her two lovers left behind, Jack and I; on board she also met the writer Laurens van der Post, something of a legend, largely self-consciously created, in his lifetime. He became her new mentor and undertook to introduce her to the literary world in London. At the same time it was clear from Ingrid's letters that, if his attitude was, above all, fatherly, it was not without incestuous undertones. Ingrid told me that van der Post had been castrated as a prisoner of war in a Japanese camp: if this was indeed so, it might explain the ambiguities in his relationship with Ingrid, and his attitude towards other, younger men who came close to her.

The six weeks in Britain were both exhilarating and bewildering; she never quite felt at ease, and her nostalgia for South Africa became worse. When she moved to Amsterdam, the sense of *dépaysement* increased. A particular source of distress was that her small rented room had no mirror. Ingrid had always been obsessed with mirrors, with the need to see herself reflected. Her dream was a bedroom and a bathroom with floor, walls and ceiling covered in mirrors. There was nothing narcissistic about it, and no vanity at all: what she needed, more and more, was the constant reassurance that *she was there*. As her confidence ebbed, this need became almost pathological.

The stay in Amsterdam – relieved by meeting some Dutch writers and poets to whom Jan Rabie and others had provided her with introductions – became, in her own words, 'a waking nightmare'. The most memorable poem ringing out like a *vox clamantis* from this darkness, was 'Waiting in Amsterdam', based on a dream about my imminent arrival. In it, the absent lover returns to a table she has set for him, but instead of sitting down, he unscrews his penis, places it on the table, and leaves without a word. She copied it out for Jack, and dedicated it to him; with another copy for me, dedicated accordingly.

On Saturday 20 June I arrived in Amsterdam – to find that, instead of the secrecy we had planned for the visit, Ingrid had already arranged radio interviews for us jointly and severally and had thoroughly briefed everybody at the NZAV (the Dutch-South Africa Society) about our impending 'honeymoon'. This, linked to her insistence that we dine at the most expensive restaurants and live it up as much as possible, and the almost impossibly high expectations we had both brought to the visit, created tensions from the first hour. These were carried over to Paris, where we lodged in a seedy but charming little hotel in the rue Monsieur-le-Prince, off the boulevard Saint-Michel. The tensions were temporarily held in check by the magic of Paris itself and by meetings with colourful and stimulating people, especially Breyten Breytenbach, who was an old friend of Ingrid's and with whom I'd been corresponding for a long time although we'd never met. Breyten had by then married the beautiful Vietnamese Yolande, a union regarded as 'immoral' in terms of South African legislation, which meant that he could not take her back to his country.

There were magical nights at the Coupole or the Sélect or on the place Saint-Sulpice, or up on Montmartre, or along the banks of the Seine. But there were also eruptions of temper, recriminations, shouting, tears. The trip was already beginning to flounder.

And then came Spain, which was to be the culmination of our travels. Before we could rent a car, I had to spend several days in Barcelona meeting publishers on behalf of my Cape Town publisher. But Ingrid refused to be left alone in the hotel, and was too scared to venture out on her own. I reasoned, argued, pleaded. To which she would respond by trying to taunt and lure me sexually, at first subtly, then blatantly, crudely, into staying. But in the end, hyperconscious of my obligations to the publishers who had made the trip possible, I had to go ahead, making appointments and keeping them. On my return the door would be locked. If I insisted, she would start screaming so loudly that people came running to see who was being assaulted or murdered. Even the management, though undoubtedly accustomed to the legendary *furia español*, became concerned. Our whole relationship was turning fatally destructive, self-destructive.

There were a few happier interludes, including an afternoon at a *corrida* – in its own right, and when it works, a performance that marries beauty and cruelty. But our time of light and lightness – inasmuch as these were evident, except in brief flashes – was over.

In a moment of quiet despair soon after the *corrida* we both agreed that it would be better for her to return to Paris, where Breyten and Yolande could take care of her, and where, we both thought, she could still turn her holiday into something rewarding. Finding it impossible to reach him by telephone, I notified Breyten by telegram. When we set out for the airport Ingrid was unnaturally subdued. As her flight was called she suddenly became hysterical and refused to go to the departure gate, throwing such a tantrum that half of the airport officials came running to add to the commotion. In the end a doctor was called, who gave her an injection. And we returned to the hotel, silent, tight-lipped and resentful.

The following day, with due warning to Breyten, the exercise was repeated, but this time in a minor key and without histrionics. Ingrid flew to Paris, and I set out for a month's exploration of Spain. Not until the very end of the holiday did I learn, with shock, in a letter from my publisher, that Ingrid had in fact returned to Cape Town.

It was only much later that the details were filled in. How her mental state in Paris had deteriorated so suddenly that Breyten had to arrange for her to be hospitalised in the institution of Sainte-Anne; how through the intervention of Roy Macnab, cultural attaché at the South African Embassy, she had been released and put on a plane. She also revealed in letters and telephone calls after my return that Jack wanted nothing more to do with her; and the only ray of light was that her period had come on time, so at least she was not pregnant as we had feared.

It should have been the end, but it wasn't. Within a month or two our correspondence resumed in all its intensity. Moments of disillusionment and rebellion were swept away by rekindled passion. Early in December I was back in Cape Town.

On the surface, everything seemed to have returned to how it had been before. Yet not really. Something had been lost; there was a touch of urgency, an almost frantic need to reassure ourselves that all was still well. But we both knew, and in vulnerable moments openly acknowledged, that our love could no longer be what it had been. The pain was almost unbearable; for Ingrid it implied a final loss of innocence, that childlike quality, as of an elf or a sprite, which should remain forever untouched by the pettiness of the ordinary world.

One particularly stormy episode still haunts my memory: it was a night in December; I was to drive home to Grahamstown very early the next morning. An argument arose and became hideous. Near midnight, beside herself with rage, Ingrid ran out of her apartment in an ugly modern block on the beachfront where Three Anchor Bay merges into Sea Point, screaming that she was going to kill herself. By this time I was so utterly worn out, and had heard the threat so many times, that I did not believe it. An hour later a stranger brought her back to the door: she had tried to jump in front of his car. We were both in shock. For hours we talked, and cried, and slowly found our way back, as always, to concern and forgiveness and love. And then, exhausted, I went to sleep. Ingrid stayed awake, and on the narrow porch outside the room, with her small writing pad on her lap, wrote the moving poem 'Plant me a Tree André', in which she dreams of a small paradise where we would plant a tree and squirrels would come to collect the acorns, and where there would be a dog to cuddle, and where there would be an open house, the windows of which would discover the day, green or gold or grey, and beautiful.

For some time we kept the embers alive, mainly by working together very closely on the polishing of my experimental novel *Orgie*, based on our letters, on our love and on Ingrid's life. It had been scheduled for publication the year before, but political intervention had forced Bartho Smit to cancel the project. Now a new publisher, John Malherbe, was going to bring it out in a particularly beautiful publication in March of 1965. Early in the new year I returned to Cape Town, and together we celebrated the occasion, not realising that it was to be our final farewell. A week or so later there was the customary telegram from her to confirm the onset of her period: once again there was to be 'no butterfly'. Over the previous two years there had always been a particular poignancy about those notes, a sense of loss and emptiness, each time a new farewell, a loss of hope, a different kind of failure, another small death. But it was also ambiguous, because in our fraught situation expecting a child would have been catastrophic.

By that time Ingrid had already met the Flemish painter who was to become, or had already become, one of her last lovers. She had spoken in glowing, suggestive terms about 'my painter'. Perhaps I should have sensed something; but I didn't.

Soon after my last visit at the end of March, for the publication of *Orgie*, in a letter dated 18 April, Ingrid wrote to announce: 28 *days on the dot, last Wednesday*. That coincided with a holiday I spent with my parents; and from Potchefstroom I went to Pretoria, where I, too, had met someone else. At the end of April, almost two years to the day since our first meeting, I wrote to tell Ingrid about the new love and my plans for the future. We had one last, devastating telephone conversation. It was like a desert landscape. Her reaction was very similar to the one with which she had thrown Nico Hagen out of her flat.

There are confusing and conflicting accounts of her last few months. About several heady affairs, surrounding the central relationship with the painter. About one or more abortions. About ruptures with friends. About an accident in which she broke her leg. About terrible financial straits, where I had to step in to help her with money.

On Monday 19 July, 1965, on a visit to Pretoria, I received a telephone call from a close friend, the author Abraham de Vries, who told me that

Ingrid had committed suicide by walking into the sea a hundred metres from her apartment. Ingrid, who could swim like an angelfish . . . ! Her body, as she had predicted in poems written since before her sixteenth birthday, and reiterated in many recent letters and telephone calls to friends, diary entries, jottings on odd scraps of paper, had been found 'washed ashore in weeds and grass'.

However predictable it seemed in retrospect, when it happened it was unbearable, and unbelievable. I felt the world grow dark in front of my eyes. For the rest of the day I was blind.

I am Ingrid. Pity, but there it is.

It was almost impossible to resist the impulse to fly to Cape Town for the funeral; but the idea of facing the world of prying strangers, the knowing eyes of friends and acquaintances, facing Jack, facing the press, was just too much. I could not turn my grief into a public spectacle; it was too private and too deep. And so I missed that ultimate tragicomedy of her funeral, where the dour members of the Jonker family, protected by security police, glowered across the grave at the special friends – writers and artists – gathered on the other side; missed the spectacle of Jack trying to hurl himself into the grave; missed, too, the second funeral, some days later, when the real friends met at the graveside again to read from Ingrid's work.

And now, I suppose, she belongs to the ages – and, sadly but inevitably, to the industry that has sprung up around her life and death. Ultimately all the world can hold on to is what she has left behind: the poetry. As for me: a handful of memories, most of them ambiguous, from a few lost and never-lost years in which Dante's doomed lovers Paolo and Francesca, did hand in hand on the dark wind drifting go.

There was an unexpected and poignant footnote to Ingrid's story only a few months ago, when Karina took me to Poland to introduce me to the landscapes of her childhood, from the first ten years of her life, before her family fled from the country devastated by its own tyrannical regime. We went to Jelenia Góra first, the lovely town with its pastel-coloured gabled facades where she grew up; and there we stayed with her aunt Zosia, who was in every respect as lovely and lively as Karina had led me to believe. From there we proceeded to Wroclaw, then to Kraków, and to the house of her aunt Iwona in the sweet-smelling wood outside Kowary, where she had spent so much of her time in those early years – building little secret houses among the trees, consorting with fairies and angels, escaping from dark and dangerous little creatures in the underbrush. On the last morning of our visit, her uncle Boguslaw Michnik arrived with his wife Anna. He brought with him a beautiful little book which his small publishing firm, WitrynArtystów, had published in 1993. It bore on the cover an all too familiar name: *Ingrid Jonker*. One of the first Afrikaans books, we learned, ever published in Polish translation – the work of a talented and enterprising academic, Jerzy Koch, from the University of Poznan, who over the years has championed the cause of Afrikaans literature in Poland. When, not long afterwards, Mandela chose to read 'The Child' at the opening of the first democratically elected parliament in Cape Town, the Polish reading public was ready to embrace Ingrid and her reputation was consecrated in the world of literature. And how remarkable, that through the intervention of Karina's uncle, this small handcrafted publication, under the title of *Tęsknota za Kapsztadem* (*Nostalgia for Cape Town*) was responsible for disseminating it so far from home – while yet keeping it within the family, as it were. Somehow, meeting Boguslaw Michnik with her, was the closing of a very special circle.

Indeed, the child is not dead, and now become a giant, is still travelling the wide world. Without a pass.

MY FATHER'S CUPBOARD

I WAS WORKING ON THE CONSTRUCTION OF A SMALL *SHADOUF*, THE SIMPLE but ingenious contraption the ancient Egyptians had devised to scoop water from the Nile and convey it to an irrigation system on higher ground. It was, needless to say, an enterprise performed under duress, as a school project for Olga, our housekeeper's lovely child, who has a very special place in our lives. Even so, I worked with great gusto and dedication. Not by any means a triumph of skill and professionalism; and Tutankhamen or Ramses would most likely have had me drawn and quartered for shoddy workmanship. But I was trying. Even though I am all thumbs when it comes to doing things with my hands. Not even thumbs: big toes. Elbows. Knees.

My incompetence has never dampened my enthusiasm or determination. On the contrary. I love carpentry tools. The more expensive and useless the better. From angle grinders, drills, electric screwdrivers or fretwork saws down to the most basic pliers, hammers and chisels, I adore them and respect them and revere them. The only thing is that I cannot use them. In theory, yes. Not in practice. But that has never deterred me.

Which is why I did not turn my eyes to the heavens or groan in despair when Olga broached the small matter of a *shadouf*. In fact, I eagerly jumped at the opportunity. And Olga loyally assisted me. Now that it is all over, I can look back and reflect on the experience – now that the *shadouf* has been finished, and submitted to the scrutiny of the class teacher, who gave us full marks for choice of materials, and for concept and planning, rather less for workmanship, and none at all for functionality.

I have experienced this kind of thing before. When I was fourteen I turned to keeping guinea pigs for a hobby. If I'd kept the number of rodents under control, it might have worked. But I started too big, and did not quite reckon with the natural proclivities of the little creatures. This meant that the first cage soon became too small. The new one was constructed on a grand scale. It was meant to house about thirty to forty guinea-pigs, and had to be tall enough for me to stand in. It was fitted with breeding boxes, recreation areas, feeding corners, a sick bay and whatever else I could think of. One brick wall was required, and that I built single-handedly. Not entirely perpendicular, but it passed my own scrutiny and the rather more strict, but still indulgent inspection of my father. He even offered to pay for the cement, and offered me an advance on the chicken wire and corrugated iron I would need. Unfortunately I had neglected to consider the timber that would be required for the large frames, covered in chicken wire, that were to constitute the other three sides of the cage joined to the brick wall. But then, we had a wide veranda running round three sides of the house to keep the fierce heat of the Griqualand West summer sun at bay; and this stoep was surrounded by wooden railings consisting of sturdy beams and trelliswork. If I sawed some of the beams in half, lengthwise, I reckoned, the remaining structure would still support the curved roof of the veranda, while the other half-width lengths would be just what I needed for the scaffolding of my guinea-pig cage. I waited for a Saturday when my father had gone hunting, and started dismantling the framework of the stoep. It turned out to be harder work than I'd anticipated, and I had to call in the help of the teenage girl, Rebecca, who was my mother's kitchen help at the time.

Rebecca, true to form, demanded a share of the future profits on the guinea-pig sales, and together we made some laudable, if erratic, progress on the cage. By the time my father came home in the late afternoon, two sides of the cage were already standing, awaiting only their covering of chicken wire. The beams for the last side were already half cut. The veranda, even to my biased eye, looked rather the worse for wear. As did my backside after my father had inspected the site. As the damage had already been done, it was impossible to salvage the framework of the stoep, so my construction could continue. And as a tribute to my father I should add that on the

Monday afternoon he actually gave me a hand tacking down the chicken wire to finish the cage.

Months later we reached the next stage, as orders for guinea pigs came in hard and fast, following a letter to a children's magazine; I had to spend hours every day hammering together small rickety cages in which the animals could be dispatched by train. After paying for the material for the cages, the costs of dispatching the guinea pigs, and Rebecca, I'm afraid there wasn't much profit left for myself. That, and the increasingly uncontrollable numbers of pets in the cage, brought about the end of the enterprise. A few score of guinea pigs had to be given away to willing and less willing friends just to get rid of them. And my father stepped in, in a characteristic way, right at the end, by drowning the last ten or twenty without telling me beforehand, in order to spare me unnecessary agony.

After that, I may add, I steered clear of investing in animals. Apart from a grandiose scheme for establishing an international organisation for the care and preservation of wild animals – but that, thank God, never got beyond the planning stage. I turned to vegetables instead. Once again I was not interested in approaching the project in a modest or even manageable way. Our house in Douglas was surrounded by about ten hectares of barren veld, in which only stones and the hardiest of thorn trees could survive. That was where I decided on planting about a hectare of pumpkins, water melons, mealies, beetroot, carrots, radishes, lettuce and even exotica like asparagus and artichokes. With Rebecca's help (once again in exchange for payment which, characteristically, turned out to be more than anything I myself ever made out of the deal) that stubborn, steely, hard-as-rock patch of earth was dug up and turned into beds square and rectangular, fertilised with manure – mainly from the cow my father kept at the time – and prepared to become a verdant paradise.

The problem was water. There was only a single water tap at the back door, apart from a half-corroded red water tank outside the kitchen. But that was not enough to discourage me. Besides, all the hard work had already been put into the layout of the garden, a hundred metres or so behind the house. With the ever-loyal Rebecca's help, we dug a furrow from the tap, across the gravelled backyard, and into the daunting hectare of newly dug scrub and slate and rock where our garden was to flourish. From there, an entire network of smaller trenches were dug, criss-crossing the garden-to-be.

It was only at this stage that a slight miscalculation came to light: from the tap at the back door to the garden the earth was actually sloping uphill. Not very steeply. But uphill all the way. No hope in hell of ever coaxing water to trickle up that incline to irrigate the beds and beds of vegetables I had foreseen in my mind's ever-optimistic eye.

Well then, the only solution would be for Rebecca and me to lug the water in innumerable buckets, in a wheelbarrow, from the house to the garden. Could that be so difficult?

Yes, it could.

Reluctant to abandon a scheme so grandiose and promising, we very bravely battled on – from the moment the school came out until the stars appeared in the evening – trying to water the endless expanse of garden-to-be. And afterwards, my father insisted that I complete all my homework before I was allowed to go to bed. Rules were rules.

It lasted for about three weeks and the first seedlings were just becoming visible above the dusty, arid earth. And then, without further discussion – except for a whispered reminder by Rebecca about outstanding debts – another vision of paradise was unceremoniously terminated.

I am sure that, secretly, even when anything seemed doomed to utter failure, my father was hoping it might succeed after all. Because, I suspect, it would vindicate a need in himself. Something he never discussed with anyone, not even my mother.

It was undoubtedly something in the genes.

In one way or another these genes persist in my children, and how they permutate and change. In most respects it seems to me they have improved.

First there is Anton, born in 1962, soon after Estelle and I had returned from Paris. Since his earliest years Anton has been an immensely creative person, particularly visually. It was a sad day when divorce, just after his third birthday, interrupted our closeness. At university, he turned towards science, specifically physics; and after his PhD he became a lecturer in the subject at Wits University. He specialised in image processing and was remarkably good at it. But just when it seemed as if his future was settled, he made a clean and complete break. Deciding that his real passion had always been the arts, he resigned from his post and became a full-time painter – a courageous decision if ever I saw one; and it made me hugely proud. On two occasions after that he obtained scholarships to the Cité des Arts in Paris; and although it was a battle to keep his head above water, the experience brought him a deep sense of fulfilment; and also brought a new closeness between us. After years of uphill struggle he has finally made a breakthrough and his work is now quite sought after. As I am writing this, he has just built a studio outside Grahamstown where he and his companion, Athinà, have moved in after the birth of their first baby, Ilyo. He could build any number of *shadoufs* without any problem.

My second son is Gustav, bright and serious, and a born critic. When I came back to South Africa from France at the end of 1968, he was two, and came to visit me, dangerously perched on top of his tricycle on the front seat of the car during the drive to my parents' home where I was then on holiday. I was working on a play, constantly interrupted by Gustav who insisted on having his nappy changed every half an hour. Once, while I was preparing something in the kitchen, he suddenly fell ominously silent; and when I went to investigate, he was on top of the table where I'd been writing. He had methodically dismembered my manuscript, crumpling up each separate page into a ball, arranging them all in a pyramid, and then perched right on top to perform one of his most basic functions. It was a moment to say, like Sir Thomas Beecham when an elephant defecated on the stage after a bad rehearsal of *Aida*: 'Manners abominable, but heavens, what a critic!'

Gustav's manners improved immeasurably. He had a brilliant career as a law student, subsequently became involved in investigations of commercial dumping all over the world, reared three beautiful and amazingly talented children with his resourceful wife Marie-Jean, and spends his time rushing from Mexico to Bangladesh to France (he is a Francophile like his father) to Italy and Bosnia and elsewhere in search of dumping practices.

*   *   *

There is another glorious potential builder of *shadoufs* in my family, who is Danie, the first of my two children with Alta. In recent years I have not seen much of him, since he exchanged an ordered existence as a computer expert in South Africa for the joys of the sea, and moved to the Caribbean where he now lives on the island of Grenada. He came home all the way from there to be at my wedding with Karina; before that, I'd last seen him on the island of Carriacou, a tiny pimple in the Caribbean.

Danie was only ten years old when we sailed on the Stockholm Archipelago with my friend and publisher Bertil Käll who offered Danie the rudder: and to my amazement and immense pride Danie held on and navigated us through a nasty storm. 'That was the day,' he told me years later, 'when I decided I'm going to live on the sea.' His tenacity and ferocious will has stood him in good stead as he navigated his colourful life past all variations of Scylla and Charybdis.

He'd grown up quite close to Anton, as we were then all living in Grahamstown. But he was already a few years old when Gustav came visiting for the first time from Pretoria. And the discovery of a new brother came as a revelation to him. For at least a year after that visit, Danie would eagerly point at every boy we passed in the street and ask, 'Is that also my brother?'

He is a son to make any father's chest swell: the way in which he combines great practical skills with his sensitivity, his sense of loyalty, his fierce convictions about justness and fairplay, his concern for others, and his belief in the brotherhood of all men.

And then Sonja, my second child with Alta. In the summer of 1981, when the four of us travelled through Scandinavia, all the way up to Kakslauttanen in Finland to see the midnight sun, Danie was ten, and Sonja not yet eight. From the time they were still quite small, they loved travelling. For Sonja there was always one condition: in every new hotel we came to, she first chose one corner of the bedroom which she would cordon off with chairs and blankets, and where she would set out her dolls and teddies and the small, furry dog which still today, a quarter of a century later, has a place of honour in her home. Once she had staked out her territory, self-contained, inviolate, the Unknown exorcised, she would be completely secure and happy, content to accompany us anywhere.

This became emblematic of the course of her life. Since long before my first marriage I'd always known that I wanted to have children, sons and daughters. But I had a very particular feeling about the bond between father and daughter. (Is there any other book in world literature which portrays this bond more devastatingly than Halldór Laxness's *Sjálfstaett Fólk* (*Independent People*)? And I knew that I would not stop having children until I had a daughter born to me. Each of my sons has a special place in my life; and I cannot think of the world without any of them. But when Sonja was born in 1973, there was a feeling that my existence had been rounded off and fulfilled. And it was only natural that we should share a closeness that will always remain inviolate and inviolable. In the power of her will, in her beautiful pig-headedness, allied to her *sympathie* with others, in her spontaneous tuning-in to the world, her inner radiance, in her relationship with her family and her innumerable pets, in her many talents, including her amazing culinary skills and her sense of humour, she is one of the most affirmative individuals I know and love in this world.

The practical genes I have transmitted, for better or for worse, to these four children, all reach back to my father. However quiet, and reserved, and placid, and imperturbable he might have appeared on the surface, I know he was also a planner of plans and a dreamer of dreams. And nothing he ever did testified to this as eloquently as the cupboard he built for my mother.

This happened in the small town of Sabie, set in the mountains of what was then the Eastern Transvaal. He used to plan for months in advance whenever she had a birthday coming up. Usually he would order things from mail catalogues – silverware, crockery, jewellery, even items of clothing. Very often there would be some disappointment involved. The jewellery never looked exactly like the resplendent pictures in the catalogue. The clothes did not quite fit. The crockery did not match anything she had. The silver was suspect. But she always made a great show of it, and feigned surprise and delight. Only afterwards she might confide in me or Elbie that the gifts might not have been as much of a success as she had made him believe.

And sometimes the surprise might be different from what he had expected, usually because he would have to hide the presents so well, knowing her incorrigible curiosity, that he himself might forget where he had stowed the gifts. Once, more than a year after a particular birthday, she discovered a box of chocolates he had hidden in a bin of chicken food, where it had melted in summer heat, and then congealed.

But in the year I turned twenty, he decided to make my mother a cupboard. No mail order this time. No driving into town or to the next town to a furniture shop with specials on display. No. My mother needed a cupboard – as she had intimated with her special brand of 'subtle' hints for a long time – and this time he would make it himself. On a Wednesday afternoon when she was out to a meeting of the Women's Auxiliary, or some church gathering, he came home from work earlier than usual, and took me to a hardware shop with him. He had with him several sheets of paper on which he had made indecipherable sketches and drawings and lists and lists of calculations.

He refused to discuss the plan or any of its details with me. It was a secret. I merely had to help him transport everything in the back of the old grey '38 Hudson before she came home.

That was sometime during the June holidays; my mother's birthday was on 16 October. For four months he spent every single afternoon except Sundays in the outroom where he had locked up his tools and materials. In front of the only window he had draped an old tablecloth. The key he carried in his pocket, even when he went to the office. He knew the extent and the unscrupulousness of my mother's curiosity. This was to be the crowning glory of his carpentry skills. During the short vacation in September, I asked him about his progress. It was going well, he grunted. But he refused to divulge anything more. Still, the look of satisfaction on his face suggested that he was indeed pleased with what was happening in that locked outroom.

I was not there for the grand finale in October, but Elbie brought me up to date. Early on the morning of 16 October my father got up and got dressed, very meticulously, and instructed my mother to do the same. Then he took her by the hand and led her round the house to the outroom, which he unlocked with great ceremony. He went in first, to draw the tablecloth curtain at the window and put on the light. From the threshold he invited her inside.

'I know you wanted a cupboard,' he said, unable to contain his glee. 'Here it is.'

My mother went inside. All my siblings, Elbie and Marita and our small brother, Johan, born just before the move to Sabie, followed on her heels.

She stared. And gulped.

'Well?' he asked. For someone as calm and contained as my father usually was, his excitement was almost palpable. 'What do you think?'

She approached, stroked the somewhat unevenly varnished wood, then opened the two doors, one by one.

'It's – it's – big,' she said after a long time.

And big it certainly was. Too big, it soon transpired, to get out through the door.

And there in the outroom the cupboard stood, for the remaining years of our sojourn in Sabie. In the end, when the family moved to Bothaville, by which time I was in Paris, the cupboard stayed behind, and had to be sold to the new owners of the house as a permanent fixture.

POLITICAL STIRRINGS

MY MEMORIES OF THE WAR CENTRED MAINLY IN THE TWO PARAFFIN BOXES IN
our outroom where my parents had hoarded scarce items: candles, white
flour, peanut butter, some tinned foods. Seen from one angle, I suppose, I
had almost no political awareness at all as a youth. From others, *everything*
in my life was steeped in politics from the outset.

My father's way of looking at the world was undoubtedly shaped by the
fact that as a young man *his* father had joined the Boksburg Commando to
fight the English in the Boer War. That is a story in its own right, and he
wrote it all down afterwards, in High Dutch, in his beautiful copperplate.
How they trekked this way and that, through the Transvaal, through Natal,
and back to the Transvaal, following one report or rumour of decisive battles
after the other, yet always managing just to miss the really important engage-
ments – Spioenkop, Colenso, Dalmanutha, Elandslaagte – in what, to me,
but not to him, became a dark comedy of errors. So I was brought up on
a diet of Boer bravery and English cowardice and atrocities, resulting in a
burning nationalism and the dream of restoring Afrikaner independence –
a version of history from which blacks were largely absent, at most
incidental.

But as a magistrate, a civil servant, my father was not allowed openly to
get involved in politics. His private opinions were no secret; but in the exercise of his duties he usually tried to be scrupulously correct. This was also
a consequence of his chosen career. Finding himself passionately immersed
in the legal profession, my father conditioned his mind, and shaped his

whole view of the world, by considering, as objectively as possible, the right and wrong of every situation, every person, every human problem.

One of the first demonstrations of this, an episode which still defines much of the image I have of him, came in 1948, when I turned thirteen, my first year in high school, and the watershed year when the National Party came to power and introduced apartheid as its official policy. For our family this was a cause for jubilation. As early as 1938 my parents had taken part in the countrywide festivities to mark the centenary of the Great Trek; my father even grew a beard for the occasion and my mother sported a full-length Voortrekker dress and *kappie* as, with other local dignitaries, they took a ride on one of the ox-wagons that trekked through the length and breadth of the country on the long road to Pretoria where the cornerstone of the Voortrekker Monument was to be laid. How well I remember the moment during the elections of 1948, when news came that the prime minister, Jan Smuts, had lost his seat in Standerton. I was already in bed, but the general commotion in the lounge, accompanied by a thundering crash, made me jump up and run to the scene to find my mother trapped up to her waist in a hole in the middle of the room, right in front of the radio. It turned out that the news had sent her jumping into the air with such energy that in coming down she had crashed right through the floor. And for years 'Mother's Election Hole' was kept as a sacrosanct memento of that unforgettable night.

Then, mere weeks after the elections, I was instructed at school to take part in what was to be my first attendance at a meeting of the debating society. The topic was, *The government should go ahead with its segregation policies.* And I had to oppose the motion.

I did not even understand the word 'segregation', nor did I have any inkling of the rules and procedures of the debating society. Naturally, I went to my father for help. It was only years later that I realised how my request must have gone against the grain of everything that had shaped his convictions as a Nationalist Afrikaner, the son of a Boer War veteran, whose whole life had been steeped in distrust of anybody or anything that might threaten the political aspirations and the survival of his people.

My father set aside his gardening for a precious hour to retrace with me the history of Afrikanerdom since the Anglo-Boer War and explain every bend and detour on that road where Afrikaners had thwarted or betrayed black aspirations and jeopardised the future of the country – all of which he understood and could explain rationally, even though, emotionally, he resented it with every fibre of his body: the Land Act of 1912, the disenfranchisement of blacks in the thirties and the way in which only Smuts's holism could in the long run ensure a just and free and safe multiracial society. Intellectually, he could defend it. But in his guts he supported, with conviction and passion, the apartheid government and would continue to do so for the rest of his life – to the extent that even though it was, strictly speaking, unacceptable for him as a magistrate to do so, he joined in due course the secret Afrikaner organisation, the Broederbond or 'Band of Brothers'.

At that meeting of the debating society, I went out of my way to plead the cause of a non-segregated society and a non-racist future. But of course my heart wasn't in it; and my side lost the debate by a large majority. Much to my own relief, and my father's when he learned about the outcome. But I had learned something which in my later life I would cherish as a vital moment in my approach to the world, at all the future forks along my road – even if it took me many years fully to grasp the meaning, and the necessity, of it. The need to think, not just laterally, but cubistically. To approach subjects 'in the round'. To try to understand why others think what they think and are what they are. To imagine someone else's thoughts from the *inside*.

I persisted for a long time on the right-hand side of the road to nationalistic salvation. I remember a conversation with my mother just before going to university, when I told her about my excitement at the prospect of meeting people of different political, moral or religious persuasions, and she responded with uncharacteristic vehemence, 'You can do what you like and be what you like. You can even become a communist for all I care. But one thing you must know: if ever you become a Sap, we will no longer regard you as our child.' A Sap was a member of Field Marshal Smuts's erstwhile South African Party, later the United Party, that lost the 1948 election to the ponderous Nationalist ex-dominee, Dr Daniel Francois Malan. Yet I should add as a footnote that when I fell in love with the pretty almond-eyed

Esther who steadfastly evaded all my approaches and whose parents were of the Sap persuasion, it was my mother who tirelessly negotiated with Esther's to set up a tryst.

Early in my first year at university there was a momentous occasion when Dr Malan was re-elected as prime minister, this time with a sizeable majority, which enabled him to unfold the whole dire programme of apartheid: the Group Areas Act, the Separate Amenities Act, the Mixed Marriages Act, the Population Registration Act, the Immorality Act, you name it, each of which the staff and students of my university, including my enthusiastic self, welcomed with waves of almost near-religious fervour as milestones on the road towards the Afrikaner's reclaiming of his identity and his ultimate republican destiny ('his', indeed, as it was a thoroughly male-chauvinistic concept and ideal). To anyone familiar with German history of the thirties these events must have appeared sickeningly familiar.

From the Cape, Dr Malan travelled on a special victory train to the north, making a halt at every station and siding to 'meet the *volk*' and receive its homage. We learned in time – the news travelled swiftly – that the Man of God would be at the Potchefstroom railway station at eleven or twelve o' clock on that weekday morning. We had classes to attend. One in partic-ular. History. The professor was famous, not just as an historian but as a Party Man. So we did not foresee any problems. But we did take the precau-tion of sending a small delegation to request permission of absence in advance. To our utter amazement Professor Krüger, widely known, and with reason, as Daantjie Donder (Daantjie Thunder), turned down the request very curtly. As a professor at a university, he said, he had no right to give us permission to miss a lecture. I got the distinct impression that if we had simply bunked, he might have turned a blind eye; but in the circumstances we gave him no room to manoeuvre – even though I remember delivering an impassioned plea on behalf of the whole class, based on the argument that as students of history we might be said to have a duty not to miss an occasion to be witnesses to history in the making. There was a shadow of a smile on his stern face, but he refused to budge. In fact – and here I did feel that he went too far – any member of the class not present during the lecture in question, would be severely punished for it.

We were all taken aback by the unexpected response. As fervent young Calvinists we had an unhealthy respect for the structures of power. In the context of a university, we dutifully acknowledged, a professor ultimately derived his authority from God. So what were we to do?

We defied authority.

Not all of us: about half of the delegation attended the lecture the following morning, as did a fair number of our classmates. But a good handful of us, having weighed the options and decided to respond to the call of history (which might, for all we knew, coincide with the will of God the Father, Son and Holy Spirit), took to our bicycles and went to the station.

It was a scene never to be forgotten. Hundreds of people were thronging on the platform. Outside, the streets were lined with vehicles of every description. Not only cars and trucks and tractors and trailers, but horse-carts, mule-carts, donkey-carts. Some of them, we learned, had come from faraway farms and outlying districts; many of the old people – all in their Sunday best, even though covered in dust, the women's flowers wilted and ashen in their gnarled hands, the men's pipes scuffed and chewed – had driven right through the night to be there on time. Most of them were clasping Bibles or hymn books to their bosoms. It was like attending the Second Coming.

The train was at least an hour late, as every halt along the road had lengthened the delay. But no one cared. And at last it came. And the Anointed of the Lord made his prophet-like appearance, solemnly clad in black, on a balcony between two coaches, flanked by his sturdy wife in hat and tailored suit, and his small daughter, an adopted German orphan. He spoke for about a minute before some secretary or lackey ushered them back into the train. But his two paltry loaves and five smelly little fishes were enough for the hungry horde. And long after the train had disappeared in a cloud much bigger than a man's hand, which left most of us covered in soot, I distinctly remember coming past an old man with a long white beard marked by yellow streaks of tobacco juice, his wrinkled cheeks wet with tears, but in his eyes a light that seemed to come straight from heaven.

At the next history lecture we were set an instant test on the work covered in the previous lecture. The true believers who had attended that class and had been duly warned about the test had no problems whatsoever; those heretics among us who had gone off to pay homage to the portly Prophet, floundered. We all felt that we had been most unjustly served, but no one complained. Some, we must have believed, have their reward on earth, while others receive it in heaven. It was only after many years had passed, when Professor Krüger asked me to check an English translation he had made of *The Hound of God*, a long dramatic monologue by the uncrowned king of Afrikaans poetry, N. P. van Wyk Louw, that he admitted, with a wry smile, that on the day of our truancy he had been conscious of only one burning desire in his mind: to be on that station platform with us. By that time I had long broken free from the bonds of Calvinism and Christian-Nationalism. But I could not help admitting to a perverse admiration for his unwavering loyalty to the dictates of his Calvinist conscience. And of course, by then I had heard him lecture on the parallels between the Ancien Régime in France and South Africa under the devastating rule of apartheid; and I could appreciate how he, like my father so many years earlier, could tragically adhere to the dictates of what they *believed* to be right while, deep down, *knowing* what it really was.

For the rest of my university career, going for one of the first major forks in my road, I somehow managed to follow two paths simultaneously: on the surface I toed the official Calvinist line, often even enthusiastically and with the sense of a 'calling', while below that surface I did my best to subvert it.

In my final year, a few months before I left for Paris, it briefly seemed as if the official path had triumphed. One day I was called in by the rector, an unsmiling granite-faced man known to the students as Stone-eye, and invited to join a very select, very secret group of young men, hand-picked as 'leaders of the future' and known as the Ruiterwag, or Cavalry Guard, generally accepted to be the junior branch of the Broederbond. On the appointed evening a small group – no more than five or six of us – were assembled on the lawn of the rector's home and called in, one by one, to appear – blindfolded? – in the middle of a circle of senior professors, where during a most solemn ceremony we were inducted into the ranks of the country's political elite, to assume responsibility for the future of our people, that small band of Israelites surrounded by a dark sea of heathens.

Of the others called up for this kind of higher service, I can remember only one individual. It was F. W. de Klerk, the future state president.

At the time, although I believe he was already chairman of the SRC, he did not cut a particularly impressive figure. His most obvious characteristic appeared to be a desire to please, and a readiness, even an eagerness, to stoop quite low to achieve it.

One of the first things I did when I returned from Paris two years later – after Sharpeville had happened and it seemed as if the country was set to change, to change utterly, was to write a letter to de Klerk outlining the events in France that had led me to revise everything I had previously taken for granted. I proposed that a meeting of our Potchefstroom branch of the Ruiterwag be called to discuss the possibilities of a New South Africa, and assured him of my readiness to take part in such a meeting. I never received a reply to my letter.

FRANCE

I FOUND MYSELF IN PARIS LONG BEFORE I EVER WENT THERE. IT STARTED WITH a passionate love affair with Jeanne d'Arc when I was not yet fourteen. I can no longer remember how and where I first met her, but it was many years before, as a homage to one of the most meaningful women in my life, I introduced her into *On the Contrary* and, more sketchily, into some of my other books. In due course I read and reread her story in many different forms, but some of the key moments remain indelibly fixed in my mind. The early encounters with the Voices, of course, which did not seem at all far-fetched to me, as from a very tender age I had the habit of wandering about the veld and talking aloud to thorn trees, rocks, scaly lizards and the odd slithery snake, and imagined their replies. The long journey to Chinon to receive her first official engagement. Cutting off her long hair and donning men's clothes to join the roughest soldiers in the kingdom on her way to Orleans.

These details of her journey were reinforced in my mind by an old story from the Boer War, no doubt apocryphal, which I could also not resist working into *On the Contrary,* and which retroactively contributed to the process of shaping a clear image of Jeanne in my mind: it concerned a girl of seventeen or eighteen who wished to accompany her father and brothers on commando against the English. But obviously this was summarily rejected. However, she bided her time and at the very first opportunity she cut off her hair, put on her youngest brother's shirt and corduroy jacket and trousers, stole a Mauser from the rack in the passage and made her getaway on the only remaining horse on the farm. She joined the first group of Boers she came across, only to discover that life on commando was not really the adventure she had expected. It was a bore. And also unbearable, in heat and cold and mud and misery. But she kept doggedly on. The turning point caught everybody by surprise. One evening the whole commando was having their meagre supper in a wide circle around the campfire. As usual, they were all squatting on their haunches. At first she did not notice that the elderly man opposite her was staring very intensely into the V of her open legs, so voraciously that he never even realised that his pipe had burned out. What she did not know was that her trousers had split right open along the seam. It was only after a while that she became uncomfortably aware of the old patriarch's stare. But not wanting to attract any undue attention she dared not move. At last she could no longer contain her discomfort. 'What's the matter, Oom?' she asked with a show of annoyance. 'What are you staring at?' He shook his head, then began to knock out his pipe very slowly and deliberately, without taking his eyes off her crotch. 'Opperman,' he said, ponderously chewing on the stem of his cold pipe, 'Opperman, you must forgive me for saying so, but I have never seen a man with such a long arse-hole in my life.'

How Jeanne emerged unscathed from her long marches with the army, was a miracle. I followed her all the way, from Orleans, to Patay, to Reims where she witnessed the coronation of Charles VII, to Paris, to Compiègne, to the tall tower in the castle of Beaurevoir from which she tried in vain to escape, to the confinement of her grey dungeon and the cruel interrogations by Pierre Cauchon, at last to the stake on the old market square in Rouen. When she was burned by the English, the traditional enemies of my people, the intimate bond between us was sealed forever.

Once fired, my imagination would not let go of France again. My love of history – after a number of years of repetitive lessons on the South African past – was first kindled by a teacher, Mr Rousseau, who in my first high-school year miraculously turned history into story in much the same way as Herodotus had first done, and who taught us, with all the feeling of a man who spoke from personal experience, about Socrates and Xanthippe.

During the nearly three years I spent in his classes he took us on a guided tour through ancient Egypt, Sumeria, Palestine, Greece and Rome, all the way past the Middle Ages and Renaissance, the Holy Roman Empire, early modern Europe, to the French Revolution and Napoleon. When he discovered how passionate I was about Jeanne d'Arc, he began to ply me with books on France. These not only fascinated me in their own right, but stimulated an immensely rewarding discovery which has remained crucial to almost everything I myself was to write in the years to come: the discovery of how many variants of the same story could coexist. Each new book on a given topic (Jeanne d'Arc, say, or Napoleon, or the pyramids) adding new facts to the others, relativised them, turning history into an infinitely variable collection of accounts and possibilities, instead of the rigid and unimaginative repetition of the same version of South African history we had been confronted with, in Standard 2, in Standard 3, in Standard 4, in Standard 5, and then again, so help me God, in Standard 6. In this way I learned to look at the past through what was once felicitously called 'the multiple eye of the fly'. With these books and the energetic discussions that accompanied them, Mr Rousseau guided me through the Wars of Religion and the Night of St Bartholomew, the glory of the Sun King and his repulsive lack of personal hygiene, the sad, big-nosed Louis XVI and his flighty Austrian princess, the writers who changed the world – the wise and humorous Montaigne, the learned Montesquieu, Voltaire with his wit and wisdom, the romantic and inventive Jean-Jacques Rousseau addicted to his secret vice . . . (about the vice I only learned years later, by which time I had already discovered it for myself, when I immediately began to make up for lost time). And then the explosion of the Revolution. The humourless and merciless ascetic Robespierre, the audacious giant Danton, Marat in his bath, Charlotte Corday a predictable successor to my Jeanne. Followed at last by the Avenging Angel, Bonaparte, who started with nothing, rose to unimaginable glory and ended again with nothing on the island of St Helena – except possibly a few bottles of Vin de Constance from our own Cape. Today, Napoleon may be one of the worst reasons for admiring France, but as an adolescent I was an unrepentant fan. Under the influence of Mr Rousseau, and for several years afterwards, I lived through a quite protracted phase of adulation for Great

Men. At university I was swept off my feet by Carlyle. And the landscape of this phase was largely inspired by France.

Literature was indeed decisive for my love affair with France too. As it happened, a number of French classics were translated, very badly, into Afrikaans during my high-school years, and my parents were happy to feed my voracious appetite. A few others, not available in Afrikaans, I read in English. And during my first year at university, as soon as I had mastered the rudiments of French, I plunged into the originals. Each one of those books helped to fill in details of the image of France, and more specifically Paris, that was taking shape inside me. Even today, when I close my eyes, I can recall the smell of those books, and recite lines or whole passages that formed the collage and palimpsest of images that came to constitute Paris, and France, in my mind.

There was Hugo who made me aware of the unspoken, often unspeakable, subconscious dimensions of a place, whether stowed away in secret alcoves and passages of a cathedral, or submerged in the sewers of the city. There was Balzac, who unfolded the whole human comedy to my eyes and taught me to respond to the challenges of Paris with, 'À nous deux maintenant'. There was Zola who initiated me, through the whole constellation of the Rougon-Macquart family, to the very entrails of Paris and provoked, through Nana, some cherished secret erections, while never ceasing to surprise me with the understanding smile with which, from behind all that wretchedness, the writer could contemplate the small foibles and follies of his characters, or the sudden shock of liquid light as the sun came out over a wet and shimmering street. These novels were to me the perfect accompaniment to the paintings of Monet or Le Nain. I read and reread the poems of Baudelaire and Verlaine, and knew that the Paris of spleen, like the Paris of ecstasy, was where I really belonged. I savoured the ironies and the wryness of Simenon, the vagabondage of Colette, the adolescent rebelliousness of Françoise Sagan, the lost innocence illuminated by Anouilh, the lucent prose of Gide. There were also plays and short stories by Sartre, who appealed to me intellectually but with whom I could never empathise.

And then there was Camus. Who promptly became, and still is, one of the Baudelairean *phares* of my life. I do not merely admire Camus, I love him. And one of the most profoundly moving pilgrimages of my life, more than twenty years after first reading *La peste*, was to Lourmarin in the Vaucluse, to stand at the simple slab of his grave overgrown by rosemary in the uncompromising sun of Provence. Camus: the indefatigable persistence of Sisyphus, the revolt-without-end, the struggle, literally to death, against injustice, against the lie, against unfreedom. He provided not only a map for my explorations of Paris, of France, but a blueprint for the rest of my life.

This was the mindset I found myself in when, like a castaway on a distant beach, I arrived in Paris, curious and intimidated, driven by all kinds of urges and desires to which I could not yet assign a name – in early October 1959, in time for the new academic year at the Sorbonne.

Paris. Already described during one of the debates in parliament during the Revolution as 'the most beautiful city in the world', and 'the fatherland of arts and sciences'. I had been there once before, at the end of my second year at university, when my parents offered to send me to Europe with a small touring group led by a Flemish-born Johannesburg teacher, Jacques van Oortmerssen.

For me, the decisive factor was that my best friend, Christie, also managed to persuade his parents to let him join the tour. And a very mixed group it was, ranging from a wealthy farmer from the arid north-west and his family to a few young teachers and a handful of students. There were also a couple of girls just out of school; and one of them, an impish, vivacious, short-haired, pretty but rather spoilt city brat, Jeannette, with whom both Christie and I almost immediately fell in love. A recipe for disaster. It certainly put our friendship to the test. But friendship was what prevailed in the end. In the middle stages of the tour Christie and I had a long discussion and nego-tiated a strategy: each of us would have two days at a time to try our luck, after which the other would take over for the next two days. 'Trying our luck', I should hasten to make clear, might involve at the utmost a brief holding of hands, not even the shadow of a kiss. And at the end of every day he and I would get together – we usually shared a room anyway – to discuss our progress and prospects.

What particularly touched me was that he agreed in advance, knowing how I'd been dreaming about Paris for most of my life, that our programme would be devised in such a way that for our few days in that city Jeannette would be 'mine'. I had feverish visions of a walk along the Seine at night, a kiss on the Pont des Arts, a Mass in Notre-Dame, a lavish ice cream on the terrace of the Café de la Paix, a boat trip along the sewers. These visions turned out to be rather unrealistic. It was midwinter, early January, the Seine was in flood, rising to the underside of the roadway across the Pont Neuf and causing the Pont des Arts to be closed to pedestrians. All the quays were submerged. Our sightseeing programme ruled out the possibility of attending Mass in Notre-Dame. The sewers were off limits. The Café de la Paix was, of course, open for business, but there was nothing romantic about its glassed-in and fogged-up terrace and the ice cream was most unimpressive and bloody expensive. I had an allowance of £60 for the whole two-month trip through England, Holland, Belgium, France and Italy, so that towards the end of the holiday I had to flog some of my prized acquisitions to other tour members to afford a haircut in Florence, an oversweet sugared pineapple ring in Pisa, and the odd espresso in Venice. And Jeannette had the sulks. After the first day I invited Christie to join us; and from then on, in spite of everything that had gone wrong, Paris became as magical as it had been in my dreams.

We had been well prepared for Paris, and for the other cities and towns of our journey. Mr van Oortmerssen was a charismatic lecturer, and during the fortnight of our voyage from Cape Town to Southampton he had given us talks on the history, the art and culture of all the countries on our itinerary. Those lectures were usually the high point of our day. But there were many other unforgettable moments on that dark-blue voyage streaked with the silvery lines of flying fish, as our ship, the Dutch immigration liner *De Groote Beer*, waded ponderously through the swell. Much fun and laughter too. Meals where a Tom Jones could have feasted to his heart's content. And dances, extravagantly enjoyed by the young teachers and some of the other students. There was also a group from some posh girls' school on board, a source of unbridled randiness among most of the younger men in our group; and most of them turned out to be seductive and provocative on the small, crowded dance floor. But Christie and I, stupid wet blankets, remained on the fringes – although we could not muster the conviction to stay away alto-gether: apart from anything else, Jeannette was on the floor. Our university, I'm ashamed to say, not only frowned on dancing but rated it as just about the worst sin in Christendom. There was a common saying in those days that at this university sex in a standing position was prohibited, as it might lead to dancing.

Not everything on the boat trip was fun and games. One night there was even high drama. I was woken some time after midnight by a persistent hammering on the partition that separated our cabin from the next one, which was occupied by six or eight of the sirens from the girls' school. The hammering was accompanied by what sounded like muffled female voices shrilling in the background. Befuddled with sleep, I unfolded myself from the top bunk where I was sleeping to wake Christie. Unsure about what was happening next door, all we could agree on was that something must have gone drastically wrong. We tried to respond to the persistent hammering by knocking on the partition from our side. For a moment there was silence. Then the hammering resumed, with what seemed to be more urgency than before. And this time we were pretty sure that we could make out from the chorus of dull shouts and screams next door several individual voices artic-ulating, 'Help! Help!'

Leaving Christie behind to deal with the emergency as he thought fit, I ran, barefoot and in my pyjamas, through the almost pitch-dark ship towards the section where Jacques van Oortmerssen and his wife and child were sleeping in rather more salubrious accommodation than ourselves. In the labyrinthine underbelly of the ship it took a while to find the section I was looking for. Minutes later, an equally befuddled van Oortmerssen joined me to go in search of the ship's sole policeman. And then the three of us, the policeman dressed in vest and underpants but wearing his official cap, and wielding an outsized baton, returned to the suspected scene of crime, where total chaos awaited us.

Only after the event could all the pieces of the jigsaw be fitted together. Among the passengers on the ship were four pretty unsavoury-looking Germans who had been deported from South Africa after having committed a series of violent crimes. But the authorities had neglected to alert the captain and his crew, as a result of which nothing had been done to restrict their movements on board or even to keep them under surveillance. Only now did we learn that the foursome had been pestering the girls in various ways during the first week of the voyage. In the course of this night, they had tried to force the door to the girls' cabin, but the girls had managed to barricade themselves inside. Whereupon the miscreants had got hold of a hand-axe and had begun to break a hole into the partition between their own cabin and the girls'. Just about the time the policeman, with our tour leader and myself pale and trembling in his wake arrived on the scene, the four Germans succeeded in breaking through the last obstacle and tumbled headlong into the cabin next door. In a flurry of flimsy short nightdresses and bare limbs the girls came pouring, shrieking and hysterical, from the cabin into the passage, where Christie and the other occupants of our own cabin were trying to set up an ineffectual barrier.

This lasted for about five seconds. Then the policeman went into action. At the first blows of his huge baton the Germans tried to scamper up the short flight of stairs leading to the next floor. But the policeman overtook them with two or three improbably large strides and managed to await them at the top of the stairs. There he grabbed hold of them, one by one, delivered a series of thwacking blows to each, before kicking them downstairs again, where they landed, dazed and bloodied. In a flurry of movements the policeman managed to handcuff them all together. Afterwards, the four men were taken to the ship's cells, where they were kept for the remainder of the journey. From that night there was a new camaraderie among us, and it was with real regret that upon our arrival in Southampton the two groups parted company – the girls heading towards Scotland, we to London, and the Low Countries, and then Paris.

Disappointing as the floods and storms of Paris might have been, there were enough memories to cherish, enough indelible impressions on which to base a very firm decision to return as soon as I'd finished my studies in South Africa. And arriving there again, in October 1959, was not just like returning to a place already familiar from memories and dreams, but like coming home for a second time.

*   *   *

Not that this 'home' was in every respect a happy or a reassuring place. France was in the middle of the Algerian War; every fifty metres along the Champs-Élysées soldiers were lined up with machine guns; already there were signs that even de Gaulle (who in my mind, ever since he had so majestically announced that he was ready to assume the powers of the Republic, had become a new Napoleon) might not be able to staunch the wounds. I had married my first wife, Estelle, barely a fortnight before flying off to Paris; and only a few months after our arrival, news from South Africa became so dire that it no longer seemed far-fetched to imagine our own cities, Cape Town, Pretoria, Johannesburg, Durban, transformed into military zones like this. And from that moment on Paris became for me the flipside of the South African reality: a persistent image of what the country *might* become, but for the grace of God.

The sense of living on borrowed time, of being strangers in a world that was not-quite-real, of living from day to day without seeming to be going anywhere, turned even moments of almost sublime beauty, discovery or happiness into glimpses of mortality, of absurdity. I no longer needed to *read* Camus, or Sartre for that matter, or even Marcel (I was still very religious), to understand what existentialism was all about: I was *living* it every waking and sleeping moment of my life. Everything I had discovered, in awe and wonder, in *L'étranger*, or *La peste*, in *L'homme révolté* or *Le mythe de Sisyphe* before I came to Paris, now took on the appearance of reality. I could no longer be sure of anything I had taken for granted in my life; I no longer knew who I was. At university, and in South Africa in general, I 'knew my place': even if I cautiously rebelled against the prevailing ideologies I was accepted. But here in Paris the city could not care a damn about who I was; or even whether I was there or not. It had no need of me. Inevitably, I was driven to existential questioning of *myself*.

And then Camus, who had been my Bible, my vade mecum, died in that absurd car accident, at Pont-sur-Yonne, just north of Sens, on the highway to Paris, at 13:54 on 4 January, 1960. Just when the gloom of depression which had surrounded him ever since he received the Nobel Prize, and even before, seemed to be lifting; just as he seemed to be finding his way back into writing; just as life seemed to be becoming, if not meaningful by any means, but worthwhile again – that is, an absurdity worth living for – a wholly gratuitous death had the last word. For me, in those circumstances, at that moment in my life, nothing could have confirmed the significance of Camus in a more definitive – a more final – manner as his death. It lent a solemnity, even a profundity, to every reading and rereading of Camus I made over the nearly fifty years that have passed since then. It meant that for the rest of my life I would never be without his shadow, or the shadow of his light.

Seventeen years later another man died, with much the same devastating effect on my mind and my life, even though the manner of it was totally different, and the circumstances incomparably so. This was Steve Biko. And in a curious way there was a line running from the first to the second.

Late in March 1960, while I was still stunned by the death of the man who had defined Paris and France for me, news came of the latest atrocity from South Africa. I have often told the story of how on that morning I was sitting on a green chair near the fountain in the Luxembourg Gardens with a bright yellow copy of Comte's *Philosophie Positive* on my lap. But the book was a mere pretext. My thoughts were very, very far away from that green garden. They were circling, like bees, around a reality 10,000 kilometres away to the south, a reality where, in a place I had never heard of before, Sharpeville, sixty-nine black people had been killed and many wounded when armed police opened fire on a crowd of peaceful demonstrators who had converged to protest against a new law that extended the obligation to carry a pass (previously applicable only to men) to black women.

I had grown up amid violence of all kinds; my generation were the heirs to a centuries-old history of violent encounters between individuals and peoples, specifically between black and white. But this massacre went beyond the customary and, in the context, beyond the imaginable. Compared to the bloodbaths and convulsions of history – the Holocaust, the British in India, Cortés and Pizarro in the Americas, Julius Caesar at Munda, the good King Leopold in the Heart of Darkness, Lothar von Trotha in German South-West Africa – this was a mere hiccup. But in the modern experience of South Africa, in the unfolding of apartheid, this was the most massive, the most cold-blooded, the most pernicious event we had yet had to face. There was something apocalyptic about it, and it was aggravated by occurring at a moment when the emergence of Africa from centuries of colonial bondage was in full swing and the eyes of the world were on South Africa. The West was anxious to exorcise its own lingering racial guilt feelings by projecting these on a scapegoat. And South Africa was so much more than a scapegoat: it was prepared to offer real atrocities, not just the semblance of bad faith. Its commitment to racism was total, and genuine. And nothing, until that disastrous moment, had demonstrated it with such conviction, such abandon, such staggering arrogance.

The shock of the event, for me, was aggravated by a strange sense of *recognition*, a feeling of: *Yes, this is it. Of course. This is what we have really been waiting for.* An early intimation came a month after our arrival in Paris, when for the first time we went to the reading room of the South African Embassy to catch up on the newspapers from home. It was not a matter of following events from day to day, blindly, a collage of disparate, disconnected moments. Now, all of a sudden, after a month, their randomness replaced by coherence, they fell into a pattern and a plan, revealing a discernible, predictable direction. An array of 'immorality' trials. Riots in the town of Paarl. Most obviously there was an unfolding court drama in Pretoria where a policeman, Sergeant Nic Arlow, was appearing on twenty charges of murder, after he had become something of a hero with 14,000 arrests to his credit. All his victims were black. Even more sickening than the crude facts was the way in which the huge public – white – interest in the case was reported. Subscription lists had been opened for the thousands of people who wanted to contribute to the legal expenses of the accused. Behind all of this, with unexpected clarity, lurked white South Africa's *fear* of blacks, fear that could only be expressed as hate. What became unmistakable, was a sense of panic, of which I'd been unaware before coming to Paris. Panic, terror, a spasm of death. How almost desperately I tried, in the diaries I kept through those convulsive months, to discover something heroic in the struggle of a small nation finding itself with its back to the wall, confronting the mounting rage and incomprehension, of the whole world. But Sharpeville broke through all attempts at justification. And as it happened, judgement in the Arlow trial came at almost the same time as the massacre. The heroic sergeant was found guilty, not of murder, but on thirteen counts of manslaughter. He was given a fine of £75, which was collected rapidly among the many people who regarded him as a hero. In the same newspaper reports, the possibility of a film on his life was mentioned.

All of this was milling and whirling through my head. I found it hard to concentrate on the news, on what was happening, in my country. I had the feeling that everything was in free fall, that an anchor, a hint of fixity, had given way and that, ten thousand kilometres from where I was sitting in that park, the place that had shaped me and the people I had known and trusted for so long, were sinking, sinking into the quicksand of history.

And for me, as I sat on the green chair in the Luxembourg Gardens in that early spring morning, the event was not something out there: the murderers were *my people*; the regime which had not only made this possible but had actively and enthusiastically orchestrated it, was the government to which I had, only a few months before, eagerly sworn allegiance by joining the Ruiterwag.

How strange, now, to think that one of my first thoughts that morning was: if my country is indeed destroying itself and going to hell, if that wretched, despicable, irredeemable old ship was indeed sinking, then I had to rush back and go down with it. I felt in need of an all-encompassing apocalyptic cleansing which might be achieved only by total obliteration. Of the country, the people, and myself.

Among the notes I jotted down in my diary in those dark days was this brief entry: *It is bad enough to belong to a people that is facing extinction – but it is pure hell to belong to a people which* deserves *extinction.*

On that morning in the Luxembourg Gardens I was saved from this fate by an incident both grotesque and utterly banal, when I was approached by an old crone in black who put out a gnarled hand to demand payment of thirty centimes for the use of the rickety green chair. As far as she was concerned, undoubtedly, my country could indeed be wiped out in a cataclysm, provided she got her thirty centimes. In a fury completely out of proportion to the moment, I refused to pay. In that case, she said, I had to get up and go. Promptly. *Sur le champ.*

Coming at a moment when I felt my whole life was in the balance, this intrusion was so totally absurd that I instantly lost my temper. But there was nothing I could do. In the background a policeman in a black mantle already seemed to be aiming in our direction and I knew that on the slightest provocation the old witch would summon him to support her. And that was how I left the open space surrounding the fountain and went to a sturdy brown – and free – bench among the chestnut trees, where I was reborn.

It is difficult, now, to summarise what that rebirth really involved. Undoubtedly, it included the horror of discovering what 'my people' had been doing all along, on what atrocities and perversions our proud white civilisation had constructed its edifice of Christian morality and enlighten-ment; I had to move towards an awareness that I would have to define my own position in the morass. I did not, could not, go into denial. Things had happened and were going on happening; at some stage I would *have* to decide how to shoulder the burden of my own responsibility. But for the moment, all I could do was to admit the devastation of the discovery and try to learn to live with it. At least, for the moment, there was no need to go back; I was in Paris, I could start by exploring all it had to offer – the newness of my marriage and all the discoveries that brought with it, my research at the Sorbonne, the music and art and philosophies and insights exploding all around me and inside me – and gradually try to probe the full meaning of what Sharpeville had made me see.

And all of this was exacerbated when the first letters from our families after the explosion started trickling through: *Things over here are not nearly as bad as they are made out to be. All the firearms in town are sold out, but there is no occasion for alarm: everything will soon be back to normal.*

What I knew that morning was that the point from which I looked at the world, had shifted: it was no longer *there*, in faraway South Africa, but definitely *here*, in Europe, in Paris.

Barely two years later, back in South Africa, when I first wrote about that morning of illumination, I approached it simply as an impressionistic piece about an hour in the early spring sunshine of the Luxembourg Gardens, the delicate mood disrupted by the old woman in black – with no mention at all of *what* had driven me to the Luxembourg, of the shock of discovery, of Sharpeville. Because at that stage I no longer wanted to have anything to do with South Africa. I was, simply, too ashamed to face it.

Would I have reacted differently if I had *not* gone to Paris – if I had been in South Africa when Sharpeville happened? Clearly I should hope that it would have hit me just as hard. Yet who knows how many defence mechanisms connected to being an Afrikaner in the midst of such events might have restrained, or at least delayed, a reaction? Certainly, there was one dimension of experience in France that had already begun to have a profound influence on my thinking even before Sharpeville, and had motivated a shift inside me which at the very least had *prepared* me for the event. In itself, it might have seemed very insignificant, yet its effect turned out to have been momentous. It had to do with our experience of student restaurants in the Latin Quarter.

The first month of our stay we were lodged in a big room in the PEN residence, a somewhat dilapidated old apartment with a posh address just off the Champs-Élysées, of all places. But afterwards we moved into a very small, ill-lit, over-furnished room above a noisy schoolyard on the rue d'Assas, at the southern corner of the Luxembourg Gardens. It belonged to a students' 'home' run by a diminutive old spinster – a word much frowned on nowadays, and with good reason; but Mademoiselle Domecq was everything of the archetype implied by it. She was strait-laced and severe, wholly devoid of humour or human warmth, attended by two morose *femmes de chambre* who could detect the smell of a clandestinely cooked chicken two storeys away. The old lady allowed us one carefully measured bath a week – not included in the rent – and nearly had apoplexy when for reasons both of economy and sinful delectation we insisted on sharing it.

In order to live as cheaply as possible, Estelle and I took at least one meal a day at a student restaurant, using coupons issued to me as a *boursier*, a student studying with a bursary from the French government. The food in these restaurants, especially the one in the rue de Vaugirard which we frequented most regularly, was a far cry from Gallic gastronomy, and varied between so-so and abysmal, relying – like several establishments immortalised by Zola and Balzac – largely on overcooked cabbage, greasy pork and spinach that looked and smelled like cowshit. But going there was a wonderful opportunity for meeting other students. Even for two tongue-tied strangers like us there was an undreamed-of world to be discovered at these otherwise dreary meals. There were students from Spain and England and Germany and Scandinavia, from South America. From Africa. For the first time in my life I sat down to share a meal with black people. It was a cultural shock so great that during the first evening I was barely able to eat.

But amazingly quickly it changed. Not only did the strangeness wear off within days, but there were other – delightful – shocks to get used to. I had no great illusions or pretensions about my academic standing. But after seven years at university in Potchefstroom, I had come to assume – or at least to hope – that if there was one subject I knew something about, it was literature. Now, suddenly, I found that many of my fellow students knew incomparably more. *And many of them were black*. This discovery was not only shattering but also invigorating. And the real significance of it had very little to do with academe: it lay in something extremely obvious, yet stunning in its implications. It had to do with the simple fact of our shared humanity. And even if, quite often, this was expressed in no more than complaints about the food, or the weather, as autumn slowly descended into winter, the similarity in our reactions and comments bolstered a new-found sense of camaraderie. It no longer mattered that we were black or white. We were all strangers in a strange land. We were all battling for survival. We were all struggling against *le cafard*. We were all eager to face the new challenges. When someone received bad news from home, we would all commiserate. When someone had a birthday, we would all drink to it.

As a consequence, when Sharpeville happened it was impossible to think neutrally of those sixty-nine people killed as *sixty-nine blacks* – as one would of necessity have thought back in South Africa. They were sixty-nine *people*. Skin colour had become irrelevant. They could have been sitting in that dingy, foul-smelling restaurant in the rue de Vaugirard with me, any evening.

This kind of experience was often repeated during those early months. In January 1960 there was a huge rockfall in a mine near Coalbrook in Natal, trapping 404 people almost two kilometres underground. Journalists from the major newspapers flocked to the scene to interview the four women married to the white miners killed in the disaster, publishing photos and life stories of each of them, while mentioning very briefly, in passing, that 400 black women were also mourning the loss of their husbands. The Salvation Army arranged two prayer meetings – one for the whites, a separate one for the blacks.

Black and white; black and white. How many variations of this scenario did I witness? – a scenario that had been ingrained in my life in South Africa: yet it was only now that it began to acquire a weight and a coherence, an insistence, which had previously escaped me. Perhaps nothing went as deeply, and persisted as pervasively, as our Saturday evenings with Grandpère Maurice.

At the office of the *boursiers*, there were always small notices advertising items for sale, or weekend bus excursions, or accommodation for rent, or opportunities for meeting French people in their homes. This one, written in an immaculate copperplate which immediately caught my attention, was an invitation to lonely strangers in need of a family, a home-cooked meal and friendly conversation to contact Monsieur Maurice Perceval at 93, rue Lemercier, in the seventeenth arrondissement. I discussed it with Estelle and we decided to risk it – mainly because in the wake of the Sharpeville explosion we felt miserable and in need of some homeliness. After hesitating for another few days, I telephoned in my still very broken French, and the very next Saturday evening we took the Métro to Brochant station, near the place de Clichy, not knowing what to expect. It was a turning point in our lives, and over the next two years we hardly missed a single Saturday evening meal. A grandfather, we soon discovered, was exactly what we most needed.

We were seldom the only guests, as Grandpère, as he insisted on being called, seemed to pick up young strangers much as a dog collects fleas. Some of them were *boursiers* like us, others were simply rounded up in the streets and squares of the city, in churches or churchyards, at the markets, in the Louvre or other museums, at concerts or various theatres. However haphazard his collection of guests might appear – usually four or at most six of us at a time – there was a shrewd method in the old man's madness. When Estelle and I were there, we would also find at least one black African as a fellow guest; an American would be counterbalanced with a Russian or a Korean; a Frenchman with an Algerian or a German; an Israeli with an Arab. In this way a microcosmic United Nations would be set up.

Sometimes our discussions would be relaxed and amusing, as when the sardonic René was talking about his travels in the Midi or his military service in Algeria. Sometimes, as when the musical twins from Madagascar held the floor, it would be more light-hearted. But often it would become excited and passionate, when Mario from Argentina turned on the South Africans. Otherwise Tai-Kun Lee, the thin, dark-eyed young man from Korea, might cast a satirical eye on world events, a perennial smile on his lips as if he were inwardly chuckling about jokes no one else had understood. Literally anybody might turn up, from a Japanese to a Spaniard, from an Austrian to an Australian, from a Chilean to an Icelander. And Grandpère Maurice knew enough about all our countries to contribute small but profound or humorous comments. He always wanted to find out more, encouraging us to bring along books and photographs which would add to our mutual understanding. This was his reply to the tensions and misunderstandings of the world; and bringing together young men (Estelle was, as far as I could establish, the only woman ever invited) from so many different backgrounds and races and cultures, invariably inspired us to return home, usually very late at night, with more understanding and more hope.

Each guest would be given his own large white serviette, tied up in a tidy roll at the end of the meal with his name tag on it. Whenever one returned for a visit, the tagged serviette would be taken from hundreds of others kept filed away in an enormous old armoire in the small salon, to welcome one by name. On one occasion, when I returned to Paris after an absence of several years, Grandpère Maurice immediately went to the armoire to retrieve my own serviette, which had patiently awaited my return.

His apartment was cramped, stacked to capacity with furniture and ornaments and books and pictures. In the little salon one had to follow a veritable obstacle course past chairs from the reign of the Roi Soleil to the pretentiousness of Napoleon III, small tables laden with old leather-bound books, coins, delicate laces. Beside the door to the passage stood a display cabinet with a satin dress that had once belonged to a lady-in-waiting of Marie Antoinette. Above the cabinet was a portrait of the lady: a rosy, round-faced, vaguely attractive but rather insipid face surrounded by an ostentatious coiffure. On the opposite wall was a portrait of her husband, an architect who had allegedly survived the Revolution, gazing smugly over the lacework of his collar, his wig tied with a satin bow.

'Sometimes I take my chess set from the drawer,' Grandpère Maurice told us with a wink. 'Then I set out the old ivory pieces, put off the light and go to bed. But a couple of times I had to get up unexpectedly in the night – and then I'd find the portrait frames empty, and the architect and his wife would be sitting here at the table, playing chess.'

The table itself appeared undisturbed after two centuries, the architect's instruments neatly arranged on one side, beside a massive old French grammar.

The walls were covered from floor to ceiling with paintings and plates and precious woodcuts, photographs and the 1,001 pieces of bric-a-brac sent to the old man over many years by his young friends from all over the world.

Just before eight o' clock our host used to go to the kitchen, where he had been working on our dinner since early afternoon. He never had any help, and consistently refused all our offers. About fifteen or twenty minutes later he would reappear on the threshold, delicate touches of light, like brushstrokes, in his long Father Christmas beard, and a broad white apron over the brown dressing gown he always wore.

'Dinner's ready!'

In the dining room the dark round table would be waiting, the heavy plates and cutlery and candles perfectly set out as in a top-class restaurant, everything gleaming and meticulously polished. The meal was never extravagant but always unforgettable, and it would never last for less than two hours. We approached it as a ritual, an act of contemplation and meditation. It became a unique experience simply to gaze at a serving spoon dipped in sauce and changing with every flickering of the light. Or to study each new mouthful of food, concentrating on its texture, its flavour, its taste as it became part of one's body. In the smallest movement or gesture one's entire personality was invested.

There was a good white wine with the entrée (a Pouilly-Fuissé, or a white Bordeaux), an even better red (a Brouilly, perhaps, or a Nuits-Saint-Georges) with the meat, usually a prime cut of beef or veal, prepared in its own *jus*, with a minimum of additives, more delicately savoury than anything, I can honestly say, I have ever tasted in another home. This would be followed by a vegetable, and a salad, a dessert served with a new bottle of white wine – usually a little-known label he had selected during a lifetime of dedicated tasting. The meal would be rounded off with cheese, accompanied by another glass of red, a small cup of very strong coffee, and cognac or liqueur, and fruit.

The guests were always served first, even though Grandpère Maurice was so much older than everyone else. It was useless to protest. 'I always serve myself last,' he would insist, 'even when I'm alone.'

Then came the third act of the evening. In the first, Grandpère Maurice allowed *us* to talk, and argue, and discuss. The second was devoted to the meditation of the meal. Now, in the third, it was his turn. There was never a fixed pattern. Some evenings he would fetch the small volume of poetry he had published forty years earlier, to read in his rich, sonorous voice, sometimes with trembling hands and tears in his eyes, his white beard caught in the candlelight with every movement of his head. On other evenings he might bring out a volume of Baudelaire, or Valéry, or even Ronsard, or Villon. Or he might open a fat scrapbook of letters and press cuttings from his long past: from the First World War, when he'd helped to nurse the wounded; or the many years when he'd worked as a banker; from his travels in Europe, mostly to Spain; or the many people, famous or obscure, he'd met during his life. On other occasions he would show us photographs for a guidebook he was compiling on the small church at Marly, where Louis XIV had often attended the service, or about the royal park where after years of battling with bureaucrats he had succeeded in having the old fountain restored. Or he would simply regale us with anecdotes about his interminable skirmishes with officials and authorities of all kinds. If at a given hour the Métro that was supposed to arrive at his station did not arrive, he might start a correspondence that could last for months, until he managed to get hold of the minister in charge to lodge his complaint; should an announcer on the radio get a single word wrong in a quote from the classics, a new succession of letters would be unleashed – each one of them a peerless example of French wit and sarcasm and poetic imagination.

Round about midnight we would become aware of the time. He possessed an amazing number of clocks, all over the apartment, each with its own rhythm, each set to a different time. This was done partly because Grandpère enjoyed savouring the separate voice of each, but also because it afforded him a peculiar Gallic pleasure to exercise his brain should he happen to lie awake at night, and draw his own conclusions. Suppose number one struck seven, followed by number two striking four, he could start calculating: number one was three hours and twenty minutes fast, number two x hours slow; and by the time number three struck eleven, he could wind up the sum, check it against number four, and then wait to make sure all the others were 'on time'.

When it was time to leave, each guest would be ritually kissed on both cheeks, Grandpère's white beard tickling one's neck. And then we would disperse through the dark streets, Israelis and Arabs, Irish and English, white South Africans and black Nigerians, Turks and Greeks; all of us restored to our common humanity in a broken world.

My immersion in Europe meant that I had, at least temporarily, turned my back on Africa. At that moment I did not experience it as a loss. On the contrary, it was an escape from claustrophobia. And there was a whole new world to discover, which, if I had previously known it at all, had existed only in books: a European world of painting and music and theatre, a world of life in a different key.

Painting insinuated itself into our lives within the first few weeks of our stay in Paris, when we were still living in the PEN residence. There was a portrait of a very young girl in a gallery just around the corner; and in the grey, oppressive early winter days she brought a sudden, shocking ray of light which brought both of us to a standstill the very first moment we saw her. She was naked, her face turned away to stare into a measureless distance of impressionistic blue and white, her long hair loosely tied up with a bright blue ribbon behind her head and half-covering one small breast; and she was clutching – a trifle too anxiously perhaps – a skimpy white cloth to the gentle curve of her lower belly. In retrospect I must confess that there was a hint of the chocolate box about the painting; but at the time the girl seemed like the perfection of pulchritude. I was reading *Lolita* at the time, and though Nabokov's young temptress had a streetwise, provocative hardness about her, none of the sweet aloofness of this luminous image painted by an unknown Polish artist called Talwinski, she did confirm a stereotype lurking in the deeper recesses of my mind. Innocence personified, but an innocence at its most dangerous, on the verge of the Fall. A hint, in the angle of her head, of the forever untouchable, the inviolable, the eternally just-out-of-reach. Belied, perhaps, by the anxiety with which she clutched her little towel? But in a way that only confirmed her air of self-awareness, self-assuredness. A beyondness.

She was ruinously expensive. At 120, 000 old francs, she was the equivalent of three full months' stay in Paris. Impossible even to contemplate. Yet we dared to ask the small round man who ran the gallery to reserve her for us, for a week. That, we assured each other, would be enough. She would be placed in the front window, where we could come to visit and to gaze on her. For a week she was ours. And the small white sign, *Reservé*, in the upper right-hand corner confirmed a secret only we shared.

A week of feverish discussion and calculation. We even checked the Bible for the parable of the merchant who had sold all his possessions to acquire one single pearl of great beauty, and the one about the labourer who got rid of everything he had in the world to buy a field in which he had found a treasure.

But no go. Absolutely and totally no chance in hell. Setting this Lolita against the journeys we could make to the south – to Spain, to Italy – or the concerts we could go to, or simply the food we could buy for that money, just confirmed how outrageous, how utterly disastrous, how impossible such a step would be.

And so we bought her.

*   *   *

Not all our encounters with art in Paris were so expensive. Often we would simply wander down the rue Bonaparte, or the rue de Seine, or along the small steep streets of Montmartre, and meticulously explore every little gallery along the way to find out what was happening. Much of it was depressing, repetitive, derivative. I even enrolled for life drawing at the Grande Chaumière, but when it came to the push I was just too timid to risk it. With painting, as with music years earlier, I knew when I was out of my depth.

But then there were the great museums: the Jeu de Paume, sometimes the Orangerie, quite often the Musée d'Art Moderne. And many Sundays, when entrance was free, the Louvre. Which in the course of our two years we methodically explored with total dedication, section by section, hall by hall, gallery by gallery. Sometimes we would spend the whole Sunday just absorbing two or three paintings, returning for more the following week. This was a luxury, an investment for the future, a journey of never-ending delight and discovery.

Yet the greatest single aesthetic discovery of those two years came, not in Paris, but in London, in the Tate, in August 1960. It was one of the most intense and profound emotional experiences of my life. I had seen some Picassos in Paris during the months before this, but even so I was unprepared for what I can now call a spiritual tsunami. Never before this day had I fully realised that the impact of Picasso was comparable to that of Michelangelo, or Rembrandt, or Beethoven.

Words like 'beautiful' simply do not express it any more. What I felt was awe. And if this was beauty, then beauty terrifying in its magnificence. The gradual deepening and widening during his early years: nothing tentative about it – even in the work from his teens there is a sureness, a self-assurance, a conviction in his exuberant but at the same time dedicated exploration of styles and influences. Then the blue works, the intimations of a world of grief and melancholy washing like rain across the canvases – but already bearing a premonition of the power looming ahead. The gradual assertion of the forces of life in the deceptive ease of *la vie en rose*, the powerful undulating yellows and browns, the awareness of the plastic possibilities of the nude. This is where it really takes hold of him: he's got to remodel the body, feel it from

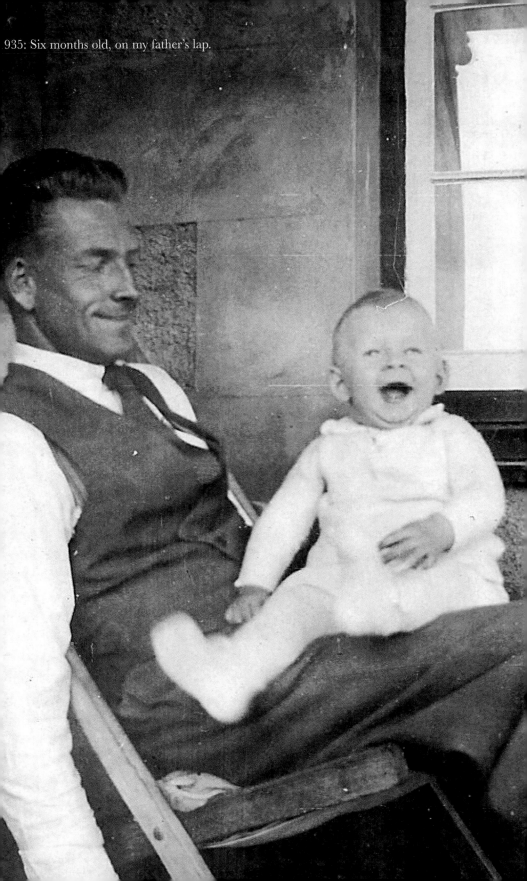

935: Six months old, on my father's lap.

1936: Some habits start early.

1938: With the Sotho nanny Aia who first made me conscious of the rhythms of language.

1938: With my sister Elbie on her first birthday.

1945: With my sisters Elbie and Marita.

1950: My father's side of the family. My grandparents and Ouma's sister, Aunt Anna, in the back row from middle to right, I am in the same row second from left, my father front row left, and my sister next to him and Johan on her left.

1950: A homemade boat on the farm dam of Oom Jannie and Auntie Dolly. My parents are far left, I am rowing.

1949:
Preparing for
a tennis match.

1953: The
pianist, before
I learned to
accept my
limitations.

1959: At the Place de la Concorde, Paris.

1963: With Etienne Leroux, Ingrid, Jan Rabie and Marjorie Wallace
in Somerset West, near Cape Town.

1963:
Ingrid on a
holiday farm in
Franschhoek.

1963:
The same
occasion.

1965: Ingrid's funeral, with her family on the left. A few friends are restraining Jack Cope from jumping into the grave. (Copyright: Cloete Breytenbach)

1966: With Etienne Leroux and Breyten in the Rue Soufflot, Paris.

the inside, get to *know* it, probe it, break it open in order to explore every possibility of scale and volume.

Cubism, burgeoning until the passionate engagement with the figure begins to spill over into the background.

Followed by one of the most moving periods: the return, the violent replunging into a redefined sense of the real: the newspaper fragments, the hallucinatory words flung at the spectator – the name of a lover, a playful song, a village. In such a way that within the construction of the whole those single, concrete moments hit you like a scream in the ears. All of this as part of the whirling, spiralling search for *essences*, in the all-encompassing creation of his own, new reality.

And then the reconstruction, the interrogation of what lies beyond facades and immediacies, in the slow movement towards the terror and the infernal nightmares and exultations of Africa, and of the Spanish Civil War. The omnipresence of the shout, the scream in colour, and *beyond* colour.

Finally, if anything in Picasso can ever be final, the latest series, the child-like rediscovery of munificent life: white pigeons, blue skies.

It is a descent into hell, an ascent into heaven – not as an inevitable progression, as in Dante, but with a shattering simultaneity.

A small moment during the hours of confrontation with this force of nature: dazed from the bombardment of the senses, exhausted, overwhelmed, I slump down on a bench in the middle of a long gallery, in need of rest, of physical and mental equilibrium. But the hard bench has no back. It is impossible to relax. Suddenly there is a back reclining against mine. All I can make out is that it is a young woman. I have no idea of what she looks like, and will never know. But for a few minutes, in the whole chaotic, tumbling world, flooded with weariness and emotion: this fleeting human touch. Leaning back, shoulders against shoulders, a brief moment of sharing. And then I can return to the crowd.

In a brilliant, light-hearted session of questions and answers after a lecture, Doris Lessing once spoke about the kind of book that leaves an indelible impression on the mind, changing utterly and irrevocably the course of one's life – for at least two weeks. But that day in the Tate did not fade away with time. It remains, along with only a very small handful of memories, a moment of radical change.

I could never write again in the way I'd done before. I could never *be* again as I'd been before.

Since the first day in Paris, I had known that this period in my life would mark my writing. More than 'mark': it would definitively decide whether I was really going to be a writer as I'd so foolhardily resolved when I was nine, or not at all. And within two months I'd started writing in a different key altogether. It turned out to be a play, based on Julius Caesar, with whom I had been preoccupied for months. A verse play, no less. It took me a week, writing day and night. And I was convinced that, if not the world, then at least Afrikaans literature, would never be the same again. Today I cannot help but cringe. It really was bad. Pretentious, derivative, strained. But it was, for me, a new beginning. Still, verse has never been my medium. The problem was that I had really no idea of what to do with prose. Until that day in the Tate.

When I returned to Paris I had no clearly formulated aim as yet, but I was conscious of a welter of possibilities in my mind unleashed by Picasso. Suppose, like him, I could try to break language open, to see what makes it tick. To put it together in new and unexpected ways. To say new and unexpected things. The revelation came at a very specific phase of my experience in Paris: I found myself in a slough of despond with no horizon visible. I was going through a period of misery about my studies: I went through the motions, but without really believing in the enterprise or being able to work up any enthusiasm about it. Attempts to change direction – originally in Netherlandic studies, later in English, focusing on George Eliot and her 'literary fortune' in France – made no real difference to the utter lack of interest in what I was doing. Estelle, who had taken a secretarial job at our embassy in the avenue Hoche to keep us going financially, had landed in her own slough. And it was spilling over into my writing. I was beginning to have serious doubts about the experiment with *Caesar*. All I knew was that I wanted to do something new. But I could think of nothing at all to say that had not already been said, and incomparably better, by others, in many languages. Yet how could I give up writing? No matter how futile it might be, it was all I had. *But it was pointless!* Even in despair there was nothing new. Language itself appeared to be a useless, second-hand garment already worn by too many others. The mere possibility of originality seemed a dead end.

Then came Picasso and shocked me out of the torpor. And I plunged in. The book was originally called *Naakfiguur, kers en ruit* (*Nude, candle, window-pane*). Not a good title. And when I turned it into a radio play, it was changed to *Lobola vir die Lewe* (*Lobola for Life*: *lobola* meaning the bride-price paid, in some black societies, by a young man for his bride-to-be). My publisher, wisely, insisted on retaining it for the novel it eventually turned into. I felt like a man possessed. It took a fortnight to write, and then I was exhausted. Afterwards it went through several more drafts, and getting it published became a story in its own right. But at that moment I didn't even care whether it was good or bad: all I knew was that I *had* to write it. Whether it would ever find a publisher was a different matter: for the time being I simply knew that I owed Picasso a kind of dowry for my own life, and this was it.

Of course I knew that I would return to 'normal' prose after that, although I was to find out the hard way that 'normal' language can be incomparably more difficult to write than experimental prose. Back then, all that mattered was that for the first time I really knew that writers are not made by the stories they carry within them, their themes or ideas or beliefs or whatever, but by their intimate relationship with language. And this was *my* exuberant and defiant and adventurous and terribly intimate engagement with the angel of language. Since then, even in the most restrained and 'ordinary' piece of writing, this sense of adventure has always remained part of me. If ever it were to become dissipated, if the adventure were to go flat, then very quietly and very resolutely, like the lover in the wonderful cummings poem, petal by petal my life will shut very beautifully, suddenly, and I will cease to be.

Art in Paris, during those two years, did not consist only of paintings and sculptures and exhibitions and museums. There was a whole world *surrounding* the discoveries that enthralled us. A world of artists, of people.

A close friend at the time was an English painter from Wolverhampton, Frank Ward, whom I met over lunch in a student restaurant one day, when we both left the place in disgust about the bad food, and caught each other's eye, and burst out laughing. He invited me for coffee in his tiny sixth-floor apartment in the rue de Condé.

From the first day I loved his work: most of it based on street scenes in Paris – market stalls, town squares on festive days, or disconcertingly voided of people, the outlines of *bouquinistes* on the Seine, the flea markets at Clignancourt or Kremlin-Bicêtre – but all of it highly stylised, stripped of redundancy and coincidence, to the verge of abstraction, with clear architectural symmetries and planes of clean, uncluttered colour: blues, dark greens, browns, an occasional shock of vermilion. A sense of space. A few portrait studies, the occasional stylised nude. I soon came to recognise in several of these studies his girlfriend, the dark-haired Margith with a shocking white face and stark red mouth and large black eyes, who unceremoniously entered his life when in the small hours of the night he was awakened by a knock on his door and found her standing on his doorstep, dishevelled and shivering with cold, having been quite literally thrown out by her boyfriend, divested of most of her clothes. Frank invited her in for a drink, and she didn't leave before noon the next day, with borrowed clothes.

Once, while we were sharing a frugal meal from a stall on the *trottoir* below, there was a hint of movement in a window opposite, diagonally down from Frank's little loft. 'Ah,' he said. 'I've *wanted* to introduce her to you. Now watch.' A girl appeared from the dark interior of the room behind her. She was wearing only a misty white petticoat and a black bra. We looked at her. She looked back. Then moved her hands up behind her back and calmly undid the straps of her bra. Flung it back into the room, and leaned forward, her elbows resting on the balustrade in front of the window. For a long time she was motionless, except for an occasional toss of her head to fling back the dark hair from her face. Then, almost gravely, with a sense of ceremony, she moved her hands down, with almost unbearable grace, and removed the petticoat. She wasn't wearing anything underneath. From across the street the small black triangle of her crotch was visible. She resumed her pose, leaning on her elbows. I had no idea how long she stood there, facing us.

Then, with the merest hint of a gesture, like waving goodbye, she turned round and disappeared.

'That's all for today, ladies and gentlemen,' said Frank with a straight face.

I did not realise it that afternoon. But from the combination of Frank's apartment in the rue de Condé, and the girl opposite, the central character in *The Ambassador*, Nicolette, and something of her life, was conceived.

It was only about a week before Frank's bursary ran out and he had to return to Britain. He was in a rage: 'If I look at some of the people who get bursaries, and have them renewed, and who fuck around doing absolutely sweet blow-all, this is bloody outrageous. Look at what I've done these last few months' – a sweeping gesture through the dirty little room with the unmade bed, the floor covered with stacks of paperbacks, and every square centimetre of space crammed with paintings and sketches – 'Think of what I could still have done! And now I must go back to that bleak, godforsaken place and try to paint without any spark of inspiration . . . !'

On the appointed day he left. At the harbour in Calais he bought three or four bottles of whisky for friends back home, but in his rage he started drinking and didn't stop before there was nothing left. Then he fell into a stupor, and by the time he arrived in Dover everything he'd brought with him – his clothes, his wretched kitchen utensils, his books, every single sketch and painting – was gone. He arrived in London with nothing.

But Frank had the invincible spirit of a young revolutionary – *L'audace, de l'audace, toujours de l'audace!* – and within a few months he'd set up a new studio in Wolverhampton with a group of energetic young painters, sculptors, actors and musicians, and started working furiously to bring art to the working classes. When I saw him again, in London, some months later, he was all fired up. Not just by the work, but by a wild affair he had going with one of the top writers in England. However, I'm sorry to say that not long afterwards he stopped painting. And when I met him again, years later, in Stockholm, he was in the wine trade, and married, and with a family.

Whatever Frank's peregrinations after the few months we shared in Paris, what he left behind has become part of my life through *The Ambassador*

– perhaps the closest to a *roman-à-clef* I have ever written. I remember how nervous I was when my friend Broder came to visit me and Estelle in Grahamstown soon after the book was first published, because the parallel between him and the character of the third secretary Stephen Keyter in the book was difficult to deny. And within minutes of his arrival at the airport in Port Elizabeth, he started talking about the book and what a frenetic process of mixing and matching it has caused in our embassy in Paris as every staff member tried to identify themselves in the story. Some of the attempts at identification were rather unpleasant, as happened when one female secretary insisted on recognising herself in all the most negative and grotesque characteristics of Anna Smit in the novel. What was more uncomfortable, was when Stephanus du Toit, the ambassador at the time of my stay in Paris, confided to close acquaintances that I must have used him as a model for my Paul van Heerden. To my mind, van Heerden was a much more sympathetic character than the real ambassador, an uncouth rhinoceros who had left some rather muddy tracks through his career in the diplomatic service.

What initially surprised and secretly pleased me was that Broder, who hugely enjoyed the consternation of some of his colleagues upon 'discovering' themselves in the book, assured me, perhaps too emphatically, of his own relief about what he saw as a conscious decision on my part not to implicate *him* in any way – while my own main concern had been that Stephen Keyter in the story might have resembled him too closely for comfort. But not long afterwards the whole thing took a dark and unexpected turn when Broder appeared to have taken his cue from Keyter, who commits suicide in the book – by shooting himself in the presence of his own family. Life can sometimes imitate art in the most unsettling ways.

In a somewhat lighter vein, although it brought some chilling moments of its own, was the reaction of South Africa's then minister of foreign affairs, the redoubtable Eric Louw, in instituting an official inquiry into alleged 'leaks' of classified information in the novel. Much of my knowledge about the workings of our foreign service, and particularly about our embassy in Paris, obviously came from close observation of the members of its staff from 1959 to 1961, particularly those individuals with whom I had regular contact, either personally or through Estelle while she worked in the embassy. But one thing I really had to invent for myself was the kind of top secret official business with which my ambassador could have occupied himself during the crisis of Sharpeville and its aftermath. What I devised, was negotiations with the French about clandestine arms deals – not knowing for one moment that this was exactly what South Africa and France were indeed involved in at the time. Eric Louw must have had good reason for his worst suspicions. But fiction can be truer than fact.

The key character in *The Ambassador* is, of course, the somewhat disreputable, defiant, free spirit Nicolette, and in its early drafts the book was named for her. (In German it was later published as *Nicolette und der Botschafter*.) And there was indeed a real Nicolette in Paris at the time, who worked as a model with Dior before she faded into more shadowy, and no doubt more interesting, recesses of the city. I first learned of her through what Broder told me about the tempestuous on-off affair he'd had with her. Born into a very rich family, she'd drifted to Paris at an early age after a childhood about which she chose never to speak, and merged into an intriguing world of bright lights and dark shadows. Broder first met her when she came to the embassy to discuss some minor consular business. At the time, the embassy was still situated on the avenue Hoche, before moving, some years later, to the Quai d'Orsay. And thereby hangs another tale. It happened in the darkest and direst days of apartheid; and on the appointed day an armed truck arrived to transport, in the greatest secrecy and under armed escort, all the classified documents of the embassy to the new address. But instead of arriving at the Quai d'Orsay, a mere few hundred metres away, the truck got lost. Disappeared. Like a needle in a haystack. And only arrived at its destination the next day. Where was James Bond when one needed him?

Broder dealt with Nicolette's negligible little enquiry in a few minutes. But the next day she was back with another trivial query. Although she was not beautiful in any conventional sense, he found her striking, and provocative; and he invited her to dinner. There seemed to be something in the air, but she was often accompanied by a fiancé, about six different ones over a period of two years, and so matters did not seem to lead anywhere. But one day, in a frisky mood most unbecoming to a budding young diplomat, Broder thrust his hands rather too deeply into the large pockets of her overcoat, and she gave him a resounding slap. He lost his temper, sat back on his desk, drew her down on his lap – all of this in the presence of the current fiancé – and proceeded to give her a brisk spanking. The fiancé was wickedly amused, but Nicolette stormed out in a rage. Outside in the courtyard she looked up at Broder's window, blew him a kiss, and called out, 'See you at the Christmas tree!'

Only a few weeks later, Broder went to London for a weekend, to find upon his return at midnight on the Sunday the front door to his apartment completely blocked by a mountain of suitcases and bags and boxes of every description. While he was still standing there surveying the scene in a mounting rage, the door to the apartment opposite opened and Nicolette appeared.

'Oh you're back at last,' she said blithely.

'What the hell is going on?' he asked.

'I'm moving in with you,' she said – the neighbours listening wide-eyed – as if that was the most normal announcement in the world.

Within two weeks his apartment was in total chaos, the floor strewn with half-opened baggage, littered with stockings, skirts and dresses, flimsy underwear, lipstick, nail polish, tampons, shoes and sandals, handbags, scissors, ribbons, crumpled paper, and torn glossy magazines. She had taken over, without any thought of his needs or comfort. She could loll in the bath for hours, then wander over to a mirror to study her reflection, naked, half-clothed or clothed, experimenting with drapes and scarves and feather boas and whatever garments she could lay her hands on. There were days when she never left the bed, and others when she put on whatever was within reach, and went out, staying away for hours, sometimes for days, driving him crazy with uncertainty and jealousy and worry, and without a word of explanation when she returned, sometimes at noon, sometimes in the late afternoon, or at three or seven in the morning.

From time to time she would get an urge to read – magazines, popular novels, manuals for make-up or carpentry or welding, once, unlikely as it may sound, a massive encyclopaedia on the great philosophers from Plato to Nietzsche, which she read from cover to cover. When he dared to ask her about it afterwards, she shrugged and said, 'Oh they all thought they knew all the answers, but they didn't, did they?'

Sex? She would turn her head sideways, or suck a strand of her long dark hair, and say nonchalantly, 'Oh I rather like a good fuck. Sometimes I even like a bad fuck. But you know, I'd take a game of tennis any day.' Eventually, when Broder actually invited her for tennis, it turned out that she didn't even have a racket, and had never had one. She could devise, and perform, the most outrageous things in bed. But she also had unnerving spells of chastity, when she refused even to be kissed. Which did not prevent her from teasing and provoking him precisely when she had no intention of satisfying his rampant lust in any way. And often, when she did consent to intercourse, she would bring an apple to bed with her and lie back munching it while he was bucking and thrashing above her, and insist that he stop the moment she'd finished the apple.

No wonder that after a few weeks he couldn't take any more and threw her out. She demurely packed all her possessions, and he helped her to load everything into the taxi he had ordered; she left, again chewing an apple. And was back within a few days. He exuberantly welcomed her and they had their best sex ever.

Once, during her second or third stay, Broder arranged for them to see a film with two other couples. Nicolette arrived with another man in tow, whom nobody else in the group had ever met. Broder refused to let the stranger go with them. Nicolette merely shrugged and went off with the man on her own. A week later she returned with the news that she'd married him. When he lost his job, she moved in with him, his mother and his grand-mother. In due course a little girl was born. Soon afterwards Nicolette left the baby in the care of her mother-in-law and returned to South Africa to live with her parents, who had previously cut off her ample allowance.

It was at this stage that Estelle and I arrived in Paris and met Broder. He was still emotionally off balance as a result of the affair. It was clear that he remained totally infatuated with the woman and that he would not recover easily. Perhaps his vulnerability was the main reason why I could not help feeling sympathetic to him; we even became friends. Estelle and I may well have been the only friends he had in Paris. In so many respects he was a very, very difficult person to get along with. His hang-ups and fixations about religion and sex, his obsessive nature: talking non-stop for hours, or retreating into a sulk for days; his habit of seeing some films – like *Cat on a Hot Tin Roof* – twenty or thirty times, and then discussing them compulsively, quoting long passages of dialogue from memory, with every syllable and inflection fixed forever; above all, his habit of locking himself into his apartment for whole weekends, listening to all of Hitler's recorded speeches day and night and at full blast . . . All of this wore down one's defences and one's patience. And yet he was such a lost soul, and when he was on a high he could be so generous and humorous and eager to share, that one couldn't help wanting to reach out to him and help assuage his terrible loneliness.

At some stage, while we were in Paris, Nicolette came back. No one knew what had happened to her husband, or ex-husband, or her child. Broder became more and more of a recluse, and more and more offensive and preposterous in his outbursts. And once he even arranged for us to meet Nicolette. That was a mistake. I had formed such a clear idea of her dangerous allure, her tantalising moods, her teasing and her provocations, her intriguing nature, that meeting the real person behind the image inevitably turned out an anticlimax. Her conversation was uninteresting, even boring, she gave the impression of deliberately trying to offend with her loudness, her chain-smoking, her drinking, the plastic-and-neon quality of her clothes and her make-up. *This* could not possibly be the person who had so completely turned Broder's whole life upside down and paved the way for his shocking death. And perhaps, inspired by Simenon's Yvette in *En Cas de Malheur*, by Simone de Beauvoir's brilliant philosophical evocation of Brigitte Bardot, by the effusions of Henry Miller, and by some of the lyrical inventions in Lawrence Durrell's Alexandria Quartet, in writing *The Ambassador* I was going in search of an image that had got lost along the way: an image not only of a woman, but of a city; of a woman-as-city, of a city-as-woman, situated in the dark heart of Dante's Sacred Wood, somewhere between heaven and hell.

In Paris, most of our monthly budget went into concerts. Like theatre, music provided a refuge and escape from the world, but just as importantly an enhancement of the world. In many ways music became even more indispensable than drama. Already at university Christie was the one who acted as my guide and interpreter, and after I'd taken over from him as chairperson of the Music Society the passion both widened and deepened. The variety was stupendous, ranging from singers like Seefried or Schwarzkopf to pianists like Kempf or Brailowsky or Rubinstein or Arrau, from ensembles like the Pasquier Trio or Karl Münchinger and the Stuttgart Chamber Orchestra to conductors like Markevitch or Cluytens or Furtwängler or Kubelik or Karajan. At that stage of my life, my belated period of *Sturm und Drang*, it was probably inevitable that the man who marked me most deeply was Herbert von Karajan. Flamboyant, yes; a showman, yes; an egomaniac, yes. But from the moment he appeared on the podium, without a score, and dramatically closed his eyes to the outside world in order to gaze, as he must have calculated very deliberately, upon an inner landscape without boundaries, he held me, and it seemed most of the audience, in thrall. I had the impression that he was not so much conducting an orchestra as incarnating the music, from the delicate, serene, ineffable quality of the Andante in Beethoven's Sixth, to the passionate, incomparable, sustained glory of the Ninth. He came to Paris twice while we were there: once, with the Berlin Philharmonic, working through the entire cycle of Beethoven symphonies; and once, in the heart of winter, with the Vienna Philharmonic, in a programme of Dvorak, Richard Strauss, Beethoven, Mozart and Schumann. This, I believed then, was the ultimate in music. I could not wish for anything more, I could not *think* of anything closer to the sublime.

Sublime, Edith Piaf was not. But unforgettable in her own way, extending the range of music in a completely different direction. We saw her in one of her last concerts at the Olympia. Barely able to walk, a hobbly stick insect who appeared at the back of the huge stage, caught in the spotlight like a dying moth, standing there on wobbly legs, her face a stark white, her mouth a red bleeding gash, the waves upon waves of applause breaking over her. From behind the back curtain one could make out the outline of hands almost frantically clutching her, steadying her, trying to hold her upright, and then pushing her forward and letting her go. For the eternity of several seconds it seemed inevitable that she would fall, crumble into a wretched little heap of bones. But then she reached the microphone at the front of the stage, and caught hold of it. The too-loud music began. The insane thunder of applause began to die away. And Piaf began to sing. The old favourites. 'Milord'. 'La vie en rose'. In a voice like a shout from a tomb, a triumphant bellowing of sound, unbelievable, impossible, coming from such a frail and rickety body, the voice of life itself, refusing to die, refusing to be silenced, the voice of humanity itself, ineradicable, inextinguishable. *Non, je ne regrette rien.*

In the moveable feast of Paris the sublime was often hidden away in unexpected corners and recesses. Going down the rue Lepic from the place du Tertre on the *butte* of Montmartre we were attracted to a display window filled with a colourful collection of ceramics: plates and bowls and mugs and ashtrays splashed with nostalgic or bawdy French songs, ambiguous rhymes and delightfully reckless illustrations. Inside it was dusky, with an inner door leading to a studio flickering with bright orange flames in the fireplace, the walls covered with antique bric-a-brac – wooden crucifixes, a death mask of Beethoven, glassware, dilapidated woodcuts, religious paintings with iconic images almost disappearing behind the patina. And in the middle of it all, hunched up in a large ornate chair like a throne, the lord and master, the artist, with a weather-beaten face like a decayed masterpiece, old Platon Argyriades.

He was a great talker and raconteur, and it didn't take much prompting to get him going. When he heard that we were from South Africa, his surprisingly bright blue eyes lit up with memories from a distant past: he could remember the World Fair of 1900, when as a child he'd joined the crowds in the streets to cheer the old president of the Transvaal Republic, Paul Kruger, venerable with his white beard and his tall top hat and a golden ring in his ear.

He'd always lived in close contact with all the successive movements washing like tides through the sea of the arts: Fauves and cubists, expressionists and Nabis and abstractionists, he'd visited the young Picasso when the painter was working in his studio in the Bateau-Lavoir here in

Montmartre; he'd been a close friend of Modigliani, with whom he'd spent many nights in conversation when the young man had fled the wrath of his stepmother and found refuge in the Argyriades household; he'd known Gide and the young Malraux, and later the flamboyant Saint-Exupéry and the taciturn Céline; before the Second World War he'd even briefly met the expatriate American Fitzgerald. Talking to old Platon was like opening the whole of the twentieth century as if it were a great illustrated book. Art and literature and history were no longer subjects to be studied, but a real and deeply lived world, a train that had set off on its journey long before either of us had stepped on to it at some forgotten station and would continue long after we had left it again.

During our many visits following that first encounter, he often took a book of poetry from one of the dark shelves in that inner sanctum to read us some random stanzas from Ronsard or Verlaine or Valéry; then his mouth would start trembling, and his blue eyes would become misty with tears like Grandpère Maurice's. He was a true Romantic, in his own way the last of a generation, a way of life. He introduced us to his wife, a small bird of a woman, with a black bonnet drawn tightly over her grey hair – but she was an unsympathetic little creature, and I think an unworthy companion: brazen and impatient and businesslike. More than once, when Estelle or I picked up one of the old man's ceramic plates or boxes to study an inscription, she would rudely snatch it away, snarling, 'Don't bother, you're a foreigner, you won't understand.' And after she'd gone out to attend to other customers or feed the fire, he would pick up the object again to explain, unhurried and smiling, a pun we'd missed or a phrase we hadn't properly grasped. The irony was that *she* was the one, I often suspected, who was out of place there and hadn't understood what her old husband was really about: his love of shaping things with his hands, taking his time, moulding them not just from clay but from love and understanding and patience and a wisdom accrued through generations and centuries. A world which Proust understood, and which exists beyond sentimentality or nostalgia.

They had no children. '*Après moi*,' he often sighed, '*c'est fini*.' He was referring, I think, not only to his family, but to an old Montmartre, an old Paris, an old world, slowly ebbing away, leaving only progress and industry and

163

technology in its wake. We, Estelle and I, had missed the last heyday of the bohemian age ranging from Picasso to Hemingway and Gertrude Stein, but how lucky we were still to live in the twilight of that world, pick up some of its lingering scents, catch in our ears the last echoes of its fading melodies.

Our time in Paris was running out. Early in January 1961 there was a curt note from the university to say that my bursary, now already in its second year, would not be renewed at the end of the academic year. Estelle had resigned from her temporary job at the embassy. Suddenly the sense of an ending pervaded everything we did, everything we could contemplate. We were back to the existential angst of the early months – even though this time, at least, we had the relative space and comfort of our spare flat under the slanting rooftop of the old building on the rue Vieille du Temple. We did what we could to fight *cafard*, but our efforts were not always successful. There was less and less money for theatre and music, which meant that in the most literal sense we had to take to the streets for entertainment. Lolita was still there on the wall, of course, to provide some flimsy reassurance – but in weak moments, when it was not so easy to fend off the truth, she already seemed to be more of a chocolate box than an immortal work of art.

There were Sundays, especially in spring and summer, when we did not go to the Louvre but chose to stroll from one open space to another – squares and concourses, even street corners, where amateur performers appeared from their secret chrysalises like strange moths to spread their wet wings. The swallowers of swords or flames, the breakers of chains, the escapists, the jugglers and conjurers and magicians, the tightrope walkers, the trainers of dogs or monkeys or rabbits or parrots or fleas.

I remember an early spring afternoon on the carrefour de l'Odéon when a burly, red-faced, middle-aged man performed in the centre of a large, ragged circle. Beside an unsteady green table on which a small glass aquarium had been placed, stood a weary young woman anxiously avoiding all eye contact with the crowd, as if she found the scene just too humiliating to face. When enough spectators had gathered the man announced that he required fifteen fifty-franc pieces to commence his next act. The woman did the rounds with a floppy hat in her outstretched hands. It took quite a while, the spectators were not particularly forthcoming with their contributions. Some simply tossed the coins in her direction, forcing her to stoop to pick them up. I could not bear to look at her haggard face, which must have been beautiful once.

At last the man took a full bottle of water from the table, and turned to his small aquarium. The crowd pressed inwards, craning their necks. In a deft movement the man retrieved a green frog from the bowl and plunged it into his mouth. Doing the round inside the circle he briefly half-opened his mouth a few times to allow us glimpses of the frog kicking out its long hind legs. Once everybody was convinced that the little amphibian was indeed inside, the man took a few large swigs of water from a bottle, and opened his mouth wide to demonstrate that the frog had disappeared.

The process was repeated twice more, with two new frogs, after longish intervals during which his sad companion went round with her floppy hat for more contributions. By this time the response from the audience was slightly more encouraging. To round off the first act of the show the ceremony was repeated with three small fishes. Once again a collection was taken by the pale, expressionless woman with the crumpled hat. Quite an enthusiastic response, this time round.

Then followed the climax: returning the inhabitants of the glass bowl to their habitat. There was only one, obvious, method: they had to be regurgitated back to life. This was done rather boisterously, with such motions and sound effects that several members of the crowd could not help gagging and retching too. And it didn't go very smoothly either, so that the man was forced – now quite breathless and his face a deep purple, with a network of throbbing veins on his temples – to imbibe another large bottle of water. But in the end the last of the little creatures, wriggling much less energetically than before, was restored to the bowl. One little fish hadn't made it. But the others seemed more or less alive.

A final round of collection, but by now most of the crowd had dispersed. The day was turning cool. The exhausted woman poured all her coins into a small trunk under the table. All around them the ground was drenched with water. In the little aquarium the fishes and frogs were swimming about with surprising vitality; only the one unfortunate fish was floating belly up on the surface.

On another occasion a large gorilla of a man, stripped to the waist to expose his once impressive pectorals and bloated stomach, was ordering a tiny wisp of a boy dressed like a clown through his paces: riding a bicycle seated backwards on the saddle, standing on his head in the man's hand, doing a handstand on his flabby biceps. After each act the boy stood to attention, mechanically – like a ventriloquist's dummy – saluted the spectators, his face drawn into a tight grimace of concentration under the huge red clown's lips painted on his thin trembling mouth, the ludicrous red blob of a nose skewed and smudged, his eyes staring fixedly at the big man. At a nod of the trainer's head, the little one grabbed an old top hat to collect the alms, then stowed it in a box and returned for the next round. Everything performed without the hint of a smile. One almost expected his batteries to run out at any moment.

Dusk was closing in by the time we left. In silence we walked down to the Seine, watching the first lights appear through the messy pencil lines of trees against the dull flatness of the water. Notre-Dame was a black blotch against the pale orange glow of the sky where it lay smudged across the rooftops, fading gradually into a dirty lilac higher up. The tall arches of a bridge were reflected in the dark green water, the red reflection of distant traffic lights stretching and shrinking on the surface.

It was the time of day when all the old and deformed or decrepit people of the city seemed to emerge on the streets like sad, angular insects drawn by the evening light. An old man bent almost double, carrying a small pail of milk; a shuffling old woman with tousled hair, brandishing a broken umbrella; a cripple hobbling along like a crushed cricket.

And at last we were home again in our small, overheated, over-furnished room with Lolita's straight young back defiant and vulnerable in her ornate frame on the wall, the bright blue ribbon in her hair. Hot chocolate steaming from two big bowls. The delicate spattering of raindrops against the window. And then the welcoming billows of our big bed.

*   *   *

There was one enterprise in which we were prepared to invest whatever little money we still had to spare, and that was travelling. We had no idea of how many years might go by before we could afford another visit to Europe, so whatever could be packed into this stay in Paris simply had to be done. When Estelle's mother came on a visit with a touring group, we swallowed whatever reservations we had about organised tours and joined her on a bus trip to Spain. Not a very wise decision, but there were good moments too, especially after we'd left the group to spend some time on the Costa del Sol with good friends from South Africa. Another trip took us to Germany, but this ended after a most unfortunate incident in the cathedral of Cologne where Estelle and I were walking along a dark aisle hand in hand, in a mood of fervent religiosity, when a fat priest with flapping black surplice descended on us like an avenging devil from hell, grabbed us by the arms and violently jerked us apart. He hissed so furiously that we were showered in spittle, '*Das ist keine Promenade!*' Which for many years effectively kept me out of Germany, and also became a turning point in my already tenuous relationship with the Church.

Altogether more memorable was our long journey through Italy in the spring of 1961 on a train ticket that allowed us to get on and off as we wished. Much of the love affair I've had with Italy over the next forty years was inspired by that first visit.

We were also able to fit into our travel programme two visits to Provence, one along the Route Napoléon, past Serres and Sisteron and Grenoble and Castellane to the Mardi Gras festival in Nice, the other to Avignon, Nîmes, Arles, and Saint-Rémy de Provence, which over the years came to represent for me the France I loved above all other regions.

We often crossed the Channel too, once on an extended drive through the Scottish highlands, but mostly to visit the man who was then my best friend, Naas, and his wife Sarie, in London. We'd first met at university, after which he'd joined the diplomatic corps and was appointed private secretary to our high commissioner in London. This not only gave us a foothold in England but opened up a new dimension of theatre, ranging from Chekhov to *West Side Story*, and from Shakespeare to Pinter. Especially after *Godot* in Paris, *The Caretaker* made something click in my mind to steer my own interest in drama in a more clearly defined direction. It also helped to shape the novel I wrote after the Picasso exhibition, as the title role enabled me to visualise more clearly the sordid, down-and-out old man who became a catalyst in the main storyline of *Lobola for a Life*.

Naas was one of the first people I approached to read *Lobola for a Life* when it was still at a very vulnerable stage. Later, when I started putting together all my notes and memories of Paris, he was the one who helped me to make sense of it all. When he noticed that I was intrigued by the diplomatic world, he made sure that I would meet as many diplomats as possible – some brilliant, some dumb, some consumed by ambition, some by women, some by dedication (misplaced or not), some by frustration, bureaucrats and technocrats and hawks and doves, chancers and careerists and schemers, plodders and inventors, men of action and men of dreams: in those days there were no women in the corps yet. I owe to him the dubious pleasure of meeting a sweet and stupid woman married to a sweet and stupid third secretary in Berne, who once plunged into a very intense discussion about the resurgence of anti-Semitism by offering her own considered view: 'You know, I have given this a lot of thought, and I believe that anti-Semitism has a lot to do with the feeling against the Jews.' I also owe to Naas an introduction to the South African high commissioner in London at the time of Sharpeville: a portly old Boer who at the height of the anti-apartheid protests, with Trafalgar Square a seething mass of screaming demonstrators, would come to Naas's office of a morning to ask him, 'Ag man, can you please get me another bag of those oranges you got me last time? They were *so* sweet.' Or who would leave the dining table during a reception at Buckingham Palace and go to the kitchen to admonish the staff who were keeping him waiting with the next course. Inevitably, Naas was a key informant and consultant in the writing of *The Ambassador*, as he later was for some of my other books. I could count on him for wit and wisdom, for spotting the smallest mistake of spelling or style or information; and for applying to it the salt of his wry understanding. 'The price of intelligence,' says Carlos Fuentes, 'is disenchantment.' And yet perhaps Naas's most striking quality is his ability to be disenchanted without ever denying the romantic in himself.

Not long after our return to South Africa, during my involvement with

Ingrid, Naas's only comment was, 'I can understand why any person might decide at a given moment to get divorced. But for the life of me I'll never understand why anyone would want to *remarry*.' And when Karina and I announced our wedding, Naas sent an e-mail entitled *The Triumph of Hope Over Experience.* In the text he commented that our enterprise was like Mandela swimming back to Robben Island.

Still, however strong his own opinions were on any given person, any given subject, he would allow me to draw my own conclusions. And that whole sojourn in Paris – including our many visits to London, and his and Sarie's to us in Paris – was coloured to a very large extent by this defining friendship.

It brought its own mysteries with it too: after one visit to London I came across a small piece of paper on which I'd scrawled a note, a bad but indispensable habit most writers suffer from. This particular note read: *Sarie's mole.* It must have been scribbled after an evening of serious imbibing, as I did not have the faintest recollection of how or why this had happened. But it was so intriguing that it kept on plaguing me for days. At last, frantic with curiosity, I sent Naas a telegram:

WHAT ABOUT SARIE'S MOLE?

A few days later a reply arrived:

HOW THE HELL DO YOU KNOW ABOUT SARIE'S MOLE?

I still do not know the answer.

It remains a footnote to those two years in Paris: so many things were still unanswered, unresolved. It had been a long experience of questions, rather than answers. Some were tantalising and rich and rewarding in their own right. Too many others simply remained unfinished business. Politics was among these issues. After my early disillusionment and nausea following Sharpeville I went through many fluctuations of conviction and irresolution. There were even moments when I began to wonder whether there was not, after all, something heroic in the stance of Afrikaners against the world, some redeeming value in their fierce beliefs. To my shame I must admit that one of these moments came in 1961 when a horde of Afrikaners from all over Europe converged on our embassy in Paris for a rugby match between the Springboks and the French, and in that wave of atavistic patriotism there was a terrible surge of melodramatic enthusiasm for a lost cause. But more often than not I was depressed by the shockwaves from Sharpeville that still persisted, in thoughts by day and dreams by night. My decision to go back filled me with self-hatred – it was a return prompted not by any deep conviction or worthy cause, but by something as banal as a lack of money.

The pervading mood was of going back to a world already lost – and *deserving* to be lost. I did not *want* to go back. I loathed the very notion of South Africa. I knew I could not, after what I had seen and lived and discovered in France, *write* about South Africa again. If I continued to write, it would have to be something radically and emphatically *different*. But how? And what? The future seemed one unending space of bleakness. The only resolve I was conscious of, the only promise I dared to make to myself, was that I would be back. As soon as I could afford it, I would come back to France. And this time I would *stay*.

In a strange, submarine way, what tugged me back was the memory of an afternoon at the Sorbonne. As I shifted into the uncomfortable seat in the amphitheatre where I usually sat during Professor Dédéyan's lecture on the late nineteenth century, I noticed an inscription on the desk in front of me. It was very simple, very direct:

MOI

And it hit me like a blow in the face. The simplicity, the starkness, but at the same time the outrageous affirmation of it. The cry of birth. The wellspring of all art.

I was here. I am.

CAPE OF STORMS
AND GOOD HOPE

THROUGHOUT MY CHILDHOOD PLACES CHANGED ALL THE TIME, EACH MERGING disconcertingly into the next: Vrede, Jagersfontein, Brits, Douglas, Sabie, Lydenburg, Potchefstroom, Bothaville. New people, new friends, new teachers, new schools, new everything, every four years or so. But there remained one constant to which we could return as a surrogate home at the end of every endless year. Cape Town. But I still hesitate to explain its magical hold on my mind. A love that can be explained is not love.

My love for the Cape involves both Cape Town and the region it nestles in. But it involves lifetimes too. My own, to start with. And also the whole biography of the town, from its infancy, with flocks of fat-tailed sheep and herds of long-horned cattle grazing along the lower slopes of Table Mountain tended by their Khoi herders, to the aggressive signs of early middle age in today's vista of skyscrapers, freeways and flyovers (one abruptly halted in mid-flight), billboards, traffic snarls, concrete aspirations, failures – and, admittedly, a few rare successes – of the architectural imagination, hospitals and apartment blocks like malignant growths, the brown clouds of urban pollution.

In spite of growing up in that string of small dun-coloured villages in the deep interior, Cape Town has been in the background of my life all the time, brooding like a huge hen over my early years. For at the start of the summer holidays every year, we would pile into my father's grey 1938 Hudson and head south. When my friend Christie went on this same kind of trip with his family – which included three boys – their father would stop after every hundred miles and give each of the three boys a hiding: even if they hadn't done anything wrong he knew that punishment would be appropriate soon. My father was more long-suffering: we only stopped to pee or have a picnic, including hot coffee from a flask smelling of tea, and cold water smelling of the canvas of the bag draped over the radiator. For two days, sometimes three, we would mark our grim progress across the plains and ridges of the interior followed by billowing clouds of dust, until we would draw up on the last rise below the Boland mountains to behold the sprawl of the city wedged between its two dark blue oceans and know that we had, again, arrived.

When we did not travel by car, we took the train. There is an enthralling quality about today's great trains of Europe – nothing quite as unique as the TGV in France, but even the more modest ones have a charm beyond the reach of any other means of transport. That soundless, almost imperceptible, fluid transition from immobility to motion; the suave, whispering seduction of near-silent speed, the landscape beginning to streak past on either side – is like entering a different kind of existence altogether. How different were the trains of my youth! The noise, the swaying, the sensation of dangerous speed, of lurching forward through the night, the inevitable mote lodged in an eye, the farty smell of coal, a veritable ode to joy that may have nothing in common with Beethoven, except the feeling of touching the sublime. The smell of the green leather upholstery of the bunks, the sound of the conductor's key rapping on the door, the gleaming lustre of the woodwork, the swirl of the water in the washbasin, the dark blue of the blankets and the stark white of the crisp sheets at night. Above all: seeing the world around you fading under a sky erupting in the flame of a Karoo sunset, everything darkening mysteriously until only the sound of the train remains in silence and space, and the glimmer of the stars high above – and then to wake up very early in the dawn of a new day and see everything changed, changed utterly, from the stark expanse of the deep interior to the luxuriant blue mountains and billowing green vineyards of the Boland, as if the world has been reinvented overnight. Made strange and wonderful and exhilarating, a new experience of seeing, and hearing, and smelling.

The whole year peeled from one like the slough of a snake, the everyday-ness of home and school terms and familiar faces scraped away to reveal a new bright tenderness beneath the surface, a holiday quality which the rest of the year does not have, and in which everything is abundant with untellable possibilities.

This annual month in the Western Cape was the single unwavering point of reference of my youth. A place of holiday, of blustering wind and blistering sunshine, of fighting with male cousins like the scowling Pieter or even the ever-grinning Willem, and falling in love – at a very safe distance – with their female counterparts, nut-brown Annatjie, black-haired Stella, freckled Miemie, evenings with storytelling uncles and cushioned aunts, days of fruit and grapes and the taste of Oom Jannie's forbidden wine, excursions to the Mother City, flooded by images of shopping in towering places with staircases that moved magically by themselves, of consuming ice cream and pancakes in the Koffiehuis, meeting strange strangers known only to one's parents at Fletcher & Cartwright's, or feeding squirrels in the Company Gardens, or taking cable car rides up to the portals of heaven, or swimming in the dark blue ice-cold seas of Melkbos. A world so remote from the space in which we lived inland that it seemed as foreign and imaginary as Jerusalem or Gomorrah or the Baghdad of Scheherazade.

It was the one point in my youth where all the loose strands and threads used to be drawn together and where, at long intervals, the far-flung relatives from my father's and my mother's side of the family could meet and be more or less merged.

We loved my maternal grandmother, who was small and rotund, with thick round glasses and a bosom made for comforting small children. Sadly, we never came to know her very well, as she also died much too early. My main memory of her is the family ritual of undertaking, every Sunday after coffee, a small pilgrimage to her already-dug grave, which was covered by a sheet of corrugated iron next to my grandfather's headstone. Visiting 'Ouma's hole' during our visits to Bedford in the Eastern Cape where she lived, is one of the abiding memories of my childhood. There was nothing macabre about it. On the contrary, to us, it was a reassuring reminder of the presence of death in life, the inescapability of it; and when at last she died, there was something wholesome about knowing where she rested, in her grave next to that of the Oupa we'd never known.

There was one delicate matter which endeared Ouma to me. When I was very small, I was allowed to share her bed: not an ordinary bed, but one that featured a huge, billowing *bulsak* stuffed with goose feathers that nearly overwhelmed one with suffocating warmth, so that it was almost impossible to breathe. But my problem wasn't so much breathing as emptying my bladder. It was quite impossible to extricate myself from that *bulsak* to reach the chamber pot in time. The consequences were predictable. But I still remember with gratitude that Ouma never divulged this to the rest of the family. She would merely mention quite casually at the breakfast table that the nights were so hot that they caused me to sweat quite inordinately.

Most of my mother's family remained unknown to us, and for several of them a detour had to be made to the Eastern Cape. There had been thirteen children, some of whom we never even met; my mother herself, born when her oldest sister, Aunt Johanna, had already left home, barely knew her older siblings. Many of these, especially the uncles, also had the disconcerting habit of dying. And so there was always something mysterious about that part of the family. One morning I woke up early from a commotion in the bathroom. I must have been about ten. In front of the mirror stood a bald man I hadn't set eyes on before in my life, shaving. I tiptoed to my parents' room. 'If you've come about the stranger in the bathroom,' said my mother, 'it is your uncle Piet.' I never saw him again. I believe he died about a month later.

Among the aunts, a few survived to leave a more lasting memory, mostly because of their robust sense of humour, their tendency either to erupt in boisterous peals of laughter, or to sit in corners trembling in silent convulsions of mirth like round jellies enjoying the mysteries of jokes we could never fathom and more often than not were not even allowed to hear. The most colourful of the aunts was Auntie Sally, who lived on a farm on the West Coast; our holidays there were among the most memorable we spent as a family. One summer she took us to the resort of Strandfontein which is now overrun by the nouveau riche, a pretentious collection of

174

architectural monstrosities; but in those days it was an idyllic backwater with hardly any permanent buildings: only during the Christmas season the farmers from the area would converge there to set up primitive but highly effective reed-mat houses that allowed the sea breezes to move through unhindered, while the swelling of the reeds in times of rain assured a beautifully cosy interior when needed. The technique, presumably borrowed from the Khoisan inhabitants of the coastal region in early centuries, is still a reminder of a long past when survival depended on tuning in very naturally to the whims and vagaries of the seasons.

I remember the long twilights following the outrageous splendours of the sunset (the spectacle Ingrid once described as 'God's little vulgarities'), when families would gather on the beach for games, or horseplay, or storytelling, and lovers would wander off in the dusk and try to imagine themselves invisible.

These were the times when Auntie Sally would have everyone in stitches with her stories about the past or her comments on all and sundry. She once cut a particularly vain political opponent down to size by voicing her opinion – she was, among many other things, a midwife – that for someone like him it would be better to stay out of public life. 'What do you mean?' he asked with an aggressive sneer. 'Because,' said Auntie Sally, 'it is quite obvious that at your birth they buried the baby and raised the afterbirth.'

Auntie Bessie and Auntie Frances were also colourful people, the former more morose, the latter as expansive as the huge farm in the semi-desert over which she ruled. And then there was Auntie Dollie, an unsettling mixture of the generous and the narrow-minded. Her greatest asset was her husband, Oom Jannie, one of the first South Africans to study abroad. He went completely off the beaten track: not to Holland, or England, or even Germany, but to heathen France. To study viticulture. Along the way, as far as we could glean from the rare unguarded remark when there were no women around, he was not, during his study years, impervious to the charms of the odd mademoiselle. I used to believe that he must have married Auntie Dollie to inflict upon himself the direst punishment he could think of for some barely imaginable transgression whose name could not be spoken, even though the outrageous memory would still, occasionally, twinkle impishly in his impossibly blue eyes. A man of wit and erudition, but above all of passion, and an uncontrollable love of life. On her own, Auntie Dollie also had a generosity of spirit, a laugh that could erupt at unexpected moments, a love of good food. But something had blighted her spirit and turned her into the impersonation of a blast of icy wind on a summer's day, dour, stern, scolding, disapproving, dissatisfied – Goethe's *Geist der stets verneint*. For some reason, all her negative feelings were concentrated in one laser beam of virulent hatred against alcohol. And as Oom Jannie, one of the ablest vintners in the country, had chosen wine to express his whole zest for life, their collision course was staked out from the beginning. Or was there, perhaps, in the early days of their love, a shared interest, a shared passion? But what could have happened to twist it into something so awfully different? I have still not solved the mystery. There lurks a book. Oom Jannie inspired one of my favourite characters in *Before I Forget*, the father of the bewitching girl Driekie with whom the protagonist shares an unforgettable summer's afternoon in a mulberry tree.

Auntie Dollie's crusade against the deadly sin of alcohol abuse led to the uprooting of every single vine on Oom Jannie's farm, destroying his very *raison d'être*, everything that had made life worthwhile to him. Regrettably, all the orchards she'd instructed him to plant after uprooting the luscious vineyards, turned out a huge success, and they prospered more than ever before, which she interpreted as a sign that God was on their side.

Most unfortunately their only daughter, Bettie, was no Driekie, and she also died young, as did Willem, my favourite cousin among their four sons. He'd inherited his father's incorrigible *joie de vivre*. No farmer, he. He studied drama, which his pious mother could not have approved of. And in November 1956 he took the outrageous decision to travel to Austria and join an international brigade of young workers in a schloss on the Hungarian border to receive refugees from the Soviet invasion and help them in the hazardous transition to a new life in the West. Afterwards, I spent hours listening to Willem's account of those midwinter weeks in the schloss and their aftermath – the excitement and the dreariness, the hard work and the adventures, the shy young Hungarian girl who briefly shared his narrow bed in the high round tower where the helpers were lodged, the intrigues and subterfuges, the exploitation and bullying and chicanery, the moments of hope or despair, of caring, of cruelty and betrayal, of unexpected generosity, the brief eruptions of passion. Much of this information was later transposed into the life of Philip, the film-maker in *The Wall of the Plague*; because ultimately, in writing, nothing is left unused.

My mother's side of the family certainly provided enough colour, stimulation and drama to keep those times acutely alive in my memory. But it was my father's family that formed a narrative backbone to those memories. They were more tightly knit – not thirteen siblings, but only five, all of them sons – and we saw more of them than of the rather shapeless, chaotic though redoubtable Wolmarans clan my mother represented.

In the centre of my father's clan, as was only fit and proper, were my grandparents, two of the most loveable people I have ever known. Biblical too, one might say. But they sprang more evidently from the New Testament side.

Oupa was a clerk in a grocery shop in Malmesbury. But he had had his day, as I found out when I discovered the book he wrote about his experiences in the Anglo-Boer War, which he wrote in a thick, hardback ledger, in beautiful copperplate, and in High Dutch, which at the age of twelve I dutifully translated into Afrikaans. To no avail; no publisher was interested. Perhaps it was not all that surprising. Oupa's war was not exactly a series of heroic feats. I turned it into something of a tragicomedy in the history section of *Looking on Darkness*, and plundered it much more extensively for the passages about daily life on commando in *An Act of Terror*. Oupa had a sense for the observation of the everyday, the ordinary face of war behind the masks of gore and glory. Had he been less scrupulous about respecting the reality of his experiences, and with a tad more imagination he might have conjured up a *Good Soldier Svejk*. But there was something endearing about his dogged determination to get through the war. Afterwards he even had one of his five sons christened in the name of General Christiaan Beyers. And I worshipped him for it.

When peace broke out he married Miemie Kotzé, the fiancée he had left behind before going off to war against the British. She was a distant scion of the illustrious Kotzebue family, and my tenuous claim to a French connection. They settled in Malmesbury and bought a house at the very top of Hill Street. He got the job in the grocery shop, and they lived happily ever after.

In many of our games over the Christmas holidays in the Western Cape, we emulated Oupa's war exploits – that is, his meanderings across the lush hills of Natal and the barren high veld of the Transvaal. When Elbie complained about being compelled to be my batman or *agterryer*, I proceeded into my dreams on my own. And one variation of the game became particularly pleasurable. The stoep of Oupa's house ran the full length of the facade, and if one hooked an arm over the railing at the end of it and hung over the edge, it was easy to imagine oneself one step up from a horseman on commando, that is, as a train driver. Which caused me from an early age to dream of becoming just that. Unable to realise that ambition, which I still feel as a lack in my life, I turned to writing, which is just another way of travelling. Is not any story an image of the journeys in the *Odyssey*, or *Gilgamesh*, or the *Divina Commedia*, or *Don Quixote*, or *Voyage Au Bout de la Nuit*?

The journeys to my grandparents were always occasions for discovery and rediscovery. My beautiful cousin Stella was one of my first loves, in the category of adoration from afar. The closest I ever came to indicate my special interest was to assure her at bedtime, on the evening before her family was due to return to their home in Johannesburg, that I would make every effort to get up in time the next morning, 'because I want to kiss you goodbye'. But the lady was not for kissing and in the early morning rough and tumble there was not even time for a shared moment away from everybody else. Which may have been the beginning of a lifelong hunch that the mere existence of love already presupposes an ending. Still, we did see each other at many year-end holidays, and we sometimes exchanged letters, and when I was at university I once actually spent a few days with the family, which was not the same.

There wasn't room enough in Oupa's home for the whole family to converge at the same time, but there were always enough of us for a festive atmosphere; and as the oldest grandchild I was often accorded the special privilege of sleeping with the grandparents in their room – on a special narrow striped mattress stuffed with dry maize leaves which made such a rustling racket that sleep did not come easily.

The time we spent in Malmesbury was crammed with adventure, most of it provoked spontaneously by the interaction among so many cousins. At home, one had the choice between Ouma's pantry, an Aladdin's cave of simple treasures as she never ever threw anything away, and Oupa's garden in which chickens scratched and turkeys strutted and Muscovy ducks hissed, and from which an endless supply of vegetables and fruit found its way to the great table that could comfortably seat the eighteen or twenty or, upon occasion, twenty-four family members assembled at mealtimes. On the underside of the table my father had written his name when as the first-born child he was invited to make his pick from the heirlooms on offer; unfortunately some of the other family members got there first after Ouma's death, which occurred within a few months of Oupa's. They carted away whatever took their fancy before anyone else could make a claim. And so Auntie Kochie, the most pious Christian of them all, went off with the loot. She was the strictest and tidiest person I have ever known, always smiling the smile of the redeemed, while sharpening knives in her steel-blue eyes. Unable to bear the merest suggestion of untidiness in any form, she used to spend hours every night making sure the whole house was spick and span before she went to bed, 'just in case the Lord comes in the night and finds us unprepared'.

When we were not in or around the house, we went on picnics – to shady spots in the village, including the graveyard; or to surrounding farms where some of the other pleasures of harvest time in the Boland were on offer, or even, on a few unforgettable Saturdays, to the flanks of Table Mountain. Or to the sea, the fearsomely cold Atlantic Ocean at Melkbos, where Ouma's sister, Great-aunt Anna, would wade into the waves in her *kabaai*, a huge, billowing white nightdress that ballooned up around her in the wind, a truly unforgettable and side-splitting sight. Poor Aunt Anna suffered in her old age – and she really *was* old, two years older than God, my friend Daantjie Saayman would have said – from dementia, and once attacked Ouma with a carving knife in the kitchen, after which she had to be taken away to the mental institution of Valkenberg in Cape Town. This shaped in me a lifelong apprehension of a deep, dark welter of forces lurking just below the surface of the most ordinary, boring or funny experiences in our lives.

Boisterous moments, interspersed with good, deep silences, all of it stewed in the searing summer heat of the Swartland region as the holidays finally drew to an end; and then someone would take us to the Cape Town station and deposit us back on the train, and we travelled ever more deeply into the night, towards the flaming explosion of a new inland dawn.

The first time Cape Town truly became part of my consciousness – in my childhood and youth it was merely part of the unexamined life – was in early August 1961, when Estelle and I arrived in Table Bay on the *Something Castle* (was it *Warwick*? *Edinburgh*? *Windsor*?) The previous two grey weeks at sea, the great majority of the grey passengers had spent in the grey smoking rooms, smoking. But in the early hours of that morning of arrival, there appeared a streak of lurid red in the sky, as if some great hand had taken up a pencil to score out the erroneous writing of the immediate past and turn the page to start again. On this page was gradually inscribed the ink-black mass of the mountain above the ink-blue wash of the sea; and as the ship drew nearer and the sky became luminous, the sprawling city assumed a recognisable shape under tumbling gulls. One of those incomparable winter days when the rain clouds dissipate to reveal, in blue and gold, the sight that already struck dumb Sir Francis Drake, as it must have Diaz and Vasco da Gama before him, and millennia earlier, Phoenicians on their way to unimaginable new worlds. Before our eyes the picture came to life. And then the Capeness of the Cape exploded in my ears with the trumpet voices of coloured harbour workers gleefully coaxing us ashore. 'Jus' look at these pale *outjies* coming down the gangway!' shouted one to a distant friend. 'White like blerrie maggots. *Aitsa*! Bring on that sun to give them a spot of colour, man.'

Aitsa: the exclamation derived from the once-hallowed name of Heitsi-Eibib, hunter-god of the Khoi people.

That was when I knew, with a recognition so fierce it took my breath away, that I had indeed come home. *Home*, a concept I had never grasped so acutely before: not during the previous years of studying in Paris, nor in those villages in the dusty heart of the country where one never dared grow too fond of anything or anyone, as goodbye was always in the air. Rilke: *These things that live on departure*. But this, now, suddenly, was *home*.

I was heading inland; I had accepted an appointment at Rhodes University in Grahamstown. But *this* was home. This was where I wanted to be.

It took thirty years before I could take the step. But when I finally made the definitive move in 1991 when the University of Cape Town found a place for me – even though it meant changing from the Department of Afrikaans and Dutch in which I'd lectured for thirty years, to English – it was like entering more deeply into myself. There was nowhere else I could so naturally be at home.

And it was defined by those exuberant early morning voices that greeted Estelle and me on our arrival in 1961 – voices spoken or shouted by people who are still not granted the dignity of their own name. Not even coloureds, but '*so-called* coloureds'. A people that began to emerge about nine months after the arrival of the first Dutch colonists, who brought with them a flag of the Dutch East India Company, the VOC; and a variety of dialects; and a very basic, fundamentalist brand of Calvinism, soon fortified by equally fundamentalist Huguenots from France: what a pity, I've often thought, that when France decided to dump some of its citizens on us, they could not have been more representative of the Catholic majority, including at least some 'pagans' and atheists of the Voltairean mould. When I dared, in passing, to make such an observation in a radio interview soon after our arrival, it led to a period of more than thirty years in which the South African Broadcasting Corporation treated me as *persona non grata*.

Be that as it may, the doughty Dutch were instructed to plant a garden for the provisioning of passing ships, tame the fringes of a savage Africa, and introduce miscegenation as the national sport. Nothing homogeneous about the new generation of Cape inhabitants then generally known as 'Afrikaners', except perhaps the many shades of brown that separate black and white. How fitting, how emblematic, that in this context the very name 'Afrikaner' should have been forged *in opposition to* the ruling class, as a sign of the heretic – when the unruly, drunken young Hendrik Bibault was carousing in the streets of Stellenbosch in 1707 celebrating the recall of the much-loathed governor Willem Adriaan van der Stel to Holland and the *landdrost* tried to silence him:

'I shall not leave!' shouted the youngster, 'I am an Afrikaner, even if the *landdrost* beats me to death or puts me in jail, I shall not, nor will I be silent.'

Very soon *language* also became a marker of difference. In this peculiar *bredie* indigenous peoples and imported slaves – from Indonesia and Malaysia, from Malabar and Madagascar and Mozambique, from Amboine and Angola – attempting to speak Dutch, the master language, transformed it into something new, a local fabrication, soon known as *Afrikaans*. Which for a century and a half marked the speakers as locals, an underclass, largely of half-breeds, speaking a patois derided as Kitchen Dutch.

This was both the strength and the weakness of the group. Weakness, because it was easy to relegate them to the margins of 'decent' society. Strength, because it meant that the language would remain identified with the deprived and the oppressed, the very roots from which the New South Africa would later grow. Towards the end of the nineteenth century the language was regrettably appropriated as a political tool by a small band of white men to challenge the domination of English and Dutch at the Cape; and when, after sickening humiliations and tribulations, they finally came to power, Afrikaans became, in its own turn, the language of oppression and power. The language of apartheid. But while that was happening, the coloured community retained it as the vehicle in which they could best express their humanity; and eventually their resistance. Which made it particularly depressing that once a democratic, largely black, government came to power, Afrikaans should continue to be suspected by many as an instrument of power, while its long history of association with the coloured downtrodden should be ignored by many of the new power elite. And sadder still is the fact that the people who had kept Afrikaans alive, initially against the battalions of political and military power, later against the hijackers who tried to establish a new language of domination, should still be largely deprived of proper recognition by the new establishment. Previously, they were regarded as too black to be allowed into the laager of power; now, except during election time when their votes are useful, they are often regarded as too white to be accepted as worthy fellow citizens. Given that almost every single coloured man, woman and child in South Africa may well be traced back to an initial act of power abuse – literally to a rape, as one can recognise it in the early history of slavery in the USA, that is, 'the original wound' in the terminology of one of the leading critics of slave narratives, Ashraf Rushdy – it remains a festering presence in the conscience of South Africa not yet adequately exorcised, or even confronted, by any regime.

It was mainly in the Western Cape, with Cape Town as its hub, where the coloured people found their home. This, above all, was what defined for me that homecoming in 1961. And not long afterwards I had the joy of being introduced to the very heart of the Coloured Cape, District Six. By then, the bulldozers had already begun to lay waste the lower slopes of the mountain where 'The Six' had teemed and pullulated for centuries. But there were still swathes of the old community left, and my friend Daantjie Saayman would take me on long walks through the once-vibrant quarter which would later form the core of *Looking on Darkness* and much of *The Wall of the Plague*. Daantjie himself was the model for the protagonist Andrea's larger-than-life fisherman father, long before colon cancer finally struck him down. This, like the Malay Quarter on the slope of the Lion's Rump, is what truly spells Cape Town for me: its indomitable, raucous, rebellious way of confirming a heretic otherness, of saying no – not only to apartheid, but to everything that tried to domesticate and inhibit the human spirit and its wild, affirmative freedom, its laughter, its compassion. And also its outrageous and jubilant way of saying yes to life itself. A yes all the more remarkable for the long darkness it had to traverse in order to return to the sun.

Much of that darkness – the darkness that lends relief and contours to the emotional and moral landscape of the Cape – was defined by slavery. For many years white historians lulled us with assurances of a relatively benign dispensation affecting slaves at the Cape, since the arrival of the first men, women and children in bondage in 1658 until the abolition of the barbaric practice in 1834. We know today that the experience was both more violent and more widespread, and assumed many more forms, than used to be believed.

Even when *A Chain of Voices* was published in 1982 and I wrote an article on the slave revolt that had prompted the writing of the novel, there was a furious and sarcastic letter in the *Argus* from a woman who found it a waste of time to write about such matters in our day and age, since slavery, she insisted, had never left any real mark on South Africa. Her attitude was a precise demonstration of what had gone wrong with South African race – and interpersonal – relations following the arguments of slave owners at the Cape in 1830. For too long apartheid historians have covered up the scar of this iniquitous practice by arguing that this country had instituted a peculiarly benign form of slavery, which is belied by the evidence.

In Cape Town, punishment of slaves ranged from the 'mild practices' involving the cutting off of noses, ears or heels to the lingering agony, sometimes protracted for six or eight or twelve days, of being left to die on the wheel after having all the limbs of the body shattered, or of being impaled on a long pole thrust up the anus and protruding through the neck, or drawn and quartered by four horses attached to arms and legs.

This was the punishment meted out to the young woman Trijntje of Madagascar in 1714, when it came to light that she had been forced into a relationship with the brewer Willem Menssink, a violent man who used to thrash his own wife Elizabeth into submission exclaiming, 'Don't you know that it is the Cape custom to live by the Old Testament?': driven to despair by the advances of the brewer and the cruelty of his wife, Trijntje attempted to poison her mistress, and murdered the child Menssink had fathered on her. For this, she was taken to the place of execution at the south-eastern corner of the castle, strangled to death, and her body tied to a forked post where it was left 'to be consumed by time and the birds of heaven'. Menssink, of course, being white, and indispensable in supplying beer to the Company, went scot-free.

This story was researched by the indefatigable Nigel Penn and published in his scintillating study, *Rogues, Rebels and Runaways*; and I still remember the little smile with which he offered me the book, saying, 'You might find something in here.' Which I promptly did, in *The Rights of Desire*.

A decade after Trijntje's death, in March 1725, the leaders of the only significant attempt at a slave revolt at the Cape were hanged and/or tortured at the same place. Among them was the young man Galant, found guilty of having murdered two young van der Merwes, Nicolaas and Barend, with whom he had grown up.

These are just two of the slave stories from the Cape that still define the texture of the place. There are so many others still to be written! Among them, the moving account of the handsome slave Titus of Bengal, who was found guilty, in 1714, of having had a relationship with his white mistress Maria Mouton and of killing her husband, Frans Joosten, on her instigation. In this case, Maria was first half-strangled, then scorched, and finally garrotted to death; Titus was impaled and left to die, then his head and right hand were cut off and exposed on a post at his master's farm.

The memories persist, like the shapes of fish in murky water. Ghosts not yet laid to rest. And it is no surprise to find that Cape Town is indeed a city of ghosts, shades, spectres, revenants. Wherever one goes, there are stories about hauntings, many of them memorably recorded in an essay by the irrepressible Willemien Brümmer, great-granddaughter of one of the most famous ghost-story writers in Afrikaans, C. J. Langenhoven. Today, the castle is a starting point for this kind of exploration. Another favourite haunt is the once lugubrious Slave Lodge at the top of Adderley Street where important functionaries of the VOC and stout burghers were allowed visiting hours at night to assuage their pent-up lust, father children on female slaves, and with Calvinistic righteousness and a sense of patriarchal duty, 'improve the quality of the slave stock in the colony'. Even early in the nineteenth century Lord Charles Somerset, then governor of the colony, was said to have imported a Scottish jock, with the very same purpose and function. They must have added a shade or two to the local ghost population.

Ghosts also frequent the Malay Quarter which still keeps its dark and dangerous memories behind colourful facades now turned into dollied-up showpieces for the chic and the trendy; and Robben Island where the hazy figure of a drowned nun sometimes shows herself in the mist; and in the stately home of Kronendal in Hout Bay to which a beautiful woman forsaken by her beloved returns to rearrange the furniture; on the noble old wine estates of Alphen and Constantia; and in Admiralty House in Simonstown, still haunted by a 'lady in white', who had hanged herself in the 'fisherman's room' two centuries ago; and of course the museum in Simonstown, where ghosts are almost as much at home as shadows. Among the regular visitors is the benevolent Eleanor in silky black who invariably leaves behind the scent of lavender; but prisoners in the basement there are also the more ominous shades of slaves, and from a turbulent past with which the present has yet to make its peace.

Through the ghosts one discovers the obvious: that in this place past and present are not opposites, not even terms in juxtaposition. It is, rather, a matter of the past *in* the present. There are places in Cape Town which exude a sense of timelessness. The museums naturally belong to this dimension. Today there are many more of these than before, the most moving of the additions being those of District Six, the Holocaust and Robben Island. The entire experience of the latter, from the moment the ferry leaves the quay to the moment it returns, belongs not so much to time and space as to a state of mind, in which the present and the most recent past – the sojourn of ANC and PAC leaders like Mandela or Sobukwe – reach back to a more distant history: to the incarceration of great nineteenth-century leaders like Makana, and all the way back to the early days of Dutch settlement – an era evoked with such remarkable understanding in Dan Sleigh's monumental novel *Islands* – when Robben Island was a holding space for prisoners, for lepers, for 'undesirable elements'. Among these was that forlorn, exceptional woman Eva (or Krotoa), the first go-between in negotiations involving the Dutch and the Khoi, also the first indigenous woman officially married to a Hollander and one of the first victims of the chain of misunderstanding that defined race relations at the Cape.

But in my childhood there was, for us, only the museum in the Gardens, where I spent hours making drawings in a small notebook of all the stuffed mammals; and then stared in awe at the Bushmen in the display cabinets, firmly believing that they, too, had been stuffed and propped up in disconcertingly lifelike postures.

But more timeless, more solid, altogether more majestic than any building, is Table Mountain itself. The exquisite terror that gripped one on a first ascent by cable car. The dassies on the top boulders. The triumphant feeling when a few of us boys could briefly evade the surveillance of parents to pee over the edge and watch the thin spray evaporating in the wind. The harbour with its ships and cranes and its promise of sailing out to the farthest unknown reaches of the earth. The coastline, an indolent painting in blue and white. The undulating mountains, past the Twelve Apostles to Cape Point, the petrified monument of the titan Adamastor punished for all eternity for his arrogant attempt to seduce the eminently seductible sea-nymph Thetis. And although one knows that Agulhas reaches further south into the ocean than this spindly coccyx of the continent, this *feels* like the end of the earth, the meeting point between two angry oceans, one warm, one cold, where everything is reduced to the elements of earth and air and rock and sometimes, in summer, fire too. There is no obstacle, for thousands of kilometres, between our uncertain here-and-now and the distant icy Antarctic.

But ultimately Cape Town is not an assemblage of places and monuments, of sites and historical spaces: it is an entity defined by its people, a kind of Comtean gathering of all who have gone before, all who are here now, all still to come in the future. The pioneers, the Great Men, the achievers, the illustrious, yes. But also, and especially, the hosts of the ordinary, the humdrum, the mundane: those who, by and large, do not make history but undergo it, as immortalised in Brecht's poem 'Fragen eines lesenden Arbeiters' – 'Questions from a Worker who Reads'.

Here in Cape Town, not only the early inhabitants of the old castle live in the memory, but so many others too. The shepherds of fat-tailed sheep, the burghers trying to eke out a living along the Liesbeek; the Khoi victims of colonialist expansion, and the colonial victims of Khoi retaliation, the mothers of many children: those who survive, or try to survive, in the wind and dust of the Cape Flats and in shacks along the dunes; the street children with big eyes and snotty noses and cupped hands who can curse blue lightning bolts from a clear sky; the bergies pushing their Shoprite or Pick 'n Pay trolleys to gathering points in subways or in parks, smelling of Blue Train and woodsmoke, of mortality and humanity. All of those, countless and nameless, who ensure that the Cape survives. And all of those who bear the names of my family, from the first Andries Brink who arrived from Woerden in Holland, after an earlier migration from Denmark, and still earlier and earlier migrations back to the dawn of humanity, to a Garden with a man and a woman and an apple that should have been a fig. In this place the footprints of the larger history merge with those of our family, private and personal, sometimes proud and often despicable. Men who cultivated fruit farms and men who raped their slave girls and sold their own children to plant a new nation, brown under the sun. Those who were recorded in history books and those who survive only in memories. Aunt Sally's laugh. Oom Jannie's blue eyes as he looks at the orchards where his vineyards used to grow. The home-made boat in which we rowed on the farm dam one Sunday afternoon when I was supposed to lie on my bed reading an unbearably uplifting book, and then the boat capsized and we were all thrashed because we had desecrated the Day of the Lord, Stella with her sleep-heavy eyes that morning when we didn't kiss each other goodbye. Elbie falling from a plum tree and breaking her arm. An entire youth in a handful of memories. The history of an entire nation in a city under a mountain. Beautiful and hideous, dangerous and comforting, disconcerting and reassuring. The Cape. The fairest Cape in the whole circumference of the earth.

BLACK AND WHITE IN CRISIS

MY RETURN FROM PARIS TOWARDS THE END OF 1961, EVEN THOUGH THE arrival in the country was marked by the brief ecstasy of acknowledging, in the exuberant voices of the coloured labourers in the Cape Town harbour, the reality of being home again, remained clouded by the overwhelming resentment I felt against South Africa following the massacre of Sharpeville. And that feeling persisted. Basically, *I did not want to be here.* Certainly it showed in my writing: that is always a reliable barometer. In *The Ambassador* I remained firmly ensconced in Paris, with South Africa still very much present. All the characters, even Nicolette, are South African, but their roots remained somewhere in the background. The experimental Afrikaans novel *Orgie* (*Orgy*) was set in Cape Town, but the setting is almost coincidental: the story was very narrowly focused on the doomed relationship with Ingrid. If there was a wider frame of significance, it came from ancient Sumerian mythology. We were all, in one way or another, myth-mongers in the sixties. In *Miskien Nooit* (*Maybe Never*) I returned to Paris, based on an unfulfilled relationship from the summer I spent there in 1966. This time the mytho-logical frame came from Scandinavia. But for me the most significant piece of writing I did in the sixties was a novel which was mercifully never published, although in many ways it paved the way for much of what came later. It was first called *Ninety Days*, a reference to the draconian new legis-lation that was passed in the early sixties, in the wake of Sharpeville, and which permitted detention without trial for a period of ninety days with

189

the option of prolonging it with further periods of ninety days each, for as long as it pleased the state.

In a second, completely rewritten, version in 1967 the novel was renamed *The Saboteurs*; and in a third draft that followed soon after, the title was once again changed, this time to *Back to the Sun*. I have no copy of this final version: in 1968, I left it with Breyten in the hope, fortunately unfulfilled, that he might one day read and comment on it. But he had a friend at the time, a dyed-in-the-wool Marxist architect who opted out of his very successful career to become a bricklayer, carpenter and handyman, and in exchange for many meals and a temporary roof over his head – although most of the time he slept in his seriously unroadworthy combi – he started renovating Breyten and Yolande's apartment in the rue Malebranche. A brilliant job he did, except that he allowed practically no space for books. 'No house,' said Jean with stubborn proletarian conviction, 'needs more than twelve books.' So he fashioned a small shelf in the wall of the living room, on which one could fit exactly twelve medium-sized books, beginning with *Das Kapital*. Everything else in the bookish line, including my only manuscript of *Back to the Sun*, was disposed of.

The immediate trigger for the novel was the arrest of a group of very young people – mainly students – in Cape Town on charges of planning sabotage and, through the transparent logic of the security police, the overthrow of the state. There was the brilliant young lawyer Albie Sachs, who was closely involved with the group of accused and later married the fiercely rebellious, headstrong Stephanie Kemp. I briefly met Albie at the time, having initially been fascinated by the story of his father, Solly Sachs, who for years had played cat and mouse with the government in their witch-hunt on communists and suspected communists; later, in London, I spent more time with him and Stephanie – who, in the flesh, I found as captivating as she had seemed in the earlier newspaper reports. For a long time I had grappled with the image of the rebel as a young woman: her special kind of absolutism, her readiness to sacrifice her comforts, her world, even her *self*, for what she – irrationally and madly, but with single-minded passion – believes in. I still do not know whether that was what she 'really' was. But that was what she personified for me. And often, in writing, perception is all. There was also Spike de Keller, whom I never met personally, but who had much impressed me in the press coverage: unlike some of the others, he had seemed to approach the plan very realistically and rationally, weighed the pros and cons, and decided to risk it – and then paid the price in prison. Many years later I came to know his mother and got a touching insider's view of the man. And there was Adrian Leftwich, who ultimately broke under police torture and betrayed his friends – after he had previously, in simulated situations, withstood pressure much better than any of the others – and was branded a coward and a sellout by many, including the relentless judge Andrew Beyers, a technicolourful, larger-than-life and in many ways frightening character. Twenty years later I met Adrian in Australia and immediately felt attracted to him as a person of deep feeling and lucid thinking, a man who through personal sacrifice and suffering had placed his life at stake – and lost. But had he 'lost'? What is the *meaning* of winning or losing in such a situation? Even an atheist can find truth in the Bible: and for me Adrian was a demonstration of the profound question raised in St Mark: *For what shall it profit a man, if he shall gain the whole world, and lose his own soul? Or what shall a man give in exchange for his soul?* Adrian Leftwich became for me a man prepared to give up the world and save his soul. And the soul of the cause he believed in. *That* he did not betray. In his own way he came, who knows, to define that difficult concept, the 'hero' and forced one to rethink all one's early preconceptions and prejudices.

What was it in that group that mesmerised me and inspired me to write a novel about this kind of experience? The characters, undoubtedly. But also the profound philosophical choice they illustrated: in a country like the South Africa of the apartheid years, what was there a young white woman or man could do to take on the massive, blunt, violent power of the state? There was much courage and heroism demonstrated by innumerable young blacks who took up the challenge, and who gave their lives in the struggle for freedom. But without in any way whatsoever misreading or underestimating the sacrifices they were willing to make, and actually *made*, what they were doing was to fight for their own freedom, their own lives. Whereas these young activists, romantic or 'misguided' as they might have seemed, were prepared to make the supreme sacrifice *for others*. They could simply have continued with their own lives of comfort and protection and prosperity. In a country like South Africa, they had everything going for them. *They were white.*

That was what I tried to grapple with in my book. I wanted, in the process of writing, to find out what drove them, what made their decisions and their actions possible, what – in *this* country, at *this* time – made *them* possible.

The book was a failure. I think I was simply not equipped to understand its real challenges. I had not lived or felt or experienced anything deeply enough to work through that situation. But what it did effect, for me, in me, was to make me deeply conscious of the *dilemma* of being white in a land like this. It problematised my own existence for myself. Sympathy, even empathy, was not enough. I needed more experience. Which was why I had to confront it again, forty years later, in *Before I Forget*. And quite possibly I didn't even get it right the second time round.

Certainly, what *Ninety Days – The Saboteurs – Back to the Sun* made me discover was the significance of failure. Which so often, in the personal sense, is infinitely more of a discovery and a revelation than success.

And it was more than a writing experience. It was also something deeply felt, and *lived.* Which may well be why, in the years between 1960 and 1970, in the context of exploring whiteness and blackness – or rather: whiteandblackness – seen from the outside, my life was relatively calm, without much drama, perhaps even without much 'progress'. But below the surface, I know now, I was probing and evaluating, or simply trying to *understand*, something more about this extraordinary difficult country. Not even by 'experiencing' much, but simply by *being there.* For future reference, as it were.

The one who played the most decisive role in shaping and structuring my political conscience, especially in the way it defined my perception of racial matters, was H – as all her friends called her. From the moment we first properly met in Grahamstown in October 1966, after the early fleeting encounter in Jan Rabie's house the year before, we both sensed – even though she tried very resolutely in the beginning to resist it – that this would change the course of our lives. It took months before our relationship broadened and deepened into love; but after that there was no possibility that my life would ever be the same.

I was simply not ready to face South Africa when I had to come back. Even in spite of the momentary elation upon arriving in Cape Town, I returned with a grudge. I wanted to go back to France at the earliest opportunity. Which I did at the end of 1967. But in the meantime I had to go on living and partly living, as Eliot had phrased it.

The South Africa I returned to, was that of Rhodes University, English-speaking, and with a long tradition of liberalism; interestingly enough, the people who impressed and influenced me most, were Afrikaans-speaking: they included my head of department, a Belgian, Rob Antonissen, one of the most erudite and humane persons I have ever met; the philosopher Daantjie Oosthuizen, a confidant of Beyers Naudé, who became such a thorn in the flesh of the establishment; the professor of German, Helmut Erbe, who had once, upon re-entering South Africa after a sabbatical abroad, been stopped by customs who confiscated from his luggage a set of photographs of Michelangelo sculptures which they took to be pornography; a teacher, Laurie Graham, who had read and travelled widely. All of them had long ago broken out of the Afrikaner laager. All of them loathed apartheid and actively supported viable initiatives for significant opposition, notably Alan Paton's Liberal Party. They interacted easily and naturally and enthusiastically with black friends, something unthinkable in my previous life. Friends like these made the transition not only bearable but often exciting and stimulating. They provoked my mind into thinking through matters that my stay in Paris had introduced but not developed far enough. Through them, for the first time in my life, I made real friends with some black people.

The fact that I did not have to return to the Afrikaner world that had first defined my image of the country, made it easier in many ways – although in other respects it created distances and barriers between me and 'my people' that nothing would ever fully resolve. I lived an in-between existence – between Paris and Paris. Which meant that I brought back many changed notions about what was happening in South Africa, but without any wish to get involved. Not only because of my immersion in existentialism, but also for all the practical reasons that had to do with making a living, I remained an outsider. And perhaps this suited me. In a way it was what I had been preparing myself for since the time of being a student in Potchefstroom: I enjoyed living 'against the grain' of the place.

Yet the mere fact that in my *writing*, the ultimate lithmus test, I still could not identify sufficiently with the country to write about it, but kept on turning like a sunflower to the defining sun of Paris, meant that I still had a very long way to go. I still did not *belong*. Nor did I wish to.

And *this* was the background against which H entered my life, newly arrived from London, with her uncluttered look at South Africa, her uncompromising beliefs in justice and equity, in truth. For her, notions like 'freedom' were not theoretical or ideological, although at the time she held quite strong Marxist convictions, but grew out of the lived experience of real individuals. At the same time she was not doctrinaire or opinionated: she came to the world with a generosity, a readiness to learn and to probe and to understand, a youthful exuberance and *joy* which nobody seemed able to resist. Everybody who met her, male or female, fell in love with her. One felt better about oneself for knowing her. She could be merciless, scathing, devastating in the face of hypocrisy or falseness or lies or bad faith, which was why she loathed apartheid and its perpetrators. But in her deepest self she was warm and loving and caring, with an irrepressible sense of humour. She had real enthusiasm. She had real joy. And she was only, when we met, twenty-four years old!

Oh she had fears and uncertainties and insecurities and prejudices as well. She had scars, and chips on her shoulder too. This was mainly because of her upper-middle-class upbringing – though I have rarely met anyone who could break so convincingly and exuberantly free from the restrictions of a specific social and political background.

H had absolutely no baggage about colour. Nor about class. She could sit down on a kerb and chat with a black beggar as readily as with a revered professor or a stern white priest. Which never meant looking either down on some or up to others. And this, in the South Africa of the sixties, still reeling from Sharpeville (and already, although no one could of course have known it yet, beginning to prepare itself for the Soweto of 1976), was something of a miracle. Precisely because she brought no conditions or preconceptions with her. She would love someone, black or white, because she related to that person as an individual. She could also hate someone, black or white, in the same way. No feeble liberal covering up or smoothing over or pretending because of colour. An individual, male or female, black or white, could be a marvel or a shit – or anything in between – without colour ever entering into it.

This is not meant to be a panegyric. I am simply trying to place H in a context, to try and explain why she hit me like an elemental force when we met; and why she made *The Saboteurs* happen when it did, and why meeting her made a difference to the way I interacted with black people, in my writing and in my life.

Only a few months after she arrived in Grahamstown, the time came for her planned journey through Africa, mainly hitch-hiking. Before she set off we drove to Swaziland and Mozambique to spend some time with Breyten and Yolande who had come south in the hope of visiting South Africa, something that was ruled out when Yolande, as a Vietnamese, was branded 'non-white'.

The trip became a journey of discovery. There was, from the beginning, a sense of 'escaping'. Even though I'd been in Europe only a few months before on another brief visit to Paris for a sabbatical in 1966, there was already a feeling of being overwhelmed by the reality of South Africa. Only shortly before we left for Swaziland there had been one of those incidents that, far from being exceptional, became the norm: a group of black people gathered on a beach at East London, expecting to meet some celebrity. He didn't turn up; the people became vociferous; the police arrived and ordered them to disperse. Something that had started in a mood of festivity, suddenly turned nasty. The police moved in with dogs and batons and guns. Then the 'incident': a little girl of three was attacked by a police dog and badly mauled; she had to get sixteen stitches to mend the wound. The police officer in charge issued a statement: the girl's parents had deliberately pushed her towards the dog in order to provoke an attack.

By comparison, Swaziland and Mozambique were havens of peace. Both Breyten and H, in their different ways, managed to make contact with anybody and everybody. We held impromptu gatherings, in hotel lounges or on street corners or in bustling markets selling fruit and vegetables, porridge and samp and beans and mopani worms and suspicious-looking pods and sausages and bundles of tripe and sheeps' heads and oxtails and tongues and containers with pungent drinks. A few times we gathered – the four of us, and innumerable relatives and friends and hangers-on – for discussions that continued deep into the night: on the situation in South Africa, and other countries in the south, and far up north, and in America and Europe; or on music; on our families, on our genealogies. On several of these occasions our eloquent and dynamic discussion leader or master of ceremonies was a man with a booming voice and an explosive laugh, Chicks Nkosi, an inveterate optimist who could hold us spellbound with his visions of the future, when all the thousands of little matchboxes that constituted the black townships of southern Africa, would wake up from sleep and start marching across the hills and plains to reclaim their freedom, and everybody in our meeting place would start cheering and laughing, shouting *Viva! Viva!* and *A luta continua!* And as we finally left, daylight already staining the sky in the east, and piled into our rented car to drive back to our sprawling hotel at Mantenga Falls, we would privately relive the stories and the laughter and the rejoicing and the slogans, and wonder, deep within ourselves, how anything like that could possibly be hoped to happen in our lifetimes.

So much of my imaginings and writing of the next decades can be traced back to that journey and its discoveries – most of which had to do with most obvious yet most magical of facts: that we were all African, that we all belonged here, and *wanted* to belong. For the first time since my return from Europe I seriously began to doubt my passionate fixation on going back to Paris. Was it not an opting out, a running away? Was *this* – this place, this deepest south, this ultimate Africa – not where I really ought to remain and take root?

Mozambique provided less of the intense interaction that excited us in Swaziland, mainly because of the gulf of language. But it was no less of an encounter with Africa. Initially, there were explosions and silences between H and me, because of her constitutional inability to say no to anyone: a youngster hitch-hiking along a route that would take us a hundred kilometres off our course, a friend she had met earlier and who wanted to know whether her son and his best friend could go camping with us, an eager elderly man who wanted to send a parcel with us to a relative living in the north of the country while we were heading south.

Not that these deviations were all annoying or a waste of time. Gradually they brought with them an indispensable discovery of what 'African time' was about. Some of it I only learned to understand in retrospect. All my life I have been hurrying – to do something, to get somewhere, even when I had no idea of what that 'something' or 'somewhere' might be – as if I was by nature scared of getting stuck without anything driving me on or luring me elsewhere. But this early, all too brief, exposure to the Africa beyond our borders marked the beginning of a shift. Towards what? I am not sure I can define it: perhaps it is by its very nature indefinable. Perhaps it is just this: that there *need* not be a specified aim or destination. H knew this instinctively. Which was why, very soon afterwards, on her 'aimless' journey through Africa, she could tune in so spontaneously to the continent. One late afternoon, as we were preparing to return to our hotel at Mantenga Falls, H found an old man in a market, a man as ageless and as dignified as a euphorbia. He had been waiting all day for a friend or relative who was supposed to take him home, somewhere in the green hills. But the person had failed to turn up, and now the old man was stranded. He did not seem unduly perturbed about it: if the lift materialised the next day, or the day after, it wouldn't make much difference. Predictably, H proposed that we take him home. Just as predictably, I was upset. While we argued, the old man stood serenely waiting. He must have known who would win the argument.

'But look!' I was fighting back, angrily and unreasonably.

'There's nothing to look at,' H said imperturbably. 'Let's just take him home. He is tired. He is old.'

'But we'll be late,' I insisted.

'Late for what?'

I turned directly to the old man, trying to bypass her. 'I really am terribly sorry,' I explained to him. 'But we have an urgent appointment at our hotel.'

He shrugged.

'Please understand,' I pleaded, beginning to be persuaded by my own urgency. 'We *must* get back to our hotel before dark.'

All he said was the single word, 'Why?'

It hit me in the guts. *Why* indeed? Why did we *have* to be anywhere at any given time? I took a deep breath and, avoiding H's brown eyes, said, 'Let's go. If you will show us the way?'

It was a journey of about an hour. The sun was down before we arrived at the old man's village. For most of the time he had a solemn little smile on his face carved with deep incisions like a Makonde mask, his timeless eyes hooded. He was sitting very straight, a posture like an aloe, in a silence that seemed to have been gathered inside him for years, perhaps for centuries and generations; but it was a radiating silence, spreading gently through the car, like something he wished to share with us. A silence of suffering perhaps; certainly of understanding, of wisdom and forgiveness.

And by the time we arrived, I felt as if all the earlier anger and anxiety and resentment had ebbed out of me. I had learned a lesson, the terms of which I could not yet explain, and which even now I am not sure I have fully grasped. But it has to do with not resisting and yet not being passive either: perhaps an acknowledgement of complicity, not in some act of commission or omission, but simply complicity in life, in the hour he had generously deigned to share with us. I had the feeling, then, of knowing, and understanding, something more about this continent which was his, but also mine. The silence persisted on the long way back; but this time there was nothing tense or anxious about it; we held hands, our fingers lightly clasped. We were together, now.

And once we finally arrived at Ponta do Ouro, our destination, and settled into the bright yellow and red cabins allotted to us, after attempting the first night or two to sleep on the beach and being devoured alive by swarms of sand fleas and small crabs and man-eating mosquitoes and all ten plagues of ancient Egypt, it was bliss. But there was a dark undercurrent too, provided by a copy of an old magazine that had found its way with us, that featured a long discussion between James Baldwin and someone called Schulberg that did the rounds and provoked endless discussion which never strayed far from the aches and agonies of the promised land, so near and yet seemingly so distant.

There were other reminders of where we came from. Almost next to the holiday cabins of Ponta do Ouro was a military camp where a detachment of the Mozambican army was stationed – melancholy-looking young Portuguese men, none of them appearing a day older than sixteen, plodding about in army boots far too big for them, and carrying automatic rifles that made them look even more like kids playing. The saddest thing about all of this was that the soldiers had brought a mascot with them, a small black boy whose parents had been killed in the war. What made it even more poignant, was that he had his own mascot, a baby vervet monkey that he took with him wherever he went, and that clung to him as if to its mother, its wizened black face more ancient than any we had seen.

The war, we learned, was not far away; was never far away. Frelimo and Renamo. Africa and Europe. The ubiquitous war of Africa and its Others. Soon, within a month or so, H would also be drawn into it when she was approached to carry messages to people who subsequently turned out to be Frelimo men. In due course the news would filter back to me, when a contingent of security police turned up and wanted to know what *I* knew about a certain Miss H and her involvement with planned terrorist activities in neighbouring states. I was duly warned: 'We want you to know that we're keeping an eye on you, we're watching you very, very closely.' Because it concerned race relations, and because I, as a white, was not supposed to get involved in the things blacks were up to.

After that holiday, if holiday it was, black would never again be simply black to me, or white white. What was intensified by this journey, was the raging turmoil in my mind about the 'place' of a white person in a black struggle for liberation. It was dramatised by the debate between the white, liberal, Jewish Schulberg and the black Baldwin: Schulberg arguing with devastating clarity and logic, trying to remain calm and to reason, Baldwin becoming ever more passionate. Logically speaking, Baldwin would point out time and time again, yes, logically, logically, you may be right – 'but, Budd, we live with pain and rage – with pain and rage.' Many years later, at the Edinburgh Festival, the only occasion on which I ever met James Baldwin, there were moments when, through the layers of weariness and disappointment that had become heavier with the years, that smouldering passion still shone through his words and set his sad eyes alight. *We live with pain and rage – with pain and rage.* Those translucent days with H and Breyten and Yolande – green in Swaziland, golden in Mozambique – brought a new, real and deep understanding of what South Africa was about, what had accumulated in its past, what marked its wounded present, and what might possibly still lie ahead. About what my own possible part in it all might be, I still could not define very clearly. But I knew that I was moving towards a moment of choice, and that there was no way it could be avoided.

A few weeks after this holiday, H left on her meanderings through Africa. For me, it was an agonising time. She was an incorrigibly bad correspondent and sometimes a month or more would go by without any news at all, when fears and apprehensions and suspicions took over. And when, always well after the event, she would report on her journey and I would realise that my fears had been groundless, even though what she had lived through was often enough to turn one grey overnight. But she would always shrug or laugh it off. I was left to conjure up images of shaky bus rides on dusty roads, with the person next to you peacefully, or noisily, sleeping with a heavy head resting on your chest or in your lap; of spendings nights with strangers in some godforsaken little hovel in the *bundu*; playing on an idyllic beach in Zanzibar, paddling in a leaky canoe or trying to catch fish with your bare hands; fighting off flies, or mosquitoes; attending political rallies in market squares and scattering in all directions to get away from police; sometimes hiding away from random gunfire in the night; wallowing in muddy water, or falling ill and being attended by strangers muttering in foreign languages; attending the funeral of a dead child; speaking to priests in white robes or dog collars, noses and cheeks flushed in alcoholic scarlet or purple, sombre as marabous; gazing at the snows of Kilimanjaro in the distance; admiring the flight of pelicans rising unbelievably high on thermals, or flocks of flamingoes ascending pink against the horizon like an early dawn; or staring in disbelief at European men in impeccable white playing cricket or bowls or croquet on a lawn at the edge of a lake; being assailed by beggars and lepers, by the maimed and the famished and the altogether hopeless; *Mayibuye Africa*.

I followed her whole journey on a map, cherishing memories that seemed more and more unlikely, dreaming about a future that seemed more and more impossible. Africa was reduced to this map, as I tried to wend my own way through Grahamstown, the small university town that had become my refuge – not a refuge from the world, but a different kind of immersion in it. I talked to white friends who had in various ways been scarred by futile or meaningful attempts at involvement 'on behalf of' others: Norman, whose experience of solitary confinement had caused him to withdraw more and more deeply into himself; Terrence, banned from interacting socially with more than one person at a time, after he had spent time in the Transkei investigating security police activities and atrocities in their vain attempts to bring to boot the murderers of a family of whites at Bashee Bridge. They had rounded up all the men and boys from mere children to venerable old patriarchs, near-suffocating or half-drowning them and forcing them to ride the broomstick 'helicopter', or taking them up in real helicopters, tying their ankles together and pushing them out to dangle upside down, and beating them, and beating them, and beating them. I spoke to black friends, some of whom had been at the receiving end of these tortures and had survived, somehow, to tell their stories. Not broken, at least not all of them, but made more resolute, more dedicated, more passionate about one day, that utterly impossible day, when the dry white season would end and rain would come down to assuage the thirsty land.

There were black students to whom I would give extra classes in the afternoons. Sometimes with unexpected results, as when one of them, a tall and gentle and always smiling man called Prins, who had a contact in the post office, started to warn me when the security police had given instructions for my mail to be opened, or my phone to be tapped. 'Be careful,' was all he would say. 'Be careful. There are eyes and ears all over the place. Don't let them catch you. We need you outside. Be careful.'

But this happened only rarely. I was still acclimatising, feeling my way, learning.

During university holidays I often went to Cape Town. Jan Rabie and

Marjorie Wallace's home in Green Point was a bazaar for artists of any description. What made it unusual, for someone with my background, was that this must have been, for Afrikaans speakers, one of the only places in the country where colour didn't matter at all. I have often wondered how many foreigners from abroad landed in Cape Town with only a single name and address: *Jan Rabie*. They were of all persuasions: from Tory or Republican to Labourite or communist, from men of the cloth to women of dubious virtue, from rabble-rousers to academics, from grave, pale researchers to extravagant adventurers. No wonder that this was H's first port of call, on the day I met her. And it was no coincidence that this was the place where our campaign against censorship was officially launched, and where I first met Ingrid.

But the real eye-opener, the real window-opener, was the opportunity of meeting 'people of colour' without any inhibition or question. For many of us, more and more as apartheid grew worse, it was easier to meet an Indian from Durban, a coloured from Cape Town, a black from Johannesburg, in London or Paris or Cologne. Because of its tradition, this could happen almost 'normally' in a place like Grahamstown. But the context was English. It was more or less expected that meeting across the colour divide would occur more readily there. The house in Cheviot Place was Afrikaans. And that made all the difference.

Some of the lasting friendships of my life began there, over coffee or red wine or one of Marjorie's inimitable *boboties* – prepared in a black pot that grew blacker and smaller every time it was used, since Marjorie did not believe in ever washing it, and simply allowed the encrustations to build up over the years, restricting more and more the little round hollow in the centre. This was where I first met the writer and academic Kenny Parker. The robust and ever-voluble Richard Rive. The poet and dramatist with the gentle smile, the shy eyes and the acerbic wit, Adam Small. And all of this, step by step, bit by bit, helped me to acclimatise in my own land, to redefine the parameters of the 'normal'. To argue and reason and fight, and to find one another, and laugh, and embrace, and learn to believe in the future.

*   *   *

There were setbacks too. When *Back to the Sun*, after three rewrites, was finally done, my usual Afrikaans publishers, Human & Rousseau, responded negatively. Both the directors, Koos Human and Leon Rousseau, wrote me well-meaning and deeply sincere and utterly damning letters. By then it was already 1968, and I was in Europe again. The letters boiled down to the same verdict: I had made, they said, what might well have been the worst mistake of my life by getting involved with H. She clearly had no good influence on me and was threatening to turn me into something I could never be: a political writer. This, they told me, went against everything that had made me a writer. They couldn't very well tell me to break up the relationship. Through a cruel and perhaps crude stroke of irony our relationship was, just then, in fact crumbling, for reasons that had nothing to do with writing.

With the exception of the devastating blow dealt me by the censors when they banned *Looking on Darkness* five years later, this was the bleakest moment of my writing career. In both cases, staggering and struggling to remain standing as currents and countercurrents of emotions tried to sweep me from my feet, there was ultimately only one decision that branded itself into my consciousness: *You're not going to get me down. You're not going to win. I won't stop writing. I'll bloody well show you.* Melodramatic defiance, of the adolescent kind. But right then it was all I could hold on to. And during that year in Paris I was pushed much, much further than before on the road to becoming what Koos and Leon had found me incapable of: a political writer. With this supreme irony, that I now believe they were right. By temperament I was never a political writer. From that time on I could not write anything that was *not* political. But that only confirmed, I think, that I was indeed not a 'political writer' in the sense in which it is usually understood. I don't think I have ever written 'about' politics. If politics permeated everything I wrote, it was as part of that much-misunderstood notion, the 'human condition'. The public, or social, dimension of the human condition. What fascinated me then, as it fascinates me now, is the concept of *story*. And it is hard altogether to exclude a political dimension from the telling of any story.

In some other respects I know they were wrong. It was not the relationship with H that was at fault: that was, and remains, one of the most wholesome and rewarding and most necessary experiences of my life. It was the *writing* that was bad, in and of itself. *Back to the Sun* may be the worst book I have ever perpetrated – and that is saying something. But that was not *because* of H: it was *in spite* of her. I was simply not yet equipped for what I tried to do at the time. But its very failure inspired me to go on. For better or for worse.

Until that moment, before I spent that second spell in Paris, life in Grahamstown had continued in its seemingly undramatic way, to prepare me for the changes that lay ahead. Many of the events that later turned out to have been crucial, happened so quietly that I myself may have been unaware of their full significance at the time.

There was my friendship with Mr Naidoo. We became remarkably close friends, yet to the end we maintained a pattern of decorum and formality. Mr Naidoo. Mr Brink. Much of our daily contact was restricted to his selling, and my buying, his vegetables: he had, beyond doubt, the best fruit and vegetable shop in town; and he could discuss his produce with much more than expert knowledge – he was a connoisseur, he loved vegetables. He had a reverence for life, for all growing things. He also had a degree from Oxford.

And there were special days, when there were no other clients around and he would offer me glimpses into his two related passions. One was the major ambition in his life: to marry a white woman. She had to be naturally and emphatically blonde. 'In all the right places,' he calmly affirmed. And he was resigned to waiting for the day when that would be legally possible. He had no doubt that this day would come. Even if he had to wait for a very long time. He would never rant and rave about the injustices of the country, the inhumanity of its laws and restrictions. Composed and quiet, imperturbable, bolstered by his firm and fervent Hindu faith, he was prepared to bide his time with a patience that passeth all understanding.

His second passion, intimately linked to the first, was his admiration of Marilyn Monroe. It was more than admiration or even veneration. It was love. One of the most frighteningly pure and focused loves I have ever witnessed. He did not have photos or press cuttings of her on his walls. But he did have one small and much-thumbed passport-sized photo of her in his wallet, which he once – only once – shared with me, without ever giving an indication of how and from where it had come to him.

One morning when I stepped into the shop, I knew immediately that something awful had happened.

'Good morning, Mr Naidoo.' I said, as every day. 'How are you today?'

'Good morning, Mr Brink.' He made a small movement with his head. 'Not well, I'm afraid.'

'What's the matter?' I asked, with real concern.

'She died,' he said very quietly.

I had a sinking feeling. His mother? A sister? A dear and special friend?

'Who?' I asked after a silence.

'Miss Monroe,' he replied. And then he started to cry. There was nothing dramatic – and most certainly nothing melodramatic – about it. Just tears that ran down from his eyes. And a single sob.

'Please excuse me,' he said, and turned his back to me.

It was as if something had closed inside him.

After a long time he turned back to me. His face was as inscrutable as a dark woodcarving.

Then he added, and that was the closest I ever saw him to despair, 'Now I know I will never get married.'

And only a few months later he died. He was barely fifty.

There was also Chief Albert Luthuli. Like the majority of South Africans, but very few whites among them, I was elated, and deeply moved, when he was awarded the Nobel Peace Prize. When he travelled to Oslo in December 1961 to accept the Prize that had already been announced the year before, it was, in fact, after coming back from my studies in Paris, the first intimation I had that there might be some hope for South Africa after all. If someone like him could be afforded this kind of international recognition, there might yet be hope. How wrong one can be. It became evident very soon that, far from relenting, the apartheid government was going to be more vicious in their attempts to silence and subdue this great man of peace. For in a country that was becoming increasingly polarised and turbulent in the wake of Sharpeville, Luthuli represented an almost old-worldly faith in human goodness, and in peaceful relations. There are indications that he was sidelined by his own people at the time when, in reaction to Sharpeville, the ANC made its watershed decision to embark on violent resistance. Living in the internal exile imposed by banning orders, kept out of reach of the public, he was forced into a private and painful existence largely confined to his home in Natal. Gradually, his memory began to fail and his ability to act or to lead was emasculated. Still, his name remained a beacon, if largely as a reminder of what the country *could* have become if he had been heeded in time.

Early in 1967, I was invited to give a series of lectures at the University of Natal in Durban – which would be my first experience of that city, apart from a visit of only a few hours immediately after my first marriage, when Estelle and I went there to place her wedding bouquet on her father's grave. When the invitation came, it was almost like being afforded another occasion of laying flowers on a grave. I immediately wrote to the authorities to ask permission to visit Luthuli. There was no answer. I resigned myself to the inevitable.

Then, a day after my arrival, there was a telephone call for me, from a senior officer in the security police. A very friendly, almost fatherly voice told me that they had considered my request but that, unfortunately, it was not possible to give me the permission I had requested. But anyway, the officer assured me, there was no point in such a visit. The old chief was no longer the man he had once been, and one should respect his privacy. And he added, as the kind of afterthought the security police are so good at, that to be absolutely frank, Chief Luthuli was a grossly overrated man. No real influence at all. Not highly regarded by his own people.

If that were true, I thought, why would the government be so strict about keeping visitors at bay, imposing such near-total silence on a frail old man, trying to deny his very existence? There were, it occurred to me, good reasons for getting to know this country more intimately than I had done over the past few years.

A pity, almost, that I was practically on the point of returning to Paris.

SESTIGERS, CENSORS AND
SECURITY POLICE

IT WAS DURING THE YEARS LEADING UP TO MY RETURN TO PARIS IN '68 THAT censorship turned really bad. The situation was surprisingly complicated. Among the events that held me in South Africa, there was the emergence of a new generation of Afrikaans writers, the Sestigers (Sixtiers); among those that prompted me to leave was the almost simultaneous crackdown of censorship. The complication lay in the fact that, in the South Africa of the sixties, neither could be imagined without the other.

Within only a few months of my return in August 1961, I received a letter from the young author Chris Barnard (no relation, I should make very clear, of the surgeon who a few years later became famous for succeeding with the world's first heart transplant). Chris was then fiction editor of the magazine *Die Brandwag*, for which I had during my student years, and even during my stay in Paris, written potboiler short stories. He offered me an opportunity of emptying my drawers of old manuscripts. But much more importantly, he broached the subject of 'a new generation' of writers in Afrikaans. This was something that had much preoccupied me in Paris. I had even written an impassioned essay for the magazine *Huisgenoot* pleading for such a new wave of writing: taking my cue from the Dutch writers known as the Tagtigers (Eightiers) of the previous century, who had swept away all the dead wood of conventional writing in Holland to establish a spectrum of bold and passionate prose and poetry that infused the Romantic movement in the Low Countries with the inspiration of Impressionism and Symbolism.

In our context, of course, it was no longer a matter of Romanticism, but all the ripple effects of modernism and existentialism. My essay wasn't published until several years later, as a kind of nostalgic backward glance, but from the correspondence with Chris it was soon evident that we were fired by the same kind of vision for a drastic overhaul of Afrikaans fiction.

Ever since the thirties, when a group of young Afrikaans poets had boldly established radical new forms of individualism, our literature had been striving to break away from the more conventional expressions that had characterised it since the time of the First Language Movement in the late nineteenth century. Various spasms of renewal had followed, but these were invariably restricted to poetry. Fiction and drama still lagged depressingly behind; and by the time European literature was already experimenting with exciting new forms of writing, Afrikaans fiction was still largely stuck in nineteenth-century naturalism, echoing, at second or third hand, the surface features of the bleaker endeavours of the form, but without the passions of the great Russians, or the genius of a Hardy or a Hamsun, let alone an Undset, a Proust or a Musil. Our fiction, as the poet N. P. van Wyk Louw characterised it, was still locked in a local, cosy kind of realism dominated by locusts, drought and poor whites.

Now came the discovery that a new generation of Afrikaans prose writers was waiting in the wings: we had widely different backgrounds and styles and interests, but one passion we shared – to bring Afrikaans literature, particularly fiction and drama, up to date with the rest of the world. Most of us, by that time, had spent shorter or longer periods abroad, mainly in Paris, and that experience emphasised the parochial closeness of the local cultural scene. Chris had not yet taken his gap year, but was preparing for it – in spite of the misgivings of his then wife. I can remember her arguing: 'I'm really not eager to go to Europe. I'm scared that it may change my view of the world, and I'm so happy with the one I have right now.' What made the comment memorable was that it exactly captured the attitude of all too many Afrikaners at the time.

Several authors had begun to move into prominence during the fifties. The early leading figure was Jan Rabie (born 1920) with his piercing brown eyes and defiant black goatee, his work strongly inspired by French writers like Henri Michaux and the existentialists during his long stay in Paris. His fiction was in no small measure one of the reasons why I ultimately decided to go to Paris myself – and one of the consolations about coming back in 1961, when he broke new ground with his passionate explorations of the Afrikaners' early interaction with Africa. There was also Etienne Leroux (born 1922), a Mephistophelian figure always obscured behind dark glasses, soon to become the leading novelist of the generation, whose outrageous satires in the vein of the myth-mongering of his time provoked the religious and political establishment with his irreverence and wit. But he presented this establishment with a peculiar challenge: as the son of a respected cabinet minister in the Nationalist government, he was not an easy target for ostracism or attack. Bartho Smit (born 1924), a dramatist, deceptively gentle in manner and appeareance. As a publisher, uncomfortably ensconced in the right-wing house of Afrikaanse Pers-Boekhandel, later Perskor, he was something of a mentor to most of the rest of us and was the moving spirit behind the quarterly journal *Sestiger* which, for the two years of its existence, became the mouthpiece of the whole group. After early work in a conventional, if charming, vein, Dolf van Niekerk (born 1923), a self-effacing loner, made an electrifying impression with his existentialist reimagining of early twentieth century Afrikaner history. The other Sestigers were younger. Adam Small (born 1936) was the only coloured writer in the group, an affirmative presence with his angry and satirical poetry, his virulent rejection of apartheid, and his brilliant play, *Kanna hy kô hystoe* (*Kanna Comes Home*), which brought Afrikaans drama up to date with what had been happening in the rest of the world: an evocation of the lives of a coloured family who are forced to bear the brunt of the only one among them who manages to break away and lead a prosperous life in Canada, until the death of the materfamilias, Makiet, forces Kanna to return home. Abraham (Braam) de Vries, born in 1937, whose eyes, forever gleaming behind thick glasses, missed nothing, soon became adept at exposing the terror and magic that lurk below the surface of the everyday. And of course Chris Barnard (born 1939), a gentle giant, revealed an early interest in the taboos of apartheid before making a decisive break with realism in favour of symbolism, and an exploration of the absurd.

On the fringes of the Sestiger group the most important new writer was Breyten Breytenbach, who had settled in Paris in 1960, while I was still there, although we did not meet until 1964, when Ingrid and I were on our disastrous way to Spain. Breyten hit the world of Afrikaans letters like a force of nature, splashing a black-southeaster of surrealism, existentialism and Zen Buddhism across the still arid South African landscape. For many years, and in the minds of many people, the appellation of 'Sestiger' applied preeminently to Breyten. Yet he persistently refused to be regarded as a member of the 'movement', both before and after his imprisonment from 1976 to 1983 on largely trumped-up charges of 'terrorism'.

Others on the periphery of the core group of Sestigers included the master of Chekhovian impressionism, the short-story writer Hennie Aucamp; Elsa Joubert with her explorations of Africa and her persistent redefinitions of the Afrikaner world and heritage; and Karel Schoeman, who rather preciously cultivated the image of the enigmatic outsider, whose delicate prose explores the human condition within a South African context. In his best work he was a consummate novelist, but he resolutely steered a course separate from that of the Sestigers.

And then there was Ingrid. Who was a Sestiger in all but name, and who produced the major poetic work of the time in Afrikaans. Her prose alone, a handful of exquisitely wrought stories and sketches, should qualify her for inclusion in the group. So did her dramatic break with the *ancien régime* represented by her father, her uncompromising rejection of apartheid, and her embracing, under the influence of Uys Krige, of the free-verse forms of Lorca and his South American successors.

What all these different talents and energies needed, was a public forum. It was Bartho Smit who used his contacts in the publishing world to obtain access, during 1962, to an existing literary magazine, the moribund *Tydskrif vir Letterkunde (Journal for Literature)*. At the time, this journal was edited by an anthropologist, Professor Abel J. Coetzee, a literary nonentity – but one with vast aspirations. In 1963 he published, in Holland, a survey of Afrikaans literature in which he presented himself to the European public as the greatest novelist in the language, and an entirely unknown individual, Soul Erasmus Smit, as the undisputed monarch of Afrikaans poetry. SES, as it happened, was a pseudonym of the same Coetzee. Eager for recognition, Coetzee was readily persuaded – perhaps conned by the smooth-talking Bartho? – to turn his little journal into a mouthpiece for the Sestigers. The title was changed to 60 (retaining *Tydskrif vir Letterkunde* as a subtitle), and all of us were co-opted as members of the editorial board. But Coetzee insisted on being allowed to write the first editorial. This was a catastrophe. Out-Heroding Herod, in the firm belief that he was doing us a favour by masquerading as the patron of Renewal, Coetzee enthusiastically presented the Sestigers as nihilists and iconoclasts. There was an immediate outcry in conservative circles, and a serious threat that Coetzee's generous government subsidy for his journal might be withdrawn.

He made a precipitate volte-face. In his editorial for the next issue he totally rejected everything he had said in the previous article, intimating that he had been brainwashed by the Sestigers for their own devious purposes, and asked Bartho to withdraw from 60. The whole editorial board resigned in protest, and while Coetzee continued to fulminate in every subsequent issue throughout the year, Bartho managed to find another publisher for our own project. In November 1963 the new journal, *Sestiger*, made its first appearance. Bartho remained the main inspiration behind it, but because of his editorial ties to APB Publishers I was asked to take over as editor of the journal for the next two years. It had been decided from the outset that we would not allow it to run for too long: we needed to put our case as clearly as possible to the public, after which we wished to go our separate ways in order to avoid being perceived as a 'group' or a 'movement' with a sinister agenda. I now believe that the impact could have been stronger had we persisted for another year or two.

There were only two occasions on which all the Sestigers came together: the first, when we decided to launch the journal; the second, when we decided to kill it. As it turned out, they were also the only occasions on which I ever met Dolf van Niekerk. The others all remained good friends – with occasional misunderstandings and blow-ups, but never serious enough to jeopardise the underlying ties.

Thinking back now, those early days inevitably appear, through the romantic haze of nostalgia, as an unforgettable experience. Why? Because we were all so very young, most of us in our twenties; we were engaged in a revolution of our own, colliding head-on with all the forces of our social and political establishment, threatened by dire punishment and violent repression, yet at the same time borne along on a wave of enthusiasm among the young generation. On both sides of the great generational divide we were taken seriously, out of all proportion. The establishment saw in us the embodiment of all the destructive forces of Satan and the Antichrist. Sunday after Sunday we were attacked from the pulpits of the Dutch Reformed Church. There were clamorous debates in parliament about our work. Our books were burned in autos-da-fé on the church squares of East London and several other towns. In due course the central political faultlines in the country – those between *verlig* (enlightened) and *verkramp* (narrow-minded) – were defined by attitudes for or against the Sestigers. There were public debates where staunch pillars of the community denounced the enemy within. One mother-of-the-nation made a lasting impression by recounting in a choking voice how, while reading Etienne Leroux's *Seven Days at the Silbersteins'*, she had been sexually aroused exactly sixty-nine times. And a patriarchal dominee assured a public meeting that this same novel was a vehicle for filth and anarchy and moral destruction, 'not only because of what is described on the pages, but most especially because of what one can imagine happening *between* the chapters'.

In a long argument with a professor who had been one of my literary mentors at university, he complained vociferously about the 'filthy language' in the book: there was no place in literature, he ranted, for a word like *fuck*. I could not help but remember Brendan Behan's response to this kind of accusation: 'But words,' he told a complaining woman, 'words are *innocent little things*' – holding his thumb and forefinger very closely together in a graphic illustration of what he meant – 'the filth is in your own fucking mind!' And to emphasise his outrage the righteous professor thumped his desk: 'And to think you studied at *this* university!' he exclaimed. 'This is a *Christian* university!' 'But Professor,' I protested, 'there is no single word in this book that I have not heard many times a day on this very campus.' 'Ah, but that's different,' he countered. 'Those are spoken words. But here in your book those words are *written*.'

Long live the written word, I thought. And fuck the rest.

The debates and arguments went on and on, becoming more virulent by the day. Inevitably, this was where censorship played its hand.

It has invariably been the handmaiden of any regime with totalitarian tendencies – most particularly when that regime feels itself threatened. Even so, in South Africa, censorship was not high on the list of priorities when the Nationalist government came to power in 1948. Not because it did not feel threatened, but because it perceived other threats as more pressing for the time being. Moreover, the presence of a large black majority, set to develop into the most important threat to continued white rule, could still be 'kept in place', through an extension of brutal colonial practices; and as most of this presence was still illiterate, the written word was not as yet much of a factor in the equation. The English were bound to criticise and attack, but they were expected to play by the rules anyway, and if not, at that stage no Afrikaner was likely to take seriously any opposition from that quarter. And Afrikaners themselves were unlikely to oppose their own leaders. Ever since the First Language Movement in the late nineteenth century the fledgling literature had allied itself most loyally to the political leadership: the language itself was largely perceived as a mere extension of the political struggle.

But from the mid-fifties it became apparent that Afrikaans literature was developing modes of expression independent of, and at times even hostile to, the ideological thinking of the new regime. By the beginning of the sixties it was no longer possible for the authorities to take for granted the unquestioning support of writers and other cultural workers; and the same kind of rift was becoming obvious between writing and religion. Nationalist policies had always depended heavily on the support of the Afrikaans Reformed Churches, and the questioning of religious doctrine, even if only by implication, was seen increasingly as a threat to the political authority of the state as well.

The groundswell of popular enthusiasm for the Sestigers, especially among the young, caught the government unprepared, which prompted hurried moves towards new forms of cultural control, specifically censorship. Initially at least, the authorities had to tread cautiously, trying not to offend either their traditional base of churchgoing, conservative supporters, or the increasingly visible and voluble younger generation eager to identify themselves with international trends that followed in the wake of the Second World War. They were, after all, the next generation of voters. If the government were indeed pushed to choose between these opposing constituencies, they were likely to turn to their traditional support base on the right; but for the time being they tried to walk a tightrope between the extremes. This provided us with some breathing space – but it was becoming more and more obvious that it could not last for long.

We tried to use the gap with a vigorous campaign against the looming Publications Control Act, gaining the near-unanimous support of English and Afrikaans writers alike. It is shameful to reflect, today, that most of this campaign still concerned whites only, just as the first wave in the renewal of Afrikaans literature by the Sestigers was predominantly white, concerned with matters of aesthetic form and expression rather than political content or involvement. Almost all the heavyweights of white South African literature in English and Afrikaans – including van Wyk Louw, Dirk Opperman and other leading poets in Afrikaans, as well as Alan Paton and Nadine Gordimer and lesser but still significant lights like Jack Cope – joined the fray and petitioned the government to refrain from acting against literature. As early as 1961 van Wyk Louw had been bludgeoned by Prime Minister H. F. Verwoerd in a notorious confrontation about an historical play on the Anglo-Boer War, in which Louw had had the 'temerity' to ask questions about nationhood.

After Jan Rabie and I had written the first few letters condemning censorship in the Cape Town newspaper, *Die Burger*, it turned into an avalanche; and on that memorable afternoon of 18 April, 1963, a group of us were gathered in the lounge of Jan Rabie's rambling old house in Cape Town, when Ingrid walked in, barefoot and provocative, and the movement against censorship officially began, and the course of my life was changed.

The petition we organised that afternoon, soon acquired momentum;

and as the battle heated up, the godfather of the censorship bill in parliament, Ingrid's father, Abraham, made such a hash of it that he lost all credibility and faded from the scene. We approached the two writers most likely to be 'acceptable' to the government, Bill de Klerk on the Afrikaans side, advocate Gerald Gordon on the English, to present our petition. On the surface, of course, it made no difference; but the censorship movement had been thoroughly discredited and the Act was launched rather lamely. Bowing to widespread pressure the government appointed as chief censor a respected professor of literature, Gerrit Dekker, who had been my main mentor at university; and when Etienne Leroux's *Silbersteins* and my *Lobola* found themselves among the first books to be submitted to the Publications Control Board, it was obvious that – for the moment – we had nothing to be afraid of. But any book that could not rely on being regarded as 'literature' – a distinction that could not but cause some embarrassment to writers – could not count on any protection. And once the censors claimed their first victim, Wilbur Smith's rather innocuous *When the Lion Feeds*, everybody realised that the hunt was now open.

Even before Sestigers and Censors prepared for battle, there had been ominous signs that the forces of darkness were being organised against anything acknowledged – and branded – as 'new'. Because what was 'new' was immediately identified with 'strange' or 'foreign': that is, strange and foreign to the core of the *volk*, the *nation*. The history of the publication of *Lobola vir die Lewe* provides a chilling, sometimes hilarious, illustration of these forces. When the novel was originally submitted, from Paris, to the leading 'establishment' publisher, Nasionale Pers, it was turned down, but in a private note accompanying the official letter of rejection, I was advised to submit it to the newly founded publishing house of Human & Rousseau. The novel was accepted, but it turned out to be very hard to find a firm that might be willing to print the manuscript, as most commercial printers had links with either the political establishment or one or other of the churches. At last an English printer was found; but when the book reached the stage of galley proofs, an enterprising Afrikaans-speaking proofreader got hold of it and made a number of impromptu, and extremely crude, translations of dubious passages which he submitted to his employers.

Immediately, the publishing process was stopped. Koos Human persuaded them to send the proofs to Dr W. E. G. Louw, then arts editor of *Die Burger*, and younger brother of the great poet N. P. van Wyk Louw. Louw junior gave his approval, undertook to give it a favourable review in *Die Burger*, and the book could be printed. Even at that stage the publishers still regarded the undertaking as so risky that they did not expect more than a few hundred copies to be sold. It was consequently stipulated in the contract that no royalties would be paid on the first 1,000 copies. Only too relieved that the book would be published regardless, I signed. However, following W. E. G. Louw's rave review, it was sold out almost immediately, and seven or eight reprints followed in due course. I am happy to acknowledge that the contract was then amended, and I was paid for the first 1,000 copies after all.

But the sense of risk, even of danger, persisted. All this had consequences on the personal level as well. There were close friends from my university days who formally broke off contact with me. I had become a traitor, an enemy, an adder in the bosom. Worst of all, I had become a 'communist', the ultimate in the vocabulary of swear words at the time. For me, the saddest loss of all came when my good friend, Koos Rupert, brother of the powerful tobacco and liquor tycoon, Anton, barred me from his house in Stellenbosch. On my very first trip to Europe, with the student tour of 1954, I had met his wife Rona and we'd become close friends. Years later, after she'd met and married Koos and I'd married Estelle, we met again in London and in Spain, and became a close foursome. Once back in South Africa, Koos became a manager in his brother's business in Stellenbosch, and I a lecturer at Rhodes. We continued to see each other regularly. The first edition of one of my first novels, written on that early students' tour to Europe when I was only eighteen, I had even dedicated to Rona; and after their marriage I'd changed the dedication to include both of them. After *Lobola*, the break came.

I'd just arrived in Stellenbosch, where they lived, for a series of lectures; and telephoned immediately to find out when I could see them. Rona answered. She was strangely subdued. After a minute or two she excused herself: their little daughter was in the bath, she explained, and needed attention. Koos came to the phone.

When I eagerly enquired about seeing them soon, he said very curtly, 'I don't think we have anything to say to each other.'

'What on earth . . . ?' I stammered.

'I assure you it is better this way,' said Koos.

It took some time to filter through: I had become an enemy of Afrikanerdom; in his position he could not risk being regarded as my friend. It would be bad for business.

Coming from him, I had no choice but to resign myself. But Rona? She was just not that kind of person. I remembered our many eager conversations, on our European tour and afterwards; all the confidences we'd exchanged, our dreams for the future, our shared love of music, of literature, of art. Her ringing laughter, her sense of humour. Something in her had been denied and diminished by what happened that day. And until the day of her untimely death, years later, I never had a chance of discussing with her the break, or the dark forces that had precipitated it.

Still, in those early days of censorship, such losses became part and parcel of a writer's life. And not everything was depressing or regrettable. Sooner or later, we all knew, the Damocles sword would fall. The media remained interested and added their buzz to the situation. Not only the South African press, but newspapers in Britain and the US were reporting on it, promoting the Sestigers to a dubious status of almost-celebrity. The problem was that even talking to the BBC was widely seen in South Africa, most particularly in the government-supporting Afrikaans press, as an act of blatant betrayal. It made us more defiant; but at the same time it was cause for concern. Being regarded as a traitor, was not an easy thing to face.

This mentality went very far back in Afrikaner history. The image of the small nation battling for survival against great odds, had fed into the Afrikaner psyche since its very origins – inspired, no doubt, by the example of the Israelites in the desert. The notion of 'us' and 'them' was part of what defined our existence. The memory of the Anglo-Boer War had only strengthened this image. To be 'cast out' was a fate worse than death.

Yet it was an image that was being redefined through our own experience. During my student years at Potchefstroom University, we had witnessed from close up, a widely admired professor of law, L. J. du Plessis, attempting to defy the apartheid establishment on moral and legal grounds. When the government retaliated by turning on him the full, formidable state apparatus of ostracism, he was crushed. Yet only a few years later, another impressive man from Potchefstroom, the Revd Beyers Naudé, took the same risk, and this time it proved impossible to crush him – among other things, because he learned to find alliances elsewhere, *outside* of the Afrikaner laager. He transformed his early, chauvinist loyalty to 'my people' to the more inclusive notion of 'our people', and in the end he became one of the enduring heroes of the struggle for liberation. But the costs were almost unbearable: for years he could not pursue his vocation as a preacher; he no longer had an income to subsist on, he was banned and persecuted in unimaginably petty ways. Still, he had the moral courage to survive, and ultimately to prevail.

As for the Sestigers, what saved us was the amazing support we continued to enjoy from the young white, Afrikaner generation. Rather than breaking us, the government risked causing a rift within its own ranks. The system survived. But it was the start of a long and tortuous political haemorrhage, fed by numerous other factors, that in the long run contributed to the demise of the National Party. Yes, they did their level best to cast us out into the wilderness: but because of the support we continued to enjoy from within the ranks of the nation, we simply refused to accept rejection. This was a moral victory, the importance of which took a long time properly to appreciate. And it was not only the young generation which supported us: with several notable exceptions, the literary establishment as a whole, including some of the poets and writers who had helped to define the very notion of 'Afrikanerdom', was essentially on our side. The divisions that began to run through all layers and dimensions of the *volk* were slowly but very surely being eroded, splintering the nation to its foundations. At the heart of this entire experience lay the acknowledgement that the 'us' and 'them' of earlier days were no longer as readily distinguishable as before: the enemy was now *within*, as suggested by Jack Cope's book on the Sestigers.

For the moment, we were still relatively safe from prosecution. The Publications Control Board was largely dominated by responsible and respected men of letters. Significantly, there were no women. Pressure from the mainly lunatic fringe on the right – crackpots like Professor Hennie Terblanche and the weighty dominee Dan de Beer of the Action Moral Standards movement, could be neutralised, even though their rage continued to simmer in the dark. And after Professor Dekker left the board, to be succeeded by a career journalist with failed literary aspirations, Jannie Kruger, ex-editor of the right-wing newspaper, *Die Transvaler*, we knew that we were living on borrowed time. The string from which the sword of Damocles was suspended, was becoming noticeably frayed.

In January, 1974 the sword fell. By that time I had had some experience of informal censorship, but not as yet any open confrontation with the Publications Control Board. In 1964 I had written the novel *Orgie* (*Orgy*). The book was, among other things, a quite elaborate typographical experiment, and Ingrid and I spent hours configuring the final version. It had originally been submitted to Bartho's publishing firm, APB; by the time I left in June 1964 to join Ingrid in Europe, it had reached the stage of galley proofs, the dust jacket had been designed, and production was well under way. But at that stage Bartho's superiors intervened, the whole project was stopped and the book was killed. The trip to Europe having delayed the final signing of the contract and the publisher was able to get away unscathed. Subsequently, an enterprising one-man firm in Cape Town, John Malherbe, offered to take over the book, payed an advance of R300 (£150), and turned it into a beautiful bibliophile edition. This was the closest I had come to a brush with official censorship. Then everything changed.

Kennis van die Aand (Looking on Darkness) marked the beginning of my writing overtly in opposition to apartheid. Even a decade earlier, in *Lobola vir die Lewe*, there had been several passages prompted by the 'South African situation', specifically events to which I had been alerted by Sharpeville and by my readings in our embassy in Paris, concerning the infamous Sergeant Nic Arlow and others of his ilk. But most of these references had been weeded out by the publishers before the book came out. This time it was different. The book depicted the coloured actor Joseph Malan as a contemporary Christ and above all, his relationship with a white woman and his torture by the Security Police. It was written largely, as Baldwin would have said, in 'pain and rage'. And my publishers, Human & Rousseau, turned it down for fear of censorship. I approached my special friend Daantjie Saayman, previously a staff member of Human & Rousseau. He was an outrageous *bon vivant*, an inveterate bibliophile, an indomitable rebel, and an incorrigible adventurer. He had once walked up the length of Africa and spent some time with a tribe of Bedouins, before returning to become an itinerant bookseller and finally a publisher. In his youth, he'd worked as a traffic cop, but got fired because during his hours on point duty in Cape Town he would sit on his motorbike reading Schopenhauer without understanding a word, he assured me. As the driver of a bus loaded with books, he would top up his education and use books to seduce any females who crossed his way, before settling down, at last, but with his spirit still untamed, with an adorable, adored, and adoring family.

When Daantjie learned of the dead end I had run into with Human & Rousseau, he was immediately enthusiastic about taking over the manuscript for his own small publishing firm, Buren, named for one of the bastions of the Cape Town castle. It was the beginning of a road of mad and wonderful adventure we travelled together, until his deeply lamented, untimely death, of colon cancer, in 1995.

The reaction to the book was immediate, and staggering. There had been love affairs across the colour bar in English novels before this, most movingly in Gordimer's *Occasion for Loving* (1960). But where this had been depicted in Afrikaans previously, it had invariably been placed in a context of moral outrage; here it was presented, simply, as a part of human experience. In fact, the main criticism a respected literary critic, and a good friend, voiced against the book was that the brown man, Joseph Malan, 'acted and reacted just like a white man'. Which was more or less what I had hoped to achieve. An ominous undertone to all the reviews, good and bad, was the question: *What will the censors say?* And depressingly, from that time on, young aspiring writers who sent me their manuscripts for comment, changed their tack: previously, the key question in the accompanying letters would be *Do you think it is good enough to be published?* Henceforth the question would be: *Do you think it will pass the censors?* A devastating comment, indeed, on the state of South African letters in the seventies.

When news came that the novel had actually been referred to the Publications Board for a decision, it led to a feeding frenzy. For weeks on end the story was front-page news. And it travelled abroad, to *Time* and *Newsweek*, to newspapers in Britain, in France, in Germany, in Scandinavia, even in Japan. Within days the book was sold out everywhere. Daantjie was eager to reprint – but knowing it might be banned, he hesitated. The financial situation at Buren had always been precarious. And were a ban to materialise, he simply couldn't risk losing all his stock and having all distributed copies returned. In terms of the Publication Act, no bookshop or library was allowed to keep it on the shelves.

Then came the news that the board had considered the book and had come to a decision: but the public had to wait for the following week's *Government Gazette* before it would be official. Daantjie was frantic. Pressurised from all sides, I decided to bite the bullet. I telephoned Jannie Kruger. When I put the crucial question, he sniggered. 'I'm sorry, my friend,' he said, with that peculiar intonation that can turn *my friend* into one of the most odious expressions in any language, 'but I'm afraid you will have to wait for next Friday's *Government Gazette.*'

I explained Daantjie's predicament to him: a simple answer could save the publishers thousands of rands.

'Sorry, my friend,' he said in his most mellifluous voice. 'But the law is the law, you know.'

'Surely,' I said in exasperation, 'as the author of the book I should have the right to know?'

'Oh, no, no,' he said, 'no, no, no, no. If you want to stay on the right side of the law, there is only one way to get an answer before it is published in the *Gazette.*'

'And that is?' I persisted.

'That is for you to lay a charge against the book yourself. You see, a complainant has the right to be informed the moment a decision has been taken.'

I was flabbergasted. 'You don't really expect me to complain against my own book?'

'Why not?' he asked blithely.

I could not think of an answer.

'Well,' he said, 'if you don't want to do that, you'll just have to wait for next week's *Gazette*. Or,' he added as a mischievous afterthought, 'just wait until this Sunday, and read it in *Rapport*. They always know everything, don't they?' He obviously knew that I wrote a regular column for that Sunday paper.

'Thank you, Oom Jannie,' I said in what must have been a rather strangled voice, using the overly familiar and slightly deprecating appellation by which the Afrikaans press often referred to him.

'Goodbye, my friend,' he said. 'And give my regards to your family.'

I was livid.

I telephoned my close friend Coenie Slabber at *Rapport*, a journalist of remarkable integrity who had helped me through many a tight spot, and told him about the conversation.

'We'll see what we can do,' he said. 'But it's not going to be easy.'

And it was while he was saying this that an outrageous idea came into my head: why not follow Oom Jannie's suggestion to the letter? My book had already been referred to the board; they had taken their decision; nothing I did could make any difference to the outcome.

I telephoned my friend Naas in Johannesburg. Within the hour he called in his secretary, who was also a good friend, and discussed with her the possibility of laying a charge against *Kennis van die Aand*. Before the end of the day her complaint was on Oom Jannie's desk. Two days later his reply, with the official verdict of the board, was in her hands. From there it was whizzed to me, to Coenie Slabber, and to his editor. On that Sunday, *Rapport* broke the news about the ban, with a photocopy of the official letter.

The following months brought an inordinate amount of hard work. Buoyed by the expressions of goodwill and support Daantjie and I received from all over the country, we decided to take what seemed then the only dignified course: challenging the ban in the Supreme Court. We had several approaches from senior counsel to argue our case *pro amici*, but the costs of a trial still threatened to be prohibitive. Some initial trepidation was overcome by newspaper reports about contributions and pledges from people all over the country to fight the ban. Most of these were in the form of small amounts from private individuals: ten rands, five rands, two rands at a time, but soon escalating into the thousands. At the same time, publishers abroad began to show interest. Daantjie somewhat precipitately accepted the first offer, from the now defunct W. H. Allen in London. Not a good choice, with hindsight. The one wonderful advantage of it was that this firm's foreign-rights manager at the time was Carole Blake, now one of the most successful literary agents in the UK: in an amazingly short time she succeeded in clinching foreign deals with twenty or more publishers in the US, Europe and elsewhere, even as far as the Soviet Union and Japan. All of this firmly launched me on a road to heady international success. Unfortunately, W. H. Allen turned out not to be a writer's best friend and in due course the association led to a devastating conclusion and deep unhappiness all round.

But for the time being, the prospects seemed good – provided I could get a translation done as soon as possible. At that stage I really did not feel confident about writing in English, but in a crisis one starts drawing on reserves one never realised one possessed. There was only one thing I was absolutely sure about: I would not play into the hands of the censors by allowing them to silence me. As an Afrikaans writer working exclusively in a small language isolated from the rest of the world, I found myself utterly at the mercy of the South African authorities. That I refused to accept. The only remedy was to make my work accessible through other languages.

Fortunately there were a few English-speaking friends more than prepared to advise and help me. Even when it came to typing the English translation, there was a way out: all my life I have typed with one finger only, which slowed down the process quite drastically; and on this occasion it was advisable to have an English text ready as soon as possible. The daughter of a good Indian friend – the man who had been the original inspiration behind the character of Dilpert in the novel – offered to do the typing. The only drawback was that she identified so strongly with the story that she was crying through large sections of the narrative, and I regularly collected completed pages of the manuscript so stained by tears that I had to use Estelle's hairdryer to make them presentable.

In the meantime our campaign against the ban was taking shape. I pledged most of our foreign advances and royalties to the looming battle, Daantjie, in a deeply touching move, sold the small flock of goats he owned on the farm of a friend in the distant Namaqualand: this had been his insurance policy for the future, the 'pension' saved for his old age. But together we prepared to take on whatever windmills the world could offer.

The Publications Control Board furnished us, as decreed by the state, with full reasons for the ban. If the matter had not been so serious, it would have led to much mirth. The three areas of offensiveness were as follows:

– Blasphemy: every single instance of the (mis)use of God's name was listed as proof of this ungodliness, including every time a character exclaimed something along the lines of, 'My God, it's hot!'

– Pornography: every act of love in the book, every reference to intercourse or the mere possibility of intercourse, featured on the censors' laundry list, with pride of place reserved for the episode in which Joseph has sex with the Dutch girl Annamaria and, outraged by his pedantic attitude, she exclaims: 'Just stop talking, Joseph, Jesus! And fuck me!'

– Endangering the security of the state: the overall set-up of a brown man and a white woman daring to love each other sexually was a frontal attack on the official government policy of apartheid, thereby placing at risk the very foundations of the ideology that kept apartheid going; moreover, the portrayal of the security police was branded as mendacious, insulting and offensive.

Our legal team comprised three lawyers who all, in due course, were appointed as judges: Ernie Grosskopf, Hennie Nel and Gerhard Kuhn. Ultimately everything would depend on the bench. We rejoiced in advance when it transpired that the presiding judge would be Helm van Zyl, a broad-minded man deeply sympathetic to the cause of literature and the arts. But then it was reported that the Cape judge president, Justice Theo van Wyk, had intervened in a manner which, our contacts assured, was entirely irregular, and insisted on taking over himself. Known as an arch-conservative, narrow-minded rightist with a number of axes to grind with liberals in general and in this matter in particular, his presence made the outcome predictable. All we could do was to pin our hopes on his colleagues: Justice Diemont, known as a fair man but one who followed the letter of the law most punctiliously; and Justice Jan Steyn, a perspicacious and humane man of culture and understanding. With luck, we thought, we might expect a verdict of two to one in our favour at best, or two to one against us at worst.

When the decision was finally announced, a full six months later, it was devastating: three-nil in favour of a ban. Justice Steyn confessed later that in his heart he supported a verdict for us; but the terms of the Act simply did not allow him to support any verdict other than one in favour of the decision by the Publications Control Board.

We could still take the matter to the Court of Appeal in Bloemfontein. But the verdict suggested that we had little hope of success there. And we simply could not risk losing any more money. Already, the trial had signalled the end of Buren Publishers. The enormous support from ordinary citizens could be construed as something of a moral victory; the continued success of *Looking on Darkness* and subsequent novels abroad, ensured a widening interest in South African literature in general in the world outside; the way in which local (Afrikaans) writers began to organise resistance against future censorship – leading to the founding of the 'informal' publishing concern of Taurus and the establishment of the Afrikaans Writers' Guild in 1975 – bolstered the cause of literature. But in real and immediate terms we had lost. And the future looked bleak.

It looked even bleaker when in the same year of our trial, 1974, the existing form of control was replaced (a move in which the later state president F. W. de Klerk played an active role) by a more draconian board, no longer allowing any more right of appeal to the courts, and placing more direct power in the hands of the minister. A new chairman of the Appeal Board was appointed, an odious little man, Judge Lammie Snyman. In this new dispensation the causes of extreme nationalism and fundamentalist religion were well served; but literature became a primary victim. The infamous *Jakobsen's Index* of banned publications, which included the work of hundreds of the greatest names in world literature, including Nabokov, Sartre, Faulkner, Steinbeck and numerous others, was expanded to well over 20,000 titles.

* * *

Censorship does not happen in a vacuum. As I was soon to find out, the fact that a book had been banned, almost inevitably made the security police prick up their ears – most particularly of course when 'endangering the security of the state' had been cited as a reason for such action. Since the ban on *Kennis* I was no longer free to come and go as I pleased in South Africa; even my visits abroad were closely monitored. From then on, my telephone was tapped and all my mail, incoming and outgoing, was opened – invariably in such a conspicuous way that it was clearly the intention to make me aware of the surveillance. Even so, initially at least, the Special Branch kept a relatively low profile. Until 27 October, 1975, that is. On that day the gloves came off.

What triggered it, was a radio interview in which the South African ambassador to Washington and the UN, Pik Botha, in his customary blustering way defended his country's racist policies and blithely denied the existence of apartheid. This was well before the explosions of 1976 and 1977; even so I felt sufficiently outraged to take on the ambassador. He was a man who believed in getting his retaliation in first.

On that date in October the *New York Times* published this letter I had dispatched in the wake of Botha's brazen protestations:

It has been reported in the South African press that this country's ambassador to the USA and the UN told Americans in an extensive radio interview: 'You are all the time referring to apartheid, apartheid, apartheid. Multinational development is not apartheid in the sense that the government is keeping peoples from one another – peoples who want to join are free to join.'

Perhaps His Excellency should have somewhat qualified his assertion. As far as individuals are concerned, people of different colours in South Africa are indeed allowed to communicate or 'join', provided they do not worship in the same churches; provided they do not attend the same schools or universities; provided they do not use the same toilets or public transport; provided they do not enjoy cultural, recreational or sports activities together (except with special permission or permit); provided they do not build their houses in the same areas;

provided they do not share government bodies, trade unions or scientific or arts institutions; provided they do not fall in love or wish to get married.

It is, the ambassador said, 'a voluntary way of life, voluntarily decided upon by all the important leaders in my country'. It should, of course, be added that this wholly voluntary way of life is rigidly enforced by probably the most formidable framework of racialistic legislation in the world and, among other things, by a vast organisation of security police who contribute their voluntary bit in the way of detentions, torture and inexplicable deaths. 'All the important leaders in my country' are, of course, part of, or appointed by, the hierarchy of the Nationalist Party.

I do not question the ambassador's right to defend his country. But I do challenge his obvious assumption that this should be done through lies and distortions.

From that moment my experience of censorship became inextricably linked to all 'the battalions of lies and the armies of hate' the Special Branch could muster to crush any individual who dared to challenge their authority as the true rulers of the apartheid state. That was when censorship revealed its real face, of which Jannie Kruger and Lammie Snyman were but the obtusely grimacing masks.

In the meantime, there had been notable developments in the midst of the Sixtiers group. Quite some time earlier, during my year in Paris, in 1968, a new journal, *Kol* (which could mean either *Blot* or *Target*), had been launched in Johannesburg by Bartho Smit and Chris Barnard, with the collaboration of some friends, including the dramatist P. G. du Plessis, the novelist and short-story writer John Miles, and the critic Ampie Coetzee. It did not last for long and never made much of an impact, but it caused a rift among the Sestigers: the Johannesburg group tended to stick to the earlier *art pour l'art* convictions of the first wave of Sestiger writing, while Breyten and I, and soon also Braam de Vries, were pushed out because of our then more overtly *littérature engagée* approach. In due course, however, and most certainly following the *Kennis van die Aand* debacle, almost the whole group shifted resolutely towards more open political commitment.

After *Kennis* had been banned, the censors abandoned whatever reservations they might previously have had about acting against Afrikaans books. They now actually appeared more eager to suppress Afrikaans texts than English ones, and writers like Welma Odendaal, André le Roux, John Miles and the satirist Pieter-Dirk Uys, among others, all bore the brunt of this shift. In the theatre, bureaucrats had a field day: as most of the theatres in the country – except some of the most exciting venues, like the Space in Cape Town and the Market in Johannesburg – were run by provincial authorities, it became possible for these managements to stop a play on the strength of only a single complaint by a member of the audience – and more than once such disapproving individuals were carefully and deliberately planted by the political authorities.

Bartho, more than any other playwright, suffered under this kind of censorship. It took years before his plays were actually allowed on the stage – and as the widely acknowledged master of stagecraft in our midst, this was particularly painful to him; once a play by him was stopped on the very morning of its opening day. P. G. du Plessis, popular with the masses and never one to rock the boat, encountered no problems. But even I was hamstrung. My play *Pavane* was stopped before it could go into rehearsal; my production of Chris Barnard's *Taraboemdery*, after a sell-out run in Namibia, was banned from performance in the Cape Province.

But the new phase in censorship – that is, the Lammie Snyman period, following the banning of *Kennis van die Aand* – hit the jackpot with Etienne Leroux's *Magersfontein, o Magersfontein*, published in 1976 and banned by the board in 1977. After that it was taken on review by three judges of the Supreme Court. By this time, the terms of the Publications Control Act had been amended to allow for the 'likely reader' of a publication to be taken into consideration, and for a committee of so-called 'literary experts' to advise the court. In these changed circumstances, and with Lammie Snyman replaced by the young and open-minded Kobus van Rooyen, *Magersfontein* was declared, in the nice phrasing of censorship judgements, to be 'not undesirable'. The award of the Hertzog Prize for literature to the book, the highest accolade of the South African Academy of Arts and Science, effectively confirmed the end of the plague of censorship in the country. Sadly, however, in recent times the ANC government under Thabo Mbeki, which has become increasingly totalitarian in its approach, has announced measures that threaten to steer the control of films and publications back to the dark ages of Nationalist rule. In this respect, as in others, the hard-won freedoms celebrated in 1994 are now exposed to the threat of ever more insidious erosion.

For *Kennis van die Aand* there were still two further hurdles to cross. In 1979, five years after the ban, it was referred to the board again on review. By this time the Committee of Literary Experts was already functioning. I approached the Revd Izak de Villiers, who was also a poet and regarded as liberal-minded, to testify on my behalf. He declined, pointing out that he was already on the committee of experts and would be in a position to act more effectively in that capacity, 'from the inside'. But when the verdict came, it was announced that the finding of the committee had been unanimous. I was shocked, after the strong personal assurances de Villiers had given me. I telephoned him to ask him why he had lied to me, which I did not find very appetising coming from a man of the cloth. He could give no coherent explanation, apart from mumbling about having been in a depression and unable to think clearly. Many years later he apologised. But I still regard that action as one of the most painful betrayals of my life.

There had been others. During my student years one of my true mentors in literature had been T. T. Cloete, and much of my lifelong involvement with literary theory had been nurtured by him. My political Damascus in Paris – first, my outrage about Sharpeville, then much more drastically my reaction to the student uprisings – had alienated him as he came to believe that I was promoting the cause of communism and had become an enemy of the state. After *Kennis van die Aand* he wrote a secret paper for the Broederbond on the ideological threat posed by writers like Nadine Gordimer, Breyten Breytenbach and myself, which was disseminated to the Departments of Afrikaans at several universities. In the University of Port Elizabeth, an entire first-year course in Afrikaans literature based on Cloete's 'revelations' was devised by one Humphrey du Randt, a literary nonentity who was in cahoots with politicians in powerful positions. This, I realised, was paving the way for state action. By that time, Breyten was already in prison, but Nadine and I were exposed. Both of us decided to take du Randt to court as an early safeguard against further action by the SB.

I approached an astute lawyer friend, Neville Borman, who abhorred the apartheid regime and relished the opportunity of issuing a suit for libel against du Randt. The learned professor, already the laughing stock of literary scholars, had been bold while launching back-stabbing attacks from within the safety of the Broederbond, but did not have the courage of his convictions in an open court. So he travelled to Grahamstown to see me personally. It was one of the most distasteful confrontations I have ever experienced. He went down on all fours on the cheap green carpet in my office at Rhodes and burst into tears as he pleaded for mercy on behalf of his wife, who he said was ill, and his poor children. Faced with this abjection I relented, which might have been a mistake. He undertook to publish apologies to Nadine and myself, to terminate his slanderous first-year course, and to pay our legal costs. Later, predictably, he attempted to renege. I undertook to intercede with Nadine. Reluctantly, she consented to drop charges, but firmly insisted on a public apology, and dictated the wording for it. I, foolishly, left the wording of the apology to the grovelling quadruped. As a result, he formulated it in the vaguest terms and kept me waiting for the promised refund of legal costs until I threatened him with another summons from Neville.

Many years later, the air between Cloete and myself was also cleared, this time in a spirit of understanding and generosity – fostered by the political changes in the country. In due course I was even invited to deliver a T. T. Cloete Lecture at Potchefstroom University.

In the meantime the censorship scene was beginning to change from inside. But, as happens so often with the nastier forms of disease, it had to get worse before it got better. At roughly the same time as the ban on Etienne Leroux's *Magersfontein*, both Nadine Gordimer, with *Burger's Daughter* and I, with *A Dry White Season*, were hit with bans, in what more or less amounted to Lammie Snyman's death rattle. A year earlier, the English edition of

Rumours of Rain had also been impounded upon arrival in South Africa, and kept under embargo for months; but when it was announced, early in 1979, that it had won the CNA Award, then the country's major literary prize, the embargo was hurriedly lifted. It was this kind of confused and cowardly action that had helped seal the fate of censorship even before it was officially dismantled.

The writing of *Rumours of Rain* was unexpectedly interrupted when a contingent of seven security police arrived at my front door in 1977 and burst into the passage without producing a search warrant. They had come, they announced, to search the house. What for? I ventured to ask. The man in charge, a lean and hungry-looking officer called Siebert, merely narrowed his eyes, and told me that this was none of my business: they would know what they were looking for once they'd found it.

I was unceremoniously ordered to sit down, Alta who'd been working in her pottery studio, was called in, 'to prevent her from alerting the neighbours', and the seven men started to ransack my study: every drawer, every filing cabinet, every bookshelf, although I did not get the impression that their interest was literary. When I suggested that if only they'd tell me what they were looking for I might help them to find it, Gauleiter Siebert very curtly told me to shut up. 'We'll find what we want, don't you worry, even if it means breaking down every brick in this house.' From the growing pile of books and files and press cuttings and notes and manuscripts gathered by the Seven Samurai I gradually formed a pretty shrewd idea of what they were searching for. Some time earlier, Breyten Breytenbach had briefly returned to South Africa, more or less clandestinely, in disguise and under the assumed name of Christian Galaska, on a private mission that might, or might not, have had to do with anti-government activities. In the course of the next year or so, the government unearthed all manner of mind-blowing 'evidence' against him, including the planned arrival of Russian U-boats in a secret hollow somewhere below Robben Island. The security police, alerted to his mission, which had already been called off by the ANC and their organiser, Johnny Makhatini, followed him throughout the country, pouncing only as he was about to board a plane back to Paris.

And it was in the wake of Breyten's visit that my unwelcome visitors arrived. It was several hours before they left – after they had also driven me up to my office at Rhodes University, squeezed in tightly between two officers on the back seat of the car, with two others in front. The remaining three stayed behind at home, presumably to keep a lookout for subversive action by my wife and our two children of five and three. In the end they left with a large box filled with confiscated books and papers, including all my notes for *Rumours of Rain*; and both typewriters.

In some miraculous way they had overlooked the first draft of the novel itself, which was in our bedroom upstairs where I had been working on corrections. In those days, through some stupid superstition, I never made any copies of a manuscript in progress, firmly believing that it was unlucky to keep more than the single original typescript. But from that day on I made sure that I kept several carbon copies of everything I wrote, one of which was mailed to friends in Europe every week.

I was on a curious high after they left. I did not tell anybody about the visit. But I did drive to a colleague's home to borrow his typewriter, and before the end of the day I wrote double my daily quota. In the end, *Rumours of Rain* was finished well before the deadline I had imposed on myself. However, Alta's anxious entreaties – for the children's sake – after that visit from the SB resulted in my holding back the manuscript for a full year after it was completed. Her concern was triggered, among other reasons, by the unnerving discovery, only a few months later, that the officers who had visited us were exactly the same men who were responsible for the torture and murder of Steve Biko. The man who drove the van in which the naked Biko was transported from Port Elizabeth to Pretoria was the same Siebert who had threatened to break my house down brick by brick.

I had attended Breyten's trial in Pretoria and used the opportunity to look in on two other trials in progress in the Supreme Court to wish the accused well; I was even allowed by the security police to spend a few minutes alone with Breyten. One small piece of information he passed on to me I found particularly touching: in the cells below the courtroom, he said, he'd noticed among the spread of graffiti on the wall one inscription that had struck him: it was, quite simply, my title *Kennis van die Aand.*

He was sentenced to nine years. But after barely one year he was hauled out of prison to face a second trial, this time for allegedly attempting to escape. Among the letters he'd smuggled out from his incarceration, with the 'help' of a young warder known as 'Lucky' Groenewald, were copies of letters addressed to several friends, including myself. How well I remember the only one that was actually delivered to me, carried by Lucky in person.

It was a shattering experience. What the tone of this letter conveyed was the devastating effect solitary confinement had had on Breyten. All I knew was that he needed help. From the first moment I had very little doubt that the whole thing had been a set-up. There was no way I could trust this Lucky person with his fake naïvety, his apparent Boere-innocence. But the over-riding impression was that Breyten desperately needed help. I paid scant attention to the specific request in the letter: that he needed R300 – quite a substantial sum in those days – towards arranging a *cavale*. I must confess that in the confused state I was in at that moment, I had no idea that *cavale* referred to an attempted escape; I did not even think of looking it up in a dictionary. And even if I had understood perfectly what my friend wanted I would still have acted in the way I did.

Lucky insisted that I destroy the letter immediately, which I did in his presence. But I did memorise as much of it as I could, and afterwards wrote that down. We arranged to meet a few hours later, by which time I had the cash ready.

At the same time I had to warn Breyten of my suspicion that Lucky had been planted to incriminate him. I went across the street from my home to a very good friend, whom I trusted completely to keep a secret, particularly a dangerous one. We conferred for half an hour. The friend concurred with my fears, but resolved that I could not turn down Breyten's desperate request. So we agreed on two things: I would compose a letter in response to Breyten's, to sound as helpful and sympathetic as possible, while still trying to convey the message about my suspicions; and I had to ensure, by planting a tape recorder in my car, that I had evidence about Lucky's role, in case he did turn out to be a spy and I had to prove my suspicions in court.

It took some time to compose the letter. Years before, in Breyten's first published volume of prose, called *Katastrofes* (1964), he had written a small story about a man buying himself a pumpkin for his birthday on 16 September, Breyten's own date of birth. The pumpkin begins to grow uncontrollably and devours everything around it, including the man who bought it. Over the years, this story had become a starting point and a pretext in many of the letters we'd exchanged. And it now seemed the obvious framework of reference for the new letter, undoubtedly the most precarious of our entire correspondence. I'm not sure that in those fraught circumstances I did a particularly good job, but I did my best to devise a story in which a pumpkin is used to deliver a message planted by hostile vegetable forces in order to save the life of some innocent potato or leek or beetroot. This I incorporated in a seemingly straightforward reply to Breyten's letter. I also included the R300. Then I slid my tape recorder under the passenger seat in my car, made sure that it worked, and drove to the house of the 'uncle' with whom Lucky was supposed to be staying.

Just before I got out of the car to meet him, I switched on the recorder.

A minute later I opened the passenger door to let Lucky in. He slid into the seat and pushed it back as far as it could go, ostensibly to make room for his long legs. The whole situation made it abundantly clear that Lucky knew exactly what to expect – and wanted me to know that he knew. As he pushed back his seat, the tape recorder on the floor was exposed in all its glory. And so we had to conduct our ensuing conversation with the recorder in full view, with both of us pretending not to be aware of it at all.

Hilarious, yes, I suppose it was. But in the circumstances, with Breyten's life in more than one respect at stake, it really did not seem all that funny. At least, I wretchedly tried to console myself after Lucky had taken his leave, I had some evidence of the attempt to frame me. And I blindly hoped that, somehow, the mere fact of the SB knowing that I was wise to what they were up to, would discourage them from proceeding against Breyten any further.

It was a vain hope.

A few months later, Breyten was brought back to the Supreme Court to face a second trial. Unlike the first time, where the trial was in the hands of a right-wing judge clearly kowtowing to the apartheid regime, the new judge attempted – within the narrow scope permitted him by the system in force – to allow justice to prevail. No further punishment was pronounced, and the state's representatives received a severe dressing-down. It was largely due to this verdict that no further action was taken, either against Breyten or those of us implicated in the trial. Only weeks before the trial, when I was in Johannesburg to confer with Breyten's brilliant new lawyer, advocate Johan Kriegler, I had asked him about my own chances following Breyten's appearance. Kriegler merely folded his hands, looked me straight in the face, and said, 'You're in the shit.'

Even before this second trial I had some further encounters with the security police. At one stage I found myself in Pretoria to appeal on Breyten's behalf against a ban imposed by the Publications Control Board on my friend's collection of poems, *Skryt*: since Breyten was then in prison he could not handle the appeal himself. However, a minefield of legalities prevented me from acting on his behalf unless I could obtain his written permission – which was possible only if the security police were prepared to pass my written request on to him. I was instructed to go to their headquarters in Pretoria and on the appointed morning I presented myself at the Wachthuis. Needless to say, I was in a state of trepidation. As a futile precaution I took two friends from Wits University with me, but they were ordered to stay outside when I was led through the heavy iron security gate that slammed shut behind me. I couldn't help thinking, rather melodramatically: *Abandon all hope, ye who enter.*

I followed someone down a long ill-lit corridor, into the intestines of the cavernous building, and was shown into an office. Its very ordinariness, its drabness, was shocking.

'There are friends waiting for me,' I informed the major in charge, a thickset man in grey flannels and a blue sports jacket, smelling of smoke and with teeth and hands discoloured by nicotine. 'Could you please tell me at what time I should ask them to come back?'

His face remained utterly expressionless. 'That,' he said in a low, even voice, 'is entirely up to you.'

I was ordered to sit, and several other men, all in sports jackets, joined the major around a nondescript desk. I couldn't help remembering my friend John Miles telling me about a visit he'd paid the SB some months earlier, also in connection with Breyten, in the lugubrious blue building of John Vorster Square in Johannesburg. One of the interrogators had spent the entire session standing with his back against a door frame without ever saying a word; all he did was to hold an orange in his outstretched hand, throwing it up and catching it, throwing it up and catching it, palpating the fruit in his large paw, then resuming the maddening throwing and catching, throwing and catching, throwing and catching.

For several hours the men in the interrogation room – which was soon clouded by slowly whirling blue smoke – kept on asking about my relationship with Breyten. Where and when we'd met. Whether he had ever introduced me to a man called Johnny Makhatini. I denied it all, trying to eliminate from my memory the small Malebranche bistro where I'd first met Johnny and had been introduced to elaborate strategies of communicating to a contact address in Paris details of plane and rail and bus timetables, which had made no sense to me, and had seemed more of a boys' game of cops and robbers than anything truly serious. Or any of a long list of other names, most of which I honestly had never heard before. Whether I believed in violence as a solution for political problems. No, I said. Whether to my knowledge Breyten was likely to resort to violence. No, I said. On and on and on, going in circles most of the time. There was a curious, uncanny sense of calm, of detachment in me. If this is it, I remember thinking, then let it be so. All I can do is sit it out.

When I tried to ask about getting Breyten's permission to handle his appeal against the censors, I was told that this was out of the question. One of the men added, quite civilly, that I was there to answer questions, not to ask them. And then a new round began. I must have been a great disappointment to them, I think. In the end, which came quite unexpectedly, I was merely informed that they would 'be in touch, if necessary'. And while that final phrase was still lingering in the suffocating whorl of smoke I was taken down the long corridor once again, back to the front door. The heavy gate clanged shut behind me again. And soon I was back with my friends.

The appeal to the censors, as it turned out, was not allowed – the criminal trial first had to run its course. So that was that.

There was an unexpected conclusion to my involvement, or non-involvement, in Breyten's trial. In Grahamstown I once again called on the lawyer who had acted for me in issuing a summons against the pathetic Professor Humphrey du Randt. With more chutzpah than most, Neville promptly telephoned the head of the security police in Pretoria, General Johan Coetzee, while I sat in his chaotic office on the very edge of my chair, chewing my nails.

'General,' said Neville, 'R300 belonging to my client was confiscated by your security men and produced in the Supreme Court in Pretoria in evidence against Breyten Breytenbach. The trial ended a week ago and Breytenbach was found not guilty. You have ten days from today to deliver that money to my office, otherwise proceedings will be instituted against you. On or before the same deadline I also want here in my office all other material removed from my client's home, including two typewriters, books and documents.' Then he slammed the phone down.

I was horrified. I expected the worst.

Exactly nine days later Neville telephoned to say that I could go to the SB offices, hidden behind an innocent-looking brown door above OK Bazaars, to collect my possessions. He was prepared to go with me.

At the iron grille behind the door Neville was refused entry and I had to go in alone. Perhaps they were going to have the last word after all. But although I was received with a chilling show of rudeness, unlike the civility shown me in Pretoria, all my possessions, including the typewriters, and – to my amazement – the R300 in cash, were shoved to me over a stained brown desk and I was told to sign a handwritten receipt and get out.

Throughout that decade, the security police was woven into the fabric of the life of every day, every night. Many nights my daughter, Sonja, then about four, would wake up from nightmares in the dark, and I would go to sleep with her; and I held her in my arms wondering for how long that would still be possible. When would the dreaded knock in the night wake us up and I would find, once again, the front passage teeming with heavy men, and this time I'd be taken away . . . ? I remember the knock, one night at exactly three, the most dreaded hour, when looking from Sonja's window I saw a light flashing on the roof of a van parked at the front door. *This is it*, I thought, aware of a strange, unearthly calm settling inside me as I put on my old red gown and opened the front door. And, exactly as I had always visualised it, a number of large men burst into the passage, shoving me out of the way as they shouted, 'Where's the corpse? Where's the corpse?' It took a while before it dawned on me that they were paramedics from an ambulance dispatched to pick up a dead body from the wrong address.

The security police inserted themselves into everything: strange sounds and voices over the telephone, anonymous death threats and obscene rantings in the small hours, letters arriving with envelopes torn or cut open or completely missing, since the point was not to intercept mail surreptitiously but always to make it very visible. My car, even though locked up in the garage, would be broken into and sabotaged in various clumsy ways. One night Alta and I were awakened by a strange whistling sound, in time to see an incendiary bomb describing a bright arc in the night sky and landing on the pitched roof, from where it harmlessly clattered down the steep side into the back garden.

And wherever we went, we would be followed. It actually gave one a curious sense of security to be under constant surveillance like that. Into town, to lectures at the university, to Cape Town or Johannesburg, once to Durban where we spent a holiday with our good friends Braam and Hannie. Even when we took the children out for a day at the beach or at the aquarium, there would be someone tailing us. One morning the family set out again, this time for the Kruger National Park for the rest of our holiday. Our blood-hound had with him only the clothes he was wearing for a day on the beach: shorts, sandals, and a very bright and colourful shirt blazing with tropical trees and parrots. By the third day in the park he was near the end of his tether. At one of the wonderful picnic spots between camps we stopped to make a *braai*. Our man-of-paradise approached me like a crestfallen parrot that had barely survived a tropical storm.

'Excuse me, Mr Brink,' he said, studying his dusty toes in the brown sandals. 'Look man, I know you know why I'm here, but I want you to understand, I'm just following orders. It was all a misunderstanding. But now I'm here and I've got no choice, I got to stay here. So if you will please just bear with me.'

'Be my guest,' I said. We offered him a piece of *boerewors* and a sandwich, which he had the decency to partake of at some distance from our family group. For the next few days we would regularly acknowledge each other's presence with discreet little waves.

In the meantime, my friend Braam had been summoned by the Durban SB for an 'interview' on my visit. It turned out that the SB had an amazing – and amusing – report on my stay in Durban, in which they had confused me with the Stellenbosch academic André du Toit. But the most hilarious aspect about Braam's visit turned out to be his addiction to smoking: every few minutes he felt compelled to clean his pipe and light it again. And every time he knocked the bowl against the large ashtray in the centre of the table the officer would flinch and grow pale. This went on until the poor man could not take it any longer: leaning over in Braam's direction he shouted in a voice trembling with emotion: 'For God's sake, man, stop doing that! You're ruining my microphone.'

The scenes were not always so amusing, the men not always so inept. What never failed to amaze me was the extent to which bumbling clumsiness could go hand in hand with shrewdness and sophistication. If one could never really risk underestimating the intelligence in the ranks of the SB, it would also be easy to overestimate them. Only one thing was certain: their dogged persistence. Once they believed they were on to something, however misguided that might have been at the outset, they would never let go. And what always brought one down to earth was the basic, and terrifying, knowledge: that these men, even – and often especially – the most bumbling among them, were capable of killing for the cause they believed in and for the leaders they obeyed like loyal dogs. They might be very ordinary people, with wives and children, set patterns of going to church on Sundays, living in harmony with their neighbours, playing with their pets, enjoying a good joke at a *braai* fire. But there was one thing that set them apart from thousands of other 'ordinary' people: they were killers. They could stand around a fire with a glass of beer in one hand and an overdone lamb chop in the other, while a few metres away a black man was choking to death in his own blood.

What I found particularly agonising was when other people were dragged into it unwittingly, innocently, and always unpredictably. There was a young schoolteacher in the town of George, in her twenties, a most talented and intelligent person, who started corresponding with me about her poetry. This is the bane of most writers' lives: not merely the demands on one's time and energy and patience, but the sense of entitlement that often goes with it. Once a middle-aged woman in Somerset East sent me a manuscript of well over 300 pages of poetry, with a blunt request for detailed comments on each individual poem. In due course I believe I've become less of a sucker, but in those days, remembering my own early struggles, I tried my best to bolster youthful – and not so youthful – aspirations; so I diligently worked through those 300-odd poems, several of them running to five or six pages, and returned them with my extensive comments. And until this day, forty years later, not even a brief thank-you note has reached me. But the young teacher in George was different. Her writing was good, original, feisty, inventive. And her letters were a treat: her acute and humorous comments on her fellow teachers, her pupils, her lodgings, her dreary daily programme. Above all the unquenchable spirit that shone through it all, her dreams of the future, her ambitions to get published. And then it stopped. Abruptly. I continued to write, to express my concern, to try and probe her silence. But nothing. For several months. Until one day a letter was shoved through the slot in my front door: unstamped, unmarked, delivered by hand. By the time I'd retrieved it from the floor, I heard a car drive off in the street, but I was too late to identify it.

The letter from my young correspondent in George was handwritten, with signs of haste and agitation. Just to tell me that, somehow, somebody had got wind of our correspondence. She had no idea of how or why or when – but to me there was no mystery at all. The first she found out about it was when she was called in by her school principal, who confronted her with one of her own letters to me. Containing some poems, remarks on personal and literary matters – and a number of rude, if witty, comments on her school and her colleagues. This correspondence had to stop immediately, she was told. The man was a communist and a danger to the state. And should it ever transpire that she had in any way tried to resume the correspondence, she would be fired from her job. I wish I could say that at some future date she wrote to say that she had not stopped writing, that she still had hopes for the future. But there was nothing. And I was left wondering how many of these young talents had been nipped in the bud, how much creative potential the country had lost, obscured by the more obvious and spectacular atrocities everybody knew about.

In at least one other episode the SB used a woman to get at me. It concerns the lovely Lise who had made such an unexpected entry into my life when the arrival of my theatrical friend Francois during the production of my play in Grahamstown forced me to share a room with her. After that introduction we went our separate ways until, several years later, I had to go to Pretoria where we found ourselves eager to see each other again. We met in a hotel on the outskirts of the city, had a pleasant meal, got carried away by a torrent of conversation, and only realised what time it was when it was already too late.

About a week later there came a phone call from Pretoria. It was Lise, in a state of consternation. She had just had a visit from a lieutenant in the security police who had shown her a photo which he'd peeled from a stack in a big envelope – but he'd declined to show her any of the others. There were two persons on the photo. She and I. In what is usually described as a 'compromising position'. The officer had been very friendly, even apologetic, and he'd assured her that he had no wish to cause her any 'discomfort'. All he wanted was an affidavit to the effect that we had in fact been involved in 'sexual congress'.

But suppose she wouldn't?

He felt very sure that she wouldn't want photographs like that falling into the hands of somebody working for a newspaper. As a journalist she was convinced, as was I, that no newspaper could risk publishing photographs as explicit as that. The others in his buff envelope, he assured her, were even more 'revealing'.

Initially I tried to persuade her to call his bluff. But after another visit from the friendly officer, we began to realise that straightforward publication was not necessarily the only way open to them. Damage could be done on so many levels, and he was beginning to wear down Lise's defences.

In the end I agreed that the best – the only – way to get rid of the man, would be for her to sign the bloody affidavit, even though I couldn't see any point of insisting on an affidavit if they already had the photos. But the event had cast a pall over both of our lives. Even if other similar opportunities would present themselves in future, we would not be interested in succumbing. There was a claustrophobic feeling of our living space shrinking almost tangibly around us.

And then so many other, smaller, less dramatic, but still slowly suffocating events happened. To arrive in Port Elizabeth for a plane to Cape Town, only to be told: But you already left for Cape Town an hour ago.

I could not have left an hour ago. I am here *now*. Here is my booking slip from the travel agent. For the next plane.

I am sorry sir, but there are no more seats available on the next plane.

Or to arrive in Australia for literary festivals in Melbourne and Sydney, at a time when there was only one flight a week either way between South Africa and Australia, and to be told that one's return booking has been cancelled. Complicated, roundabout enquiries brought to light that the cancellation was effected by the SB.

All of this conspired, to put it mildly, to complicate my life throughout the seventies and eighties. The pressure never lifted. Not even when I travelled abroad.

The first time this happened was in 1974, when a film company took me to London and Paris as an advisor and an interpreter. It was the first time since my year-long stay in Paris in 1968 that I found myself in Europe again; and after the unrelenting pressure of the years in between, particularly after the banning of *Looking on Darkness* which had first publicly branded me as a 'danger to the security of the state', it was bliss to feel all that weight shifted from my shoulders. I could breathe free air again. So I thought. Until, on the return flight to South Africa, the plane came in to land at Johannesburg and the nondescript, middle-aged man seated next to me started up a conversation. The usual bland questions: How did it feel to be back home? Where had I been? For how long had I been away? Halfway through the chat, just after I had mentioned London and Paris, he leaned back in his seat. Without looking at me, he said with quiet satisfaction:

'Yes, yes, I know.' And then, reciting in a low monotone, he said: 'You left Johannesburg on 28 March, on flight number SA210. In London you stayed in the West-Two Hotel in Bayswater.' That came as a surprise as I myself hadn't known where the group would stay upon arrival: it had all been arranged by one of their contacts abroad. My neighbour persisted: 'Then, on 3 April, you left for Paris on flight BA186, and you stayed in the Hôtel du Vaugirard.' Another surprise, as something had gone wrong with the bookings the group leader had made and from the boulevard Saint-Michel we had simply set out in search of a hotel, which we found around the corner in the rue de Vaugirard.

There were more surprises in store. My indefatigable companion took a small notebook from his pocket and proceeded to read the names of all the people I had met on the journey, most of whom had been unknown to me before. At the end of the recitation he restored the notebook to his pocket. Only then did he look at me. With the hint of a smile he said, 'Welcome back to South Africa.'

That was when I really knew I was back. And what it meant to be back.

The accumulating weight of all of this was becoming a burden I could not bear any longer. Unless I found a way of writing about it, the situation in the country would threaten to submerge and paralyse me. A key event that opened up this possibility was the death in detention of an Eastern Cape man, Mapetla Mohapi. From about the middle sixties deaths in detention had become a feature of the deteriorating situation, exacerbated by new laws about detention without trial, first for ninety days, later 180 days. Turning ever more stringent and arbitrary as, forty years later, the Terrible Twins, Bush and Blair, the South African government became obsessed with 'terrorism'. In 1969, the murder by the security police of a Cape Town imam, Abdullah Haron, made headlines around the world, particularly through the indefatigable efforts of an Opposition member of parliament, Catherine Taylor. The case ended inconclusively, but more and more people became perturbed about detainees dying after slipping on bars of soap, falling down stairwells, tumbling from tenth-floor windows, or hanging themselves on shoestrings or makeshift ropes from window bars.

Mohapi's death became another cause célèbre after Donald Woods, editor of the *Daily Dispatch* in East London, took it up. Woods could be a formidable investigator, as became clear some time later when he became involved in the life and death of Steve Biko. I must confess that, though I met Woods several times before and after Biko's horrendous death, I was initially not enamoured of him. I applauded the causes he fought for, but not his ego. My impression, perhaps wrongly, was that he tended not to see the wood for the Woods. Much later, after his controversial escape from South Africa, he made a much more sympathetic impression when we spent some time together in London. Another person who played a crucial role in supplying me with many hundreds of pages of the court documents I needed for my book was the Durban attorney Griffiths Mxenge, who was most gruesomely murdered by the SB a few years later. It was only very recently that I learned, from the horse's mouth, that the man physically responsible for duplicating and passing on to me the documents was his articled clerk, Bulelani Ngcuka, who in due course became the director of prosecutions and is married to the deputy president of South Africa, Phumzile Mlambo-Ngcuka.

In the end, there really was no incident 'invented' in *A Dry White Season*. The book became the repository of my life, the lives of numerous of my friends during the seventies, and information gleaned from a number of crucial trials, inquests and investigations from that period.

It was never plain sailing: this was due, in part, to the harrowing nature of the raw material I worked with. The writing of only one other book in my life turned out to be more distressing to me, and that was *The Other Side of Silence*. But it was due, also, to an event that happened on 18 August, 1977, very soon after I'd started writing and which so disrupted the process that I came very close to abandoning the novel. This was the event that led, a few weeks later, to the death of Stephen Bantu Biko.

Only a day before his arrest I'd had a long conversation, in the tearoom at Rhodes University, with friends in the Department of Politics, who knew Biko well and could wax eloquent – even though they were normally quite hard-boiled realists, even cynics – in discussing this charismatic young man's impact on black politics, particularly in the Eastern Cape. And now came the news of his arrest, in Grahamstown itself, a few blocks away from the house in which I sat working on a novel about a fictitious black man arrested, and tortured, and killed, not by nameless grey shadows in the security police, but by people known to me, who in the recent past had searched my home.

The days that followed Biko's arrest were chaotic, and rife with rumours. It was only on 13 September that something definite came out of the confusion: Steve Biko was dead. The first statements by the unlamented minister of justice, Jimmy Kruger, announced that he had died following a hunger strike. One speaker at the National Party congress which was then taking place in the Transvaal, a man called Christoffel Venter, stood up to congratulate the minister who, he said to applause, was such a democratic leader that he even 'allowed detainees the democratic right to starve themselves to death'.

Kruger's famous statement at the congress, reverberating around the globe, was that, 'Biko's death leaves me cold.' Afterwards he claimed that the Afrikaans expression, *Dit laat my koud*, does not mean *It leaves me cold*, but something like *I am sorry, I am neutral about it.* At the annual meeting of the Afrikaans Writers' Guild, a month later, I proposed a motion that was adopted unanimously, to confirm, very simply, that *It leaves me cold* means *It leaves me cold.*

Gradually more of the truth filtered through, and at the inquest into the death in November the full state version of the event was presented, starting with an account of the 'extensive brain injury' sustained by Biko, an 'abrasion to the left forehead' and other 'numerous but superficial injuries'. In spite of the brilliant and dramatic cross-examination by Sidney Kentridge and George Bizos, the magistrate predictably found that, 'on the available evidence the death cannot be attributed to any act or omission amounting to a criminal offence on the part of any person.' Even so, this event has remained a defining moment in the contemporary history of South Africa;

and in spite of the official finding, the evil machinations of the security police had been exposed more relentlessly than ever before.

As far as *A Dry White Season* was concerned, however, my paralysis continued. It seemed obscene to resume writing. How could I indulge in fabricating a fiction – no matter how extensively it was based on fact – when in my immediate vicinity a man had been tortured and killed in such a way? It was one of the few times in my life when I felt like agreeing with Theodor Adorno who argued that after the Holocaust, poetry was no longer possible. For several months I could not write at all. I felt so drained and sickened by it all that I could not even join in any of the public demonstrations that followed Biko's death and the government's decision, a month later, to ban almost twenty political, religious and cultural organisations, thereby making public resistance to apartheid virtually impossible. Only when Nadine Gordimer telephoned to invite me to join her and Athol Fugard in a statement of protest did I drift out of my paralysis. Very slowly, life came ebbing back. And in the course of many discussions with those closest to me, above all Alta, I came to realise that writing – and most pertinently, writing *A Dry White Season* – was not an obscenity, or an irrelevance, but an imperative.

To a large extent the press, all the public media, had been gagged. Public demonstrations were illegal. Most of the organisations that had previously orchestrated resistance to apartheid, had been silenced. But in this oppressive silence there was one voice that could still be heard, no matter how maligned or suspect it had become for many: the voice of the arts. For me, the voice of fiction.

At this time a group of students at Rhodes University asked me to address them about the road ahead. I told Lynette, the young woman who had come to talk to me, that I really didn't see much point in it. She was one of the most persuasive, positive, courageous young people I had met in years, and in the past I had always accepted her invitations. But this time I wanted to decline. The odds had become too great.

She stood up and looked me straight in the face. 'If that is really the way you feel, I shall go and tell them. But then, next time we have a students' meeting, we can take as our topic what to do if people like you no longer want to talk to us.'

I accepted.

The next morning a crowd of staff and students gathered in the quad. I spoke about the imperative never to stop protesting, never to give up, never to take no for an answer. I probably summoned up Camus, as always. And, taking my cue from Artaud, I built up to a rather melodramatic, overheated conclusion:

> We shall shout our resistance from the rooftops. And when we are no longer allowed to shout, we shall speak our truths. When we can no longer speak, we shall whisper. And when they forbid us to whisper, we shall signal through the flames.

Rabble-rousing, purple prose indeed. But I was desperate.

And after that, slowly, but fired by a ferocious resolve, I returned to the novel.

But that was not the end of it. When the book was finished, I sent it to my Afrikaans publishers, Human & Rousseau. Following the earlier fate of *Looking on Darkness*, they decided – with good reason, as it turned out – that in the prevailing climate they could not risk publication. After that, I turned to my three friends at the University of the Witwatersrand, Ernst Lindenberg, Ampie Coetzee and John Miles, who had previously founded the informal, ad hoc publishing firm of Taurus, and brought out the clandestine edition of *An Instant in the Wind*. This novel had not encountered any problems with the censors, presumably because even though, like *Looking on Darkness*, it dealt with a love relationship between a coloured man and a white woman, it was set in a rather remote past. *A Dry White Season* was contemporary, and it dealt with something more explosive than interracial sex: the pornography of the security police, and the efforts of an ordinary, unremarkable Afrikaner to bring to light the darkness and the institutionalised violence that underlies apartheid.

When it was time to publish *A Dry White Season*, Ernst, Ampie and John could not risk taking any chances. They still had the list of subscribers compiled at the time *An Instant in the Wind* was circulated; but they also had to make sure that there would be no leaks at the printers. Their solution was to find a small Indian firm where nobody understood Afrikaans. To make doubly sure, they delivered the manuscript without any title or author's name attached. This information was divulged only on the very last day of printing.

There were other hazards along the way. I had to have regular contact with my 'publishers', preferably by telephone, to deal with queries as and when they arose. Knowing from experience both bitter and hilarious how vulnerable all phone conversations were, the solution we found was to use as our reference a thesis on the poetry of Breyten Breytenbach recently written under my supervision by Annari van der Merwe, today the publisher of the prestigious firm of Umuzi. We were naïvely satisfied that this would eliminate all problems. But there were a few that could not be foreseen. Foremost among these was John's tendency to forget bits of key information. In consequence, when we'd arranged for them to call me at a public telephone or a friend's house at, say, eight o' clock in the evening, there might be a most unexpected call from John at ten in the morning or three in the afternoon. A flustered, badly disguised voice would ask, 'Sorry, man, I've forgotten what number we're supposed to call you on tonight. Can you please tell me again?' Which would result in an endless new series of explanations, diversions and reroutings.

Amazingly enough, the book came out, apparently without a hitch. I had flown up to Johannesburg for the occasion, and in the bookshop of a mutual friend we met, long after hours, to put the 2,000 printed copies in padded envelopes and address them to the names on the mailing list, with a printed slip in each to inform the recipients of the price, and to assure them that if they did not want the book they were welcome to return it to sender.

As far as I know, only a single copy was returned; and nobody failed to pay.

A week later the book was banned, but by that time the full print run had been dispatched, and the printer – still none the wiser – had been paid.

There was a final piquant twist to the story when about two weeks later I went to London for the British launch of the book. I was waiting for the boarding call when two solemn men in flannels and sports jackets and wearing telltale grey shoes, turned up beside me and invited me to step aside with them. I was taken to a wooden partition in a wall. Behind it was a door leading to a small room, concealed so neatly that nobody could possibly suspect its existence without prior knowledge. Inside were a group of six or seven men. In the middle of the room, which could have been a waiting room at a station, was a long low table; and on the table sat the black Samsonite suitcase I had checked in only minutes earlier.

I was invited – the word they used more than once – to write down a full list of the suitcase's contents. They studied the list, then invited me (that word, once again) to reflect, just in case I had forgotten something. I accepted the invitation, duly reflected, added another few handkerchiefs and one pair of underpants, and handed the list back to them. Da capo. Another moment of reflection. A red jersey added to the list. No more? No more. Are you quite sure? I'm sure. You can vouch for it? I hope so. Are you really, absolutely sure? I think I'm sure. The *primus inter pares* approached the suitcase, undid the two clasps, then straightened his back and turned round to face me.

'For the last time,' he said, 'are you sure?'

I sighed and nodded.

He opened the case and stepped backwards. One never knows with terrorists.

When there was no detonation, several of the others approached the table and gave a helping hand. Every single item was removed, inspected from all sides, professionally evaluated, and placed on the open space on the low table next to the suitcase. Once it was clear that there was no contraband or explosives or booby traps among my nondescript possessions, the leader of the pack beckoned one of the others to follow him, and they disappeared through the door which was no door.

Ten minutes later they were back.

'You may go,' said the top brass. Whereupon he invited me to repack my suitcase. I swallowed the rage that had been building up steadily inside me and did his bidding.

Only as I picked up the case to leave did I venture to ask, 'Do you mind telling me *why* I was detained?'

'You were not detained,' said Numero Uno. 'You were just invited to—'

'I know,' I said as calmly as I could. 'To tell you what I had in my suit-case. But I really would like to know what you were looking for.'

A long pause. Then, now visibly irritated, the spokesman said, 'All I can say is that we received a tip-off.'

'About what?'

He stared hard at me. 'That you were trying to smuggle copies of your book out of the country.'

'But could you please explain,' I said, exasperated, 'why anybody would want to smuggle copies of a book that is banned in *this* country to a country where it is not banned and where it has already been published?'

'You may go now,' said the Grand Inquisitor.

And this time I thought it wise just to do as he said, while there was still a chance of catching my plane.

In 1984 it was time for another review of the ban on *Kennis van die Aand*. This time there was no problem. Kobus van Rooyen, who had grown consid-erably in the new liberal dispensation he had brought to censorship, did not hesitate to set the book free – albeit with an age restriction of eighteen. Even then the finding was not without a sting in the tail. When my then paper-back publisher, Fontana, applied to the Publications Appeal Board for permission to export their English paperback edition to South Africa, they received the following report:

> The Committee of Literary Experts advised that the work could not on account of its literary characteristics or merits, be protected against undesirability.
> – There are no qualities in the novel that compensate for the cardinal defects noted in the report.
> – An example of the crude intermingling of sex and religion is found on page 187, and page 393.
> – Absolute sophistication and literary or theological insight cannot be expected from the reasonable likely reader of this book.
> – It is not only a very mediocre novel, it is at times a non-novel; non-literature. This is not the result of amateurish blundering and

bungling, but rather that of sophistication but essentially trite and superficial manupulation [*sic!*]

- What has given serious offence is the way biblical and religious material in general have been employed to gain artistic plausibility and significance.
- The attitude of the author and storyteller is one of bitter hate and resentment.
- To expect his readers to accept the sacred terminal experiences in the life of Jesus Christ as symbols or metaphor of sexual satiety as in this particular novel – that is going too far.

They had dropped the original charges of pornography, blasphemy and endangering the security of the state, only to morph into literary critics.

Yet it would not be entirely true to regard the abandonment of censorship as an unequivocal victory for literature, for the arts generally. What was decisive in this development was the overall context in the country, particularly since the Soweto uprising of 1976 and the murder of Steve Biko a year later, with its immediate aftermath, the banning of nineteen political organisations and a general clampdown on the press freedom. Predictably, these dire events led to an increased persecution of all forms of opposition – a process that persisted, visibly, with the repression and the successive states of emergency in the country during the eighties, until even P. W. Botha could no longer contain it and subsided into apoplexy. But even while this was happening, there were growing signs of panic in the government's frenetic attempts to manage the situation. International sanctions were beginning to hurt the regime. Locally, a United Democratic Movement was established as a front for the exiled ANC; trade unions, permitted by the government in a desperate attempt to relieve the pressures accumulating within labour, introduced open defiance and challenges to the authorities on the floors of factories; demonstrations and various forms of opposition gained momentum in the churches, on the university campuses. The security police simply lacked the manpower to counter all these challenges at the same time. The desperate measures they were driven to, included the worst excesses of torture and repression the country had yet witnessed – but once again the very excesses signalled the breakdown of the system. And in the midst of all this turmoil, the arts were no longer regarded as a serious threat. Especially for a regime not noted for its interest in reading. P. W. Botha himself was reputed not even to read newspapers.

South Africa was finally ready to face the challenges of democracy. Except that, regrettably, democracy is seldom permanent unless an electorate remains constantly alert against abuses. What a pity that today, after some fifteen years of this new experience, the old reflexes should appear to be preparing for a comeback – sponsored by the very people who, under apartheid, had suffered most under the lack of freedom of speech. But we know, depressingly, that a battered child is often likely to become an abusive parent.

HAPPY RETURNS

CAST THY BREAD UPON THE WATERS, SAID THE PREACHER, FOR AFTER MANY days it will return to thee. The poet Uys Krige was more cynical: 'If you cast your bread on the water,' he warned, 'you must not expect to get a Christmas cake in return.' I couldn't help remembering this when I thought about unexpected responses I have had to my writing over the years.

One of the most moving letters I have ever received, about ten years after the publication of *An Instant in the Wind*, was from a woman in Scotland who sent me a few pound notes, asking me to buy flowers, to put on the graves of Aob/Adam and Elisabeth. It was painful to explain to her that they were fictitious characters.

An overwhelming letter once came from a woman in Belgium. She gave no address, but the letter bore the postmark of a town near Charleroi. There was no need for me to answer, she insisted. She merely needed somebody she could write to, and for some reason my books had convinced her that I would be that person. Her life was in a mess, she said, and she *had* to unburden to someone or she would go mad. From then on, for more than two years, she bombarded me with letters. Occasionally there would be an interval of a week or two, once even a couple of months, but on average there would be three or four letters a week, running to five or eight or ten or upon occasion even twenty or thirty pages, on very thin blue paper, in a handwriting that fluctuated between primness and wild extravagance. The contents varied just as much. She was married, but had just begun an affair with another man; in due course a second lover started drifting on and off the stage. She also had suspicions about the affairs, real or presumed, of her husband. The story became as complicated as any soap opera on television. I kept waiting for a letter announcing some kind of conclusion, or a request for advice (which she seemed to need rather desperately), or simply informing me that this was The End. But it never came. Eventually the letters just stopped coming.

The reaction of women readers to the portrayal of Andrea in *The Wall of the Plague* was strongly divided. I had some very angry attacks and denunciations; at the same time it was gratifying to receive from female readers some of the most enthusiastic and supportive encouragement I have ever had for any of my novels. One response I found particularly touching, deeply moving in fact, came from a young woman in France who wrote to me that she had identified so strongly with the character of Andrea that she had been prompted to write me the story of her own life in reply. Her letter ran to just over 300 pages. I tried to persuade her to find a publisher for it, but never heard from her again.

Another response that left me speechless with gratitude came from a young black South African woman who had spent most of her life in exile during the apartheid years: after reading *The Wall of the Plague*, she told me, she decided to follow Andrea's example and return to South Africa to face her own challenges.

And then there was Herr Böhlke. This happened late in 2000. The handwriting was a spidery scrawl that suggested old age, or severe pressure. The letter came from Hanover in Germany and bore rather unexpected news. He, Rainer Böhlke, had reached an age where he had to start thinking about death and its aftermath. He was lonely, had no children or living relatives, and having taken a liking to my work he was wondering whether I would consent to being his sole heir.

I must confess that my thoughts immediately turned, most unworthily, to a fortune in the not too distant future. I visualised a schloss on the Rhine. And I wrote back to express my empathy and appreciation, indicating that, yes certainly, if that was his wish, I would consent to his generous request.

It took a while before I heard from him again, and from then on there were repeated interruptions caused by the vagaries of the postal services. But the correspondence did continue. Then came a request: in view of his great appreciation of my work, and given our most satisfactory agreement, would I possibly consider sending him the original manuscript of one of my books?

I thought about it very carefully. But, in the final analysis, what was a manuscript compared to a schloss on the Rhine?

So I obligingly chose a manuscript of *On the Contrary* and airmailed it to Hanover.

Then: silence.

It must have been about six months later when my agent telephoned from Zurich, to tell me about a most unexpected conversation she'd just overheard between her colleague and a visiting American crime writer, Henry Slezar. This writer had just published a new book, the dedication of which intrigued the agent. And in reply to her query he told a fascinating story about an elderly German reader who had contacted him some time before to enquire whether he would consent to being the old man's sole heir. Et cetera. In this case the correspondent obsequiously asked for a dedication rather than a manuscript.

The agent called Henry Slezar to the phone and we had a rather heated conversation in which he swore that he would expose the whole affair on the Internet. For all we knew, there might be scores, hundreds, of writers all over the world nominated as heirs to Rainer Böhlke. And imagine them all, it occurred to me, turning up at the graveside and clamouring to take possession of their schloss. A theme worthy of Dame Agatha Christie.

However, Slezar had barely touched base in the States again when he died very suddenly. But I was still seething, and started dispatching numerous letters, all of them by registered mail, to Hanover. Needless to say, there never was the shadow of a response.

But when all else fails, writers do have one recourse: the last word. And in the book I was then writing, *The Other Side of Silence*, I renamed the most despicable character I have ever created, and called him Böhlke.

BACK TO FRANCE

THROUGHOUT THE SIXTIES THE DREAM OF RETURNING TO PARIS KEPT haunting me. It was only in 1968 that the possibility of a permanent return became possible, but halfway through 1966 there was a shorter, if still momentous, visit. After five years at Rhodes it was time for my sabbatical. It had been planned as a celebratory return to the city where I had been born a second time. But things turned out rather differently. To begin with, after the breakdown of my second marriage, I was feeling miserable. But I refused to change my bookings for Paris. I *needed* to go back. The result could have been disastrous, but as it happened, it became one of the richest summers of my life. If I close my eyes now, it's faces I see first. The faces of artists of all kinds. Most vividly Jan Rabie and Marjorie Wallace, who were staying with Breyten, so that for the first fortnight of my visit I found a small room squeezed in tightly under the roof of the little Hôtel du Senlis a few doors away from theirs. Some years later I also spent some time there, and this was the only occasion when we nearly fell foul of the *patronne* of the Senlis. A captivating young Dutch artist-cum-political-activist, Connie, came to visit Breyten, and in the small hours of the night I walked her back to the apartment of a mutual friend, Marion – to whom I shall return in due course – in the rue du Dragon. But halfway there I persuaded her that the Senlis might be worthwhile investigating, and we turned back. After a few glasses of *vin chaud* in the Mahieu, on the corner of the boulevard Saint-Michel and the rue Soufflot, we proceeded to the Senlis. Paris hotels can be very snotty about guests in one's room, so I smuggled Connie in surreptitiously and climbed the four storeys to my garret room. It would be overstating the case to describe it as 'small'. It was minuscule, not much bigger than a medium-sized suitcase; and my single bed more or less filled it wall-to-wall. The only way to cope, was to drag the little bed out to the landing and settle on the floor. More than the Kama Sutra was required to execute our manoeuvres on that tiny rectangular space. But we managed; and we didn't care much for sleeping anyway.

At sparrow's fart the next morning Connie was on her way. I heard her descending the four flights of stairs. And then, as she came past the concierge's cubicle, there was an explosion like Krakatoa erupting.

I stumbled out to the landing, grabbed the forlorn bed, dragged it back to the room, heaped our bundle of bedding on top of it, wriggled myself into my clothes and hurried downstairs to prevent the murder of a pretty foreigner. But barely two storeys down, the cacophony on the ground floor died away. Either Connie had been killed, or she'd managed to escape from the clutches of the concierge. Hoping for the best, I hastened back to my room, stripped off my clothes again and dived into bed. Not a moment too soon: seconds later there was a thundering sound on the stairs and without bothering to knock the *patronne* burst into my room, gasping for breath as if she'd just run an uphill marathon.

I raised my dishevelled head as if I'd just woken up and asked in a daze, '*Qu'est-ce que c'est, Madame?*'

She looked this way and that, went down on her knees to peer under the bed, then got up again, shaking her head in bewilderment.

'Did you – was there – have you seen a young woman coming past here?' she stammered in apoplectic, impotent rage.

'Past here?' I asked. 'From the roof or to the roof?'

She withdrew to the landing, looked up at the *vasistas* to the roof, once again shook her head, uttered an explosive '*Merde!*' and stomped downstairs again without another word.

But to resume. While Jan and Marjorie were occupying the spare room in Breyten's apartment, I stayed in the Senlis. Which meant that I wasn't present to witness the amazing spectacle of their departure which rounded off their visit. But I was kept abreast of it during the full ten days it lasted.

They were to leave from the Gare du Nord. Jan, meticulously organised person that he always was, probably the last vestige of his dour Calvinist upbringing, wanted to make sure that absolutely nothing would go wrong. Very early one morning, ten days before D-Day, Breyten was woken up by what sounded like an earthquake on the stairs. By the time he arrived at the front door, Jan and Marjorie had left with five large suitcases: their visit to Paris followed a voyage of many months through the US and Europe, and they had accumulated a mountain of luggage. Halfway through the morning, they returned from the Gare du Nord. It transpired that, considering their train – ten days later – was due to leave at eight, they had risen at five to catch the first of their buses to the Gare du Nord, where they arrived an hour and ten minutes early.

The next morning, there was a repeat performance, thundering down the six storeys from Breyten's apartment to the ground floor, and from there to the bus stop – only this time they left at a quarter-past six. On the third morning they left at five-thirty. From there on they fine-tuned the performance, adding or subtracting a few minutes every day, until on the morning before the day of their departure they had perfected the exercise. On the last morning we were all on the pavement of the rue Malebranche to wish them bon voyage. Everything was set for a model departure.

But just after ten o'clock they were back: there was a railway strike and their train could not leave.

Three days later the trains were back on schedule and Jan and Marjorie finally managed to leave.

The rest of that summer of 1966 turned into something of a merry-go-round, ranging from a wild affair with a young English woman who unnervingly reminded me of Ingrid, to a singular episode with a sylphide from Sweden, Mia, whose name was really Gunilla, and who shared my bed for a fortnight on the explicit condition that there would be no sex: I fell head over heels in love, but as a man of some honour I abided strictly with the rules. A mad time, as she had become mixed up with a crowd of hippies on the banks of the Seine, and some louche characters on the fringe, including a one-eyed

Moroccan who kept the younger generation supplied with drink and pot. Most of my nights during those two weeks were spent looking for Gunilla and extracting her from potentially life-threatening situations, to which she was serenely oblivious. After our fortnight of burning chastity she proceeded on her way, to Italy, to Czechoslovakia, to God knows where. There came a footnote to the episode when I visited Gothenburg for a literary festival in 1988 and in the queue of a few hundred people wanting their books signed, a beautiful middle-aged woman turned up, placing her book in front of me without a word. Only as she turned away, she spoke the words 'Maybe never', the title of the novel I'd based on that episode. And as I looked up, I recognised the Gunilla of twenty years before. I called out her name. She glanced back, briefly smiled, and walked on. The next person in the queue was already waiting. Impossible to go after her. What had remained so painfully unfulfilled in that long-lost summer, was destined to remain so forever.

There was more unfinished business during the same summer of 1966: I had seen a striking young actress, Elyane Giovagnoli, act in a Ionesco play in Montparnasse, and promptly fell for her – but as I was due to leave for London two days later, there was little chance of doing anything about it. The next day I visited a florist near the theatre and launched my private War of the Roses: arranging for a red rose to be delivered to the stage door every day for the next month. When I came back a month later, I immediately went to the theatre again. This time I left a bouquet of roses, with a note to set up a date for the next evening after the show.

I was there well in time, not knowing whether Elyane would turn up at all. But she did. And she was even more beautiful than I'd remembered. There was a slightly halting beginning to our conversation. But then we ordered something to drink, and soon we were launched into what promised to be an evening redolent with possibility. She was sparkling, witty, smiling, laughing, her almost-black eyes lit up in a festival of light.

Just when the time came to propose a follow-up meeting, a newspaper vendor came past on the broad pavement. Even from a distance I could see the large black headline:

Verwoerd Assassiné

I beckoned to the vendor and bought a paper. Unbelievable as it seemed, the news was true.

'You'll have to excuse me, Elyane,' I stammered, almost incoherent with excitement. And started running.

It was at least a kilometre to the rue Malebranche where I had my room with Breyten and Yolande, but I ran all the way. And burst into the apartment. Breyten was sitting in the narrow lounge with an old friend, the Rhodesian sculptor Keith MacKenzie. Yolande had already retired.

Within minutes she was awakened, the newspaper was read and reread. I called for a celebratory drink. As soon as the glasses were filled, Keith asked in a tone of dark suspicion: 'What are we drinking to?'

Only then did it hit us: Keith had quite strong leanings to the right, and he was an admirer of Verwoerd. Some days later he even attended the funeral service the South African Embassy had arranged. Not having any suitable outfit of his own, he borrowed Breyten's rather tight-fitting black suit from his wedding, six years before, and donned a hat with an ostrich feather stuck into it. He had no shoes. On the evening of the announcement the atmosphere was highly charged. Keith was glowering at us, clearly just waiting for a sign of celebration. And he was about twice the size of Breyten and myself combined.

It was Breyten who came to the rescue, with a show of diplomacy that has always stood him in good stead. 'Let us drink to South Africa,' he proposed. Which we all, solemnly, did.

During the rest of that mad visit there were frequent meals, impromptu or arranged, al fresco in someone's garden in a suburb in the summer or under the falling plane leaves in autumn, with a haphazard assortment of painters and sculptors and film or theatre directors and actors and writers and poets, published or unpublished, with hangers-on from a fringe of fire-eaters or sword-swallowers or chain-breakers, and miniaturists and maximalists, and weavers and lithographers and musicians, singers and sinuous sparsely clad dancers, long-fingered mimes, all eating pasta and swilling wine and talking non-stop, bickering or smooching or occasionally making love soundlessly or noisily in the background.

Once we were in a garden with grey and blue walls and shutters, outside the villa of the benevolently smiling, luminous eyes of the COBRA painter Corneille. Often in the rambling apartment which Pierre Skira, lean and pale and angular, shared with his dark-eyed Chilean companion Cholie, off my favourite Paris street, the rue Mouffetard. My ideal summer lunch: wandering down the full length of the Mouffetard, zigzagging drunkenly yet purposefully from one tried-and-trusted stall or shop to the next of a Sunday, engaging in serious conversation with each seller, collecting the ingredients for the meal: a *terrine de campagne* and obviously *pâté de foie gras*, a few cheeses, including a Soleil covered in raisins, a chicken roasted on the spit, or some slices of *rôti d'agneau,* a special red wine with a handwritten poem on the label, fresh tomatoes, a baguette or a *pain de mie*, fruit, a slice of *millefeuille*; and then a leisurely stroll to the Luxembourg gardens to regale oneself on a chair beside the Fontaine Médicis, caressed by the sound of water and enthralled by the sculpture of the two smooth and sensual lovers, Galathea and Acis, under the dark, louring Polyphemus, preparing to crush them under his terrifying black rock.

Some of the artists were hovering shadows on the edge of our familiar world, but left an indelible impression. An angular figure moving furtively from shadow to shadow, then lurking in a dark entrance while his equally ascetic woman scouted for a café not infested with familiars: Samuel Beckett. Two small, rotund figures, Tweedledum and Tweedledee, distressingly bourgeois, emerging from a theatre and exchanging some observations, humorous or banal, before disappearing into the night: Eugène Ionesco and his wife. Sartre, ugly little man on a stage during the student riots, ensconced in an alpaca jacket, scowling at his audience through thick glasses that exaggerated his aquarium eyes. I thought of Sartre years later when my friend George Weideman told me about his encounter with a vagrant in a Cape Town street: 'Excuse me, sir, but I just want to say you must have very strong eyes to look through those thick glasses.'

Other faces and memories are much more defined. One of them is Gerard Sekoto, the grand old man of African painting. But what a melancholy experience to meet him – the archetypal man with a great future behind him. He didn't seem to have done any work for years, ever since a plane transporting a number of his paintings crashed on its way to an exhibition. Since then, he believed that any future exhibition of his work would be sabotaged by unnamed forces. Of course this safeguarded him against the possibility of real failure. As far as I could make out, he used to be one of the great debauchers of Paris, a brilliant jazz musician who'd drunk himself to the brink of death in Montmartre, but like some of his predecessors in New Orleans, he had a reputation for giving his best performances when he was drunk. During his period of dissipation he was picked up by a woman who took him home to her apartment one night and then kept him firmly under her wing. Yet not one of his friends had ever seen her: if there was a knock on the door she would whisper through the keyhole, '*Qui est là?*' and then withdraw to call Gerard. And when he opened, all the other doors would be firmly closed. One could hear her shuffling about on slippers, but nobody ever saw her. I could not help imagining a story of a woman who didn't exist, yet completely dominated her husband's life with her invisible presence.

For years he'd stopped drinking, either on his doctor's or the woman's orders. But the week before I met him, he took to the bottle again, because the possibility of a new exhibition had finally materialised. In the course of our evening together he was mostly incoherent. It would have made a fascinating, if perplexing play: no matter what was being discussed, or what anybody might ask him, he would doggedly pursue his own line of thought, staring straight ahead into the distance with his tearful round eyes, his beard already turning white, his hands – which could wield a paintbrush with such colour and mastery and fantasy – occasionally clenched in fists, and letting go again. Possessed by his esoteric dreams, or nightmares, he seems to wander through the streets around the place de la Contrescarpe, mumbling, enfolded in his loneliness as in an African blanket. One of the zombies apartheid has let loose upon the world, wandering ghost, sad and terrifying dreamer.

Another of these lost souls – but still redeemable, with the embers of an old African fire smouldering behind his often bloodshot eyes, was Mazisi Kunene, responsible for most of the banned ANC's organisation in London and Europe. Much later, at the time when Mandela was released from prison and our transition towards freedom began, he returned from decades of exile and we became very close friends; I dedicated *Imaginings of Sand* to him. The most moving moment of our friendship was when, just before the elections of 1994, he invited me to accompany him to the home in Natal, high on a green hill, where he had spent his childhood and where his parents had been buried during his years in exile. It was his first visit since he returned, and there was something almost sacred about the moment he went on his knees to greet the dead. What had kept him alive all those years was his poetry. He was the most dedicated, almost obsessive, poet I have ever known. No matter how busy his schedule was (and during the years as ANC representative abroad, and later, lionised as a poet at many festivals in many countries, his days were crammed with commitments) he would get up before dawn every morning and fill notebook after notebook, in his elegant handwriting, with his Zulu poems. And if the writing had to be interrupted for breakfast or a visitor, Mazisi would – with something of a wistful smile – close his book and put away his pen, sometimes at the end of a line and sometimes in the middle, and continue from there, without a moment's hesitation, the following morning.

After his return to South Africa, he was a much more forceful presence, as a person and in my life, than in the sixties in Paris. But from the very first time he entered the little garret apartment in the rue Malebranche where I stayed with Breyten and Yolande there was something unforgettable about him. A unique kind of dignity. Perhaps, I often thought at the time, a peculiarly *Zulu* dignity. Which showed even when he was sad and despondent: then he would come to visit, and put a *kwela* record from the townships on the tinny little turntable in the lounge, and close his eyes, and start dancing, in one spot, round and round, very slowly, while the tears came running down his furrowed cheeks. Even in those early days, long before his hair became as white as the snows of the Bokkeveld, his cheeks were much-furrowed. Suffering shows. Exile shows. After a while like this, he could smile again, his indomitable little smile, and draw back his broad shoulders – there always was a massive quality about his body, even in sorrow – and face the world with his dignity restored.

And when one of us was depressed, it would be Mazisi who would put an arm around our shoulders and say, 'Don't worry, man. Tomorrow we go home.' Always that parting line, 'Tomorrow we go home.'

Even the first time he set foot in Paris his peculiarly Zulu pride and dignity was in evidence. All he had to guide him, was a piece of paper on which he'd written the only address for a friend he'd been given. Meticulously following his instructions from the Gare du Nord, he'd taken a Métro to the station nearest to his contact address. But that was in the quarter of Denfert-Rochereau and he found himself in a bewildering labyrinth of streets. Looking round, he saw a policeman in the distance and approached, crumpled paper in hand. This Mazisi thrust into the hand of the gendarme, who turned out to be very helpful. He pointed the long arm of the law up a narrow street and said, '*Là-bas.*'

Mazisi didn't know a single word of French, but immediately took this to mean 'lapa', which is the Zulu word for 'that way'.

Afterwards he explained: it didn't come as a surprise to him that the gendarme had addressed him in Zulu: that, in his view, was only natural. But what had surprised, and pleased, him was that the Frenchman had immediately recognised his interlocutor as Zulu. From that day, Mazisi had a soft spot for the French.

Something of Mazisi's melancholy was also noticeable in Lewis Nkosi, but we never became particularly close. Unlike Mazisi, the bottle never had a soothing, humanising influence on Lewis: he became steadily more aggressive and obnoxious. But I have the impression that the mellowing effect of ageing has rounded the edges of the abrasiveness with which he used to protect his vulnerability; and in recent years I have become more able to appreciate the broadness of his humour and the sharpness of his wit.

We spent some evenings of heated discussion, in which I was impressed by his critical faculties: he was undoubtedly the most acute South African critic in those years. But our real mutual mistrust began, I now believe, with the publication of *Looking on Darkness* in 1974. In London, Lewis came to one of the discussions that followed the launch, but he left before we could talk. I heard subsequently that he hated the novel. It surprised me when he later published his own *Mating Birds*, which revealed strange parallels with my book.

In Paris, when all of that was still in the future, I was aware of nothing as much as a sense of distance; we could never embrace, as Mazisi and I could. The sadness in him had, at the time, too much arrogance to let anyone come very close. Which makes it all the more gratifying that the last few years seem to have eased the relationship, highlighting more what we have in common than what separates us.

There was at least one other South African artist who marked my life with the sadness of his exile. This was the painter Nico Hagen, whom I had first met just after I'd moved my belongings to Ingrid's flat after meeting her in April 1963. On that day, Nico, with whom Ingrid had just had an affair, turned up out of the blue to introduce his bride to her. Not so long after this he left for Paris. At some stage he got divorced and married a young woman with whom he had a baby. Even during my visit in 1966 I'd heard rumours about the couple in their new surroundings: how they would pack their baby in a groceries basket on Saturday nights and set out for a night of partying, moving from one spot to the next until, when it was time to go home in the early hours, they would realise that the baby had been left behind somewhere. Then they would have to retrace their steps, sometimes for hours, until the lost basket was found again. Everything was going downhill. A couple of times Nico fell ill just before the opening of an exhibition so that he couldn't finish his canvases in time. Although many people recognised his talent, he just couldn't break out of the spiral of bad luck and looked for solace in the bottle. The wife left him with their baby. I often heard about Nico's misfortunes. But it was only towards the end of 1968, a month or so before my return to South Africa, that I saw him again. Many years after that, after he too had returned to South Africa, we met again.

And immediately clicked. That was when I really came to value his work. But that year in Paris was a low point in his life; and it didn't take more than a glance to realise this.

I hadn't had much sleep the night before, having just broken up with H, and when I was awakened by a violent knocking on my door I was in no mood for guests. But the moment I diffidently opened the door, Nico came tumbling across the threshold, stumbled over the small flokati on my floor and ended up on all fours against the opposite wall, large and angular but in a bad shape, like a dishevelled Viking.

'What the fuck?' he exclaimed, scrambling clumsily to his feet and steadying himself against my table as he stood there swaying and trying to focus his wild eyes. In his hand he had a half-full bottle of red wine.

'Good afternoon,' I mumbled, still confused as I struggled against a bad headache.

'It's not a good afternoon,' he said. 'It's a fucking awful afternoon.'

'Well, a fucking awful afternoon to you too then,' I said.

'Why are you so formal?' he asked aggressively.

'Sorry,' I said, 'for a moment I confused you with somebody else.' A colleague of mine in the Afrikaans Department at Rhodes seemed, in those circumstances, the spitting image of Nico.

'He's a cunt,' said Nico.

'He's actually a very nice bloke,' I said.

'I tell you he's a cunt.' He snorted, half turned towards the table he was using to steady himself, and in a wide gesture swept all the papers to the floor. 'What's all this shit?'

'I'm working on a translation,' I said, making an effort to remain patient.

'A translation of what?'

'A novel for teenagers.'

'Fuck teenagers,' he said. 'Is there nothing better you can do?'

'I need the money.'

'Fuck money,' he snarled. 'Selling your soul, that's what you're doing.' He came a step or two closer, swaying precariously on his feet. 'Look here,' he said, struggling to find the right words. 'Look here, my man. You're a bloody genius, hear what I'm saying?'

'That's balls,' I said.

'I tell you, you're a fucking genius. You're a great writer. I've never read anything you wrote, but I know you're a great writer. So how come you're translating this kind of shit?' He spilled wine on the scattered pages at his feet.

I stumbled forward to salvage what I could, but he eluded me, spilled some more wine, this time on the white flokati, lost his balance and landed sprawling on the bed.

For a minute or so he was silent while I kneeled to gather the remains of the manuscript.

'Is that a turntable on the shelf?' he suddenly asked. 'Why don't you play us some music?'

I obliged with a Haydn cello concerto.

'Mmmm,' he said approvingly. 'Mozart. The double violin concerto.'

I made a fatal mistake. 'I don't think Mozart wrote a double violin concerto, Nico,' I dared to counter him. 'Actually, this is a Haydn cello concerto.' I reached for the sleeve and handed it to him. 'See?'

'See yourself.' He flung it away, pushed me back and started conducting, spilling wine on the little carpet. Then stopped in the middle of a phrase to demand, accusingly, 'Why the fuck are you listening to Mozart?'

'I'm listening to Haydn because I think it's divine.'

'Divine my arse. You shouldn't be listening to music at all, you're supposed to be writing deathless prose.' Before I could answer, he offered me his bottle. 'Here, take this. Present for you. It'll help you through the dry patches.'

I made a grab for it before he could spill some more.

'Well, aren't you going to pour some?' he asked. 'Or are you too fucking high and mighty?'

I sidestepped his grasp and picked up a glass from the wash-stand in the corner, dutifully poured myself a tot, raised the glass to him and took a sip.

'God!' he said. 'Aren't you going to offer me some? It's *my* wine, you know. You bloody shit. You despise me, do you?'

I quickly poured some for him and tried to keep the bottle out of his reach. He stood up to raise the glass, but lost his balance and ended up kneeling on the floor, most of the wine soaking into the once-pristine long hairs of the flokati.

'So why aren't you writing?' he returned to the attack.

'I've just finished a book on Provence.'

'What the fuck has Provence got to do with it?'

'I've just been there to do a travelogue.'

'Why?'

'Well, I thought—'

'Ag fuck it, man,' he exploded. 'Don't lie to me.'

'Why would I lie to you?'

He leaned in my direction. 'Let me tell you something, my mate. I'm in the High Command. You got that? I'm in the High Command and you and your kind will be the first ones we wipe out.'

'Then wipe us out,' I said. 'I'll just go on writing.'

'Oh dear God,' he groaned, pressing his hands to his head and kicking over his half-empty glass. 'You. You. *You!* You know what you are? You know what you can do? So why are you wasting time listening to Mozart and writing naught but simple shit?' He broke off and started singing. 'And then you write about Czechoslovakia.' He checked himself. 'Or Provence. Or whatever. *Why?!!!*'

'I told you. I've just been there.'

'I know you've just been there. Don't keep on repeating the same shit. Why don't you start *doing* something with your life?'

It was weird beyond any telling of it. Hilarious at times, maddening in between – especially as he kept on spilling wine. But with something unbearably disturbing about it too. As if, despite his incoherence, his non sequiturs, his wild threats and accusations, he was taking my life apart, breaking me down, exposing all the uncertainties and doubts and vulnerabilities deep down.

'What do you want me to do?' I asked in desperation when I couldn't take it any longer.

'Go and get yourself a gun and go home. The war of liberation has begun.'

I tried to placate him. 'If that's what you want,' I said, 'I shall do it.'

'Good,' he applauded, then poured the last few drops of wine into his glass and promptly upended it on the floor. He offered me his left hand. 'Congratulations. And welcome to the struggle. You're a good sort and a true friend and a bloody shit. Don't fuck with me, my friend.'

There seemed to be no end to it. But suddenly I heard Breyten's steps on the staircase outside and hurried out to look for help. Risking our lives jointly and severally we escorted him down the six flights of stairs. It was almost impossible to dissuade him from looking for sustenance in a bistro; but at last, under the pretext of wanting to see his paintings, we coaxed him into Breyten's small red 2CV to take him home. But we had no idea of where he lived, and had to rely on his directions. It took an hour before he ordered us to an abrupt stop in a wholly unfamiliar part of the city. From there we had to support him under both arms as he showed the way. A mere block from where we'd left the car an unsteady old *clochard* joined us with a merry '*Salut, les copains!*' It must have been at least half an hour before he finally peeled away from us, convinced at last that the journey was not going to end up in a bistro. It was a descent into hell. Every few yards Nico would start haranguing every stranger who crossed our unsteady way:

'Brothers, friends! Listen to me. I tell you, if I were a man I would have addressed you in the tongues of angels.'

Every time, with increasing effort and shortening tempers, we managed to pull him away. At the most unexpected moments he would break free and try to run in front of passing cars. A pandemonium of hooting and curses marked our progress from street to street.

'Why are you so full of shit?' he would stop to ask. 'You're not fucking human beings. Don't you have the guts to shout? Tell the world to fuck off!' Whereupon he would do just that to the very next man, woman or child who came past.

I lost all track of time. It must have been another hour before we finally forced an address out of him and he dragged us to the avenue de Breteuil. After breaking away one last time in an attempt to barge into a *parfumerie* to buy wine, and threatening to break down the place when he couldn't find any, he dumped us in front of his apartment building where he finally managed to wiggle a key into the door and escort us inside. An unexpectedly upmarket building, all marble and mirrors, where fur-bedecked old women sat among potted aspidistras watching television behind glass panels; but Nico staggered past all this, across a courtyard, to a wretched grey passage at the back of the building, and two storeys up a dirty concrete staircase to his room, a miserable dive with a narrow stretcher as the only piece of furniture, piled high with filthy blankets. In one corner was a washbasin filled with paintbrushes. All along the walls stood empty frames and paintings and drawings, finished and unfinished, some with clothes draped over them.

I straightened his bed. As I tried to pick up an abandoned painting from the floor, he took a flying leap to tackle me, misjudged the angle and dived with his forehead into the wall. With blood and tears streaming from his head and nose, he remained propped up against the stretcher, refusing all our offers to help.

We stayed for a while, trying to plead with him, but now he remained stubbornly silent. All around us were examples of his work, mostly unfinished. Among them one large painting, a haunting canvas, some anatomical monster like a half-formed bloody foetus that had been shaken from a spoon into an empty plate. A title had been splashed across the canvas in uneven letters: *Viens dogdog*. With a subtitle, in brackets: *It could have been so different.*

'You know what?' Quite unexpectedly. He looked up at us: 'You know what's wrong with you two? You're too fucking human. That is why you're writing such shit.'

By now he seemed to have calmed down.

Breyten went over to wipe the blood from his face. But Nico shook his head angrily.

'This isn't blood,' he said. 'It's red tears.'

He moved out of the way so that we could get past.

As we reached the door, he suddenly called out, 'Listen!'

We stopped to look at him.

'Let me tell you about Afrikaners,' he said.

We waited.

He moved as if to get up, but then decided against it. 'Listen carefully.' He began to articulate with exaggerated clarity: 'I shit – you heard that? – I *shit* – on the *fucking* – that's exactly what I mean – on the fucking *cunts*

– you understand what I mean? It's exactly that – the *cunts*.' He nodded, and sighed. 'You may go now.'

On a recent long tour through South Africa with my favourite friends Gerrit and Marina, we found, in Burgersdorp, a charming restaurant in a well-restored building bearing the name of Nico's House and learned that it used to belong to Nico Hagen. And that he'd died.

It could have been so different.

Another friend from the world of art was a writer from the Cameroon, Mbella Sonne Dipoko. I loved his novel *A Few Days and Nights* which, in spite of its lightness of tone, has unexpected layers below the surface. What I found in many ways refreshing about him – something rather extraordinary, at the time, for an African writer in Paris – was his lack of interest in politics. 'Love is so much more important, don't you think?' he said more than once. 'I mean, one needs a lifetime to get to grips with love – there just isn't enough time left for politics.'

Mbella died some years ago, much too early. He was young and strong, with the build and the broad shoulders of a boxer, but he had a charming, gentle disposition and the heart and eyes of a child. He'd come to Paris to study law, but soon abandoned his studies and devoted himself full-time to the café life, a university in its own right, and to women. Not as a Casanova, and certainly not as a scientist; but as a true *amateur*, in the best French sense of the word.

He was having a hard time finding a room. The old story: he would telephone a number gleaned from a newspaper or a noticeboard at the university, the landlady would express interest, even enthusiasm, and they would arrange for him to come round – but when Madame discovered that he was from Africa, she would suddenly remember that the room had just been taken. After a few months of frustration even Mbella's good humour started wearing thin. For a while a good friend in a students' residence in the Cité Universitaire provided a way out by offering Mbella the space under his bed to sleep – sometimes alone, sometimes with a girl.

But then the friend had to return home and Mbella had to find a new shelter. Distress all around, until the friend suggested that Mbella simply stay on, under the bed, without alerting the new lodger. It worked well for a few nights, but the new occupant of the bed turned out to be a man with an active interest in politics. Every night there were vociferous political discussions, many of which began to upset Mbella deeply. For the first week he managed to keep quiet, but then it became too much even for a pacifist like him and one night he raised his hand from under the bed and expressed his unqualified dissatisfaction with what had just been said. Pandemonium. But when the consternation subsided and Mbella was allowed to have his say, the rest of the room was so impressed that he was promptly granted leave to stay on. And when the new man in the bed had to leave, everybody agreed that Mbella should move from under the bed and take his place on it. The authorities were left in the dark, and for several months Mbella slept like a king and royally entertained an impressive succession of eager French girls. Only when one of these became too loud was he asked to leave.

One evening, in April 1968, many things came together. A protest meeting against the regime of the colonels in Greece had been organised in the Mutualité. This is something that defines so much of the fascination of Paris: not just its cosmopolitan quality, but the fact that nothing, absolutely nothing, can happen anywhere in the world without people getting *passionately* involved. Even so, this was a special occasion. The Greek colonels were indeed threatening *us*, every one of us. All the freedoms we were enjoying in Paris, were jeopardised by the threat to one seemingly remote – but shockingly close, shockingly intimate – part of the world. Ninety per cent of the audience must have been Greek. The remaining ten per cent represented the rest of the world. Barely a month after this protest we would all march through the streets of Paris shouting in support of Daniel Cohn-Bendit, *Nous sommes tous des Juifs allemands! We are all German Jews!*

Most of the speeches were fierce and fiery. The evening began with a young girl who seemed to have mistaken that demonstration for another, as she broke into a passionate defence of Black Power and a ferocious condemnation of the assassination of Martin Luther King. Not a word about Greece. But a cry of outrage: 'We've had enough of martyrs. Now we need something *more*: the violence of Stokely Carmichael is the only possible solution.' How prophetic those words came to sound during the month of May! The *solidarity* of resistance against autocratic authority: students all over the world began to protest – against Spanish oppression, against tyranny in Portugal, against American atrocities in Vietnam.

Then came Melina Merkouri. Those in the audience who only knew her from *Never on a Sunday* were stunned by the electricity of her presence, the passion and conviction of her rage:

> I have come to talk to you about Greece. Not the timeless Greece of the sun, but the torn Greece of today. Not the stones of the Parthenon, but the stones of prisons. The sons of the gods have been turned into slaves.

Leading up to the ecstatic *Death or Liberty!* was the cry of *Thanatos!* which sent seismic vibrations through the entire hall.

After the speeches, more music. The Theodorakis Ensemble, playing with stoic faces but with instruments of fire. A young crippled girl, Maria. Singing with a voice that did not sound human at all: it was is if the earth itself was erupting from that narrow, maimed female body to reach out to the heavens; it became that voice possessed by duende that Lorca once wrote about in an immortal essay about an Andalusian flamenco singer who followed an ordinary performance with an outbreak of unmatched fire:

> *La Niña de los Peines* had to tear her voice, because she knew that she was being listened to by an *élite* not asking for forms but for the marrow of forms, for music exalted into purest essence. She had to impoverish her skills and aids; that is, she had to drive away her muse and remain alone so that the *duende* might come and join in a hand-to-hand fight. And how she sang! Now she was in earnest, her voice was a jet of blood, admirable because of its pain and its sincerity, and it opened like a ten-fingered hand in the nailed but tempestuous feet of a Christ by Juan de Juni.

And after Maria came a male singer. Then the incendiary Melina once more: theatrical and inflamed, seducing the microphone, undulating across the stage, throwing her hair backwards and forwards, closing her eyes, spreading open her arms, thrusting her breasts at the audience. Without the duende quality of Maria, but with an unmatched sense of theatre and spectacle, that drove the audience wild and caused the entire hall to reverberate with the cry of *Thanatos!*

And I had an ecstatic thought, which I wrote in my journal before I went to bed that night: Suppose we could all come together in the Mutualité one day in the future, thousands of us, all spontaneously breaking into *Nikosi sikelel' iAfrika*, with the same passion tonight's Greeks have demonstrated in their *Thanatos!*

Outside in the throbbing night, with the breeze cold on my flaming face, I remembered how a friend had once asked me what I regarded as one's *ultimate* possession: what would remain, what would matter, on the day one lay prostrate at the feet of an executioner? I had always imagined, in such a moment, the presence of a woman, a last touch and expression of love. But on that night I suddenly knew that freedom was something as warm and physical and as *necessary* as love; and that *this* might well be what remains *in extremis*.

POWER IN THE STREETS

MAY, 1968. IT IS HARD TO EXPLAIN TO ANYONE WHO WAS NOT THERE, BUT I know there is no way of getting out of it. Above all, it is a crucial moment from the past I *have* to revisit, mainly for myself. Certainly, much of it was directly connected to the events in the streets of Paris during that famous month of May. In my diary from those turbulent times I find this small note:

> God, what a year. The most extraordinary of my life. The most beautiful, the best, the worst, the fullest, the emptiest, the most meaningful, the most confusing.

But that year began as a quest for H. After her months of wandering through Africa, I followed her to Europe in December 1967, hoping that this long absence would bring about the mutual rediscovery and confirm what we had both been hoping for. That miracle did not happen. And yet it was a wonderful year for us. Weekends or weeks in Paris, in London, in Scotland, and at last in a seemingly endless journey through Languedoc and Provence – reading, reading, talking without end, in dingy rooms or on sunlit terraces, in dark-green fields or among the grey rocky slopes of the Alpilles, on brown benches in town squares in the dappled shade of plane trees, at small round tables in cheap restaurants in lost villages with names like the titles of poems; getting soaked in an unexpected shower in Roussillon when all the ochre hills appeared to dissolve and came washing down towards us in streams of red and yellow and we had to strip off all our clinging clothes to dry ourselves in the new sun; attending summer concerts in Avignon or Orange or Carpentras; dining on a terrace among the folds of the Montagne Noire near Carcassonne, with Madame Marinette's incomparable ratatouille or tender duckling or lamb prepared with thyme and rosemary picked in the mountains; listening on a derelict radio in an unprepossessing Hôtel Côte d'Azur far from the Côte d'Azur to news of Russia's invasion of Prague; or spending a night in the long grass beside the swift and shallow stream at La Malène in the Gorges du Tarn; battling against the exhilarating wind on a slope of Mont Ventoux or fighting off dive-bombing mosquitoes below Daudet's mill outside Fontvieille; huddling in a tatty little circus in Sault, and coming back to find our Hôtel de la Poste locked, so that I had to undertake a perilous climb along gutters and treacherous ivy up to our room, only to find myself at the wrong window and landing next to the bed of an elderly woman who broke into hysterics and woke the whole establishment with her screams.

H first came over to Paris a day after my arrival, and immediately there was the feeling – renewed every time we met again – of resuming from where we had left off, as if there had been no interruption at all. But I made the mistake, I realised only much later, of being too greedy: not content with the admittedly brief, but exhilarating past we had shared and with the present we were exploring in Paris, I also wanted to secure the future, driven by an overwhelming sense of insecurity and, perhaps, by fear of loneliness. Of course this could never work – not with H's uncompromising honesty about relationships. The only solution was to decide not to be blinded or restricted any longer by expectations which, in the circumstances, could not but be unrealistic. We would face the rest of the year with open minds, live as fully and as deeply as we could, but without burdening each other with presumptions or hopes which would press too heavily on the present.

There was a sense of release in this. And there were indeed splendid moments. Many of them unforgettable. Sometimes hilarious: as on the day when the two of us were ensconced in her small bedroom in London, from which I emerged naked into the large Victorian lounge, on my way to the bathroom, to find her formidable father sitting at a small ornate table at the window, bent over his dossiers and documents. We had no idea that he had come back a day early from the family's estate outside East Grinstead. He had his back to me, but I was already in the middle of the room. Never had such a short distance seemed so vast as I retraced my steps across that wickedly creaking floor, back into the precarious safety of her room. I still don't know whether he had seen me. His British – Victorian – sense of decorum and propriety might well have saved me from something worse than death.

Other moments had a touch of the sublime. Concerts or theatre (the Lawrence plays at the Royal Court, Beckett's *Oh les Beaux Jours* in the Odéon, Bach's Christmas Oratorio in the Salle Pleyel . . .), sunsets on the Seine or the Thames, children playing in the Luxembourg Gardens or on Hampstead Heath.

Yet throughout the year, everything was pervaded by a sense of an ending; and this was marked by several separations, usually for a few weeks at a time, but sometimes for a few months, as we prepared, consciously or unconsciously, for the end. Then the miraculous discovery, when, literally, all had been said and done, was that what we had anticipated as an end, turned out to be a new kind of beginning: like a piece of music in which the key has changed.

This was why the events of that May hit me with such ferocity. I was in London on a brief visit to see, after the first of the partings from H, whether we should try to resume the relationship. On Friday 3 May I left Paris in a cloud of tear gas after the closure of the Faculty of Nanterre and the invasion of the inner courtyard of the Sorbonne for the first time in seven centuries (except for the violation of its space by the Nazis) had provoked violent student demonstrations.

For several years the new state-of-the-art faculty had been sitting on its site outside Paris – an ultramodern complex of buildings, with ultramodern amenities, but with no provision for the needs of young people *outside* of study hours. There had been petitions, deputations, memoranda, discussions, negotiations, protest meetings and street demonstrations, but French bureaucracy grinds more slowly than the mills of God. In 1968, much of the education system was still functioning according to the rules and rhythms determined by Napoleon in 1804. In the Sorbonne, more than 30,000 students in the humanities had to use a library with only 400 seats; to attend a lecture one had to queue for more than an hour – and then be happy to find a seat on the floor or a windowsill; if you were working on a thesis, you could count yourself fortunate to see the prof for perhaps five minutes a month.

For generations the protests had been going more or less unheeded, or at least without tangible results; but it so happened that in this Year of Our Lord there happened to be a different kind of Angry Young Man on campus: the turbulent, red-headed Daniel Cohn-Bendit. Earlier in the year he'd already run into trouble with a minister who'd visited the faculty to open the long-awaited swimming pool. Cohn-Bendit demanded more say for students in university matters; the government, as always, prevaricated. Two weeks before the explosion in May, the students convened a meeting in one of the lecture rooms. Permisson was refused. The students responded by carrying the professor out into the passage and continuing on their own. That was when the rector ordered the university to be closed and police to form a cordon outside. Cohn-Bendit and five other student leaders were summoned to a disciplinary hearing on Monday 6 May.

This was what had triggered the protests on Friday 3rd, when I left for London. How many rowdy meetings had I attended under the imposing dome of the old university chapel and among the symmetrical arcades surrounding the quad. But that Friday there was a different kind of unrest in the crowd. Fired up by what had been happening elsewhere in the world over the previous months – in Madrid and Barcelona, in Rome, in Tokyo, in the US and Latin America, most recently in Germany – there was a sudden movement to storm the lecture rooms and 'take over'. Then came rumours that a group of ultra-rightists were on their way to the Sorbonne, armed with sticks and crowbars, one of them even with a meat cleaver. At the same time, from all directions, came the familiar braying of police cars. In a flash the whole Sorbonne was surrounded, allegedly to keep right and left apart.

The rector gave the order for the police to move in and 'clear the building'. Within minutes the first clouds of dirty yellow tear gas were billowing up from the pavements. After my return from London the news had spread

1967: After Ingrid, in Grahamstown.

1980: At the founding meeting of the Soweto PEN Centre, with Ahmed Essop, Es'kia Mphahlele, Nadine Gordimer and Sipho Sepamla.

1986: Addressing an anti-apartheid students' meeting at Rhodes University.

1987: Visiting Dakar with a group of Afrikaners to meet the ANC in exile.
I am in the second row, second from right.

998: With Ariel
Dorfman in
Mandela's cell
n the prison on
Robben Island.

2006: With the Russian soprano Anna Netrebko in Salzburg.

2007: With Carlos Fuentes and Nadine Gordimer in Johannesburg.

2006: In Sarajevo, with Antjie Krog in the striped shirt, and the French ambassadorial couple, Geneviève and Henry Zipper de Fabiani.

1998: With Olga.

2006: With my sons Anton and Danie at the restaurant of The Cock House in Grahamstown, the British Settler home where we lived in the 70s.

2006: Wedding with Karina. Back row: my children Sonja, Danie and Gustav. Sadly, Anton couldn't make it.

2008: Karina.

2006: My birthday celebration with Karina.

2007: With Karina and Nelson Mandela
in his Cape Town home.

with unbelievable speed, and students came from everywhere to join in the fight. They came on foot, by bus, by train and Métro. That afternoon there were 10-12,000 of them in the boulevard Saint-Michel. And police too: not the ordinary gendarmes but the most vehemently loathed riot police, the CRS, recruited from the ranks of veterans from the Algerian war, and mineworkers and jailbirds and all manner of *durs*: men who were not interested in playing games. When they struck, they meant to maim.

One street after another was cordoned off. No buses or cars were allowed to pass. Small groups of protesters were rounded up and marched off to the rows of waiting Black Marias, the *paniers de salade*. They had to keep their arms above their heads; and as they approached the police vehicles a black wave of waiting police engulfed them. One car coming down the rue Cujas was stopped, the doors torn open and the young girl behind the wheel was dragged out by five men armed with batons. It seemed like forever before she fell down, blood streaming from her mouth and nose; and as she collapsed one policeman gave her a last kick in the back.

From all sides the cry went up: '*Libérez nos camarades!*' For a while a new tear-gas attack forced the students to withdraw. Then small groups of youngsters started tearing off the steel grids surrounding the trees along the boulevards. This was followed by traffic signs and the grilles protecting shop windows. One group started breaking up the cobblestones, revealing the layer of sand below.

'It's the beach!' the cry went up.

'Back to the sea!' shouted the crowd, as if Jean-Jacques Rousseau had risen from the dead.

Then a new police attack began: ten or twenty *paniers de salade* came hurtling down the boulevard, sending students diving in all directions, followed by new columns of CRS hurling tear-gas grenades. And so it went on for most of the weekend. By the time I returned from London, late in the evening of Monday 6th, the Latin Quarter was in a state of devastation. The whole area around the Sorbonne had been cordoned off by police armed with Sten guns and *matraques*, wearing helmets and carrying shields, like unwieldy medieval warriors, surveyed by a helicopter circling like a vulture.

At one stage a young American came up to me, gasping for breath, wiping blood from a wound on his forehead: scrambling furiously to find new cobblestones from the broken street, he asked, 'By the way, what are we demonstrating about?'

What, indeed? By that time Nanterre, or the obsolete and inadequate facilities of the Sorbonne, had long faded into the distance. It had become part of a much wider and deeper Revolt of the Young. And I find it fascinating, today, to page through my journals of those tumultuous times:

I cannot agree [I wrote a week or so after my return to Paris, in a moment of reflection between outbursts of sound and fury] with violence or vandalism or chaos for its own sake. But what I do find horrifying is that a situation should have developed in which otherwise serious-minded and responsible young people should be driven to a point where they see violence as the only effective means of protest at their disposal.

The young generation has always been, almost by definition, revolutionary. Without this, the world would have been fossilised, petrified, long ago. One is reminded of the poet van Wyk Louw's words about the real danger in any society residing in an entire generation coming and going without protest. But today's *kind* of protest is radically different from the timeless 'clash of generations'. It is more violent; it has its origins in an all-encompassing despair.

Of course, many of these demonstrations are still rooted in 'local' conditions: antiquated systems of education in Spain and Italy; a smouldering anti-Nazi conscience in the Axel Springer media monopoly in West Germany; resentment against the absolutist communism of the Novotny regime in Czechoslovakia; rage against the Johnson administration and its grotesque blundering in Vietnam, and so on. But this still does not explain the peculiar passion that informs all these explosions.

The nature of the world in which this young generation has grown up, has caused the gap between their way of life and that of their parents to be greater than any comparable chasm in history. Today's youth lives in the world on the far side of the deluge and beyond the traditional assurances and the soothers of conscience represented by religion and mercy: this generation, born after the Second World War, can no longer be surprised or shocked by anything. In a world where Hitler's camps, the atrocities of the Congo, the horror of Hungary, the massacre of Vietnam, the extermination in Nigeria have become commonplace, there is not much room for hope or patience. To do nothing, or to offer only passive or non-violent resistance, merely allows evil to proliferate around you. The Martin Luther Kings who try to stop violence with reason or gentleness are murdered themselves. In this way an entire generation is driven back to the calm and moving dialectics of Camus: in a utopian world there will no longer be violence; but *we* do not live in such a world, and for us, in some situations, it becomes necessary to assume the audacity and responsibility of violence in order to come a little bit closer to peace. Our world is not absolute, but relative: injustice can never be eliminated, but it *can* always be diminished. And for that violence may sometimes be necessary. Truly responsible freedom is never offered to one as a gift: it has to be claimed, and conquered. Here in France, today: the reasonable demands, the pleas, the peaceful demonstrations, of a century have not changed anything – now it is time to grab with force.

In a different kind of society it might still have been possible to achieve change without violence. But any reasonable person must realise that 'the correct channels' for peaceful change in our society have become hopelessly blocked. No existing political party in the country offers space for the needs and aspirations of the youth any longer. The impossible bureaucracy in which both capitalism and communism have become bogged down offers only the possibility of slow suffocation. The time has come to spell out that this revolt which has been raging in the streets of Paris over the last few weeks is directed just as passionately against the totalitarian communism of Moscow as the imperialism of the US or the outdated despotism of a Franco or a de Gaulle.

The essential characteristic of today's 'unorganised' society, as one of the 'prophets' of the present revolt, Herbert Marcuse, has pointed out, is that it has become a society of *consumers*: we are required more and more, like people attending a national festival in South Africa, to sit back and expect to be *fed*. The positive, creative influence of the individual hardly exists any longer: throughout his university education the student is required to conform; the labourer no longer has any relation with the product he helps to produce. This danger, already signalled so clearly by Marx, has become a strangling reality.

All of this has been aggravated by what Ortega y Gasset, approaching it from the opposite end, characterised as 'the revolt of the masses': our overcrowded world simply no longer has space for the individual. This also means that 'domestic affairs' no longer exist: what happens in South Africa or Bolivia or Biafra or Vietnam is of immediate relevance to the rest of the world. Every European is intensely concerned by the slightest convulsion in the Third World – which explains why this revolt in Paris is directed as much against the disgrace of Vietnam as against the constipation of the French education system.

It is not only the *fact* of exponentially increasing numbers in the world that is important, but everything linked to it, including increasing longevity, which forces the young generation to wait that much longer before they can assume a place in society. Considering that people younger than twenty-five in many countries form fifty per cent of the population and that they are all constrained in a system in which they have no effective say, it is only natural that their frustration should have reached boiling point. And the members of this young generation have assimilated their world much faster than their predecessors: through the mass media they have become more fully informed about this world. They have fewer inhibitions – and more urgency. Thanks to the Pill their patterns of sexual behaviour have changed irrevocably. And it is *this* generation, that has matured so much faster and is prepared to assume responsibility for it, that is now being treated like children.

Previously, they would simply have been expected to shut up: and they would not have been aware of the general extent of their frustration. But now they have full access to the mass media. They *know*.

And for that reason their resistance has become so spectacular and impressive. Which is why they find their inspiration in the awareness, as Éluard has said, that they are no longer a handful, but a crowd.

Every state has learned to allow a certain measure of protest. But this small space for manoeuvring becomes, itself, part of the system of containment against which today's rage is directed. And now it must break out. It is only understandable that in the process today's young generation should align themselves morally with the Third World, which still comprises Fanon's 'wretched of the earth'.

This goes beyond a 'political' surface. The present generation is appalled by the top-heavy overload of laws and institutions and regulations and procedures that stifle all initiative and all long views of the future. That is why they feel the urge to rush in and start doing something about it on their own. They may not have a 'programme'; they may not even know exactly where they are going. But for the moment it is enough to know, and to articulate, that this world is no longer acceptable. Across its chaos and its sordidness, they hurl the defiant, outraged '*No!!!*' of Antigone. They are no longer content to 'play the game': they are opting out. *They* are the ones who have to live in tomorrow's world: at the very least they demand a say in it.

It is illuminating to look at the heroes' gallery of today's generation: Mao Tse-tung and Ho Chi Minh, Fidel Castro, the charismatic Che Guevara. It is easy to raise objections against these names, but these objections make no difference to the *fact* of the role they are playing in the present winter (or early spring) of discontent. What all of them have in common in the eyes of the youth of the world includes: resistance against obsolete social and political structures; a readiness to fight against imperialism (even if old Mao has been doing quite well constructing his own form of imperialism); a focus on social change, whether one agrees with the specific forms or direction of such change or not. It involves, in short, concepts of 'continuing revolution', mostly derived from Trotsky, and philosophically expressed in Camus' notion of *l'homme révolté* – the conviction that the human being can only manifest her or his humanity by ceaselessly rebelling against everything that threatens that humanity. It is not a rebellion by virtue of what still has to be attained or achieved, but by virtue of a quality which already exists within the individual and has to be *affirmed*.

I rebel, therefore we are, argues Camus. In this resides the remarkable awareness of *responsibility*, the social dimension, the altruistic commitment, of the new revolution. But at the same time it is, of course, an *absurd* revolt, because it can never finally 'achieve' a 'result': it can only, ceaselessly, redefine itself in the process of moving forward. New structures emerge within the act of destruction itself. Which suggests that much of it, especially when it is seen from the outside, may appear romantic or misguided. But I must confess that what I have witnessed over the past two weeks – the *way* in which students have organised their entire microcosm, avoiding unnecessary violence or damage, the way in which they have drawn an entire community into their movement – has unexpectedly provided me with the vision of a new world which may just be becoming visible on the horizon, and a new kind of human being who is no longer as inconceivable as it might have seemed until only days ago.

The new generation has seen all the horrors that threaten a true globalism – and surely, globalism (provided it never ceases to respect the local and the individual as its starting points) is the only 'politics' in a world that has to cope with the actual population explosion. These horrors can all be reduced to the two containing systems of race and class: and this is why our Parisian revolt, like that of the young generation in other countries, primarily targeted the manifestations of these two systems. Which is why it also, intimately and immediately, concerns South Africa.

This was the Paris I returned to on Monday night, 6 May. The streets in and around the Latin Quarter looked like a battlefield: there were buses overturned on the pavements; in the boulevard Saint-Germain the wrecks of four burnt-out cars were still smouldering; the whole area was heavy with the smell of tear gas.

A mass meeting had been organised for the following evening on the place Denfert-Rochereau, a joint venture arranged by students and labour organisations – something that had rarely, if ever, happened before. Tension was building up, and yet there was a carnival atmosphere in the streets. In many places impromptu barricades had been erected, setting up lines of police and young protesters opposite each other. What struck me was how similar they were in many respects, apart from the overall age difference. The demonstrators: the keen youths barely out of school, overeager for 'adventure'; the scholarly types with thick-rimmed glasses fascinated by the opportunity of turning philosophical concepts into practice; the hormone-driven youngsters in search of a quick fuck; the labourers in blue overalls, treating it either as a picnic or a serious engagement with the normally invisible representatives of the power establishment; the solemn ones waiting for apocalypse and epiphany; the light-hearted ones in search of fun and spectacle.

Opposite the slowly moving masses churning towards Denfert-Rochereau, the phalanxes of police: a study in endless contrasts – the eager youngsters straining at the bit like untrained young horses; the older, battle-hardened, cynical men awaiting their orders with grim patience; those leering at passing girls who swing their long hair and their tantalising short skirts; those with eyes bloated from lack of sleep.

It was indicative of my outsidership at that stage that I was unable to remain part of the demonstration until its climax: I had a theatre ticket and did not want to miss my show. A mere week later I would not even think of playing hookey. As it turned out, the mass meeting did not lead to any climax: the demonstrators dispersed peacefully, all the bistro terraces filled up with young people clustered in grave discussion or drinking to what had happened, or not happened, or might yet happen. But it was clear, by the time I came back from the theatre, that nothing had been resolved. And throughout the rest of the week one could sense a huge confrontation gradually and irresistibly gathering momentum.

On the Thursday, at a massive sit-in in front of the Sorbonne, there was an attempt at a rapprochement between the demonstrators and the Parti Communiste, after the unexpected alliance between workers and students which got the party's knickers in a knot. It led to the venerated old poet Aragon being sent to address the young generation that had previously been among his greatest supporters and admirers. Not this Thursday.

I have never witnessed such a public humiliation and rejection of a previously admired figure. His attempts at explaining the reluctance of the PC to enter the fray earlier (that is, before most of the large French factories went on strike in sympathy with the students), were roundly booed. 'Thirty years of betrayal cannot be wiped out by a ten-minute speech!' shouted his unruly audience. And when Aragon left, he was a broken old man, his proud white mane subsided into thatch, his broad shoulders bowed.

Then came the mass meeting on Friday afternoon, the 10th, once again on the place Denfert-Rochereau. It turned into a surprisingly festive occasion and at the end of it we turned back peacefully, some 30–40,000 students and young workers streaming down the boulevard Saint-Michel, singing and laughing and shouting slogans, happily resolved on 'occupying' the Latin Quarter for as long as it took – that is, until the police cordons around the university had been withdrawn. In the meantime, Cohn-Bendit and a group of students and professors – including two Nobel laureates – left for discussions with the rector to negotiate a peaceful resolution of the impasse. The overall mood was so light-hearted that I could not foresee anything menacing or even interesting developing from it; and I strolled to the neighbouring sixth arrondissement to visit a woman I had met only recently. She was from Trinidad, a passionate person with strong political convictions and it was, at least partly, her unmitigated rage against South Africa that had intrigued me. She was small and slight, with long black hair and the body of a dancer. At our first meeting she'd insisted on telling my fortune from her Tarot cards, which from the outset was such a transparent ploy ('You've just met a young dark woman from a remote part of the world who is going to play a dramatic role in your future') that I should immediately have been warned. Oscar Wilde: *I can resist anything, except temptation.* And Marion was intriguing, and attractive, enough to keep me cautiously interested. Moreover, she was not a person to take no for an answer. Nor was I in a mood to turn such an opportunity down. But it soon became clear that this would never work out, and so we did the unwise thing and decided to be 'friends'. Still, this evening went particularly well, with engaging, even hectic conversation and some good wine and calypso interspersed with Mozart; and it was well past midnight before I returned to the Latin Quarter.

My journal continued:

During the few hours of my absence everything had changed. Impossible to get home via the boulevard Saint-Germain, so had to cut along the rue Monsieur-le-Prince. From there, all along the boul' Mich', up along the rue Soufflot and then the rue Saint-Jacques, students building barricades. Many of them as young as fourteen or fifteen. Amazing organisation: while scores of them are digging up paving stones or breaking down traffic signs, the awnings in front of shops, anything they can lay hands on, others are reinforcing the barricades. Even cars are pushed or dragged into the constructions. Hundreds of young men and women standing in rows to pass on the building material. Facing each barricade, a narrow no-man's-land, then the rows of armed police with helmets and shields. Here and there a brief, angry altercation. But everywhere there are monitors ready to intervene. '*Au travail! Pas de provocation!*' Working, working like ants or bees. I'm trying to get through with a manuscript Marion has given me under my arm. It takes a hell of a detour, up in the rue Gay-Lussac, over several barricades. Then along the rue d'Ulm, yet another barricade, past a cordon of police to the rue Saint-Jacques, a last barricade, then into our rue Malebranche. The police have drawn their cordon in an irregular circle all around the Sorbonne. What has happened is that the student barricades have now started forming a second circle around the first, concentric to the inner one. Dante would have approved. I leave the manuscript and collect my camera. Just in case.

From time to time students break into song. The Marseillaise, the Internationale. Some start chanting: *CRS – SS!* They are quickly stopped by the marshals. Something is building up, building up, in spite of the exuberance on the surface.

Minutes later news comes that the Cohn-Bendit delegation has left the rector's office empty-handed.

'Then we stay right here where we are!' a chorus of voices goes up on the nearest barricade.

By this time scores of people who have gone out for the evening have become trapped between the two armies: the barricades are too high to scale, and the police refuse to let them through. Among them are a number of old people and small children. Many of them simply sit down on the kerbs or on thresholds, or lean against walls, shivering in the night cold, perplexed and scared.

Fifty metres from there an ominous motion ripples through the police. Not much: just a momentary stiffening, a tensing. Almost immediately afterwards the first volley of tear-gas grenades explodes, sending clouds of dirty yellow gas billowing across the street. The attack on the rue Le Goff has begun. Within minutes it is repeated in the rue Saint-Jacques, where I have taken up my position in the dark doorway of our wine shop. Further off, in all the adjacent streets, the volleys are reproduced. Like Guy Fawkes gone wrong.

The students have started singing the Marseillaise.

The slight night wind is forming small gusts and flurries. For a while the smoke is driven back towards the police. Their black cordon wavers, withdraws a little distance, then reforms. There are a few moments of utter silence as the two armies hover. Ten, twenty metres from me, to my right, from the top of the high students' barricade, suddenly, a hand is stretched out and a small shred of crumpled paper – a sweet wrapper? a shopping list? a phone number no longer needed? – comes fluttering into the dark street, swerves and sways erratically, then lands on the dirty cobblestones. No one even seems to notice it. Yet there is something momentous about it.

And as if it was a sign – the decisive signal – all hell breaks loose.

From behind the police lines two black trucks suddenly emerge from the night – the lines open to let them through – and move very slowly, like monstrously out-of-scale metal insects, towards the students' barricade. The youthful mass erupts in shouts and screams as it lets loose a barrage of stones. From the upper windows on either side of the street onlookers start pelting the police with whatever comes to hand: the contents of rubbish bins, flower vases, chamber pots. Without warning, the two trucks start spraying huge jets of water into the crowd, sending scores of bodies flying backwards. At the same time volley after volley of incendiary bombs are shot and hurled at them. The sky has become a churning mass of yellow-black smoke through which red and orange flames are flickering. The awning of the vegetable shop has caught fire. It is doused again by the water cannons. In a black swarm of outsize commando ants what seems like thousands of police are now swarming up and over the barricade. More and more of the fire bombs explode. In the rue Gay-Lussac, barely a hundred metres away, the first few cars have been set alight by the police bombs, exploding like rolling thunder that causes the whole area to shudder.

As barricade after barricade is taken, the students fall back, setting fire to all the cars they come across, trying to stem the advance of the police.

On every barricade, and through most of the open windows over-looking the street, radios are blaring, all of them tuned in to the same station. Professor Monod is speaking. We recognise his voice from meetings during the past few days. He is pleading with the police to allow the people trapped between the armies to escape, to evacuate their wounded. Every few minutes the programme is interrupted to broadcast emergency messages for doctors and nurses, requests for medicine, bandages, ambulances –

But the ambulances are stopped by police. So are Red Cross vehicles. Several of these, in fact, have their doors torn open and their drivers and paramedics pulled out and beaten up in the street. Fleeing students and wounded people try to escape into apartment buildings on either side of the street, but the police storm in after them and drag them out. Their flailing batons look eerie and unreal in the smoky night. The screaming and shouting, the wailing sirens, the cries of the wounded, of young girls beaten with truncheons or kicked with heavy boots, the rumbling thunder of exploding tear-gas grenades and more lethal mortars turn the night into a nightmare from Daumier or Gustave Doré.

As the day begins to break the streets lie devastated and exposed. High up in the rue Royer-Collard small groups of students are still fighting; elsewhere everything is deserted. Here and there individuals are squatting on shattered pavements, supporting broken heads with bloody hands. All along the rue Gay-Lussac, uphill and down to the Luxembourg Gardens, the black carcasses of burnt-out cars lie strewn about as if some gargantuan baby has broken all his toys. Here and there a sobbing girl wanders through the ruins in search of who knows what.

The long rows of black police vehicles are waiting for the wounded and the arrested to be herded in (most of them have first been driven into courtyards and lobbies to be beaten up) and driven off. One old man approaches from a nearby building in a flapping white night-shirt, to remonstrate with the police – until he too is grabbed unceremoniously by the front of his shirt and flung in among the turmoil of bodies already inside. And then a small, pale girl in a red dress arrives to add her own pleading to his – perhaps he is her uncle? or grandfather? But she, too, is picked up by the arms and legs, her bright red dress rucked up to her hips, and thrown into the truck amid the cheers and jeers of the berserkers in charge of the operation. One by one the trucks drive off.

At a given moment, from the top of the long, wide rue Gay-Lussac, a single policeman approaches, his black cape swirling. He is bellowing like a lone bull. In both hands he clutches his long truncheon, swinging it this way and that, smashing all doors and windows along the way, until he disappears around the far corner of the boul' Mich'.

And then there is only silence.

Exhausted to the bone I arrive back in our building where a bizarre sight awaits me in the courtyard: the occupants, in curlers and flapping gowns and striped pyjamas, talking and arguing and gesticulating and shouting like madmen: some want the huge front door to be locked and barred to keep out intruders or crazed police; others want it thrown wide open to offer refuge to the fleeing and the wounded – or merely to admit *un courant d'air*, a breath of air. And in the middle of all this stands our old concierge, holding her false teeth in one hand, hysterically interrupting all the diverse actors in this macabre comedy to narrate to all and sundry, at the top of her voice, the story of her life and the details of the flowers she once grew in her garden long before she came to this goddamned building.

In my room I try to lie down. I am exhausted. But sleep is out of the question. Off into the new day I blunder again. By this time a new crowd is already gathering like swarm upon swarm of bees in the boul' Mich', shouting with a rage that makes me shudder: *Libérez nos camarades! Libérez nos camarades!* Followed by: *Gestapo! Gestapo!*

Monday 13th. Yesterday the inquisitive bourgeoisie arrived in their Sunday best from the smarter suburbs to stare at what the restless natives have been up to.

Another demonstration has been planned for tonight. Afterwards the students will occupy the Sorbonne, the workers their factories. A number of senior professors have resigned in protest. Ministers and syndicate leaders are scurrying from one meeting to another. There are more than a million people in the streets – no longer only students and workers, but academics, lawyers, film stars, doctors, industrialists, farmers, housewives.

The power is in the streets! they chant. *The imagination is taking over!*

Saturday 25. At eight o' clock last night the whole of France came to a standstill for ten minutes. In houses, in cafés, in bistros, in the besieged factories, on street corners and pavements, everywhere they clustered around TV sets and radios to listen, as in other moments of crisis in the country's recent history, to General de Gaulle's response to the situation. After the weeks of violence and near-chaos and all the desperate attempts to leave it to Pompidou and others to find a solution, the hour has come for the General himself to intervene.

But what an anticlimax! This was not the de Gaulle of the Liberation, of the Algerian war or the putsch of the army generals. This was just a very confused old man speaking. Never before has there been such weariness and pathos in his *Vive la France!*

This must have been, effectively, the end of the de Gaulle era. The general may succeed in staying in power for some time to come. In his shrewd way he may manage for a while longer to manipulate the situation for his own benefit. I can well imagine the nation, exhausted and dazed by anarchy, rallying around the old man in desperation. But it cannot last. Last night was the moment of his fall. Only a year ago this would have been unthinkable.

Does this mean that something similar could also, in a not too distant future, happen in South Africa? And should that miracle happen, where will it find me: here, 10,000 kilometres away – or there where it will be happening? More and more, in these chaotic days, I do wonder where I really belong.

I'm not scared to be caught in a clash with the police. But what would be the *point* of it? I am deeply concerned by everything that happens here. But it is not *my* society. This was brought home most stunningly by yesterday's events.

After a long night in the streets – a few of us were in a small restaurant in the rue des Écoles when yet another street fight broke out and the *patron* helped us to get through a back alley; but then there was no way of getting home and we had to join the mass of demonstrators and fight on through the night – there was a brief pause in the morning before we went to the place de Clichy for the big march, more than a million people, to protest against the government's decision to keep Cohn-Bendit out of the country. A sense of madness taking over, Nietzsche's *Umwertung aller Werte*. The cabinet seems to have given up all hope of taking control of the situation: almost all the original demands of the protesters have been met, but still it goes on. Because the demands have been mere symptoms of the deeper anguish behind the revolt: the need for a new kind of society, a new set of values. (We can only hope that we will be spared Mao's Red Guards!)

Through the heart of Paris we marched and marched. Chanting

slogans. Many of them outrageous or funny. Many not so funny. *De Gaulle to the gallows!* Returning every now and then to the key line: *Nous sommes tous des Juifs allemands! We are all German Jews!* In the circumstances it made sense. Excluding Cohn-Bendit from negotiations meant excluding, demeaning, humiliating us all. And yet something inside me felt uneasy about it. This is what I cannot stand about mass demonstrations: the glib simplifications. The denial of the one thing that matters: individual lives, sensibilities, needs, hopes.

Then de Gaulle's speech. And another night of madness. At two o'clock in the morning the crowd storms the police station in our quarter where a fleet of cars and *paniers de salade* have been drawn up as a shield. When the first of these explodes it turns into yet another scene from old-fashioned representations of hell. Soon all the vehicles go up in flames, a red sunset through the black clouds of smoke. And then scores of police vans come charging from behind and a counter-attack begins. A cortège of makeshift ambulances – mostly private cars with red crosses taped to the sides – arrives to cart the wounded off to the impromptu hospital wards that have been set up inside the Sorbonne. Even wounded police are transported there to be nursed by students: once again it is the discipline in student ranks that amazes me. When scuffles do break out from time to time, there are always monitors and marshals available to restore order.

The day breaks, yet again, over a wasteland of torn-up streets, broken trees, telephone booths and newspaper kiosks overturned and destroyed. Even the sun seems reluctant to rise through the clouds. It is raining over the burnt city. From the kerbs and cobblestones blood and soot are washed away by the weeping rain. The streets are littered with soggy, dirty newspapers with the news of de Gaulle's futile address. On one destroyed barricade a door that has been torn from its hinges still stands propped up, bearing its legend like a defiant slogan: *WC Dames.*

Slowly, slowly, the city staggered through the mess. After two weeks, the strike had spread everywhere, paralysing everything, from banks and postal services and public transport to petrol stations, turning Paris into an Amsterdam of cycles and pedestrians. Everybody was on strike, from the prostitutes in the rue Saint-Denis to the gravediggers of Père Lachaise and the other sprawling cemeteries where macabre stacks of unburied coffins were piling up. The prostitutes generously offered to provide their services for free on nights of major demonstrations. Rats were scurrying everywhere. Scenes from Defoe's *A Journal of the Plague Year* and Camus' *La peste* were chillingly coming true in our everyday life. Every evening we gathered in Yolande's kitchen, grimly to count our remaining, dwindling stock of tinned food, packets of pasta, *berlingots* of long-life milk, dry biscuits, wine. No sugar left. No bread. It is a singular deprivation to live without mail. No letters from home. No money coming in. On the plus side: no tax forms to fill in, no accounts, no tirades from friends complaining that I owe them letters. No regular newspapers. From time to time I had to telephone H in London to find out what was happening here.

In *Le Monde* Robert Escarpitt wrote: *No mail, no transport, soon no more radio or television. France is truly approaching its Golden Age.*

In the main thoroughfares the army started clearing up the burnt-out skeletons of buses and cars, but in the side streets the battlefields remained untended. With no trucks to collect rubbish, no street-cleaners to get rid of rubble and litter and dirt, there were whole neighbourhoods invaded by bins and boxes and bags of every description. And after a few days of summer sun, followed by an all-pervasive drizzle, the city was beginning to succumb to the smells of death.

The situation had its lighter moments. Somewhere in the southern suburbs a hundred soccer players occupied their stadium to demonstrate their 'solidarity' with the strikers. One evening the city's artists threatened to occupy and close the Musée d'Art Moderne, but when they arrived at the museum they found it already locked up, and abandoned their protest. The city's writers occupied a building and started talking – which is always an unwise thing for writers to do.

Talking had indeed become the main occupation of the city. For once in their long history the French had enough time to talk. And everybody took part: in the streets, on the open squares, in bistros, in occupied factories and offices, in the Sorbonne, above all in the Odéon theatre:

This must rate as the most spectacular occupation of this month of May: when the students took over control of this playhouse and the manager, the legendary actor-director Jean-Louis Barrault handed it over with a grand gesture and a memorable line: 'Today Jean-Louis Barrault is dead!' Now the theatre has been transformed into a 'permanent tribune', and whether one visits it during the lunch hour, or in the early evening, or at two or four in the morning, it is always filled to capacity, with hundreds of people hanging like weaver-birds from the decorated balconies; and for twenty-four hours a day, seven days a week, the discussions continue. On the Cultural Revolution. On the Third World. On Vietnam. On students. On the potato harvest in Brittany. On Johnson's foreign policy. On modern art. On new trends in psychology. On Sartre and Marcuse and Guevara and Mao and de Gaulle. On everything in heaven, or on earth, or in the waters under the earth. With deadly seriousness. With humour. With rage. With passion. With wit and finesse and histrionic gestures. Sometimes a cabinet minister gets up to speak: and it is allowed, provided he awaits his turn, because there is no priority in this free tribune. A miner with blackened hands has as much licence to speak as a clergyman or a disciple of the president. Farmers, teachers, lawyers, students, stripteasers, factory workers, everybody speaks.

One powerful farmer, like an overgrown potato, rises to his feet to say, 'Comrades, this is what I want to say. I mean, where I come from, we are working like hell. And we have a lot of potatoes. That's all I have to say.' And then he sits down again.

Another is more to the point: 'Comrades! I am worried about all this talk of revolution and change. How do you think you're going to make a revolution with the French? We are too set in our ways. Take the lot of us in Auvergne, where I come from. We have four beds in a bedroom and everybody in the house uses the same basin to wash their feet. This is how it's been for weeks and months and years, for generations and for centuries. How are you ever going to change that? Who *wants* to change that?'

High above all the orators there is a banner taped to the proscenium arch which proclaims in huge letters: *EVEN A CHAMBER POT CAN FLOWER.*

Perhaps, in the long run, *this* is the sense of our revolution: a rediscovery and a celebration of the imagination.

It is a veritable funfair of slogans and ideas, most immediately visible in the rash of posters that have begun to spread across public buildings in Paris. There are enough of them to fill a voluminous anthology. Manifestos of Trotskyists, Maoists, Marxists, Anarchists, Fetishists, Sadists, Sodomites, Naturists, Gaullists, Dadaists, Filatelists – all the isms of the century. And quotations – from Valéry: *The wind rises: we must try to live.* Or Victor Hugo: *The truth lies concealed under words like a field under flies.* And many forms and turns of wit: *Any view of the world that is not strange is false.* Or: *If a madman persists in his madness he arrives at the truth.* Or: *Only the truth is revolutionary!* Beneath which someone else has written: *Only the revolution is true!*

This is a wonderful safety valve for a society under pressure. And yet it becomes claustrophobic after a while. There are *so* many flies. And the truth remains so obscure and timid in the presence of the sun.

Talking, talking, talking, a continuous happening. But there is something terrifying about so much talking while rubbish bins accumulate around you and the burnt-out wrecks of cars are lined up along the streets and the queues in front of banks and food shops grow longer. Among the piles of stones young girls are doing the rounds to take collections for victims of violence and workers who have lost their jobs, and the many victims. In the shacks of the poor the children are crying for bread.

In the midst of the convulsions in the city it is often impossible to remain in contact with what is happening *inside* me. All I know, through waves of increasing fatigue, is that in a space still beyond the reach of reason and logic, these momentous events are beginning to shape, darkly, a deep-seated political and moral unease about the many things set in motion by Vietnam, by the Greek protest meeting, by the attempts of the French government to suppress the protests with brute force. Even in my dreams I can hear the chants: *CRS – SS! CRS – SS!* And at one stage, when the telephone lines were cut, students moved into the churches and started ringing the bells to accompany the cadences: Ta-ta-ta, ta-ta! Ta-ta-ta, ta-ta! Until the whole city was reverberating with it. All I know for sure is that, in the process, I have irrevocably become a 'political person'. From now on it would be hypocritical to imagine that politics can remain a separate, clearly demarcated territory within my overall experience. It is everywhere, it permeates everything. It cannot ever again be set apart.

Will there be room, in later years, amid the chaos of those impressions, to remember the frail, dark girl in the Malebranche crying in a corner over a glass of wine after her boyfriend has stormed out?

In a way this is precisely what marks the whole earthquake: every individual, every group or *groupuscule*, every political faction, every separate corner of experience (students, artists, musicians, actors, gravediggers . . .) may bring to it a more or less subjective or private memory or expectation, an individual chip on the shoulder – but what makes it remarkable is that all of it is happening at the same time, and the co-incidence forces everything to merge and fuse into a much larger, massive social movement. A small group of students on the barricades has set in motion something a whole society will have to include in future assessments of their world. I am sure that much of it will dissipate again. But I am just as sure that no one who has been touched by it, however fleetingly, will ever completely forget that moment when the *possibility* of a new society became visible – a society of *participation*, which happens spontaneously, not because a national assembly or a dictator is demanding public endorsement for decisions or actions implemented from somewhere 'up there'.

When even our crusty old concierge stops me at the front door one morning with a hearty '*Dis, camarade!*' I have to accept that the world has become a different place.

For what seemed like a space beyond the reach or flow of ordinary time, the turbulence continued with unpredictable ebbs and flows. The government's stupefying decision to ban Cohn-Bendit from returning to France after he had slipped out to muster support elsewhere, unleashed a new cycle of violence; then he proved, like the Scarlet Pimpernel he came more and more to resemble, that he could match them every step of the way by promising that he would be back – and materialising in the courtyard of the Sorbonne on the evening of 28 May to keep his appointment exactly as and when he'd threatened to do. And yet another frenzy of violence convulsed the city. There were indeed moments when it seemed as if the whole place was going to go up in flames.

In the very heart of the eruption, de Gaulle disappeared. Just like that. It may well have been the closest, since 1870, that France had come to the abyss. And the numerous attempts at clarification or explication that subsequently appeared, including the old man's own version, have not completely settled the question. A masterpiece of military planning? A desperate attempt to 'get out' and shove the mess on others? Certainly, in the few days of his absence, rumours had a field day: de Gaulle had fled and was going to resign; de Gaulle had escaped to Germany; de Gaulle was consulting his generals and planning a military coup . . .

And then he was back. Once again he addressed the nation. This time it was not the weary and almost desperate old man of the previous speech. He had rekindled some of the old flame that had inspired his people during the Nazi occupation, or brought new hope to a torn and wretched land sick of war and confusion, when he announced in 1959 that *I am ready to assume the powers of the Republic.* Not everyone was fooled by it, of course: and in retrospect one had to acknowledge that – even though he himself might not have been prepared to concede it at the time – this was really his farewell to power. A year later he was gone: in Thackeray's unforgettable words it was time to shut up the box and the puppets, for his play was played out. But it *was* a masterful performance. At the same time it was one of the most memorable demonstrations in our post-war world of *sic transit gloria mundi*. Even in South Africa, at that time still gasping for breath in the stranglehold of apartheid, it should have brought a small, chilling reminder of the way in which all regimes with totalitarian tendencies must reach their end. At the time of our own student revolts in 1969 I had the occasion to remind Prime Minister John Vorster of what had happened in France. His reply, as I have noted elsewhere, was flippant – and, in its own obtuse way apocalyptic: *I wish you a good night, in spite of the curlers in your hair* – but it is satisfying to recall, today, that our own hourglass was very slowly but surely running out.

By mid-June the French government had stormed and taken back the Sorbonne; a plain-clothes policeman had climbed to the top of the Odéon, torn down the red and black flags and hoisted the tricolour; the small group of hardliners who called themselves the Katangese, under the command of an ex-mercenary known as Lucien, was driven from its stronghold in a wing of the Sorbonnne. And slowly life in the exhausted city returned to its previous rhythms and occupations.

There was a sense of futility and deep disappointment about it all. One accepts that 'life must go on'. But was *this* the only way in which it could have happened? Was it worth the price? As I write this, forty years later, France is again in the throes of social constipation. So many of the issues of 1968 are still unresolved. There is only more weariness, and disillusionment, and cynical resignation all around.

And yet . . . !

All of us who lived through those days of madness and exhilaration and dreams and impossible hopes in which we realised our own 'Ode to Joy' – in whatever form it manifested itself, building a barricade, throwing stones at a phalanx of armed police, making love with somebody encountered in the heat of the moment, scaling walls, uprooting traffic signs, braving odds to deliver a message, dragging a bloodied victim to the safety of some stranger's apartment, addressing the crowd in the Odéon, or simply allowing oneself to be dragged along by a demonstration, walking through deserted streets at four or five at night, crossing over the dark arches of bridges guarded by dark lines of police, inspired by the anticipation of love or cherishing its memory as one moves to, or leaves, the room or apartment of a lover, and hearing far, far in the distance the rumours of warfare – will bear with us, inside our blood and memory, the spark of that discovery: that all is never lost, that the impossible can come true, that the most overt political act can be the most intimate. The humdrum of ordinary days may tone it down, or temporarily mask or muffle it, but it cannot be obliterated, it cannot be ultimately denied. *It was there. It happened. And having happened, it may happen again.* Perhaps not in such a dramatic way, but still as a presence in the mind, a small glowing ember against the winds of the world.

Through all the upheavals I never stopped writing. There were many interruptions, of course. But behind it all, and in between, my little portable typewriter was prepared to submit to all my onslaughts. During the first months of the year, there was a novel – mercifully never published, at one stage called *Ballad of the Boer*, and at another *Death of a Bee*. This was inspired by a famous essay on bees written by Jean Paulhan – the author of that great aphorism, *Not everything needs to be known*. In the essay he argues that if you hold a bee in your hand and try to smother it, it is bound to sting you before it dies – a negligible thing in itself, but if it hadn't been for that, there wouldn't have been any bees left in the world. The idea for the novel was fine, but the execution execrable. The storyline was partly inspired by *Antigone*: my main character was a dour farmer who kills the son who dares to challenge his authority, and then forbids his daughter to bury the body; when she disobeys, she is also killed, and it is found that she is pregnant by the black labourer. I also followed the outline of *The Waste Land*; but it was too 'literary' and contrived. At that stage, after the failure of *Back to the Sun* I was low on confidence, and urgently needed this short novel as a lifeline. But it was turned down, rather scathingly, by my South African publishers, Human & Rousseau. They felt, once again, that H had been my kiss of death and that for as long as I was with her I would not be able to do anything worthwhile again.

Even the physical act of the writing was problematic. In the midst of the uprising my small typewriter broke down and there was no way of getting it repaired. Marion was kind enough, albeit with a hidden agenda, to lend me hers. But then, just as I was getting warmed up, this second machine also collapsed. I had to go on in longhand for some time, but at last I was on my way again. Not that it availed much. If only I'd read the signs correctly, I could have let the story die a peaceful – and, in retrospect, well deserved – death. As it was, I had to keep hoping all the way to the final verdict before I gave up.

After that, I thought of writing a non-fiction book on the student revolt; and H was eager to work on it with me. But once again my publishers killed it in the bud. The climate in South Africa, they argued, was so negative about this whole experience – and they made it clear that they subscribed wholeheartedly to the notion of these worldwide revolts as a 'communist-inspired plot' – that there was no prospect of its ever being published.

I was having my own doubts about communism. Although I had been sympathetic to some aspects of the Marxist view of history and of litera-ture, I had always been suspicious about both its utopian overtones and its devastating practices under Stalinism. The 1956 invasion of Hungary had effectively killed off any lingering doubts I might have had. Aragon's appear-ance among the students in May 1968 had strengthened my disillusionment. And if further evidence were needed, it was provided by the brutal squashing of the Prague Spring in August 1968 – coming at the very moment when H and I were planning a visit to Czechoslovakia.

During that year, as the American offensive against Vietnam intensified and more and more atrocities came to light, I developed a romantic admir-ation for Ho Chi Minh. I even had a poster of him in my little garret room. And at one stage I wrote a long poem against Lyndon Johnson's criminal involvement in what had once been French Indo-China: this was published in the rather staid literary journal *Standpunte*. As I served on the editorial board, my contributions *had* to be printed. Within days the security police raided the offices of the publishers and confiscated all the copies. This placed the political establishment in a serious quandary, as there were several cabinet ministers on the board of directors of the publishing firm. But then Uncle Ho came out in defence of the Soviet Union's action and I removed his poster from my wall. Another small ridge of hope on the political rock face on which I was hoping to find a toehold, had flaked off. It seemed, more and more, as if I would never find a system of thought or belief that could inspire enough trust or confidence to harbour my own uncertainties and yearnings. I was, indeed, living in a crumbling world. And more and more I was forced to acknowledge that there was no point in finding anything *outside* myself to provide a platform or a starting point. Whatever I could use to construct a future action or involvement, would have to come from within myself.

Ever since the outbreak of the student revolt I knew that sooner or later I would have to make up my mind about going back to South Africa. Living in Paris was, in itself, the reward for being there. There was a sense of freedom I simply could not experience back home. But the revolt had placed it all in the balance. So many of the interminable discussions in the Odéon and else-where had focused on the peculiar exchange between the individual and her or his social context. There was suddenly something hollow in being where I was, 10,000 kilometres away from the place that had shaped me. I honestly didn't think it 'needed' me. In the larger context I was readily expendable. I was not, nor could I ever be, in the full sense of the word, a 'freedom fighter'. What I had was, at most, a pen. A broken typewriter. But even that seemed, at such a distance, preferable to sitting on such a distant sideline.

Yet what could I really do, by going back? Every bit of news that filtered through from South Africa was enough to turn my stomach. The parochial smallness of it all. The myopia. The sickening arrogance. Even within the severely restricted territory of my own, immediate interest, writing, the novel, there was nothing in South Africa that attracted me: how could one go back to do what almost everywhere else in the world was already old hat? I did not have the stomach to fight battles from the day before yesterday.

On the other hand, what was there I could really achieve in Europe, where I would have to be measured, in a foreign language, against writers ten years younger than myself, who in the context of their own world were already so much more experienced, in their world? Unless I gave up writing alto-gether. Yet that was the one thing I could not contemplate. No matter at what low ebb I found myself, writing remained all I wanted to do. All I *could* do.

Here in Paris I was beginning to despair about the power of a majority within a democracy. How could it be ethically acceptable for fifty-one per cent of a nation to have a decisive say in the affairs of a nation, in its present, its future? Yet how much worse was it in South Africa, where not a minority was excluded from the making of decisions but a vast *majority*?

From the journal notes of those days:

My beautiful, damned, despicable land. Already the plague has entered so deeply into its very fibres and sinews that no salvation seems possible. The terrible sickness of intolerance. Over these last few months I have totally and irrevocably broken free from that life. I cannot take the pettiness and viciousness and dull stupidity of that world any longer. It threatens every grain of creativity in me and in 'my people'. I'm no longer interested. I cannot even think of attempting my book on the student revolt any more: it would, at best, be seen as 'furthering the cause of communism'.

To what extent is even *thinking* of writing in that context, in that language, a show of dishonesty?

But what else can I offer? I cannot handle a gun or blow up a building or maim children.

The alternative remains writing. But how can I think of that if nothing I may be interested in saying will be tolerated, will even be *allowed* to be said? It is no longer a matter of wanting to have the right to argue in favour of an alternative, let alone to defend it. It is the mere *notion* of an alternative that is being denied.

And so: Must I stay here and shut up because I lack the means and the talent to say something worthwhile?

Or must I go back where even the attempt to say something worthwhile may be suppressed?

Poor old Hobson.

'Why,' Marion asked that night, 'can't you stop *planning* your future? Why don't you just give up planning and unplanning yourself all the time and try to *be* just what you are?'

Perhaps that in itself was an aspect of the problem. It is the 'masochistic ecstasy' the political essayist Stanley Uys once spoke about. The Afrikaner's idea of heroism: to stand alone against the world. And even when you break away from the system, from the laager, you still find it necessary to define yourself in relation to that same system. That is the starting point of why we are so screwed up.

This is when I find some comfort in Basho:

> In the autumn wind
> There will at least be
> A lotus to sit upon
> For eternal peace

The break with H, inevitable for so long, came soon after our return from a wonderful voyage through the Midi. It was a devastation for which there were no words. And yet it also brought a strange, shocking illumination. Thinking about the violence I had lived through during that long year, and about the revolutionaries – Guevara and others – who had inspired it, I slowly began to see beyond the immediacy of 'activism'. Gradually, but unstoppably, I began to think (because, as a writer, there was no other way I *could* think about it), not only of the actions that constitute change or mark revolutions, but the *context* within which such actions become possible. Over the years I have often reduced it to the glib formula: for those who do or die, there also have to be those who *reason why*. But I do believe there is a grain of truth in it. And although, of course, there are gifted people who can assume both these responses to the world, writers by and large belong to the second category. Which meant that if I decided to return, it did not *have* to mean defeat or failure. There could be something very creative about such a choice.

And perhaps there was another way of looking at it: late in November several of us planned a trip to Amsterdam to be with Breyten at the opening of a major new exhibition. There was some talk about where to spend the night: Belgium, or the north of France? It was Pierre Skira who came up with the final word: 'Ah well, the night is everywhere the same.'

Perhaps the choice between going and staying might not be decisive after all.

Even at that stage I was still trying to think of ways and means to bypass the finality of such a decision. But on 16 November we received two visitors, Prins and Marais, who brought a sudden end to all the dithering. They were not 'representatives' of any organisation or grouping in South Africa: they simply came to see the rugby Test match between the Springboks and Les Bleus of France. One was a businessman, the other a journalist, and they moved very close to the establishment. In the course of the meal we had together on the Saturday night after the match, they provided me with a very clear view of my position in Paris. Given the present climate in the homeland, my closeness to Breyten might soon narrow down my choices to very few. Damned in advance by our friendship, I might soon not have any guarantees about 'effective action' back in South Africa.

What it brought home to me was the awareness that my presence was beginning to curtail Breyten's own choices. I'm pretty sure that in the course of that year he'd had ample opportunity to see that I was not 'revolutionary material'. His concern about me, and the closeness of our friendship, might soon become a burden to him. That alone was enough reason to make up my mind. But there was my own life to consider as well.

For a brief period I thought of moving to Amsterdam instead: after the exhibition I stayed on for a few weeks to explore the possibilities, and found that the Free University might indeed be willing to accommodate me. There was even, briefly, the attraction of a blue girl who lived on a riverboat with nine cats, an artist with streaks of paint on her face, dirty fingernails and a provocative, explosive nature. But I realised that this would merely postpone the final and inescapable decision. My place, for better or almost certainly for worse, I now knew, was back in South Africa. I would not slink back in despair, but assume the burden, above all the responsibility, of a choice made lucidly. *To be there.* Even – and perhaps most especially – if *being there* might mean living on a sinking ship.

It was no longer, as it had been in 1961, a reluctant and resentful choice: going back because I had no other option, because my money had run out. This time I *wanted* to return. Not because I was hoping for 'victory', whatever that might mean; not because I was either masochistic enough to sink with the ship, or determined enough to try and 'do' something about it. But because this was what I had to do and wanted to do, a decision that came from deep inside me and was no longer imposed from outside.

À nous deux maintenant? Maybe. But there was little defiance in it. More grim determination. And even a new and strange sense of happiness. At long, long last writing was being integrated into the woof and warp of my whole life. And I couldn't wait to take up the challenge.

I went to London for one last week, and then H came back to Paris with me for another. All of this had been plotted at the time of our parting in October. We knew it might be disastrous. Or simply a mistake. By that time she was already in another relationship. But in some indefinable way we felt that we owed it to one another. There were days of real agony. But above all there was a belief in the profound necessity of that decision. It brought a strange kind of happiness with it. An inner freedom such as neither of us had known for a long time. If it was a parting, we also knew that we could never again be truly separate. Each had been assimilated as part of the other. And forty years on we still knew that it had been the right thing to do. The only thing.

HOME SWEET HOME

WHAT 1968 HAD BROUGHT HOME TO ME, ABOVE ALL, WAS THE REALISATION that however solitary a writer's work might be, as a *person* one is irrevocably linked to others, to an entire society. Even if the relationship with that society might be antagonistic, hostile, rebellious, angry or destructive, its existence cannot be denied and will always be part of whatever comes out of it. And this time I *wanted* to find out where I came from, what had shaped me, what had made that entire society what it was, for better or for worse.

The first novel to come out of this mindset was *Looking on Darkness.* Even so it took several years for it to reach the point where I could start writing.

It began with the title which, in its original Afrikaans form, was inspired by St John of the Cross to whose writings I was first introduced by Breyten and who, in one of his meditations, distinguished between *nocturnal knowledge (la noticia vespertina)*, which is the knowledge of God through his various manifestations within the temporal world, the kind of knowledge a lover might have of his beloved, through the mingling of their bodies – and *daytime knowledge (sabiduría matutina)*, that immediate and total communion with God which really lies beyond the reach of mortals. What inspired me was that phrase, 'knowledge of the night', or, more literally, 'knowledge of the evening'; and because roughly at the same time I started reading Dostoevsky's *The Idiot*, those two worlds soon started interacting in my mind. I wanted to explore the notion of the idiot – as Dostoevsky defined and complicated it with, among so much more, the fusion of Christ

307

and Don Quixote in one mind, one figure, with a hint of Erasmus thrown in, and further nuances inspired by Sartre's magnificent study of Flaubert in *L'idiot de la famille*. The very first paragraph became a variation on Sartre's opening:

> To know who I am. To define myself through the why and the how of her death. To enumerate and name it all, trying to determine not what a man can know of man, but simply what I dare to know about myself . . .

My first idea was to write a novel about Christ being reborn into the world of the twentieth century. In itself not all that original an idea; but I became fascinated by the possibilities of this birth taking place in South Africa in the throes of apartheid. It seemed inevitable to me that in such circumstances he could in no way be white. He would *have* to belong to the oppressed, to Fanon's 'wretched of the earth'. Of course there was, specifically, that moving passage from Isaiah 53: 'He hath no form nor comeliness; and when we shall see him, there is no beauty that we should desire him. He is despised and rejected of men; a man of sorrows, and acquainted with grief; and we hid as it were our faces from him.'

But I could obviously not conceive of it as a moral or political sermon. I wanted to write about my own childhood and youth, the stories and the people that had made me what I was – not as autobiography or memoir, but as fiction, as an intimately lived world transposed by the imagination. By writing the life of a coloured man – rejected by the white power establishment, but also not acknowledged by the black majority struggling for their own liberation – I hoped to distance myself from my subjective involvement with my own life and to come to grips with some of the larger issues of my time and my country.

Having become deeply involved with the theatre immediately after my return, the choice to make my main character an actor, was almost inevitable.

And because I wanted to tell a *story*, not write an essay; and because storytelling has always, for me, in one way or another, been vested in love as the key to the life of an individual, a central impulse in the novel had to come from what is, surely, the central impulse in life: love. I believe that the one moment in Joseph's life where he comes closest to what life is about, is the one where he contemplates his own imminent death and thinks about what his very last wish would be: to make love with his Jessica for one last time.

Jessica. In several respects, *Looking on Darkness* was a way of finally taking my leave from Ingrid. But Jessica in the book is not Ingrid, and was never intended to be. There is a closer link. Among the treasures I brought back with me from Paris was the memory of H. And in the course of working on the novel, the whole course of our love came to life in me again. The first few months of caution while we were both huddling to protect our bruises. Until a magical naked day in Bains Kloof when we moved into a dimension where love finally became a possibility. The endless white beaches of the Eastern Cape at Kenton-on-Sea, where one could walk for miles and miles, without clothes and without encountering a single person; ramblings in the forest outside Grahamstown: one unbelievable night when everything was glittering with fireflies, and we stood among the trees under the moon and I held her face between my hands and said, in my most intense discovery of the Other I had ever had, 'This is you'; her returns from the Hogsback where she went from time to time to meet with a remarkable priest, Father Mark, who knew not only about things spiritual but about the needs and the importance of the body; hours and hours spent talking and laughing and caressing and being together in silence – all of which in due course finding its way into the novel.

Then her leisurely wanderings which took her the better part of a year, through Africa, back to London. Followed by the year we'd shared there and in Paris, until the devastating moment of the decision to part. Perhaps, in retrospect, it was unwise to construct the book around our love. I was too close to the experience, too overwhelmed by it, to do justice to the character of Jessica. Later, in *An Instant in the Wind*, I could stand back and allow Elisabeth to 'talk back' at me. For many years I almost compulsively fell in love with all the female characters in my novels, so that a measure of male possessiveness possibly curtailed their freedom and their fullness as *people*, as *individuals*; but at least, from Elisabeth on, they began to assert their independence. Until Hanna, in *The Other Side of Silence*, took the final step to emancipation by making it almost impossible, physically, for me to fall in love with her. I like to think that, indeed, I did not 'fall in love' with Hanna: I learned, more simply and more momentously, to *love* her. And not in spite of her hideous deformities, but *because* of her essential humanity.

My working pattern of writing for *Looking on Darkness* deviated from the normal. My usual inclination, when I start out on a novel, is to get the first draft done as quickly as possible. If it is a mess, as it often is, it can be cleared up later: at this early stage I merely want to get it out of my system. So I may write twelve or eighteen hours per day. In the very final stages, after the four or five or twelve stages in between, this may even increase. But for this book I imposed a pattern of three pages per day on myself. I began soon after my return from that second long stay in Paris. By that time the relationship with H had ended, I had come back to South Africa, met Alta, and we were married. We were in the process of renovating an old Settler house we'd bought, and I knew that this would occupy most of my time. Also, Alta was pregnant, and Danie was expected late in June, and that, too, would not allow me to keep to any regular hours.

The regime suited me. It left enough time for contemplation every day, and even though it stretched out the writing time on that first draft to extraordinary lengths, I relished the opportunity it gave me of really soaking myself into the novel. It also made the text much longer than I'd ever planned, as I found I could move deeply into every phase and facet of Joseph's life – which to a large extent became also my own life.

Having just come out of the production of Camus' *Les Justes*, the whole theatre experience fell naturally into place. But for some sections, particularly those dealing with Joseph's years in Cape Town, living in District Six, I needed the enthusiastic guidance of Daantjie Saayman. In a way, therefore, it was poetic justice that Human & Rousseau declined to take the risk of publishing it and I could give the manuscript to Daantjie, who had been its godfather since its inception.

There was another inordinate delay, as my very dear friend Rob Antonissen, who was also my head of department and who'd been my mentor ever since I came to Grahamstown, had fallen ill with cancer, and I couldn't face the idea of finishing the book unless he had read the manuscript. And it was one of the most terrible days in my life when it became clear that he would not be able to do it, and that it was beginning to weigh very heavily on his mind. But at the same time I knew – and I knew he knew – that asking him to give the manuscript back, would be like a betrayal; because that would make it clear that I did not expect him to survive. It became unbearable. I needed to set him free, to release him from this obligation; but that might be a death sentence – from someone he desperately needed to believe in his recovery.

I discussed it with Rob's wife, Liesje, and with his daughter Rike. They knew exactly what was at stake. But they both agreed that the presence of the manuscript in their home was becoming an unbearable weight on his mind.

To this day I believe that my removal of that token of trust was like a final sentence. And the end was not long in coming after that.

I could only hope that dedicating the book to him, even if he could not know it, would be, at least for those of us who survived, an affirmation of a friendship that had been one of the most precious things in my life.

When I'd dedicated *The Ambassador* to Ingrid, that had been a consecration of our love. But six months after the publication of the book, she died; and the dedication had to be changed. In Rob's case, the *In Memoriam* had been, from the beginning, an act of dedication.

Apart from writing and the theatre, the heightened creative urge I brought back from Paris also drove me to explore other forms of expression. For several years photography became one of my main preoccupations. As a teenager I'd started experimenting with painting, only to find out, after a few overambitious exhibitions, that enthusiasm was no substitute for talent. But photography presented me with new possibilities of satisfying a preoccupation with the visual dimension that had already informed much of my writing and my interest in the world. I began to spend twelve or fourteen hours a day in the darkroom. In those days, I worked almost exclusively in black and white, which seemed to me the closest I could get to writing poetry. Colour is a major component of our perception in the natural world;

by excluding colour, the view becomes 'unnatural', which enables one to highlight other attributes, of tone, of form, of perspective, of texture – just as in poetry, language is to a certain extent made 'unnatural' by shifting syntactical form to the background, making it possible to foreground features like rhythm or imagery. Or phrased differently, the unit of communication in prose is the sentence, while in poetry it is the line, the verse. In photography, it seemed to me, elements of line and form, removed from their everyday context, acquire a heightened intensity and can be used in an almost plastic way. I'm not sure that at the time all of this was done consciously: it happened over the years, through immersing myself in the work of some of the great photographers – Cartier-Bresson, Ansel Adams, Capa, Salgado; in South Africa, Paul Alberts, Chris Jansen, Cloete Breytenbach, and above all David Goldblatt with his battered Leicas, who I am still proud to call a friend. There were shifts in my choice of subjects too. Initially, when I was still more spellbound by colour, landscapes were my main subject. In Paris, abstract shapes began to predominate. Soon, a fascination with the body, specifically the female form, took over. I began by returning to negatives of Ingrid; but soon a number of new models made their appearance. I even produced a book of figure studies, *A Portrait of Woman as a Young Girl*. And then I stopped, packed away my equipment and for many years hardly ever touched a camera.

Why? In part, it had little to do with photography as such, and more with South African narrow-mindedness. The young girl I'd used as a model for 'Afternoon of a Nymph', the main story in the book, came from a family where nudity was as much part of the everyday world as music. In the sequence of images she wanders through a sylvan landscape with a flute, and everything is suffused with musicality. She brought an enthusiasm, an inventiveness, and a radiant innocence to our working sessions. But neither of us, nor her parents, were prepared for the outcome. As soon as the book was published, the local bookshops were besieged by hormone-driven teenagers who came flocking to leer at their classmate. She became the butt of crude jokes and the kind of viciousness only the young are capable of. For me it was one of the most disillusioning moments of my life.

It was exacerbated when, in a quite unexpected way, my young model's best friend also became a victim. On one or two occasions she had come with us on photo sessions, just as the model's sister or one of her brothers had accompanied us on other occasions; one morning I impulsively invited the friend to join in as it occurred to me that the story of the nymph might be neatly concluded if, before falling into a sleep, she handed over her flute to someone else. Without a moment's hesitation, she stepped out of her clothes to take part in the session, and some really good photos came from it. When the films were developed, I gave the girl some proofs to take home in a large envelope. Stupidly, I had never considered that her father was a Presbyterian minister. When, totally unsuspecting, she proudly and happily went to show him the pictures, he nearly had an apoplexy. But he never came to discuss it with me: instead, he confronted the parents of my original young model and started fulminating about the sinfulness of the body, the corruption of minors, and threatened prosecution. Fortunately, my model's parents were more than able to talk him out of it, and it was only much later that I learned about the father's reaction. The anger I then felt was provoked, above all, by discovering how something which had been pure, joyous, youthful innocence had been retroactively sullied and corrupted by the misplaced piousness of a man of God. When, not long afterwards, *Kennis van die Aand* was hauled before the censors, it confirmed some of the worst suspicions I already had about the mindset that informed the system.

But abandoning photography also had a much less dramatic reason: by publishing my photographs as a book, I had turned my favourite hobby into just another part of my main job. It was no longer pure escape or pleasure. It lost the magic that had first lured me to it. And the next step was inevitable.

In other ways the first few years after my return also provided new ventures into the territory of black and white. On a visit to Brazil in 1970, there was a small excursion to the less salubrious outskirts of Rio, which I undertook purely as an act of homage to H, who had then been doing research for years on charismatic African churches in London. On this in many ways disturbing evening I attended a Macomba session in a bare, barn-like hall in a backyard, where an altar had been set up with cheap painted images of Jesus, the Virgin, Joseph, the Magi and assorted angels and saints. Under the watchful eye of a leader figure, wearing a blue cap, a long yellow Nehru tunic and white sandals and carrying a white book, the audience starts dancing. Both they and the leaders stop several times to smoke from ever-ready pipes, presumably filled with marijuana. 'Prophets' in white robes mingle with the dancers, attending to individuals who appear to be approaching an orgasmic explosion as they await possession by the Spirit. The music becomes more and more urgent. Some of the dancers are going wild, collapsing on the floor, their limbs beginning to jerk in seemingly uncontrollable spasms. Until one dark-haired girl loses all control and with hair tumbling wildly over her face, she starts uttering shrill bird-like sounds; the others begin to clap their hands and stomp their feet while they move more and more frenetically, whirling like dervishes. The girl's beautiful face becomes contorted as she starts foaming at the mouth, screaming and shouting uncontrollably, rushing this way and that, colliding with every-body in her way. Until the leader, unperturbed, approaches her, removes one of the numerous necklaces from his scrawny neck and drapes it over her. With shocking suddenness she stops, her face becomes singularly serene, almost shining, as if illuminated from the inside, and very quietly she returns to her seat. She is followed by several others, coming to climax, before they fall silent, or start sobbing silently, and meekly sit down again.

At last they all bow in front of the candles set up around the hall, kneel in front of the leader, bow to the prophets, and withdraw. Some are joined by boyfriends, and the couples disappear into small cloakrooms where they change into day clothes. And then they leave quietly, carrying the robes of their ecstasy in small bags. Then the audience, too, disperses. And on the pavement in front of the hotel a group of voodoo candles remains burning peacefully in the night.

OPTION CLAUSE

RELATIONS WITH PUBLISHERS HAVE ALWAYS BEEN OF IMPORTANCE TO ME. THEY involve so much more than business. So the decision, in the early eighties, to move from W. H. Allen to Faber & Faber was unnerving. Although I had been embarrassed by Allen's sensationalist approach to their edition of *Looking on Darkness*, I spent several quite happy years with the firm – thanks, mainly, to Carole Blake's wonderful work as foreign-rights manager and cordial relations with Robert Dirskovsky in the PR department and several of the editorial staff. Later, when the lovely Amanda Girling became my editor, I really began to feel at home; and even more so when a close friendship developed between myself and the fellow South African, Aubrey Davis, who took charge of the editorial side of my dealings with the firm. Apartheid had driven Aubrey from South Africa, and there was so much we shared – from a loathing of the politics of the time to a nostalgic attachment to the country itself – that my ties with W. H. Allen seemed assured. The only cause for uneasiness was the dizzying rate of staff turnover. More than once I would arrive at 44 Hill Street to find that, apart from Aubrey, there wouldn't be a single face in that imposing building which I recognised.

Then Aubrey also left. He joined the agency of Hughes Massie; and although he never tried to exert any pressure, I began to consider the advantages of being represented by an agent. The crunch came at the end of 1979, when W. H. Allen 'forgot' to submit *A Dry White Season* for the Booker Prize, after both its predecessors, *An Instant in the Wind* and *Rumours of Rain*, had been short-listed for the award and *Rumours of Rain* had actually been runner-up.

I remember the consternation with which Francis Bennett, then newly appointed as managing director, conveyed the news to me. I got along extremely well with Francis and we have remained friends to this day, but his concern forced me to start thinking about a change – especially after he quite frankly broached it himself.

'I want you to know,' he said, 'that, after what has happened, should you decide to move elsewhere, I'll understand completely and respect your choice.'

There was one problem in my own mind, however, which I mentioned to him: 'What about the option clause?'

He just shrugged dismissively.

It was at the time, and perhaps still is, a traditional part of an author's publishing contract to grant the publisher a right of first refusal on the next book. But every single publisher I consulted in those years – including W. H. Allen – assured me that 'nobody pays any attention to it'. And so, when the matter came up after Faber & Faber made an approach to Aubrey, I also did not take it seriously. Even so, I did mention it to Francis again, just before he joined the merry-go-round into and out of W. H. Allen. Like the other publishers, he assured me that the option clause had no legal validity. He added that if at any stage I required written confirmation of the fact that, as MD, he'd given me permission to leave W. H. Allen, he would be happy to oblige. Not long afterwards, following a request by my counsel, I approached him for such confirmation and he readily gave it.

It turned out that such an agreement could be legally binding only if I had offered something in return, even if it were no more than a token amount. But neither Francis nor I was aware of this; and counsel did nothing to enlighten us.

I was not interested in approaching publishers before I actually had a new novel in my hands, and so there was some delay before I handed the manuscript of *A Chain of Voices* to Aubrey for submission to Faber. Even at that stage I suggested that he contact W. H. Allen in writing to make quite sure there would be no complications, but once again he made it very clear that an option clause was not binding and that we should simply go ahead. At some stage there was a letter from Allen's to remind me of the clause, but Aubrey just shrugged it off and told me to do the same.

It was only when *A Chain of Voices* was published by Faber in 1982 that the shit became airborne. By that time there was a new MD in charge of Allen's, one Bob Tanner, known in the trade as One-and-Six; I showed his letter to Aubrey, who once again dismissed it. At any rate, he said, Tanner was a newcomer to W. H. Allen and had no idea of what the situation had been before I'd left.

Tanner informed us that legal proceedings would be forthcoming. Bluff and bluster, Aubrey assured me. Assuming that he spoke with the authority of a respected agency like Hughes Massie behind him, I followed his advice to ignore the letter.

Allen's, who had by then lost most of their serious writers apart from Bernice Rubens, apparently needed some public bolstering and decided to press for prosecution. The trial was set for January 1983. I travelled to London. That was where everything turned serious. To begin with, Hughes Massie refused my request for a refund of my travelling expenses and accommodation during the trial: the matter, they said, did not concern them. It was something purely between W. H. Allen and myself even though the negotiations had been conducted between Aubrey as the representative of the agency, and me. They did graciously offer me the services of their counsel, at my own expense, though; but no one thought of pointing out that this might lead to a conflict of interest, given that this person had been acting for Hughes Massie for years and should have been expected primarily to protect their interests, not mine. Aubrey, who had been the kingpin in the negotiations leading up to the trial, was moved out of the action, and soon afterwards was made redundant by the firm – nothing to do with the Allen business, of course, I was assured: purely a matter of internal reshuffling – and I was left out on a limb. The Massie counsel strongly pressurised me to settle out of court, which would obviously have suited their agency. By that time the costs were piling up alarmingly: not only W. H. Allen's exorbitant claim of £30,000 for compensation, but all the legal costs to date. I would be ruined financially. In the circumstances, and with no impartial advisor to turn to, I yielded to the pressure and agreed to settle on the opening day of the trial.

317

There was a huge party at Allen's and they celebrated with unseemly haste before the ink on the settlement was dry.

The saddest part of the whole unpleasant business was that I never saw Aubrey again. He could not find another job in publishing and had to resort to making sandwiches for some fast-food concern. Not long afterwards Herta Ryder, who had left Hughes Massie to safeguard her integrity and set up an agency for children's books on her own, conveyed the shocking news that Aubrey had been murdered in a rather sordid incident. This was heartbreaking. For my daughter Sonja too, who had become close friends with Aubrey's lovely little Victoria.

In due course, following Herta's advice, I went to the wonderful Liepman agency in Zurich, who had previously been my subagent for Germany. Hughes Massie hobbled along and in due course disappeared from the map.

One of the really good things to come out of the whole mess was a life-long friendship with Herta Ryder, to whom I subsequently dedicated *An Act of Terror*.

I'd first met Herta in her very small cluttered office at the Hughes Massie agency, where she was almost invisible among the books and paintings. She had, for paintings, the kind of compulsion a gambler has for betting, and her favourite artist was the British painter Bernard Dunstan. Most of my own collection of his work – oils and etchings and gouaches – came from her. She had the habit of first keeping a new acquisition in her already over-crowded office until she felt she could smuggle it home past her husband John, a typographer who had spent his most creative years with The Bodley Head. He, too, knew all about compulsion. When we talked about his wartime experiences – some of them quite hair-raising, like when he was dropped behind the enemy lines in Belgium as a spy – he had no hesitation recalling what to him had been his most exciting experience during the war: when, in a very old book in a library, he had come across a perfect specimen of the letter *A* in a font that had become almost extinct.

There was a very specific reason for the close friendship that quickly developed between Herta and myself. She told me that in 1935, while still living in Germany, her fiancé had been in the SS. She was a Jew; when she fell pregnant her young officer forced her to have an abortion. It was very much a backstreet affair and it was botched to such an extent that she could never have children, which became the greatest void in her life. It was the end of their relationship; and soon afterwards she fled to Switzerland, and eventually from there to England, where she entered the world of publishing.

When Herta discovered that I had been born in 1935, at the very time she'd lost her baby, I became, for her, the child she would never have. She began to give me paintings on every occasion we met: she had the touching habit of giving away precisely the ones she liked most. Once she and John took me along to a small village in Surrey, near Glyndebourne, where friends were housing the overflow from her own collection. I was invited to make a list of all the paintings I would like to inherit. There were priceless works among them. What I specifically remember, apart from the Dunstans, were a Vuillard and an Augustus John.

These wishes were duly recorded in her will. But sadly, after Herta's death her will was not executed and I felt too bad to mention it to John on the many occasions I visited him again. When I made discreet enquiries after his own death, nobody seemed to know what had become of the paintings. I have often wondered about the rest of the treasures they had amassed in their small flat in Richmond – the artworks, the music, the first editions of *Ulysses*, Hardy, Caroll, Wilde – and I can only hope that they found the cherishing homes they so richly deserved.

What mattered to me, was not the books, or the music, or the paintings, as material objects, but the way in which Herta's life was left incomplete by leaving her wishes unfulfilled at her death. So much remained unfulfilled for her. By the time she was brought down by the cancer that took her away, the one thing she was still looking forward to was the undertaking by the German government that her family would receive compensation for the property confiscated by the Nazis. Next to paintings and books, travel had been Herta's main passion; but during her life there never was enough money to travel as widely as she would have liked. John had never been keen on travelling much, but Herta still had so many voyages lined up. When the money came through at last, it was too late. That feeling of 'unfinished business' left her depleted. And for those of us who had known and loved her, there was something terribly unfinished, and unfair, about it all. For me, the only consolation was that, after she had seen several of my books through to publication, even though someone else took the credit for doing it, at least with *An Act of Terror* I could express something of the closeness and the gratitude I had felt for her for so long.

Even after the court case about that damned option clause was all over, the attitude towards such clauses in the publishing world did not change much, as far as I know; but I should think that people would act a tad more cautiously in future. And I know that several publishers simply dropped the iniquitous clause from their contracts. For myself, it ended on a positive note when Faber decided magnanimously to take charge of all my liabilities. And for several years, until I moved to the welcoming embrace of Secker & Warburg, Matthew Evans and Robert McCrum, and most especially their brilliant, shrewd, generous, loveable foreign-rights director as well as deputy chairman, the legendary Tony Pocock, happily took care of my publishing needs. It was the end of the single dark chapter in my writerly career abroad.

WRITING THE DEEP BLUE

I'VE MET ARIEL DORFMAN SEVERAL TIMES, IN PLACES AS FAR APART AS CAPE town and Stockholm and Galway and Duke University, and our encounters have always been immensely stimulating. But there are two that will always stand out, commemorating as they do a life and a death. The first was a visit to Robben Island, with the parents of Amy Biehl, in a small group guided by Achmat Kathrada, who had been one of Mandela's close friends in prison. Standing in Mandela's small, sober cell with Ariel, was truly one of the most intense moments of my life. It was an encounter, not only with the spirit of Madiba, but with unfamiliar depths in ourselves. Some time after this, a visit to Chile provided a rich opportunity to plumb other deep places inside our friendship.

This was a gathering of writers from three of the southernmost countries in the world – Chile, South Africa and Australia. The encounter was titled *Writing the Deep South*, although someone in our Santiago hotel accidentally announced it as *Escribiendo el Azul Profundo* (*Writing the Deep Blue*) instead of *Escribiendo el Sur Profundo*. It was arranged on Ariel's initiative, and the main organiser was Jorge Heine, the Chilean ambassador in South Africa at the time. The idea was to arrange three annual meetings, in each of the three countries involved. But after Jorge returned to Chile at the end of his South African tour of duty, our local organisers made a hash of their arrangements for the second year and so the rest of the project was, regrettably, shelved. The Chilean delegation included Ariel, as well as Antonio Skármeta, author of the novel *Burning Patience*, on which was based the beautiful film, *Il Postino*. Among the Australians were Peter Carey, the Aboriginal writer Roberta Sykes and Helen Garner. The South Africans were Nadine Gordimer, Mongane Wally Serote, Zakes Mda and I. Along the way we were joined by a Mapuche poet, Leonel Lienlaf, who brought the poetry of his people and their 'alternative geography' into focus, including rivers that run from Above to bring their stories of the ancestors down to us. After looking at a variety of themes and issues, it was Wally who suggested what became the key theme of all our deliberations: *Unfinished Business*.

Nadine was accompanied by an unknown young West Indian man, Ronald Suresh Roberts, whom she had chosen as her biographer. He turned out to be an obnoxious person who seemed to have appointed himself as an official delegate and who interrupted almost every time Nadine spoke, even in completely private conversations. She might start a story about something she remembered from, say, September 1958 when he would imperiously interrupt, 'No, no, Nadine, that was in October 1959 . . .' He soon became quite insufferable, and the delegates were unanimous in regarding him as an embarrassment to the whole travelling conference. It came as no surprise when, in 2004, Roberts blatantly broke the terms of their agreement and Nadine fired him. In retaliation, he turned the biography into a scandalous attempt to insult and humiliate her.

I was incensed by the book and would never have read beyond the first few chapters had I not been asked to review it. The biography became one of the most unpleasant literary events of the year in South Africa. Since then, Roberts has turned his writerly attention to Thabo Mbeki, publishing an embarrassing hagiography to which the brilliant cartoonist Zapiro responded with a picture of Roberts ensconced so deeply in Mbeki's backside that it seemed impossible to extract him without surgery. Obviously, Nadine's standing is such that the malicious back-stabbing by Roberts caused no dent on her reputation, whereas Roberts has become a laughing stock.

The conference started in Santiago, then moved to Valparaíso, and south via Concepción, all along the Andes until the *cordillera* broke down in a string of snow-topped, smoking volcanoes, to Valdívia. On the way to Valparaíso, we spent a morning at Isla Negra, where Neruda had lived for an important part of his life. The front of the building had been altered, disconcertingly, but I suppose inevitably, to accommodate the needs of tourism. But once we had made our way beyond restaurant and shop and public spaces, the house was undisturbed. It is a long and narrow edifice, every nook and cranny crammed to capacity with the bric-a-brac the poet compulsively collected throughout his life: bottles in weird shapes and many colours, woodcarvings, a variety of large painted figureheads from sunken ships, pictures and ornaments from Asia, Africa, South America, India, God knows where, covering every square centimetre of space – interrupted by windows overlooking the turbulent sea beyond a sandy beach with piles of bizarrely shaped black rocks. The bedroom is upstairs, relatively bare, with a wide panorama from the large bed across the whole bay.

Outside is the boat where Neruda usually spent time drinking with his friends: there is a huge bell which he used to strike to let all and sundry know when he was in a mood for drinking. When he did not feel like having guests, he would hang out his pirate's flag. His grave lies just beyond the flag, flapping gently in the breeze.

Standing there in the high wind, I recite soundlessly in my mind two of my favourite lines from Neruda:

I want
to do with you what spring does with the cherry trees.

And while we are still assembled around the boat, a busload of small children – eight- to ten-year-olds – arrive. Ariel starts talking to them – a brilliant lecture in geography, history and anthropology. He shows them newspapers with the photos of our group in it. And suddenly we are all stars, and have to sign our autographs. Not all of the kids have paper, so a number of them have their small hands signed. A moment I will never forget: standing on that high rise above the sea, signing and signing and signing small hands shaped like starfish.

Back in Santiago, Ariel accompanied us to the cemetery. And that is where the second of my epiphanies with him takes place. We pass the rows of enormous, ostentatious baroque sarcophagi where members of notable families lie buried. Among them is also the monumental grave of Salvador Allende – perhaps too ostentatious for a man with his reputation, although one understands the wish to make it imposing. Then we follow a flight of stone stairs to the tomb which lies below the ground. And as we assemble in front of the grille, a small procession arrives: an elderly man, a retired railwayman from Valparaíso, we learn later, with his sister and her daughter. Without paying any attention to us, he grasps the bars in his hands and calls out at the tomb where Allende lies buried: '*Compañero!*'

We all freeze to listen. The old man continues, in spite of his sister's efforts to silence him – obviously conditioned by so many years of not daring to speak out in front of strangers, not even now, in the wake of Pinochet's arrest. He continues: 'It's me, *compañero*. I have come to tell you that they've caught the bastard. At last he's going to pay!'

Once again his sister, terrified, tries to intervene, motioning anxiously towards us. But Ariel steps forward and places an arm around his shoulders. 'You needn't be scared, *compañero*, we are friends. We are with you.'

The old man starts crying. He half turns towards us and starts telling the story of how he was tortured. And about a family member, a woman nine months pregnant, who was also tortured. In the process her labour pains began and she gave birth to a baby surrounded by her torturers. And then – it takes a while before he can utter the words – the baby, too, was tortured to death. It goes on and on. Before he has finished we are all in tears. It is an inside glimpse of a country still torn asunder. What we are witnessing is the suffering of a people who can only now begin to face their terrible past. It is profoundly reassuring to think that, whatever its glaring mistakes, and however much still remains unresolved, South Africa's Truth Commission has at least *tried* to look its own past in the eyes.

After we have said goodbye to the railwayman and his family, Ariel guides us to the monument for the disappeared, the *desaparecidos*: just a simple, long wall on which the thousands of names of the victims have been written. On one side, against a railing, someone has left a sheet of paper and a few roses: it bears a simple inscription in large, clumsy capitals: *I HAVE BEEN TRYING FOR 22 YEARS TO FIND A PLACE WHERE I CAN LEAVE A FLOWER FOR YOU.*

Has this not been the most devastating consequence of the Truth Commission too – the many mothers who still do not know where their dead lie buried? The often-repeated plea: *Just show me his bones, that I can sleep again.*

That, and the passionate phrase that reverberates around the world wherever atrocities have happened: *Nunca, nunca, nunca mas! Never, never, never again!*

A resolve among all of us on that trip: as writers we have nothing with which to counter the horrors of history, except our words. But surely that should never be underestimated. In a society under siege, as South Africa was for such a long time, while we have the word, our humanity remains confirmed. And even after the darkness has passed, we need the word to continue discovering or rediscovering the truths hidden in that obscurity.

THE PINK SHOE

AN HOUR OUT OF THE LOVELY CITY OF KRAKÓW, STAND THE BLUNT watchtowers in the barbed-wire enclosure where the cattle-trains stopped and the sign above the wide gate still says *Arbeit Macht Frei*. Oświęcim. Auschwitz. A space still beyond the grasp of the imagination. I had to battle everything inside me that drove me to revolt; but there was a morbid compulsion that forced me to go through with it.

I had gone to Dachau twenty years before, to research an article for the German magazine *Stern*. I was given carte blanche. But because it was 1986, in the middle of the states of emergency that marked the darkest circle of the hell of apartheid, I could not resist following, step by macabre step, the rise of the Nazi Party and Hitler's march to his ultimate madness and death. Not that it was easy: except in Bavaria, I found people curiously reluctant to talk about that past; in Nuremberg it was almost impossible to find the Zeppelin Feld where the great rallies had taken place, and the court of justice on the Fürthertstrasse where the post-war trials had been held. There followed the unsettling discovery in the courtroom – once we'd located the crucial number 625 which seemed to have been deliberately misplaced – that all courts of justice, from the ones in which my father had presided in my childhood, to the one in Pretoria where Breyten had been tried, to this one in which Goering and Hess and Kaltenbrunner and Donitz and their accomplices had been herded together, have the same smell. Dust, and wormwood, stale tobacco, and old sweat, and perhaps fear. An overwhelmingly human smell.

Then on to Dachau. Most of the barracks have been demolished – unlike in Auschwitz, where they have been left intact. As a result, what dominates in Dachau is one's exposure to space. To openness, blankness, emptiness. It comes as a shock, and yet it is so utterly logical, to discover that during all the years when the camp was in use there was a ban on leaving a mark of any description anywhere – wall or beam or bunk or chair or table. Is it not one of the most basic urges that define us as human, the need to make signs? Is it not the last and most definitive of our needs, when everything else falls away or is stripped from us: to leave a mark? To say *I was here*? When *that* is taken away, we are deprived of the very last possibility of recording our presence and our passage.

It is all the more shocking in a place like Dachau, to be forced to face the proliferation of graffiti from our own time in the camp. The silence of that past – the cacophony of today. And in the midst of all the other obscenities, in one of the two restored barracks on the site, marked with the bold statement of a date, 28.6.86, a mere two months before my visit, the final blasphemy, a swastika.

Moving through the museum, one is confronted, every inch of the way, with huge photographs documenting every step in the process that led from the exuberant early demonstrations of nationhood and rediscovered identity after the devastation of 1918, via the celebrations of law and order, of rules and laws and regulations, the terrifying logic of the System – every little ramification of it replicated in the South Africa of my own time – to its culmination in Nuremberg, and in this place. It soon becomes overwhelming. It is nauseating. Yet there is no escape. When I become claustrophobic, physically and morally unable to face another photograph, another torture rack, another torn piece of clothing, and try to escape to a window, to breathe, to see fresh air and open space outside – all there is to see is the place *itself*, the stark and very simple reality of the space where it happened, where each of those atrocities took place. Inside, the mementoes, the records, the representations – outside, the real thing.

Everything must have looked so different then. From all the records, all the photos, the overwhelming impression is of *bodies* – thousands upon thousands of them in the workplace, at the roll calls, in the mass graves, inside the barracks: the three-tiered bunks, so narrow that it would seem too small for a single person, but with three, four, five, six of them crammed into each. And now this sudden emptiness, this sham of serenity that shockingly reminds one of a Buddhist stone garden, in which the past reverberates without end.

But there is no resolution. What is the 'sense' of torture, of atrocity, of a place like Dachau, or Auschwitz? Suddenly, remembering all this, I recall a later visit to Prague, to the stark beauty of the Jewish cemetery, to the small museum with its documents of the children transported from here to Treblinka: the pictures drawn by those children in the camp; the one that will forever remain unforgettable: a bright butterfly, drawn by a small Dutch boy – accompanied by a phrase in a childish scrawl: *Hier heb ik geen vlinder gezien. Here I have seen no butterfly.* Could *this*, in any way, perhaps, point towards the elusive 'sense'? Is torture, as it is generally argued, the final denial of the humanity of the other, because without such denial, surely, it cannot be done? Hence, the initial 'branding' of the other as non-human, as deviant, or miscreant, as Jew or Black or whatever? Or could it also be the opposite – by doing something inhuman to the other, I confirm the humanity within myself and express my disgust with it? Because I *know* what pain means, I can torture another and thereby relish the fact that it is not being done to myself? Is that why, in an act or a system of torture, there always lurks an ideal of the absolute, of purity, of something greater than ourseves: an ultimate justice, Christianness, Aryanness, Whiteness . . . ?

Some individuals can rise above this, or break out of it. I thought about it – how could I not? – when Karina and I recently visited Mandela. The opposite of what Barbara Masekela's husband Henry said after his release from prison and torture: *The only thing that suffering has taught me is the uselessness of suffering.* There are many who think and react like that: they are the ones who arrive in positions of power, later, and take their revenge for what they have not learned. Because to them suffering is useless, they can inflict it on others. What makes Mandela not just different, but the opposite, is that suffering has opened a space within himself in which he can discover the deeper humanity in which he can be with others. One also experiences this with Desmond Tutu. That is why, every time one comes away from him, even after a short moment of sharing, there is a sense of being more fully human, of having glimpsed what 'being human' may truly and fully mean. In Mandela's case by having personally plumbed the depths of what he suffered with others; in Tutu's case by having so deeply shared the suffering of others that he has assumed it as his own.

And Auschwitz takes and tests the measure of suffering, the limits and the possibilities of pain. Of endurance. Trying to take in everything that can be seen in these neat, precise rows of barracks – the Nazis were nothing if not meticulous and tidy; they must all have been very obedient as children – is of course impossible; the mind cannot compass it. What remains fixed in the mind are details. In Dachau it was the bunk on which prisoners had been tied, spreadeagled, to be flogged; and the splintered remains of a cane lying on it. In Auschwitz, because of the way in which all the people who had passed through there – women, children, men – are now represented by the most banal of objects, *things*: mountains of shoes, of children's clothing, of spectacles, of combs, of chamber pots, of small suitcases with names written in bold capitals, of hair spilling from canvas bags. Of all the things I will remember from Auschwitz, this is what will haunt me until the end of my days: one small pink shoe; a single long, thick, blonde braid hacked from a woman's head. Only last week, looking for something else, I came across a magazine from the seventies about the house in Grahamstown in which our family lived at the time. It ends with a glimpse of Sonja: *Little Sonja Brink went tripping off there in her pink shoes. She twinkled at us, refused to talk or to be photographed, and disappeared.*

Here, too, a small girl once twinkled and went off, leaving a single pink shoe behind. On the way, possibly, to the gas chamber. Still refusing to talk, seventy years later. And yet, how eloquent the silence of that small pink shoe. I remember a philosopher once talking about 'the interminable silence of things'. And of one blonde braid, which must have been the crowning glory of a young life. Silent now. Collecting dust, yet shining through the gloom.

Through two small objects, two mementoes of a world once real, a world once lived, small lost moments of joy, of being, of existing, Auschwitz has gathered, for ever, all the unbearable lightness of being. A child's shoe, a girl's braid.

What remains in the end is aways – and only – words.

I remember Rilke:

Aber weil Hiersein viel ist, und weil uns scheinbar
alles das Hiesige braucht, dieses Schwindende, das
seltsam uns angeht. Uns, die Schwindendsten. *Ein* Mal
jedes, nur *ein* Mal. *Ein* Mal und nichtmehr. Und wir auch
ein Mal. Nie wieder. Aber dieses
ein Mal gewesen zu sein, wenn auch nur *ein* Mal:
irdisch gewesen zu sein, scheint nicht widerrufbar.

In the translation of J. B. Leishman:

But because being here is much, and because all this
that's here, so fleeting, seems to require us and strangely
concerns us. Us the most fleeting of all. Just once,
everything, only for once. Once and no more. And we, too,
once. And never again. But this
having been once, though only once,
having been once on earth – can it ever be cancelled?

THE UNDISCOVER'D COUNTRY

I SUPPOSE IT IS INEVITABLE THAT AS ONE GROWS OLDER, THE PROGRESS OF one's life is marked by deaths. When one is young, these deaths are a mere hiccup in the flow of life. Moments, occasions where the unforeseen, even the unthinkable, breaks into the ordinary and places it in another light, a new context. Gradually, almost imperceptibly, they become more and more seamlessly integrated into the flow of life itself. I must confess that on my travels I never miss an occasion to visit a graveyard, to read the tombstones and wonder and fantasise about the people resting below them.

What remains a shock is news of the deaths of lovers: a body that has been so close to you that its contours become part of the lines that define yourself – and suddenly it is no longer there. It is like losing part of your-self, a limb. And its phantom will continue to haunt you. For me, Ingrid, inevitably, was the first. I haven't been to her grave for many years. I may not even find it today. But the day of her death I can never forget, and how I went blind, and how the world suddenly became a strange place, as if a huge, invisible hole had opened up somewhere to let in a cold wind from elsewhere, which nothing could keep out any more.

In due course she was followed by others. Sometimes I only learned about their passing much later, months, even years. Stephanie with her wide smile and her freckled shoulders. Paddy and her drawings in the sand; and how we fell asleep at the fringe of the sea and only woke up when a small wave came rippling across our feet, and the shape of her hands and the music of her voice. Elisabeth brilliant and luminous, always arguing, always questioning, never content with easy answers; shivering in the wind that carried the sweet smell of the pine forest, as her thin thighs turned blue in the cold. There must come a time when one is surrounded by more of the dead than the living. Until, gently or violently, one is gathered up with them. The congregation of the dead. Not all of them lovers or loved ones. Just friends, casual acquaintances, even enemies. People who used to be there and no longer are. There may be some among them of whose passing I haven't even heard yet. And others of whose deaths I've learned, somehow, somewhere, only to find out much later that the news was false. It can be unsettling. I remember at least one person, quite recently, of whom I'd already taken leave in my mind; and then, out of the blue, one day, there he was again, among the guests at a lecture or a launch or something, as if nothing untoward had happened; and it was so unexpected that when he came to me and I shook his hand – not a cold or bony hand at all, but warm and sweaty exactly as I remembered it – before I could stop myself I blurted out, 'But I thought you'd died long ago!'

There are other deaths that will never fade from memory. In October 1993, I was telephoned by the frail-care centre in the old-age home in which my father, then eighty-eight, resided. He had suffered a series of small strokes and was in a coma. I flew up to Johannesburg and from there drove to Potchefstroom, where I found him in a sorry shape. Since his late fifties he had suffered several heart attacks – once I had to rush back from Finland because we thought it was the end – but he had always managed to recover. But this time it seemed serious. And during the week I spent in the old-age home, sitting at his bedside most of the time, I was aware that this was a final goodbye. He never regained consciousness, so there was no chance of exchanging some last words – and what would we have said if it had been possible? He did feel discomfort and pain, however, or so it seemed to us. And it was a harrowing experience to see him suffering and struggling, but unable to do anything about it. From time to time I took one of his hands in mine. Gnarled and burnt by years of sun, compulsively working in his garden, they seemed so out of place on those stark white sheets: more talons than hands. He never gave any sign of being aware of my presence at all.

Except once, very briefly, when he did open his eyes and looked at me, and it seemed the mere shadow of a smile appeared on his face, but that might have been wishful thinking. For the rest, he just lay there, sinking, sinking slowly, and clearly suffering, but unable to go.

It became unbearable. And then the moment came, one morning when I went down to the frail-care centre from the flat where my mother still lived. The door of his ward was closed, but I opened it from the passage, to find two nurses working with him, washing him and changing his pyjamas and his bedclothes. I turned away towards the passage so that they could finish their ministrations. My father had never had any self-consciousness about being naked in the house; if my mother had always maintained a sense of propriety, he could not care less. But there was something about the scene that morning that pierced me to the quick. His helplessness in the hands of the nurses. Reduced to just a body. Not even a body, just a wretched bundle of bones covered by a parchment of skin. Curled up like a foetus, wholly defenceless, moaning almost inaudibly as they handled him with brusque efficiency.

It did not last for more than a few seconds. Then I found myself back in the passage, leaving the nurses to finish their sad little task. As soon as they had done, they came out, smiled at me and motioned at me to go in.

I went to stand by his bedside. He was lying on his back now, his rough farmer's hands like the claws of a big bird involuntarily clutching and unclutching on the white sheets, his eyes closed, the hint of a grimace on his lips, and that ceaseless low whisper of a moan coming from somewhere deep inside him.

In a slow but unstoppable way my whole life with him and my mother came reeling past me. The way he held me against his body when I was small. How strong and reassuring his sinewy arms were. How he had taught me to swim. And tennis. He'd never been a demonstrative person. When I had done well at school, he might touch my shoulder briefly; and even that was excessive. But the smallest hint of satisfaction, let alone pride, was enough to make me feel light-headed. All my life I'd been searching for a clear sign of affection. It had happened from time to time, but rarely, and always muted, restrained, never unambiguous.

Over all the years there had been a distance and a reticence. There were occasions, especially when the family had gone on holiday, when we could all laugh or sing together. But when there were only the two of us, we couldn't find the words or gestures to express our closeness. It may be an exaggeration, but I believe I can trace it back to my very first conscious memory. We were still living in Vrede. I could not have been much older than two and a half, because my mother was still pregnant with Elbie, who was born shortly before my third birthday. That was why she couldn't catch me, one day when she wanted to give me a hiding and I ran away. Through the garden and the red earth of my father's vegetable beds, under a wire fence, across a couple of streets, to the red-brick building of my father's office, where a black policeman was standing outside warming himself in the sun. He wanted to know what I was looking for. I glanced back over my shoulder, saw my mother approaching from a distance, and grabbed him by the arm: 'Where's my father? I want my father!'

'Come with me,' said the policeman and went on ahead of me, down a long bare passage to the office.

I was saved!

But it was a pyrrhic victory. Yes, my father welcomed me, smiled, even – if I remember correctly – briefly folded me into his arms.

But then he told the policeman to take me back to my mother.

Which was only to be expected. What else could he have done? But that compound feeling of safety and betrayal has remained with me for the rest of my life. Mostly I forgot about it. But there were a few times in my life when the memory did return, most lucidly a few years ago when Athol Fugard asked me about my earliest memory. That was when I realised how that subaquatic memory had remained with me all the time. And I presume it also came back on that terrible, unforgettable day when the black man came to our house to ask for help after he'd been assaulted by his master and by the police; and then my father had come home from his game of tennis and told him that he couldn't help, he had to go back to the police – the very police who had assaulted him.

There were so many other things that were unscrolled in my mind as I stood beside the freshly made bed: my father on a hunt, or skinning a springbok with long, precise strokes of his sharp knife; my father on his high magistrate's bench, copying the evidence on his foolscap pages; my father digging or watering in his vegetable garden; my father in the fowl run, while I sat on a nest teaching the hens to lay eggs; my father smashing a lob on the tennis court; my father, wearing his floppy little sun hat, on one of his compulsive walks, ten or fifteen kilometres every day: was he trying to clear his thoughts, or was it meant as exercise, or perhaps – a depressing suspicion from later years – as a way of getting away from home?; my father in his black tailcoat and hard white collar among the elders in church; my father on one of our Sunday afternoon family walks, squatting to shape a small dam on the dirt road for my sister Elbie to pee in; my father under the reading lamp in my room checking my Latin declensions and conjugations; my father telling us bedtime stories with wonderful codas and cadenzas that could leave us limp with laughter; my father with the newspaper on his lap in front of the fire; his endless patience, his unexpected quips and straight-faced jokes. All of it now reduced to this small bundle of dry skin and bones.

It was the indignity, more than anything else, that overwhelmed me. Even at times when we had found it hard to communicate, even when there were great distances between us, I had always been in awe of his gravity, his composure, his quiet dignity: the very fact of being unable to reach out and touch him, had always confirmed that he was someone special, someone literally set apart. And all that had now been eroded, broken down to this pathetic little heap, mercilessly exposed to the eyes of the world.

I still don't know how it happened. But at a given moment I found myself standing over him with his pillow in my hands, preparing to push it down on his face. He might put up a struggle, brief and weak, I knew, but then he would succumb, and it would all be over. I could not bear it any longer. I was sure that if I were to ask him and he could respond, he would beg me to help him out of this into the peace of death.

I was ready to do it. There was no one else near. In a minute or two I could go out and find a nurse and they would confirm that he was, thank God, dead. Nothing and no one stopped me. And yet I could not proceed.

335

I dropped the pillow. I was trembling all over. I was crying. But I did not do it.

An hour or two later I left. The nurses had confirmed that he was 'stable', that he might well remain in that state for days, for weeks. I could have spared him that, but I hadn't. I drove back to the airport, caught a plane back to Cape Town. When I arrived home, there was a message from the old-age home to say that he had died. Not even died: just slipped quietly out of reach. The next day I flew back to attend the funeral.

How often, in the years since then, have I recalled that moment of decision, trying to probe its silence, trying to explain to myself what had happened, what not; what had driven me to that moment – and then held me back.

I think, now, that if our love had been straightforward and uncomplicated, I would probably have gone through with it. For his sake. To make it easier for him. To rid him of his pain and of the indignity. But if I *had* done it, it would also, at least to some extent, have been for myself. Because *I* could no longer take it. There might even have been bitterness in it. Resentment. Or shame. Perhaps, however preposterous it might seem, revenge. For what had *not* been accomplished between us. For what, between father and son, had *not* happened, had *not* been said. And all of these impulses made it impossible to go through with the deed.

It made me realise, forced me to acknowledge, that I *could* commit a murder if it came to it. That I was capable of it. But I also knew that there were boundaries inside myself which I cannot cross. Boundaries which, ironically, my father himself, with his strict code of justice, of right and wrong, had inculcated in me.

My sister Elbie – known to South African readers as a wonderful writer of juvenile books, Elsabe Steenberg – died three years after my father, when she was not yet sixty. She'd suffered from multiple sclerosis for many years. For me, the most lasting memories of her go back to our childhood. All those games in which she had to fetch and carry, serve and sustain, warn and watch. All those secrets she was expected to keep. All the paths on which she was supposed to follow me. But only for as long as it pleased her. Pushed too far, she was sure to rebel and tell me exactly where to get off. She could be as calm and reasonable as my father, but she also had his wry sense of humour, and she could laugh with unbridled joy if something really tickled her.

She certainly could write. By the time she was fifteen she finished her first novel. Not far-fetched, blood-curdling inventions like my own early efforts, but adult stories about relationships and quiet fulfilment and loss. She turned to me for help, after she'd contacted a secretary to type the manuscript of that first novel, and only then discovered that she would not be able to pay the professional fee from her pocket money. Our parents were furious about her rashness, but I stepped in quietly and typed out the whole thing during my matric examination. When it was returned by the publisher she started on her second manuscript without missing a beat. She had a will of forged iron.

When we were kids, the only way of resisting her when she put her narrow foot down, was by playing the invented game of 'Auntie Paya'. It was more my invention than hers, and I still find it amazing that she ever consented to it. This consisted of her putting on a hat and a dressing gown of my mother's to play the role of a munificent mother figure who was to be approached only in dire circumstances, in which case she could not refuse any request, no matter what was asked of her. I shamefully turned it into a way of getting anything I wanted; and because she had a holy respect for rules, she would grimly hand over whatever I begged for. A doll, chocolates, a favourite pillow, sometimes even money, of which I somehow was always short. But in mitigation I should add that when I knew that *she* really wanted something very badly, it would make me glow with pleasure to surprise her with it when she least expected it.

After my return from Paris, we sadly began to grow apart, mainly because of strong differences on politics and religion, and on matters like divorce and remarrying. And as her illness progressed and in sheer desperation she turned to all kinds of unscrupulous quacks and con men, the distance between us grew – smoothed over only on very special occasions, as when a small group of close friends learned of her wish, when she was already bedridden, to reach one last time the summit of a mountain near the family's holiday home in the Eastern Free State, and achieved the near impossible by carrying her up in a wheelchair. It happened not so much because *they* had made the decision, but because Elbie had *believed* it to be possible. And her ferocious faith at times even inspired a sceptic like myself.

Curiously, she never read my work and I never read hers; yet each would fiercely defend the other whenever there was any need to unite against the world outside. And deep down, there was a blood link that held us together, even when it became impossible to talk openly about our differences. And then, in the last years of her life we recovered the early, innocent trust in each other that had made our childhood such a miraculous place to live in and return to.

My mother died quite recently: when I started writing this memoir she was still alive, and we were waiting, not solemnly but serenely, for her hundredth birthday. About a year before that, she'd woken up one morning and told the nurse who had come to tend to her that God had come to visit her in the night and had told her that he would soon be back to fetch her – there were just a few bits of business he still had to wrap up. I was in Johannesburg at the time and when the matron of the frail-care unit telephoned my sister Marita with the news we drove down to Potchefstroom to say goodbye. With her one could never know. We couldn't take God on his word – he'd failed her so many times – but just in case.

She was in a lucid and happy mood when we reached the home, and she didn't seem depressed or even sleepy. In fact, the nurse on duty told us that when she'd come into the ward early that morning with her coffee tray, my mother was content to be moved into a sitting position; and when the nurse momentarily turned her back to attend to the patient in the next bed, she quietly pulled away the back of the nurse's slacks and poured her whole cup of coffee into the gap. Quite a light-hearted leave-taking it turned out to be, as she happily slurped up the cup of yoghurt she always enjoyed with such relish on our rare visits. The whole day seemed to be bathed in a gentle and smiling light.

But it was not the end. God must have jumbled the message – he must also be getting on in years – but whatever it was, he did not turn up for the appointment. And then, months later, when everything had settled again, and it had been tentatively agreed among all of us that nothing would happen before 16 October, when her century was full, she very quietly, mischievous as always, sidestepped God and slipped away before he could show up.

But tonight, writing this chapter, there are three deaths that somehow remain particularly painful to come to terms with. The first was Rob Antonissen. He was Flemish, and head of the Department of Afrikaans and Dutch at Rhodes when I arrived there on a miserable August day in 1961, after the two years in Paris. Rob very nearly didn't make it to the station in time: he'd been working on an article and waited till the last minute to rush to the station, and the train was only an hour late instead of its usual two or three, so there was a wild race, and Rob made it by the skin of his teeth before the boom slammed down over the railway line. The stationmaster and several of his sidekicks came running to berate him, whereas Rob, flustered and frantic, his long overcoat flapping in the wind, gesticulated and apologised and tried to explain while Estelle and I heaved our luggage from the compartment on to the platform. It took quite a while to sort everything out and then we all collapsed with laughter. I'd been rather diffident about accepting the post at Rhodes, as all I'd known about Rob was his reputation as the fiercest literary critic in South Africa, but I'd desperately needed a job and was prepared to make the best of it for a while, until I could land something less daunting. But in the end I stayed for thirty years and Rob became one of the dearest and closest friends of my life. A man of dazzling erudition who could read eight or nine languages, Greek and Latin among them, loved music and painting and sculpture, was passionate about the theatre, and dreamed about becoming a conductor.

And there was his sense of humour, which could be as expansive and ribald as anything ever thought up in Flemish painting or writing. Bosch and Bruegel and Ensor were in that laugh, and Timmermans and Streuvels and van de Woestijne. I can still hear – and see – him laugh, folded double, his eyes streaming with tears and his glasses misted up, his nose changing shape, every pore in his face exuding joy. Only someone who had suffered deeply could feel fun so profoundly.

His family was adorable too. His lovely and lively wife, Liesje, and three daughters, Rike and Helga and little Elsje. There had been a boy too, Dirk – the first son born in the family for a generation, and the only one to pass on the Antonissen name. He'd been born soon after their arrival in South Africa, and the whole family in Belgium had been living for the day when they could see him. It took several years before Rob was able to go on his first sabbatical and they boarded a ship to Europe. On the day of their arrival every member of the family, even distant cousins and uncles and aunts, were on the quayside to meet the four-year-old little Dirk. But there was no little Dirk. He'd died during the voyage and had to be buried at sea, and communications in those days, just after the war, being what they were, it had not been possible to transmit the tidings to the family. Not one of them ever recovered completely, even though the depths of their Catholic faith helped them to bear what many others would not have managed to.

From the first days of our years in Grahamstown Rob and I were friends. To me, it was like discovering the world anew. The depth of his feeling about the good and the bad of it, was unfathomable. He was one of the only people I have ever known who could make me think that there must be something about religion after all.

He read every manuscript I produced in those years – with an acuity and an understanding that never ceased to amaze me. He never pulled his punches. He wouldn't allow a suspect comma or full stop to pass without thorough motivation and explanation. At the same time he could be generous in his praise. But what mattered was never the praise or the condemnation, but the *understanding*. More often than not he made me understand what it was I'd really been trying to say. And what he shared was not just his insights into literature, but the fullness of his humanity. In the eleven years and one month I knew him I may have learned more about writing, and about living, than in the whole rest of my life.

And then he died. Cancer. He was fifty-three years old. Don't try to tell me there is justice in the world.

At one stage, as so often happens, the cancer went into remission. The doctors pronounced him 'clean'. There was no sign of the malignancy left. We arranged a small celebration at our home to welcome him back to life.

340

All his closest and dearest friends were there. A week later the cancer was back. From then on the descent was steep and brutal.

When the brief September holidays began, Alta and I went to her parents in Gordon's Bay. I visited Rob just before we left. He was shockingly frail. But his bed was littered with music scores and when he spoke about Bach and Mozart, his eyes were still bright.

About four or five days into the holiday I woke Alta up in the night.

'Rob has died,' I told her.

'How do you know?' she asked, aghast.

'Because he'd just come to me in the night,' I said. 'To say goodbye.'

It was not a dream. It was much too clear for that. I knew that he'd been in the room. And there had been nothing sad or dark about the visit. He had to go, he'd told me. And he didn't want us to mourn. It was a good thing to go.

Later in the day Liesje telephoned. He'd died at precisely the time I had awakened Alta.

Then there was Daantjie. A larger-than-life man. With a larger-than-life laugh. Daantjie could speak ten or twelve different accents without any trace of a language. A gourmet of the female sex. And a lover of words. No one I have ever known could turn language inside out as Daantjie could. If he couldn't find an existing word for what he wanted to say, he would invent one – or three, or seventeen. Nothing in his life was done, or said, in half measures. He was a specialist in crudeness and fulmination. At the same time he was passionate about literature, and he could quote from Shakespeare or Donne or Whitman or Dylan Thomas or Joyce or Zola for hours; literally for hours.

In his young days, when he drove a 'book bus' through the country, he'd regularly summon up the help of these writers to lure girls into the cramped but welcoming space of his bunk.

Daantjie was a lover, most especially, of physical activity. Walking, cycling, swimming. A lover of the sea. A lover of mountains too. He took me along to the Cederberg once. There wasn't a peak or a slope or a rock formation he didn't know by name. He was as strong as a bull. And he lived life fully and recklessly.

I remember him telling me once about a walk up Jonkershoek Mountain outside Stellenbosch, one Sunday morning, with his son Neel. How, on the way down, his foot had caught on a protruding tree root and how he'd started falling.

'I fell,' said Daantjie, 'and I fell and I fell and I fell. It went on forever. I remember thinking, if I had a book with me now I could finish reading it before I hit the bottom. And still I fell. At a given moment I could see my arse coming wheeling down past my ears. And still I fell. I think, if you consider it properly, I haven't stopped falling yet. I'm *still* falling.'

There was nothing he wouldn't do for a friend. I'm sure his family often suffered because of his unbelievable generosity towards others. What he couldn't stand was hypocrisy and pretence. Then he would be relentless. Apartheid and its practitioners he hated with a very particular virulence. And why shouldn't he? He was immensely proud of being a descendant of the first mixed marriage ever performed at the Cape of Good Hope. To hear him talking to a group of brown fishermen at Hout Bay, or a team of builders in what remained of District Six after the coloured inhabitants had been expelled and their houses bulldozed, was to rediscover not only a language but all the human joys and sorrows and excesses that went with it.

Then the cancer got to him too. He put up a fight as ferocious as any in his life. But in the end he succumbed. To see him waste away – pale for the first time in his life, I'm sure – struggling to find words, keeping his eyes closed when the light became too bright, was to learn the saddest thing about death. One's only consolation is that his ashes were scattered in the Cederberg. And that something of the spirit of Africa was kept alive by a man who could live, and love, as deeply as Daantjie Saayman could.

The third death was very different. This was not someone who had lived long and fully. It was a child of only a few months old.

In those days, the early seventies, our very special friends, Gerrit and Marina Geertsema, often came down to the Eastern Cape to visit us. Sometimes we would all go down together to the not very comfortable beach house we then had at Kleinemonde, about fifty kilometres from Grahamstown. At other times they went on their own. On this occasion they brought their two little boys with them, Luka, then about four, and the baby, also Gerrit, whom we hadn't met before. They'd been looking forward to this trip enormously. Gerrit was a great fisherman, which he still is; and they had a few hectic months in the theatre behind them. They needed this break.

But early on the third or fourth morning they came back from the sea, and needed a doctor. The baby had taken ill. I took them to our doctor, who decided immediately that they should rush him to the hospital. I had to go off to a lecture. When I came back, the child was dead.

There are things the mind cannot grasp. Not even with hindsight.

I remember going to the undertaker's in the afternoon, with Gerrit. Mr Inggs was a collector of vintage cars, and the entire backyard of his tumble-down premises was crammed with the carcases of ancient vehicles. We had to pick our way around, and past, and over the remains of long-dead cars, and then go up a crumbling staircase, to a back porch stacked with coffins that seemed as decayed and second-hand as the cars. When we knocked, there was a long silence. Then the door was opened on a chink. And a very pale, very round face emerged at roughly the height of my navel. The whole conversation that ensued took place between Mr Inggs and my midriff. There was something Dickensian about him: he was small and rotund, with an expression of chronic sadness applied to his face, and he was dressed all in black, with a black bowler hat on his head. He had no voice, but spoke in a sibilant whisper.

Extending one soft round hand first to me, then to Gerrit, he sighed, 'My condolences, sir.'

I explained our business. Mr Inggs came as close to beaming as was proper in the circumstances.

After that we had to find suitable outfits for the funeral. Gerrit and Marina, being on holiday, had nothing formal to wear, and Gerrit and I were nowhere near the same size. Some friends were approached and we duly retired home to mix and match – Alta's experience as wardrobe mistress came in useful – and the next morning we tried our best to look solemn and dignified. Gerrit wore a black jacket, the sleeves of which barely came down to his elbows, and he couldn't do up his shirt buttons. He had to make do with sandals.

The day broke wet and wretched. In pouring rain we drove to the cemetery. There were only the four of us, Marina and Gerrit, Alta and I. And Mr Inggs, of course, who approached with the small white coffin, barely the size of a shoebox, in his arms. Gerrit took it from him. For a minute or so we stood waiting, not sure about what to do next. Then Gerrit handed the coffin back to Mr Inggs, and the small hole was filled with mud. All the while the rain came down steadily.

Nobody could face going home. As we drove around for a while, the rain unexpectedly started clearing up. In the uncomfortably bright new sunshine we drove out of town and found a small stream under wet, dripping trees. There we stopped. It was too wet to get out. We just sat quietly together. Nobody spoke. What could there possibly be left to say?

Yet there was something unbelievably wholesome about the togetherness in the car. An awareness of a bond of friendship that gathered up the time we had spent together and the years ahead. The image of that slithery, dark, muddy hole where we'd stood together in the cemetery. The half-repressed memory of the baby we'd buried. Knowing that this would remain with us, till death us did part.

BLACK AND WHITE
AFTER THE FALL

AT A RECENT CAPE TOWN BOOK FAIR, I SPENT SOME TIME IN CONVERSATION with Fred Khumalo, the Insight and Opinion editor of the *Sunday Times*. For many years, one of the most depressing aspects of returning to South Africa after a trip abroad used to be exposure to the standard of local newspaper reporting. This has changed considerably in recent years; and Fred is one of the bright stars in the new firmament. After spending much of his teenage years among criminals, dagga smokers and scavengers of various kinds – 'in a crazy swirl of booze and drugs and sex' as his publisher describes it in the blurb to his autobiography, *Touch My Blood* – he turned to journalism.

What makes Fred special, is his ability to mingle the hilarious and the deeply serious. Many of the darker moments, in his essays, his weekly column in the *Sunday Times*, his autobiography and his novel, *Witches' Brew*, are illuminated by flashes of often irreverent comedy, whereas his humour often careens on a bedrock of human need or greed.

On this occasion, something in our conversation triggered a memory to make me realise, anew, the extent to which this country has changed in recent years. When I came back from Paris at the end of 1968, I was adamant that one thing that had to change in my life was interaction with black people. What particularly interested me was, predictably, the world of writing and journalism. And within a week or so of my return, just after my first newspaper interview about the year in France had been published, there was an opportunity I couldn't miss under any circumstances. It was a request for an interview from a black journalist, Harry Mashabela, working for the *Star* in Johannesburg. And talking, now, to Fred Khumalo, that memory hit me between the eyes. What was now so easy and relaxed – so 'normal', in fact, that one needn't think twice about it – had been, in the last days of 1968, a major enterprise. First of all, Harry Mashabela and I could not meet in a public place: the lounge or foyer of a hotel, a restaurant, a pub, whatever. He was black, I was white. We were not even allowed to have a drink together. Which meant that we had to arrange a meeting in the house of friends. Harry felt that it would not be advisable for me to come to Soweto, so I turned to the few friends I had in Johannesburg. They were writers, publishers, journalists, people of culture and open minds. Or so I'd thought. After Paris, it hadn't even occurred to me that there might be a problem. Only when the first one I approached started fidgeting with embarrassment did I realise that meeting Mr Mashabela might not be as straightforward as I had anticipated. Some of the excuses and explanations had to do with the family ('Well, you see, we have small children in the house. They won't understand.' Or: 'Look, you know me, *I* don't mind. But my wife . . .'). Some with social relations ('I hope you'll understand, but if my friends found out about this I'll be in trouble.' Or even: 'I'm not sure how I can explain such a visit to my domestic. I mean, how can I expect her to come into the lounge and serve a *black* man?'). Or with work ('You must realise that I work in public relations. We depend on our clients. My job may be on the line.').

Recently, as I was reading the magnificent autobiography of the human-rights lawyer George Bizos, it struck me in an almost sickening way: how easily, how *naturally*, it came to him, in the circumstances in which he entered South African society, even as an immigrant from Greece, to campaign for the victims of apartheid, to find himself surrounded by other people who shared his outrage about oppression. This was true for many others – academics or writers with an English background. Very dear friends like Nadine Gordimer and Athol Fugard. Not for a moment do I underestimate the effort it cost them to identify with the deprived and persecuted majority in the country. The obstacles they had to overcome, the humiliations they had to suffer. But whatever the cost, all they had to do was to follow their natural instinct. 'Human rights' was what they breathed in every day of their lives. There might be endless hurdles placed in their way by 'the system'. But they could always count on the solidarity of like-minded people. On the other hand, to be an Afrikaner, to come from a family and a home and a social environment where apartheid was not a hateful idea or a foreign concept, but something that defined the parameters of the 'normal' – that was something else altogether. And because Afrikaners had such a *beleaguered* sense of identity, of identity under threat, the possibilities for normal discussion and argument were almost non-existent.

It went further than what theorists have called 'colonial cringe': one felt that in such conditions the individual's very existence was at stake in every utterance, every attempt at compromise, every attempt at reasoning. And over the years Afrikanerdom had devised diabolically efficient ways of dealing with 'aberration'. During the Anglo-Boer War, dissidents were summarily dealt with – often executed. To be branded a 'traitor of the *volk*' was devastating. Since identity itself was tied up with, determined by, the *volk*, expulsion from that safe laager was a form of death. Very few individuals could deal with it. Which was why it was so much more difficult for a man like the Afrikaner Bram Fischer to campaign for the oppressed than for someone like Sydney Kentridge. If Nadine wanted to talk to a black writer, she could invite him or her to her home. At the time I returned from Paris and found myself in a strange city, Johannesburg, this was not possible.

In the end we did find a solution. If I remember correctly it was my friend Naas who offered us his lounge. And then everything went smoothly. Harry Mashabela and I spent a most stimulating and heart-warming afternoon together. He filled me in about what had been happening in South Africa in my absence. I told him about Paris. About Mbella. About Gerard Sekoto. Harry was particularly interested to hear about the student revolt. Not just the events themselves, but the inspiration behind them. The writings of Che Guevara, of Régis Debray, of Fidel Castro. We spoke about Marcuse and Camus. I told him about Amiri Baraka, then still writing under the name of Leroy Jones, and his recent volume of essays, *Home*.

Meeting Harry was a prelude to the new chapter in my life that began with my return to South Africa. I was eager not to lose the momentum I'd found in Paris. And over the following years it did become easier to cross the barriers into a territory where a notion of 'belonging' was not determined by political or racial prejudice, but by shared interest, by privately formulated *choice*. Even so, it remained difficult. I lost a number of friends, several of whom I had previously regarded as 'close' or 'good' friends. But this was a price I was prepared to pay: having made my choice in Paris, I knew what I was returning to, and accepted that it would not be plain sailing.

My family was part of the problem. Among my siblings, Marita and Johan had an almost immediate sympathy and understanding for my situation. Not Elbie. And politics remained a bone of contention between us until the end. My parents were mortified by the shift Paris had occasioned inside me. My mother's somewhat more relaxed, liberal attitude made contact easier. But my father, the member of the Broederbond, son of a Boer who had fought against the English and whose whole life had been tied up with the struggle for Afrikaner identity, was not to be swayed. His sense of right and wrong, which had inspired his career as a magistrate, could make him understand reason. But that was intellectually, never emotionally. On my return from Paris in 1968 I quite simply represented everything he found abhorrent. What had happened in many other families might have torn us apart. And within the family we deeply loved one another! In the end, after a long and painstaking process, we did arrive at the only solution that could possibly have worked: having discussed all the implications of our respective positions, we acknowledged that we could never agree on politics in South Africa again. The only course past that irremediable difference was to agree, rationally, that we would never, ever discuss politics at home again. It was, and would remain, off-limits. And in this way we navigated a careful route that took us through the straits.

Only once after that, I remember, my father discussed one of my books with me. He faithfully continued reading them all as they appeared; but he would never refer to them, not ever. My mother could do that without any problem. She might differ, even object. But it would never be an obstacle between us. The exception, for my father, was *A Dry White Season*. As a magistrate who'd worked with the police all his life, he was shocked to his foundations by the portrayal of the SB in the book. 'All I want to know,' he asked me, 'is this: is it true, or did you make it up?' 'It is fiction,' I told him. 'But every single fact in it is based on the truth. Everything has been documented and presented in one court or another.' He never referred to it again.

That was the situation within the family. In my working environment things were made a bit easier by the fact that Rhodes University had a long tradition of liberalism, which meant that, at the very least, contact across the barriers of class and race was not automatically frowned on. Although Rhodes could not match the ideological openness of large universities like Wits or UCT or possibly Natal, it did offer a space where people of different ideologies could meet and interact and discuss; and a broadly based opposition to apartheid imposed an awareness of shared interest. Yet the fact that some of the most enlightened minds, including some of the most principled opponents to apartheid on campus were Afrikaners, encouraged an accommodation of divergent views. One of these, Daantjie Oosthuizen, professor of philosophy, provoked an unprecedented furore in Afrikanerdom, by divulging in a scholarly article something which subsequently became generally accepted as historical fact: that the revered president of the Transvaal Republic, Paul Kruger, who had led the Boers into war against Britain at the turn of the century, had had a black ancestor. Today I can foresee a time when many white Afrikaners may go out of their way to claim 'authenticity' by unearthing black ancestors. It is something I myself have quite eagerly pursued. And although, so far, I have only found some fascinating near misses, I have not yet given up.

At one extreme, on the Rhodes campus, there were still old colonial types who habitually looked down on 'locals', and even more so on 'natives'; at the other, there were a number of extremist diehard Afrikaners who were heroically carrying the torch for God's own people bent on defending their small, threatened, white territory against foreigners and black, indigenous, heathen masses. And at both extremes the Anglo-Boer War was still being fought every single day. But in between there was a broad, tolerant, even generous, space where open discussion was possible, resistance to government policies ethically and philosophically grounded, and a shared future for an as yet only dreamt of South African nation a viable topic for negotiation. In this space there were even a few black individuals. Not all of them were members of the academic staff, or of the student body. But at least some of them were accessible. They could be drawn into discussion. Their opinions and contributions were regarded as vital.

For quite some time such contact inevitably remained fairly restricted; nevertheless, there were open windows that provided views of the other side of the South African moon, something almost wholly unthinkable on an Afrikaans campus.

Sometimes I became despondent: why should it be such an effort for a white person to go in search of opportunities to meet black people? After the publication of *Looking on Darkness* this changed drastically, and effortlessly. But even before that there had been some events that cast new – and often deeply unsettling – light on 'the South African situation'. One of the first was an invitation, in the second half of 1970, to deliver the Gandhi Memorial Lecture at the Phoenix settlement outside Durban.

I was invited by a man with an overwhelming personality, Mewa Ramgobin, who was married to Gandhi's granddaughter; and for many reasons it was to me an occasion not to be missed. There was also something celebratory about the visit as it was the first weekend Alta and I spent away from home after our marriage. As it turned out, our son Danie was conceived there.

In many ways it was a strangely unnerving visit. We hadn't realised that Mewa was under banning orders, which meant that he was not allowed to receive visitors. As a result, there was little opportunity, apart from the lecture, to meet people from outside the settlement. Mewa himself showed only too clearly the emotional scars inflicted by his solitary lifestyle. Fifteen years later, when he published the novel *Waiting to Live*, I recognised in it much of the repressed emotion and anger which we'd witnessed from the outside, at a distance, during that weekend in 1970. But at the time there was only the unforgiving hardness of a still-unresolved rage. And I remember thinking: this, more than the blatant suffering inflicted through imprisonment and persecution and torture and humiliation and even death, may ultimately be among the cruellest testimonies to apartheid – the fact that it deprived innumerable people all over the country of a full emotional life; the way it has restricted and inhibited the range of their human possibilities.

The way in which Mewa reacted to what had been inflicted on him, was to become harsh and domineering in his relations with others; his need always to be in command, to make decisions on their behalf, to inhibit *their* freedom. In the daytime Alta and I were barely allowed to be alone on our own for even a minute. He insisted on reading every word of the lecture I had prepared for the gathering; he wanted to impose changes and additions – and he was offended when I refused. For better or for worse, I told him, this was *my* speech.

This is the place where Gandhi spent much of his time in South Africa. And something of his spirit – the much misunderstood 'passive resistance' of *satyagraha*, the non-violence of *ahimsa* – can still be imagined there. Even though during that depressing weekend there was little sign of his greatness of mind, his humility, his blitheness, his sense of humour. His memory, I felt disturbingly, had become harnessed to a predictable and definable cause, to a narrow, personal interpretation of a specific doctrine of resistance. Part of the secret of Gandhi, I have always believed, was that he was not only *against* certain things – but that he could also, wholeheartedly and positively, even exuberantly, be *for* the things he truly believed in. In some respects he might be regarded as a forerunner of Tutu.

What in some ways made a more lasting impression on me than the smouldering anger in Mewa, was the reactions of his two young sons, eight and six years old, to the conditions under which they were forced to live as black people in a country dominated by a white minority. Before his banning, Mewa told me, they had once taken a walk along a beach in Durban where children were cavorting on the swings. The two boys wanted to join the other kids, but Mewa stopped them.

'You can't go there,' he said.

'But why, Daddy?'

'Because those swings are for white children only.'

That, said Mewa, was where the political consciousness of the younger boy began: a virulent hatred for all whites. On one occasion he even asked his father not to give him any toys for his next birthday.

'Why not?' Mewa had asked.

'I want you to buy me a gun so that I can shoot a white man.'

The reaction of the older boy had been quite different. 'You know what?' he told Mewa after the walk on the beach. 'When we get home I want you to make us a swing too. And then we'll invite all the children, the white ones too, so that they can see we're not as bad as they are.'

What I did realise after that conversation, was that I certainly could not blame Mewa for holding the views he did. Through his account of what his younger son had said on the beach, I came closer to understanding the father.

There was a huge audience at the lecture. I met Griffiths Mxenge there, the lawyer who later supplied me with hundreds of pages of court documents on deaths in detention, which I used for *A Dry White Season*; and his wife Victoria, impressive in her dignity and fire; and Rick Turner, a charismatic activist and lecturer, murdered a few years later in front of his family by the security police; and numerous others who in later years helped to shape my consciousness. The lecture itself began as an exploration of Gandhi's philosophy, the way it shaped his life, and its possible application to our dire circumstances of that time. Towards the end, the focus moved to Bram Fischer who was by then terminally ill in prison; and I added my voice to the many others that had begun to clamour for his release. What this country needed right then, I argued, was precisely a man like Fischer: someone with his integrity, his belief in what black and white shared in South Africa, his unshakeable faith in human dignity that transcended racial difference, and in the freedom that would inevitably, and gloriously, come to this benighted land.

The lecture had unexpected consequences. Some time afterwards, after Fischer had been released to die in the home of his brother, I was invited by his daughters, Ruth and Ilse, to deliver the funeral oration in Bloemfontein. I was prevented from accepting by the one action of my father's which I have never been able to forgive. He had been complaining of chest pains for some time and I knew that over the past twenty years he'd had several heart attacks, at least two of them serious. At the time of Fischer's death my father had made an appointment with a doctor. Then he learned about the invitation from Bloemfontein, and promptly cancelled his doctor's appointment. If we declined the invitation to the funeral, he said very calmly and very firmly, he would reinstate his appointment. Otherwise, whatever happened, would be on my head.

I had no choice but to send the text of my speech to Bloemfontein with friends. But it was with great resentment and a feeling of having betrayed Bram Fischer and his cause that I watched them drive off.

On that unforgettable day, as Fischer's death was mourned, as his life was celebrated, over a non-existent grave, the state having refused to hand over even the ashes of the deceased to his family, I remembered the weekend at Phoenix. Those two young boys and their reactions to being kept away from the swings on the beach because they were black. And Mewa Ramgobin. The man he had become. The man he might have been.

Cry, the beloved country.

The weekend in what was then still Natal added to a growing feeling of malaise in me. The elation that had marked my return from Paris was beginning to wear off. The realities of the South Africa I'd come home to were proving too strong for the expectations and the idealism that had buoyed me during the first months. My involvement in the theatre, directing Camus' *Les Justes*, had kept disillusionment at bay for a while; meeting Alta and getting married brought a new lease on life. But the disheartening reality of the everyday world was becoming too insistent to ignore. There was an underlying hopelessness in the situation. The reception of the Gandhi lecture had provided some new impetus to my faith in the future. But the reality of Mewa's existence in banishment, corroborated by so much other evidence of the impasse the country seemed to have reached – the hardening racism of whites, the despair and anger simmering among blacks, particularly the young generation – was draining my energy and stifling my optimism. In my journals from that time, there are more and more comments on an 'inner paralysis' that was gnawing away at my wish to *do* something, and at my more and more urgent need to *write*. 'This impotent and unbearable anger about what is happening all around me – the blunt stupidity and entrenched inhumanity and ritual cruelty that marks white society – the more I see of people the less I can believe in them and the more I need to find refuge in "humanity", which can be a dangerous illusion . . .' And the visit to Phoenix Settlement was a definitive milestone on this road.

The gloom only began to lift once I was able to immerse myself in the writing of *Looking on Darkness*. Then came the unbelievable uproar about the banning of the book. This also had an immediate effect on my daily life. There was a seemingly endless avalanche of letters and telephone calls not only from places scattered across the map of South Africa, but from Stockholm and Stuttgart and Seattle and Santiago, from Tokyo and New Delhi and Aix-en-Provence and Laos and Yaoundé and Buenos Aires, you name it. More pertinently, I was approached by strangers in the street who wished to shake my hand and wish me good luck. Others turned up on my doorstep, or in my office at the university. Some of the correspondents and visitors were chancers who assumed that I must dispose of unimaginable riches and would love to share these with them. Some were genuinely in need. A number of old acquaintances wrote to say that they wanted to break off all contact as they felt they could no longer be associated with someone like me. In most cases it was a relief, but a few of the letters did hurt.

Many of the strangers who got in touch were black. As if the ban had suddenly broken down all the traditional barriers. For every person that turned his back, there were five new friends. For every white who was peeved or offended, five blacks were interested. It did not mean that my black readership grew exponentially overnight. But the ban on the book had a ripple effect in the black community. People who would never read it, came to know about it. And with the traditional obstacles cleared away, my possibilities of making contact with fellow South Africans were suddenly unlimited.

A few years later this was confirmed by the publication of *A Dry White Season*. Not all the contacts stimulated by publications and bans could, by any stretch of the imagination, be called 'normal'. But at least the possibility of personal relationships had been created. And much of what ensued during the following decades was determined by these beginnings.

One of the consequences of the ban on *Looking on Darkness* and its subsequent publication in so many countries was that a heavy international workload was added to my schedule. Even though I tried to limit my commitments to what seemed only strictly necessary, I was travelling more and more of the time, including up to eight or nine trips abroad a year, to conferences and symposiums and launches and literary festivals and universities in Europe, the US, South America and Australia. It brought about meetings with a number of writers who were household names and had taken a place of honour in my reading – and in my lecturing – over many years. The Congolese Tchicaya U'Tamsi whose wisdom was always illuminated by humour. Amiri Baraka with his verve and flamboyance. James Baldwin in whom a deep bedrock of sadness underpinned everything else. The fatherly Chinua Achebe who was like an aloe that had taken root in a foreign land, and whose great concern was children's books: 'It is a fallacy to think we can teach our children. They teach *us*. They teach us how to fly. Because children can fly, you know. *We* are weighed down by possessions.' Ngugi wa Thiong'o, as alert and unwavering as a fishing eagle. More recently there was the beautiful Chimamanda Ngozi Adichie, her figure as poised and graceful as her prose. There were also exiled South Africans like Bessie Head, with whom I developed, in Australia, a special and at times deeply moving rapport; the often truculent but always stimulating Lewis Nkosi, and innumerable others. More and more over the years I had encounters with representatives of the ANC in exile – in Melbourne, in Amsterdam and London, in Dublin and Edinburgh, in Copenhagen and Helsinki and Stockholm, even in Moscow and what was then still Leningrad. These meetings often started formally, even cautiously, but invariably they became hearty and exuberant, even celebratory; more than once they marked the beginning of friendships which still endure.

Inside South Africa, the seventies and eighties became more and more harrowing. In the long run it was almost impossible to find time for writing. Hardly a day went by without someone turning up at my front door to ask for help. These visits were often concerned with personal or domestic matters: someone who needed money to pay school or university fees; someone who was threatened with eviction unless the rent was paid; a woman who needed money to buy clothes for her children, a man who had collapsed in the street and needed to go to hospital, a boy who had been abandoned by his parents, and an ancient, wizened old man whose only son had died and who now had no one to take care of him . . . There were, inevitably, opportunists and chancers too. One teenage girl, a consummate little actress, arrived at least once a week, pretending to be a different person with new needs every time; a small, spruce man with an amazing command of English and who went by the name of Milton, who usually turned up with a basket of fruit, and more than once tried to sell me the plums or lemons he had just picked off my own trees at the back of the house; a large, boisterous woman who arrived at my front gate in a storm, safely ensconced under a wide umbrella while I became soaked to the skin in the torrential rain. 'Can you please give me money to buy a shop,' she demanded imperiously. 'Then I won't ever bother you again.' 'I'm sorry,' I apologised, 'but I'm afraid that is a bit steep.' She shrugged and looked at me as if she was doing me a huge favour: 'Then how about wheels?' 'Wheels?' I asked, flabbergasted. 'A car,' she explained. When I regretfully declined, she said condescendingly, 'All right, then just give me bus fare.' On another occasion she wanted money to buy school shoes for her children. I telephoned the shop to enquire about the price, then presented her with the exact amount. She refused to take it. 'That will be Ackerman's,' she said. 'You may buy shoes for *your* children at Ackerman's. But *I* shop at Cartwright's.'

Most of those in need I directed to organisations where they could be helped. The Black Sash. Local charities. Doctors. Hospitals. Lawyers. Where it was feasible, I tried to step in myself. Sometimes by helping pupils at school or students at university with their work, or by spending time with young would-be writers on their manuscripts. There was a young man, Raymond, whose dearest wish was to become a photographer. For several weeks I gave him lessons, and at the end of the course I gave him a camera to set out on his own. A few times there was no pretext: spontaneous friendships developed and ran their course, driven by their own momentum. Such a man was Kenneth Mdana, who first came to me in the wake of the ban on *Looking on Darkness*. We started talking, a conversation that continued until I left Grahamstown, almost fifteen years later. Kenneth was an incredibly resourceful entrepreneur, always with a bee in his bonnet, a new scheme hatching. To set up a shop. To set up a brick-making concern. To become a journalist. I dutifully became involved every time. The problem was that his schemes almost never worked out – in part, because he did not believe in gradualism. Kenneth thought big. Mindful of my vegetable-growing days, I fell for each and every scheme. I'm still not sure how many thousands went down the drain in this way. And yet, somehow, Kenneth made me believe that it was always worthwhile: and if there was a failure now and then, or even every time, there was always the firm assurance that next time it would work.

The last scheme we were involved in was his translation of *A Dry White Season* into Xhosa. It started with the loan, then the gift, of a typewriter. Then a second typewriter. Then long stretches when I had to 'keep him going', to buy him time for writing. The entire process took years and years. But he saw it through. In the end the translation was published, under the title *Umqwebedu*. It was not a commercial success. But I shall always be indebted to him for the glimpses he afforded me into his life and the life of his people. And for the equanimity – no, the uproarious good humour – with which he managed to surmount every obstacle that came his way. The break that was caused by my move to Cape Town at the end of 1990, was an irreparable loss. He contacted me only once, to let me know that his wife had died; he needed money for the funeral. But the rest was silence.

It was not always possible to respond to calls and cries for help. There were those people who found themselves in more hazardous circumstances – not just debt, or legal or administrative or career problems, but personal agony which seemed to be irremediable, caused by the simple, deep, terrible fact of living in the wrong country at the wrong time. Several times I was drawn into families where things were falling apart impossibly. One such moment will remain with me forever.

I can still see it: the old man standing opposite me, quaking with rage. But his stooped shoulders, whose usual squareness suggest the confidence of a man who knows that God is on his side, betray the underlying pain. On a chair against the wall his wife is slumped, sobbing quietly, a motherly hen disturbed in her brooding; and on the edge of the narrow bed sits a young man, pale, his blond head bowed, but with a body rigid in defiance. 'It would have been easier for me today,' says the father, his voice trembling, 'to have been told that my son was dead. Rather than *this*.' I feel like an intruder in this intimate and agonising scene. What I am witnessing is more than the gulf which separates generations: it is, in a family context, the breakdown of one system of values and the affirmation of another; the shattering of an image the world has long taken for granted, that of the Afrikaner monolith. Half an hour earlier, the young man, a postgraduate student in my department, telephoned me and asked me to come to his digs. He had just informed his parents that he was in love with a girl who, like himself, is the child of an Afrikaans-speaking church minister – except that, in terms of the South African racial laws, he is white while she has been classified 'coloured'.

'What will become of us?' asks the old man in horror. 'I shall lose my job in the church. Not one of our friends will speak to us again.' This, to him, is more important than whatever may happen to his son.

'He is still our son,' the mother whispers in quiet desperation; her husband does not even seem to hear.

I plead with him not to tear his family apart, but he stubbornly refuses to give an inch. The Bible tells us, he argues, not to consort with the animals of the veld. I get the impression that the mother may be open to more understanding; but during the rest of our conversation she is very deliberately sidelined by her husband; and when they leave, the break seems to be complete. For as long as he refuses to reject the woman he loves, the young man will not be regarded as the son of the family.

It pleased me to find that in his own way he was as stubborn as his father. He stayed with his girlfriend; in due course they were married. Some years later he became a lecturer at the same university. His father resigned from his position in the church. I do not know whether there ever was a reconciliation. Perhaps, when the political change in the country came, it may have been too late for this family.

At the time this was only one episode among innumerable others I had to tackle during those middle years of the eighties. It was the first time in my life that I had to turn away from writing for several years: the demands of every day had simply become too much. The most difficult to handle were the cases of families where a father, or brother, or cousin, or child had been picked up by the security police and had 'disappeared'. There was so little I could really do; on my own, certainly, I was powerless. Once again I had to turn to others for help – organisations like the Black Sash, contacts in parliament or close to it. There was a lawyer friend who very often was prepared to pursue such cases. Without charge. Two or three times I ventured to confront the SB myself. I came to know much more intimately than I would ever have wished the inside of their depressing grey offices hidden behind a seemingly ordinary door on the floor above OK Bazaars in the centre of town. But behind that wooden door was an intimidating steel grille; and once that slammed shut there was no telling whether it would ever be opened again. Those visits began long before I was summoned there in my own right, to recover the papers and typewriters the SB had confiscated from my home, or to 'answer a few questions'.

Needless to say, such interventions, or attempts at intervention, were not always successful. There were in fact, some very distressing moments. I remember being visited one Saturday afternoon by a distraught young man. During our conversation he burst into tears and sobbed so violently that he became incoherent. Only after several cups of tea did he recover sufficiently to tell me his story.

He was a first-year student at Rhodes, the third of seven siblings. Since his early childhood he had dreamt of studying, but to proceed to university from a coloured township was almost unthinkable. However, his family had soon realised that he was unusually gifted and after long discussions with his class teacher and his school principal, they started preparing for the big step. From the age of twelve he himself had spent every spare hour doing all kinds of odd jobs – from gardening and washing cars and running errands for white housewives to doing bookkeeping for shopkeepers and charity organisations – so as to earn money. Until at last, two years after finishing school, he had saved enough to register for a BA at Rhodes, planning to proceed to a law degree afterwards. It was tough, but the whole family was prepared to scrape together their puny resources to keep him going, and two kind white people, a teacher and a lawyer, had signed surety for a loan.

Then, three weeks before he came to see me, he had received an unexpected visit from two white strangers who took him to the Botanical Gardens where they started discussing his studies with him. They were surprisingly well informed about his background, his family circumstances, his future plans and dreams. And they were exceedingly friendly. After an hour or so they came to the point. They had been following his progress at Rhodes and they were impressed by his potential. Aware of the odds against which he had to battle for success, they were prepared to offer him a job for five years, until the completion of his LLB; in addition, they would pay him a monthly retainer, enough to supply his family; he would even have enough pocket money left to take care of some of his needs beyond the merely basic.

And in exchange?

Oh not much, they assured him. Not much at all. It would take up very little of his time. A few hours a week would be enough.

But what kind of work were they talking about?

It took them a while to get to the point. He must be aware, they said, that there were some students at Rhodes – only a small handful – who were not interested only in studying but who were involved in all kinds of activities that could harm the lives of other people. These miscreants were well known to the authorities, but it wasn't always easy to obtain hard and pertinent evidence against them. It was of vital importance to the whole student community, to the welfare of society, that such nefarious activities be brought to the attention of the authorities. There was no risk involved, none at all. He could go on with his studies and nobody would ever be any the wiser. All that was required of him would be to report, from time to time, to these two gentlemen on specific individuals on campus. What was said in certain lectures. Who attended which meetings. Nothing out of the ordinary. No risk at all. The sort of thing he would be noticing anyway. The only effort involved might be a brief report from time to time. And just think of what he would be getting in return . . .

He felt his throat contract. But it was impossible to refuse outright. There was something in their attitude, something below the surface, an expression in their eyes, that made him hesitate. He told them he needed time to think.

Of course, they said. Take all the time you need. We're not pressing you. Just think it over. Think of your studies. Think of your family.

A week later they were back. As generous and friendly as before. This time there was an almost imperceptible shift in their attitude. He was still free to take his time, of course; but at some stage they would need an answer. They counted on his co-operation.

That was when he dared to ask them outright, 'You want me to spy on my friends?'

They seemed hurt. That wasn't a word they would ever use, they assured him. It was a matter of simple observation. And of communicating only what might be harmful to others. It was to *prevent* untoward things happening. Nothing more. Surely the safety of his community was important to him? An environment in which he and his family could live a decent life and in which all his ambitions could be fulfilled. He should think of his hard-working parents. Of his brothers and sisters. They all stood to benefit from his decision.

They would be back in another week. Would that suit him?

He wanted to tell them to go and never, ever to come back. To fuck the hell off. But he couldn't. He was too scared.

The day before he came to me he tried to remain incommunicado. For the first time that year he didn't even go to lectures. But in the afternoon, downtown, near the cathedral, they came and stood on either side of him. He had never even seen them coming. One moment he was sauntering on his own, the next they were there, smiling and friendly.

Back to the Botanical Gardens. So . . . ? He must have had time to think it over properly?

He tried to ward them off. But they had a way of circling and circling around him with their remarks, their questions, and then suddenly moving in.

Well . . . ?

He needed more time. It was a difficult decision.

Nothing difficult about it at all if his studies and his future were important to him. If he cared about the welfare of his family. And his own.

And what, he suddenly dared to ask, what if he said no?

They were sure, they said with their unwavering smiles, that he wouldn't be so short-sighted.

But really, he insisted with last-ditch bravado. He *had* thought about it. It was very tempting. But no. He couldn't. He respected his professors. He was close to his friends. They should please forgive him, but he couldn't.

'Perhaps you haven't really thought about the alternatives,' said the older of the two, a man who bore a stale smell of smoke on him. 'This is for your own good.'

'What are the alternatives?'

The man didn't exactly smile. The expression on his face was more one of commiseration.

'I'm sure you wouldn't like to think of alternatives,' he said.

In a last gasp of boldness he managed to ask, 'So you're not really giving me a choice, are you?'

'Oh no, it remains your choice. Absolutely. We wouldn't think of pressurising you.'

They got up. They would be back in two days. They hoped he didn't mind, but they really couldn't wait much longer.

Now he was here with me. There was no one else he could turn to. But what could I do? Going to the SB myself would be useless. They would simply deny all knowledge of him. Asking my lawyer friend Neville to intervene, would make things incomparably worse for the student. I could approach other friends – in psychology, in politics, in sociology, in any number of other disciplines. But they would all be dead ends.

And tomorrow the two men would be back.

Seldom in my life have I felt so impotent, so useless. All I could urge him to do was to persist with saying no to them. And then to come back to me. But how would that help? There was nothing, absolutely nothing, those people could *not* do.

When I saw my young visitor off at the front door, a pale blue Toyota pulled off from where it had been parked on the far side of the street.

I remained standing at the door watching the young man walk away.

He never came back.

I had only his first name, which made it difficult to make enquiries. But I did manage to pick up his traces from two of his professors. All they could tell me was that he'd stopped coming to their classes. I got hold of his home address and was received with hostility and open suspicion. He had 'gone away', was all his mother was prepared to say.

Worst of all, by far the worst, was the sickening thought, afterwards, that it might all have been a ruse. He himself might have been planted by the SB to fulfil some sinister design of their own.

And yet I shall never forget the expression of utter hopelessness on his face that day he came to me.

My own situation was becoming steadily more difficult. During the eighties the government, threatened from all sides, changed the law governing military conscription. At the time I went to university, when only a restricted number of new recruits were absorbed into the army, their names were drawn by lot. It so happened that I was not among the chosen. Over the years, military service became ever longer: from a few months in my time, it increased to two full years, followed up by compulsory annual camps for many years. Now, in the eighties, it was announced that even men of fifty-five could be called up, and we were all required to register. The actual selection was to be random. This new measure was something I had never bargained for. All I knew was that I would not face this kind, or any kind, of conscription. But I wasn't going to wait quietly for a possible call-up to materialise. In the circumstances I had only one choice. I wrote an open letter to the minister of defence and to President P. W. Botha and made public my stance of refusing to obey any call-up.

Interestingly enough, the call-up never came.

But there were other potholes and traps along this road. The End Conscription Campaign was gaining ground throughout the country, particularly on the university campuses; and on more and more occasions I was invited to address the opponents of the system. It was quite a quandary. To dissuade anyone from obeying a call-up for military service was branded treason, for which there was a heavy prison sentence. On the other hand, not heeding the appeals of young men who needed to be encouraged, would be, to my mind, an even worse kind of betrayal. The only solution I could think of, if solution it was, was to accept such invitations to address dissidents wherever in the country they found themselves. All I could reasonably, and legally offer them, was a talk on the nature of individual responsibility. I cannot urge you not to go to the army, I would tell them. But there is one thing I can do, and am doing now: that is to remind you that no one can compel you to act against your own will. *You do have a choice.* Don't ever forget that. You have a choice. You must also know, however, that every choice has its price, and this price may be painful and high. That is ultimately for you to decide. The only truly important thing to remember is that you do have this choice. If you cannot accept the challenge, that is your decision. But whatever you do decide to do, never forget that it will be you, and only you, who takes the decision.

What overall effect these talks had, if any, I don't know. But I do know that I received a significant number of letters from young men who had emigrated to Holland, to Canada, and elsewhere, rather than do their military service. I may not have been responsible for any of this. But at least I tried. There was not much else I could do.

It was a situation in which individual action, however well meant and however precisely targeted, had become demonstrably futile. This, among many other reasons, was why the expedition to Dakar in Senegal, in July 1987, became such a watershed. Shortly before, one or two groups of influential businessmen had travelled from South Africa for discussions with members of the ANC in exile; but this time the aim of the Institute for a Democratic Alternative in South Africa (IDASA) was to bring the ANC in contact with Afrikaners from a variety of backgrounds – politicians, artists, writers and journalists, academics, jurists, educationists, leading theologians, businessmen, student leaders, a rugby captain. In great secrecy, the imprisoned Mandela had begun to talk to a few representatives of the South African government, including the ministers of justice, constitutional affairs, foreign affairs and even a reluctant and volatile President P. W. Botha. Significantly, he did not meet F. W. de Klerk who, presumably, was still regarded as too rightist to be trusted. 'To us,' wrote Mandela in his memoir, 'Mr de Klerk was a cipher . . . he seemed to be the quintessential party man, nothing more and nothing less.' But not one of us, and presumably very few members in the ANC in exile, were aware of this. In the group that assembled at Jan Smuts airport on 6 July, not one had any idea of who the others would be. And the government did its best to intimidate and discredit us. On our return to Johannesburg on 20 July, after a journey that included not only Dakar but also Ouagadougou in Burkina Faso and Accra, our passports were confiscated amid indications that P. W. Botha had actually given an order to have us all arrested. Only the forceful intervention of Pik Botha, minister of foreign affairs, saved the day. Even so, somebody had tipped off the extremist AWB, the Afrikaner Resistance Movement led by the notorious Eugène Terre'blanche, to ensure that, even if we were allowed back, we would be welcomed by a rowdy and militant mob. If we had not been smuggled past the demonstrators in ones and twos there might well have been a violent confrontation.

Apart from this, there was ample evidence that during the delay at the airport our luggage had been tampered with before being released to us. I found a mysterious set of red billiard balls in my suitcase. More importantly, the journal in which I'd made copious notes of the whole trip was missing. Fortunately I had anticipated something of the kind on our stopover in Paris and left a complete set of photocopies with my publisher. The moment my original journal went missing, an official in the French Department of Foreign Affairs dispatched the copies in a diplomatic bag to Cape Town from where they were couriered to me in time for the series of public meetings on the Dakar event which I addressed, sometimes on my own, sometimes with the member of parliament Errol Moorcroft.

For months in advance, there had been secret scurryings between the members of the group and the two main organisers, Frederik van Zyl Slabbert and Alex Boraine, previously leaders of the Opposition in parliament, and afterwards founders of IDASA. In Paris, their contact and fellow organiser was Breyten; and the whole enterprise was sponsored by Danielle Mitterrand, wife of the French president. We were all enjoined to keep the whole enterprise secret. And I still find it something of a miracle that to such a large extent the secret was respected sufficiently to ensure that the SB did not abort the whole enterprise.

For many of the travellers there were, initially at least, other worries: it was revealing, and amusing, to note, during the first few days of the trip, that the overriding question in the minds of all those brave hearts, all of them leaders in their field, people to be reckoned with, was: *What will my mother say if she finds out?* I cannot recall a single man in the group who was concerned about the fathers. But it must say something about the make-up of the Afrikaner psyche that we were all deeply apprehensive about the reaction of our mothers.

The ANC delegation was led by a young and confident Thabo Mbeki, even at that early stage introduced as the 'crown prince' of the organisation. In Dakar he introduced himself by saying, 'I am Thabo Mbeki. I am an Afrikaner.' Shades of *Ich bin ein Berliner*. Several delegates became good friends of mine. There was Essop Pahad, who is now the minister in the office of the president. There was the ebullient Steve Tshwete, and the scintillating intellectual Mac Maharaj, with his amazing command of English. His most touching moment came when we spoke about something as simple as where we came from. 'The longest period of permanent residence I had in my life was my years on Robben Island.' There was the warm and inspiring Barbara Masekela who would be my candidate for the first woman president of the country, who later became ambassador in Paris, and subsequently in Washington. The Washington residence welcomed me when Franklin Sonn was in charge there: another lifelong friend from Dakar – although he initially formed part of the 'internal group'. Lindiwe Mabusa, another poet, was in the ANC delegation too and was among the exiles whom I visited again in Lusaka a year or so later; now high commissioner in London, she, too, offered me the hospitality of her residence during visits. A few of them I'd met on other visits abroad, most importantly and endearingly Kader Ismael, whom I had first met in Dublin, and whose erudition and love of the arts and flamboyant turn of phrase won and warmed my heart from the outset. Today we are neighbours.

Apart from the wide-ranging discussions, the witty repartee, the in-depth exchanges – not only during official sessions but at the night-long get-togethers where differences were explored, agreements sealed and celebrated, lasting friendships forged – added new dimensions, new ways of seeing and thinking, to many of us. There were some exceptions too, like the historian Hermann Giliomee, who remarked to me within the first few days, 'You can't trust these people', Lawrence Schlemmer and one or two others, who – in their own way of seeing – refused to be 'duped' and developed an even more profound distrust of the ANC than before. With hindsight, I suppose some might regard them as the first in our group to 'see the light' and to become disillusioned with the prospect of a future ANC government. Yet I am not so sure that the situation was as simple and obvious as that. A number of members from the 'internal group' have undoubtedly shifted their positions – or 'grown', or 'developed'? – over the years; it seems to me that the same may be said of the ANC group from outside. Certainly, a person like Mbeki cannot be, cannot be *expected* to be, the same person he was in 1987. At *that* moment, I still believe, there were enough people on both sides who made it possible to believe that a radical renewal of South African society was actually conceivable, and that we could play a part in it.

It was, for many of us, the first true glimpse of a New South Africa. The dream was no longer *just* a dream, an illusion. It had become attainable, whatever the odds. One should never forget that at that very juncture the country was in a mess: the rapid rise of the United Democratic Movement had rendered South Africa practically ungovernable; and the extreme violence with which the government tried to stem the tide, was a sign of its growing desperation. Never before or since has terrorism in one form or another been so widespread in South Africa, most spectacularly in the programmes of systematic and universal torture and state-sponsored murder and explosions introduced by P. W. Botha and his successor. And even those of us who are in revolt about the waves of violence the country has to face today as I am writing this, should pause to consider how nearly irredeemable the situation had become in 1987.

There was something that had always struck me on my journeys abroad, since long before Dakar: it was the observation that whenever two South Africans, one black, the other white, met on foreign soil, surrounded by people from every imaginable country in the world, these two would be the ones who, in the course of an evening, would drift together and acknowledge each other as brothers or sisters. There was a memorable occasion in London when an expatriate black South African met a white compatriot who had come on a visit, and vociferously confronted him: 'You fucking Boers! When we're in South Africa, you despise me and vilify me and beat me and throw me into prison. You don't allow me into your restaurants or hotels or cinemas, you refuse to drink with me, you kick me off the sidewalk when you meet me, you degrade and humiliate and insult me at every opportunity and in every possible way. And then you expect me to love you?!' He paused for a moment, then added in measured tones, 'And I *do!*'

Dakar was the living illustration of this almost fateful bond that, in spite of all, tied us together. We arrived in Senegal as members of two delegations, divided by a fair deal of hesitancy and suspicion; when we left, we were – with the exception, perhaps, of a few disgruntled cynics in the 'internals' and two or three manipulators with hidden agendas among the exiles – members of a single group of South Africans. What we had seen was the vision of a shared future. What we had achieved was to prove that violence did not need to be the only option: negotiation had become a viable alternative; to talk, to discuss, was now the obvious way. And, as Thabo Mbeki pointed out some years later: together, we had reduced the fear of change among blacks and whites alike.

There were many unforgettable things about Dakar. Its smells and sights – of dirt and dust and shit and flowers and ozone; its brightly coloured birds and markets, its throngs and sudden spaces, its vistas of an ever-present dark-blue sea, its outrageous and brightly coloured textiles, its lambs roasting on the spit in streets or backyards, its straggling chickens and mangy dogs, its tall men in stark white *boubous*, its stately women with piled-up colourful braids and headgear, its laughing children with wide smiles and cascading laughter. There were parties and receptions to welcome us – in halls and on terraces and in yards engulfed with foliage, in the presidential palace – but always we returned to our meetings and discussions, in a tumultuous and never-ending celebration of the discovery and the affirmation of everything we shared and which was so much more than what divided us.

The key moment was a trip, by boat, across the narrow strait that divides the mainland from the island of Gorée, where long ago, as Toni Morrison reminds us in *Beloved*, over sixty million slaves were incarcerated before being transported to the States. Thousands perished by jumping off the small boats that transported them from the portals of the House of Bondage to the waiting ships. This meant almost instant death in a feeding frenzy amid the lurking sharks. But these captives were the lucky ones. For the others there was a lifetime – or generations – of slavery ahead. Crowded, in tears, in the small space of the front entrance, in the stifling embrace of two curved flights of stairs, we were shaken to the bone, moved more deeply than anything most of us had ever felt before. And there were some who voiced the almost impossible hope that, like this house of the death of dreams, Robben Island might one day become a station on humanity's road of hope, that Long Walk to Freedom Nelson Mandela was already secretly writing in his small cell, in preparation for the day he would walk out of there himself, a walk he never doubted, but which for us, there – even in spite of the new shared hope we had discovered – seemed impossibly far away.

There were other stations on our road. In Ouagadougou there was the daunting experience of being transported in open buses, escorted by phalanxes of outriders that recklessly sent all other traffic scattering in all directions: daunting not just because of the death-defying ride itself, but because of the thousands of people along the road, who ululated and danced and shouted to welcome us as the 'liberators of Africa'. Few ironies could be as shattering and humbling as this. And the feeling was compounded by a monstrous and magnificent reception at the palace of President Sankara. Surrounded by deafening music, mostly freedom songs in which Mandela's name seemed to be repeated in every line, we were fed and feted for what seemed like hours. After which His Excellency took charge of the festivities. He harangued us for a very long time, interrupting his own boisterous flow of words with wild shouts of rage or joy; and then he ordered us to dance for him. It was not an invitation but a command. Even a staunch Calvinist like Beyers Naudé was imperiously instructed to obey. Was it, I wondered, the only time in his life that Oom Bey was forced to dance? I must admit that I could not find it in me to comply. I don't think I have danced on more than five or six occasions in my entire life, persuaded more by inebriation or infatuation than by conviction or ability. It is something I simply cannot do. On this occasion there was the additional inhibition of an innate refusal to obey instructions – most especially if these were issued by what appeared to be a raging madman. And so, defying the presidential command, I simply faded away among the abundant trees with their massive, wide-spreading foliage. Although several people have assured me that I have completely misread the intentions and the character of President Sankara, I must confess that it neither surprised nor deeply saddened me when he was murdered most foully only a few months after our visit.

There were at least two unforgettable events during our visit.

First, we were transported in our open buses to a ceremony in which we were all invited to plant trees in what seemed like a fertile spot surrounded by drought-wasted plains. We were invited to partake of a heady brew in massive pots, which had to be decanted into calabashes after breaking, not very effectively, the thick layer of dead flies covering the surface. I have often wondered what happened to those rows upon rows of trees after the death of Sankara. Perhaps the wilderness has indeed burst into flower. But I'm not so sure.

The second occasion was the laying of a foundation stone for a future Monument for Freedom. I have no idea whether it was ever erected. And perhaps Sankara was not exactly the person to sponsor such a momentous enterprise. But the concept was moving, and with Thabo and Oom Bey working together at fixing the somewhat nondescript stone with scoops of mortar, one could not help but feel moved. This sentiment was marred afterwards when a handful of our group members called a meeting to object against the symbolism of the freedom monument, and most especially against the songs and chants that accompanied the ceremony. They were particularly mortified by the jubilantly repeated chant of *Botha au poteau* – *Botha to the gallows*. I must confess that I felt rather buoyed by it.

Accra was a less outrageous experience, and a long discussion in the faded glory of Nkrumah's House of Assembly, huddled behind pillars and monuments that reminded one of nothing so much as Hitler's architecture in

Nuremberg, had moments of heady dialogue. But the problem with the visit to Accra was that most of the visitors were by then disastrously afflicted by a virulent stomach bug. The scum of flies on the beer immediately came to mind. As a group we were a sorry sight. I somehow escaped the plague, but only just. On our way home, in Paris, it caught up with me and I arrived at Jan Smuts airport in a very shaky state to face Botha's spectacular wrath.

The flight with Air Afrique, from Dakar to Paris, was something of a nightmare – there was a delay of several hours at the airport, while someone fetched a manual for the mechanic who squatted on a wing trying to decipher the instructions; it was a shade worrying that he held the booklet upside down. But at least the flight itself was relatively uneventful, unlike the trip between Dakar and Ouagadougou, and then from there to Accra, where no places had been reserved and hundreds of would-be passengers simply stormed the plane to secure seats on a first-come-first-served basis. In addition to suitcases and holdalls, several small iron baths and basins and large wooden boxes had to be accommodated – as well as any number of live fowls tied together in bundles by their yellow feet, and even an unruly, farting goat.

This was not the end of the Dakar experience. Its ripple effects continued for a long time and occurred in often unexpected forms. Less than two months after our return I left for Moscow. The trip was organised by the ANC, with Barbara Masekela the driving force behind it. While we were still in Senegal she'd suggested that I might enjoy going to the Moscow Book Fair in September. As far as the SB was concerned, I was travelling to London to see my publishers. There, my dear friend Tony Pocock, who loved anything remotely connected with cloaks and daggers, whisked me off to Aeroflot in Piccadilly where the pulling of some strings helped us to avoid the legendary queues at the Soviet Consulate in Bayswater. We were welcomed by a Comrade Pruntov who greeted us with surprising friendliness, presented me with an application form and took my passport, with which he disappeared through the red curtains behind which a massive black iron grille could be glimpsed when someone entered or left. In less than half an hour he was back. The visa had been approved.

I had been prepared to wait for a few days. This came as an unexpected windfall. It gave me an opportunity of attending a particularly good production of *Fathers and Sons*, a not unfitting preparation for what lay ahead. And the next day I had time to lunch with Essop Pahad and his family. Dakar had brought us quite close together, but the context was always public. Here, in his home, with his wife Meg and his two attractive children, Amina and Govan, everything was relaxed and congenial. Mandla Langa also came round, and it was the beginning of another friendship, pursued in many other cities, and in due course at home.

Our hectic conversation, like popcorn on a hot plate, began jumping in all directions. Essop's bonhomie is infectious; but the undertone of melancholy is unmistakable. And over all the talk looms a striking lithograph with a quote from Neruda:

> And you will ask: why doesn't his poetry
> speak of dreams and leaves
> and the great volcanoes of his native land?
>
> Come and see the blood in the streets.
> Come and see
> the blood in the streets.
> Come and see the blood
> in the streets!

Inevitably, much of our talk also centred on 'home': going back, resuming the lives interrupted so many years ago. There was a running argument between Essop and Meg about where they would settle: he preferred Johannesburg, but she didn't approve. She'd had enough of concrete jungles. Before coming to London they had spent ten years in Prague: her choice was Cape Town. But they might, literally, meet each other halfway and opt for Knysna, where he'd spent many holidays as a child, or Plettenberg Bay.

As I took my leave much later in the afternoon, I was offered a packet of ANC coffee from Kenya.

'We'll drink it together over there,' said Essop.

'It may have lost its flavour by then,' I cautioned.

'What do you mean?' he exclaimed in mock indignation. 'It's going to be one of these days, man, I tell you. One of these days. The coffee will still be fresh.'

Mandla accompanied me to the Tube. After the somewhat boisterous afternoon the steady drone of the traffic sounded monotonous and grey. We drew back into ourselves. I walked huddled over the small packet I was carrying like precious loot under my arm. Mandla walked inclined towards me as if he, too, wanted to claim possession. Perhaps we were both imagining the flavour of that coffee: the smell of tomorrow. *One of these days.*

The next afternoon I arrived at Sheremetyevo airport where there was just enough light to make out the birch woods marking the end of the tarmac. I was released into the care of my personal guide, Irina Filatova of the History Department at the Moscow State University, accompanied by the deputy director of the Book Festival, a large, ponderous, blond man beaming goodwill but unable to utter a single word in English. Irina was articulate and friendly and extremely knowledgeable, an invaluable guide, if rather severe and serious. In the course of the week I spent in her company I never saw her smile, and she seemed to frown at any hint of levity. I remember an evening when we returned to my hotel from a performance of Rimsky-Korsakov's *Tsarevitch*, when I noticed the numerous Soviet soldiers all around us, taking their evening stroll in rows of three or four, or ten or twelve. There must have been well over a hundred in all. 'It looks as if the whole Red Army is out on the square tonight,' I remarked. Irina gave me a shrivelling look.

'The Red Army,' she said indignantly, 'is much, much bigger.'

After a depressing meal of cabbage in one of the hotel restaurants, Irina took her leave. I made my way to my drab little room on the tenth floor – but with a spectacular view of the illuminated St Vassily on the Red Square – past the omnipresent matryona keeping watch like a flabby Cerberus. She had massive hairy legs, brown slippers, grey mesh stockings up to the knees, headscarf, and an utterly unsmiling face like a clump of bread dough. I was tired, but too excited to think of going to bed. So I did some half-hearted unpacking into the rickety cupboard and ventured out again. Past Madame Cerberus, down to the ground floor, along the side wall of the Kremlin, and to the square. By this time St Vassily was dark, and there were few people about: one small cluster across the empty expanse of the square, near the preposterously ornate GUM store; another in front of Lenin's mausoleum with its motionless guards.

On the way back, now more than ready to succumb to weariness, I was accosted by two very friendly young girls – they couldn't possibly have been older than sixteen or seventeen – who presented themselves as Anna and Svita. Both wore heavy make-up, with exaggerated but rather beautiful big black eyes. They could speak a smattering of Italian, no English. I was invited to join them in a taxi to wherever it was they lived. Intrigued, but suspicious – surely they were too young to be prostitutes? but what on earth would two such young girls be doing on Red Square past midnight? And why *two*? – I explained that there were people waiting for me. Then what about tomorrow night? Give me your phone number, I said. And I'll call you at six tomorrow evening. The number was readily – too readily – proffered, and bemused, but relieved, I returned to the Hotel Rossiya.

The next days were a jumble of impressions. The Book Fair. The State University. Various institutes and departments, all involved in one way or another with Africa. Several of my interlocutors could speak a studied, but correct Afrikaans. (Apart from Holland, this must be the only country where my books are translated, not from English, but from Afrikaans.) The Writers' Association, housed in a splendid old mansion which Tolstoy was said to have used as the setting for the Rostov family's house in *War and Peace*. The New Arts Theatre where *The Seagull* had its premiere. The splendour of the Underground. The Kremlin.

And then, also, the Lumumba University where for twenty-seven years South African students, sponsored mainly by the ANC, had come to study.

I had been looking forward very eagerly to meeting them, and as it turned out, it was one of the most poignant encounters of my visit. But first I had to be welcomed – if that is the word – by the rector, Comrade Vladimir Stanis. I had been warned by a very distraught Irina that the man was an egomaniac and an insufferable tyrant who in any 'dialogue' insisted on being the only speaker. With a rector like that, it occurred to me, who needs a Stalin?

But in the flesh – that too, too solid flesh – he was much worse than anything I could have imagined. In all my travels I have met only one other man as repulsive as Vladimir Stanis, and that was the cultural representative of France in Sarajevo, Francis Bueb. My first thought, as he came bursting through a tall padded door into the vestibule with its orange chairs, aggressive pot plants and a long row of unaligned electric switches on the wall, was that he would fit perfectly into a photograph of any South African Nationalist cabinet.

Flanked by his deputy and a fumbling, sweating registrar who desperately tried to keep up with an attempted translation, the rector thundered on histrionically as if he were addressing a crowd of at least fifty. His pinkish, porcine eyes remained fixed on me as he spoke, pausing only to ask whether I was sure I had enough paper to write down everything he said.

His peroration consisted mainly of a panegyric on his institution, its student numbers and its faculties. A major component of the courses in all faculties, he boomed, was the shaping of patriotism, and its interaction with internationalism. After about ninety minutes I interrupted by asking Irina to inform him of what we had already told him at the outset: that we had arranged a meeting with our students at four o' clock. We were already ten minutes late.

'They can wait!' he thundered.

At that point we rose and proceeded to the nearest door. He gawked at us, his small, bulging pink eyes gazing uncomprehendingly.

A small group of South African students was waiting in a classroom. One of them was a young man with an unbelievably beautiful baby on his lap. They were all young. Some had arrived only a few months before. Several had been in Moscow for six years or more. I made a few introductory remarks about the present state of our country; and then we plunged into exuberant, even boisterous discussion. I shall never forget the wave of warmth and passion that came from them as they spoke about *our* land, *our* past, *our* future, *our* dreams. All they really wanted to know was *when* I thought they could go back, *when* we would all meet again.

When they had first arrived in Moscow, I learned, they had been welcomed as guerrillas. For Russians, Irina assured me afterwards, that is the highest form of life. They were treated as heroes. But in all the adulation nobody seemed to consider that they were, basically, *human beings*. People far from their homes, devastated by loneliness and nostalgia, eager for human contact.

I used up more of my notebook pages to write down their urgent requests: photocopies of specific Acts of parliament: the Group Areas Act, the Black Authorities Act, the Citizenship Act, the Aliens Act, the Bantustan Citizenship Act. They also needed copies of the constitution of any bantustan, books like *The Interpretation of Statutes*. Publications on Aids. Or novels, short stories, any writings by any South Africans. 'And, ag man, *sommer* anything in Afrikaans, man.' Anything that sounded and smelled and tasted like home.

It was almost unbearably sad. But at the same time there was this deep hope – a hope *against* hope – that all this misery would not be in vain. That some day, some day, it would be over and they would go home. The young man with the baby on his lap pressed the child against my chest, which it promptly and happily peed on, repeated over and over with tears on his cheeks, 'We're going home. I tell you. We're going home.' All these tough guerrillas, these tough supermen, these heroes from the Struggle: oh yes, oh yes for sure, they would be going home one day. And the regime that had done *this* to them, would have a lot to answer for. Again, as so often in the past, I felt, while we huddled in a scrum, pressed tightly together to share the warmth of our bodies, that it was not the murders, the atrocities, the maiming and the torture which might, in the final reckoning, be ranked as the worst evil perpetrated by apartheid, but *this*: this violence done to human spirits, these emotions stripped naked, this mindless suffering of individuals and generations, of these anonymous young people in this classroom with me – people whose names had suddenly been scorched into my memory, this Thabo, this Mikluho, this James . . . each with a history, a biography, a living archive and a litany of experience.

There were two follow-up meetings of the encounter at Dakar: in July 1988 a group of Afrikaans academics and writers from inside South Africa met their counterparts from the ANC at the Victoria Falls. And in late November 1989 there was a large meeting at Marly-le-Roi outside Paris. The first happened in one of the darkest moments from the last convulsions of apartheid, the second only months before de Klerk's historic announcement on 2 February, 1990 on the moratorium on executions, the unbanning of liberation movements, and the release of prisoners, including Nelson Mandela – although at the time of our meeting we had as yet no inkling about the imminence of that event.

The Victoria Falls meeting took place in an almost festive atmosphere. For most of the travellers from South Africa it was the first opportunity to make personal contact with the erstwhile 'enemy' and the discovery of shared professional, literary and moral interests made it a deeply moving experience. We encountered some smaller annoyances. On 'our' side there was the presence of an academic widely suspected of being an agent of the SB. There were also, as invariably happens in literary circles, animosities and long-standing feuds among some of the participants. It was amusing to see some of the 'internal' visitors flaunting their credentials by trying to prove that they were better Marxists than anybody in the ANC, while several ANC members went out of their way to demonstrate their deep understanding of the Afrikaner psyche and their admiration of Afrikaans literature. The difficulty in hammering out a joint resolution to everybody's satisfaction was an indication of persisting difference; but taken as a whole the conference was something of a triumph for sanity, creativity, inventiveness and goodwill. Once again it seemed that the likelihood of a shared future was becoming more than just a possibility; and the final goodbyes were said amid copious tears.

The most contentious debate of the meeting concerned the desirability of supporting the international cultural boycott of South Africa. I had always been strongly opposed to it: an economic boycott, yes by all means. A boycott of foreign investments: yes, indeed. A sports boycott: yes. But a cultural boycott? If one has faith in culture as a territory where meaning is produced, and in its power of changing minds and attitudes, I still believe that one should bombard a recalcitrant country with culture, not isolate it. But I was persuaded in the end that as an emergency short-term measure, and as a means of demonstrating solidarity of black and white cultural workers, it might deserve support.

Among the most unforgettable contributions to the sessions were those of the fine, and immensely likeable, poet Keorapetse 'Willie' Kgositsile, who was subsequently named as the first Poet Laureate of the new South Africa, and Albie Sachs, whose early achievements as a lawyer and his impeccable credentials during the Struggle and being blown up in a car-bomb attack in Mozambique that left him permanently scarred, resulted in his elevation to the post-liberation Constitutional Court. Albie is one of those rare people whom you can meet after an absence of many years and continue from where you last left off. His love of art, his appreciation of women, his clear and incisive mind, and his sense of humour have, over many years, made him particularly dear to me. As for Willie, the Falls marked the beginning of a lifelong friendship. What I shall never forget is his account of reactions from friends within the ANC to some of his writing. There was one poem especially, dedicated to his wife and using the moon as his central image, that had elicited much negative comment. How could he, his friends argued, write about the moon, and a woman, and love, while he carried on his body and in his mind the scars of imprisonment and torture, of an escape from South Africa to Botswana, of unimaginable deprivation and suffering? It was the old dilemma Brecht outlined: how to write about flowers when that implied remaining silent about people being tortured and killed. (Neruda again: *Come and see the blood in the streets.*)

But I am not silent about such things, Willie insisted. For me, being a poet means being able write about the moon and to tell a woman that I love her in such a way that everything else – the suffering and torture and deaths and misery – that I have witnessed or experienced, can be *sensed* in what I've written. What I write down on paper must bear the full weight of what I have *not* written explicitly.

Many years later, at a London launch reading by J. M. Coetzee of his novel *Disgrace*, I was told by our mutual publisher, someone in the audience asked the author, 'Mr Coetzee, don't you find it strange that we should be here tonight discussing literature while bombs are falling in Kosovo?' And John laconically replied, 'Frankly, no.'

A year later, at the Marly-le-Roi meeting, it was Albie Sachs who brilliantly took up this theme in what was intended as a discussion paper within the ANC, 'Preparing Ourselves for Freedom', which stimulated one of the major cultural polemics in the transition towards the New South Africa. 'What are we fighting for,' asks Albie in this seminal paper,

> if not the right to express our humanity in all its forms, including our sense of fun and capacity for love and tenderness and our apprecia-tion of the beauty of the world? . . . A.N.C. members are full of fun and romanticism and dreams, we enjoy and wonder at the beauties of nature and the marvels of human creation, yet if you look at most of our art and literature you would think we were living in the greyest and most sombre of all worlds, completely shut in by apartheid.

There were several new faces among the participants too: the effervescent and delightfully affirmative Cheryl Carolus, later to become our high commis-sioner in London; the urbane and smiling Trevor Manuel with his rapier mind and his built-in bullshit detector; Stuart Saunders, vice-chancellor of the University of Cape Town with his broad cultural background and his surgeon's eye for detail, who a year later made it possible for me to make the move from Rhodes to the Cape.

Although by this time such encounters no longer had the gloss and surprise of the first, it had, in retrospect, a dynamism that infused all the discussions with moral and mental electricity. Although we had no idea of the changes that were to happen a mere three months later, there was a vibration in the air that sharpened the senses and created a sense of expect-ation. Nobody really expected anything dramatic from F. W. de Klerk, but the tide of history seemed to be turning. Govan Mbeki and Walter Sisulu had already been set free; there were huge marches in all the major cities, change seemed unstoppable. This meant that many of our discussions had a nuts-and-bolts quality, and through the meeting a future that was already much more than wishful thinking was being prepared.

The talks were led, as before, by an ebullient van Zyl Slabbert and a trenchant and determined Alex Boraine on the 'internal' side and Thabo Mbeki on the other. The high point of the visit was a session in the Assemblée Nationale attended by French parliamentarians and journalists and almost the entire diplomatic corps. This was very different from our debates in

Accra or Burkina Faso. This was a true meeting of Europe and Africa – and we were right in the middle of it.

Long before this event, Marly-le-Roi had been, for me, the magnificent green park where Grandpère Maurice, on the first Sunday of every month, arranged for the fountain, the tallest *jet d'eau* in France, to be turned on at his expense, and he played host to the Sunday crowds that converted the park into a live and vibrant Seurat painting. But through this visit a dimension was added, not only to Marly, but to Paris. And certainly to my awareness of Africa *in* France, and France *in* Africa.

It is not easy to capture, today, the mood in South Africa in those last years of the eighties. On the one hand, the situation seemed to be getting completely out of hand. The pressure from the United Democratic Front became more and more irresistible, yet the government's only response was violence and more violence. The murders committed by the SB became more frequent. Buthelezi's Inkatha Freedom Party, funded by the government, was becoming increasingly bloody-minded and provocative. The generals in the security establishment seemed to have become a law unto the themselves. And as invariably happens when a small man finds himself in power, surrounded by big bullies and a seemingly endless supply of weapons and strategies of mass destruction, P. W. Botha grew more arrogant by the day, his lust for apocalypse ever more unquenchable.

Yet at the same time the forces of resistance were growing. A kind of general madness was informing public life. Botha's attempts at playing two games at the same time – the man of violence, and the great reformer – were heading for disaster. Even as he was pushing his henchmen to acts of more outrageous violence, he was having clandestine discussions with Mandela about change; and he started setting free leaders of the struggle. Mandela having refused to leave prison before all his colleagues and comrades had been allowed to go, Botha initiated, in November 1987, his own programme of 'atonement' by liberating Govan Mbeki. Very strict regulations about his freedom of movement, access to public forums, the right to address meetings were imposed. But Govan Mbeki simply refused to pay any heed and went ahead with impunity.

When Mbeki visited Port Elizabeth he received a tumultuous welcome. At the end of the rally he sent a message that he wanted to meet me. I was whisked away to a back room where I came face to face with one of the legends of the struggle. There wasn't much time to talk, but his interest – in what was happening among whites, among Afrikaners, in my writing – was astounding. I told him that I was planning a trip into Africa and hoped to see Thabo soon. At that time Govan hadn't seen his son for over twenty years. Was there any message he would like me to convey to Thabo?

'Tell my son,' he said holding his forefinger straight up in front of my eyes, 'tell him his father is like this.' Then he bent the finger at the knuckle. 'Not like this.'

His eyes were lit up with fire, but they were smiling too.

I did see Thabo. During 1988 I planned a visit to Lusaka to meet those members of the ANC in exile who had by then become close friends. Also, I had begun my new novel, based on the imagined assassination of P. W. Botha and for that it was imperative that I visit Lusaka.

While I was at it, I decided to stop over in Gaborone, in Botswana as well, and in Harare. At that time Mugabe was still widely regarded as a messianic figure on the continent. And I remember that when I was trying to arrange a writers' conference at Cold Comfort Farm in Zimbabwe, the priority wish on the list of all the South Africans was to meet Mugabe. The second was to meet the Cuban ambassador. But it was the visit to Lusaka that meant most to me. It was, by then, almost a year after the Victoria Falls meeting, and I couldn't wait to see Thabo, and Barbara, and Lindiwe, and Steve, and Penuell, and so many others again. We spent a few unforgettable days together, surrounded by the shrilling of cicadas, or by the flapping of huge, exotic moths that fluttered past like falling flowers. Again, we spoke breathlessly, incessantly, about that distant – and yet so close – country in the south which was the main focus of all our thoughts, and about our yesterdays, and our present, and above all about our tomorrows. I met Barbara's husband, Henry, scarred and wizened by pain; and a breezy Reggie September, who at the time of the first free elections, was delegated to invite me to stand for parliament. Once again there was the feeling of being embraced and enfolded, with warmth and generosity and enthusiasm. Once again there was the conviction that soon, soon, we would all be home again, together.

I remember a lazy morning with Thabo and his wife Zanele: in the shady garden overgrown with flowers, and in the lounge with its paintings and lithographs on the walls, and Beethoven's Ninth in the background; and Thabo's impish smile behind his pipe as he said, 'Don't forget to tell the people back home what it was like to visit a terrorist in his house.'

The only disappointment about the visit was that Oliver Tambo could not make it to Thabo's house in time before I had to catch my plane home.

THE RUINS OF SARAJEVO

FROM THE ASSASSINATION OF ARCHDUKE FERDINAND IN 1914 UNTIL THE recent ravages of ethnic cleansing Sarajevo has been the very image of the torn city.

When the invitation came to an annual literary festival in the fractured Bosnian city, neither Karina nor I had any hesitation about accepting; not even the chaotic arrangements for getting there, and obtaining visas and permissions and God knows what else, could put us off. And in mid-May of 2006 we set out. All went well as far as Belgrade. There, rather than waiting at the airport for eight hours to catch a connecting flight of less than an hour to Sarajevo, we arranged to be taken by car over the last lap. The organisers provided a driver and a car, but nobody warned us of the state of the road, which condemned us to five and a half hours of shaking and shuddering hell. But that was only part of the ordeal. Because so much of Sarajevo was still in ruins after the war, it took another hour of tortuous winding along narrow one-way lanes before our good-humoured young driver, Vito, deposited us in the middle of the city, in a deserted and derelict market beside a dug-up main road, led us into a foul-smelling backyard, up a shaky staircase to the second floor of what remained of a wretched-looking building that turned out to be quite beautiful on the inside. This, we learned, was the Centre André Malraux, where we were handed over into the trembling hands of the festival organiser and director of the centre, Monsieur Francis Bueb.

It took Monsieur Bueb a while to realise what was going on as he was very much the worse for wear, having evidently spent most of the day exercising his right arm. He was clutching a glass. To his lower lip an extinct cigarette was stuck as a permanent fixture. Through fumes of alcohol so thick they could be cut with a knife, he stared at us with eyes the colour of raw pork liver. After some time Vito, still unruffled and smiling, managed to convey to Monsieur Bueb who we were, whereupon we were welcomed with a theatrical gesture that caused most of the contents of his glass to spill on the floor. With the help of the driver he managed to stagger to his feet and start picking his way across the floor past haphazard piles of books and boxes. This took a considerable amount of time, but at long last, our host lunged forward to embrace, first myself, and then Karina, licking our cheeks, first left, then right, from chin to eyebrows. Once the slobbering was over, he grabbed my right hand and started pumping it as if to draw water from a well, while trying to pick his way through a long sentence. He had problems pronouncing all the consonants that had formed in his mind; at the same time it required his utmost concentration to remain standing. What he tried to say was, quite simply, that this was the French way of showing hospitality. However, the demonstrations of his hospitality were marred by disappointment upon his discovery that I was not black, and that, even though he had been fully informed of the fact since the beginning of our correspondence about the festival months before, I was not single.

We still had to go from the Centre to the French ambassador's residence where, as Monsieur Bueb had informed us well in advance, we were to be lodged. But he insisted on first filling us in on all the details of the pending festival and his role in it. As he himself did not appear to have much clarity about the organisation, and as several laborious refills of his glass were necessary to nudge him on the tortuous way from one word to the next, we seemed stuck there for the night.

The conversation was not helped much by the lapses of memory that impeded Monsieur Bueb's progress through the syntactical difficulties of his peroration. During one of the long pauses, when we began to fear that he might have fallen asleep, I made the mistake of trying to keep the conversation going by enquiring about Vito who had excused himself for a while.

In response to the question, Monsieur Bueb slumped from his chair and landed on the floor. Before we could rush to his side, he rose to his knees in a very histrionic manner, started digging into his pockets, dropping, once again, his glass, and brought out a knife. Anxious not to provoke, we remained glued to our seats. As we sat watching, Bueb held out the knife towards us. I was expecting him at any moment to start declaiming, *Is this a dagger which I see before me?* when he suddenly dropped on all fours and started digging into the slits between the floorboards, muttering to himself all the while. After several long minutes a wide smile formed on Bueb's red, wet lips, and he launched into a convoluted explanation from which we finally gleaned that Vito was driving errands for the Centre only in his spare time: his real occupation was to dig for unexploded bombs after the war and dismantle them.

At this stage the young sapper returned and patiently, but clearly with barely suppressed hilarity, helped Bueb back to his seat; in his presence there was some progress in the conversation. We learned, thanks to eager promptings from Vito, some of the basic facts about the arrangements made for our lodgings and for the unfolding of the festival. And soon afterwards we eagerly rose to be driven to the *résidence*. But not before Bueb had once more demonstrated his version of 'the French way' by working in long, liquid movements with his copiously salivating tongue across most of the surfaces of our faces.

Once again Vito picked his way through a veritable maze of streets, until he reached the *résidence* high up on a hill from where the lights of Sarajevo lay spread out below us. Strange to think how such a sad and scarred landscape can be camouflaged by the graceful concern of the night.

For the rest of our visit we were entertained lavishly and with the kind of grace one readily associates with *la belle France*. By the time we left, the ambassador, Henry Zipper de Fabiani, had been joined by his vivacious wife, Geneviève, who had come from Paris, where she mostly resides with their children, to be the perfect hostess. And on the Sunday in the middle of our stay the ambassadorial couple took us and the poet Antjie Krog, who also attended the festival, on a wonderful excursion by car to the art village of Mostar. We were enchanted by the beautifully rebuilt bridge of the town. It did not take much effort to imagine it as the architectural jewel Ivo Andrić had immortalised in *The Bridge over the Drina*.

The events of the festival were badly organised and badly attended, the microphones didn't work properly, the simultaneous translations were chaotic and unreliable. Most of the time we spent trying to dodge the unbelievable Bueb, a caricature of officiousness and bad taste. We found that several other guests were in the same boat. Antjie confided to us that when she'd first been approached by the man, she'd desperately tried to evade him, believing he was a beggar off the street.

The opening ceremony took place in the shell of the library, a magnificent old building with galleries and arches and the melancholy splendour of an interrupted past, when hundreds of thousands of books were destroyed by fire. Part of the building was deliberately left unrestored, to keep the memory of the recent war alive. The solemn atmosphere of the place was disturbed by the presence of Bueb, stumbling about in the background, from one pillar to the next, occasionally talking loudly to himself or invisible interlocutors, commenting on the events, gesticulating, stopping only from time to time to refill his glass or locate a new one. I constantly had to remind myself that this person was here to represent France and its culture.

How could such an obscenity have come about? Bueb himself was most voluble in filling in the background at length: it transpired that at the height of the war, or in its immediate aftermath, in some way or another, for some reason or another, Bueb had decided to drive from Paris to Sarajevo with a carload of books. While everybody else was occupied with providing essential services, rescuing the wounded, restoring water supplies or electricity, Bueb turned up in the devastated war zone and began to distribute books – an act that immediately captured the imagination. And as the violence settled down and the city gradually groped its way back to a semblance of normality, Bueb stayed on. Perhaps, initially, and in those circumstances, it had not been so far-fetched an idea to install him in a position of cultural influence. But how it could have outlasted the public embarrassment, the lasting insult to the reputation of one of the world's great cultures, remains a mystery.

Thank heavens, there was much else to do. Even a walk through the winding streets, past the endless cemeteries of Christians and Muslims killed in the slaughterhouse of the Balkan war, brought unimagined riches to light: the dramatic contrasts between small, colourful potholed backstreets with makeshift stalls and small shops selling all manner of arts and crafts to the swarming crowds.

There were special people and events that, in the end, defined for us what Sarajevo is really about. This included meeting with my good friend Rastko Garić whom I'd first met some years earlier in Split and who had travelled all the way to spend time with us and discuss the two of my books he was now translating into Croatian. It was Rastko who took us into the backstreets and to a small, tucked-away eating place where he encouraged the owner to unveil his treasures to us and helped us to look more deeply into the strange and sad society in which we now found ourselves. Halfway through the meal the chef arrived at our makeshift table: he had learned that we came from South Africa and wished us to know that he'd visited Johannesburg in 1975 with a soccer team. What he wanted to know was, 'Are you still treating red peoples apart, or are it better now?'

There was also the brilliant film maker Éric Valli who came to meet us in the *résidence* and whose animated conversation, eloquent hands and all-seeing eyes lent new meaning to the place. His beautiful film *Himalaya* made me think of what he might have achieved had he ever been able to fulfil his dream and make a film of *An Instant in the Wind*.

And there was a man whose name I do not know, who also sharpened the lines of the image Sarajevo evokes in my mind. He was a medical doctor, middle-aged but appearing much older as if he were carrying too much of the weight of the world on his shoulders. After Antjie Krog had spoken at the conference on the Truth and Reconciliation Commission and the importance of telling our own stories, he made a brief contribution from the floor. During the war, he explained, he had been commissioned to help deal with the crisis, working day and night to dispose of the dead and comfort the living; the circumstances were almost unbearable. Like his colleagues, he was taxed to the utmost. It was not the physical suffering that became too much to bear, but the devastation of one's very notion of 'humanity'. 'There were so many stories,' he said in his broken English. 'Too many. I could not cope with it all. Even now I cannot sleep at night. I see all those faces. I feel I am bursting with all the stories I *must* tell. But there is no one to tell them to. Nobody wants to listen. And that is the worst.' He broke down and burst into tears. It was one of the most terrible things I've ever had to grapple with: the notion of a society, a nation, with *too many* stories – and no one to tell them to. And it brought with it a wholly different perspective on the real atrocity of war.

But if Sarajevo acquired, for us, a specific human face, it was above all that of the remarkable young Serbian woman, Boba, whose beautiful features framed in dark hair revealed the light and darkness she had experienced in this city: how can we ever think about Sarajevo again without hearing her telling about her wartime experience when she had to keep count of the innumerable corpses day after day, in order to make sure the numbers would not be distorted by either side, and how the place became a city of the dead – men, women, children, all now sadly laid to rest in their separate cemeteries.

What she told about her own life in the midst of death, brought back a remarkable lecture, 'On the Dark Side of Twilight', I'd heard in 2001 when I was a visiting professor at the University of Wisconsin in Madison. It was given by Branka Arsic from Serbia, and dealt with 'the dark, unarticulated, evil forces in the Balkans', and most fascinatingly with the legendary figure of 'the Kosovo Maiden' who appeared on the battlefield after the decisive battle between Ottoman Turks and Serbs in the thirteenth century. According to Arsic, this battle, lost by Serbia, meant the end of Serbian literature and Serbian history for 600 years, causing Serbs to exist, from then on, only as spectres in the world: it is no accident, proposed the speaker, that Bram Stoker should have situated his vampire in the Balkans. The nameless maiden appeared on the field littered with the dead, the living, and the half-dead, in search of the body of her slain lover; but he was not to be found, and she could not turn herself into an Antigone because it was impossible to distinguish between the living and the dead, and consequently to decide who could be buried. It ends most inconclusively – and, for a legend, most maddeningly – because she simply disappears in a cloud. Since then, it would seem, this tragic country has been condemned to exist between life and death, between to-be and not-to-be; and Boba's observations lent terrible substance to it.

But she did not speak only about the dark aspects of her experience. She also told us about the picnics she and her friends had organised right in the middle of the war: dressing themselves in clothes of the boldest colours, shiny reds and shimmering greens and deep blues and outrageous yellows, and then walking openly up the torn hillsides to have their meal in the resplendent sun, exposed to all the eyes of the city and to the bullets of any sniper, simply to affirm life in the face of death, and to defy the forces of evil that were trying so desperately to destroy all the signs of human presence and beauty. I could not help but remind myself of the late seventies, when Breyten was in prison and his sister Rachel would ask for permission to visit him for Christmas: and then she would open the basket she had taken to Pollsmoor with her, and take out the many lengths of material she had brought along, the boldest reds and greens and purples and yellows she could find, and wrap herself in these from head to toe, as if she were a living, human Christmas tree: no conversation was necessary, simply standing there like a feast of colour, was enough: because she knew that, as a painter, finding himself in prison where the only tones he was allowed to see were grey and dun and khaki, nothing in the world could bring him so much joy, and reassure him so much about the vibrant signs of life, than colour, life-affirming colour.

SALZBURG: A STATE OF MIND

THERE HAVE BEEN SO MANY TRAVELS OVER THE YEARS, LIKE FAVOURITE BOOKS opened and savoured and returned to; so many unforgettable moments, each of which has trapped within it, like a piece of amber enclosing an insect, an essence of my experience of the world. I can close my eyes and call them up. The mound of Tolstoy's grave covered in dark green moss among the lyrical birch trees in the forest on the Yasnaya Polyana estate, an embodiment of perhaps his most memorable story, 'How much earth does a man need?' Or Ibsen's grave, a simple slab bearing the writer's name under a soundless, endless drift of leaves in an autumnal Oslo (Rilke: *Die Blätter fallen, fallen wie vom Weit . . .*). A leisurely voyage in the *Trollfjord* along the west coast of Norway, from fjord to fjord, past the bright reds and greens and yellows of the houses of Bergen to the darker seclusion of Ålesund or Trondheim in their deep havens to the spare magic of the island of Lofoten and up to the northern edge of the world at Nordkapp and Kirkenes. Or the severe extremes of Iceland, where everything in the visible and everyday world has a counterpart, underground and invisible, where hidden and unexpected entrances open from our world into the other – here, via a bole of a tree, there the mouth of a cave, elsewhere a rock formation with weird crevices. In almost shocking contrast, the ferocious sun-scorched plains and mountain ranges of Mexico. To wake up in our room in the Hotel Catedral and see the plumes of smoke from the magic mountain of Popocatépetl and his consort, the Sleeping Lady, Iztaccihuatl, or to drag oneself up the endless brown stairs of the Pyramids of the Sun and Moon at Teotihuacan, or stare in awe at the staggered sides of the Mayan temple of Nohoch Mul in its dark forest, its name – Water Stirred by Wind – as enthralling as its architecture. Otherwise, I return to a scene of dust and sun, of quick little lizards and a flickering of bright red and green *colibris*, sunbirds, in the foliage of bougainvilleas in Bamako, Mali, where I lean on a parapet overlooking the sluggish meandering of the broad Niger which one can follow all the way inland to the dream palaces and temples and libraries of another mythical place, Timbuktoo, with its ancient scrolls and books dating back to a time when this country boasted more splendour than most of its contemporary empires in Europe. Yet another shift in the mind, and there are white and blue houses on a steep slope of Santorini overlooking the wine-dark sea, or the crumbling, ageless, sunlit columns of the Parthenon. From there, it is but a wink to the luminous brown walls of Dubrovnik, and a wedding in progress on the town square, where suddenly the festivities are interrupted just as the bride – visibly pregnant – in pale green and the swaggering and swarthy groom are preparing to mount the stairs to the church: a sultry young woman comes round the corner, embraces the groom and starts kissing him voraciously. The father-in-law gives a few menacing steps in their direction. The bride collapses in tears. The stranger drapes herself around the groom's neck; and then, very suddenly, the two of them start running, round the corner of the church, and off in the direction of the city wall. Then back again to the most distant north, at Kakslauttanen in Finland, beyond the Arctic Circle, a midsummer night amid stunted oak trees hundreds of years old, under a pale and muted light in which a dull red fireball drifts soundlessly along the horizon without ever dipping behind it, while unbelievably cold dark streams rush along the white pebbles on their beds down the curve of the earth. Another memory flip, and I am in Jerusalem, from where I travel to many other Old Testament places familiar from my violent childhood, the once-walled Jericho and Megido, the biblical Armageddon, with its remains of God knows how many cities layered like a palimpsest of ruins on top of one another, from floating weightless on the Dead Sea to gasping in the thin clear air of Mount Sinai, from the barren brown heights of Masada and the caves of the Scrolls at Qumran, which I later saw in the magnificent Shrine of the Book in Jerusalem, on a day of unbelievable white heat to the fertile valley of the Jordan – entering the world of the essential mythology that had shaped and informed my childhood and seeing it transformed into reality. Conversations chiselled into my mind, with Rabbi Moshe Semer, and the fearless author David Grossman, anticipating another meeting, in Norway, in 2002, with Amos Oz. But the watershed experience of that day spent in Israel was a visit to the Palestinian university of Birzeit. I'd read much about the conflict in the Middle East; in Salzburg and elsewhere I'd had long and passionate encounters with Palestinian writers. I had an unforgettable discussion with Hanan Mikhail-Ashrawi when she visited Cape Town years earlier. On several occasions before his untimely death I'd also shared the deep wisdom and gentle humanity of Edward Saïd. But this immersion into the terrible reality of that tragic place, the land and its people, shook me as few other experiences in my life have done. It was like a rediscovery of the evil heart of apartheid. The way in which Palestinians, among them some of the finest people I have ever come to know, are subjected to one of the cruellest reigns of oppression in the world, and the web of hypocrisy and lies that, on the Israeli side, attempts to obscure and distort the truth. During this visit a particularly shocking event occurred when the small house of an old Palestinian man was flattened by the bulldozers of the Israeli army because he had dared to erect a tank on his own roof to collect the pitiful raindrops that fell on it. I saw the network of modern tarmac roads constructed for use by Israelis and the wretched little side roads to which Palestinians were confined; saw the olive groves – in many cases the sole means of subsistence of Palestinian farmers – uprooted and demolished by Israelis; saw the proliferation of new Israeli settlements deep inside Palestinian territory, established in contravention of all laws and agreements, merely to enforce Israeli presence and power in a territory not their own. I had seen this before, in the context of the oppression of blacks by whites in South Africa. I had heard all the pious excuses and explanations. And when I think back today, I cannot banish from my memory the terrible remains of Dachau and Auschwitz: for although Israel has never embarked on a genocide on the scale of the Holocaust, the ethnic cleansing this country is inflicting on Palestine amounts, morally, to a slow and minor-key copy of these camps of death. I fail to understand how a people that has staggered from the terrors of the Holocaust could subsequently proceed to do unto others what had been done to them.

All of this is projected, and focused with laser intensity, on a spectacular confrontation between a young Israeli writer and an incensed and beautiful Palestinian woman at a conference in the Schloss Leopoldskron in Salzburg, where some of the most memorable moments of my life have been passed.

My first visit to Salzburg, and in many ways still the most unforgettable, came at the very beginning of the nineties when Schloss Leopoldskron brought together, for two full weeks, sixty or seventy writers, academics and readers from thirty-odd countries to discuss the impact of the Fall of the Wall on the world of thought and culture.

As always, it was the very nature of the schloss as a venue which was vital to much of what happened during that fortnight: the marvellous old building that still bears the theatrical imprint, especially in the library with its secret staircase and the Venetian Room, of Max Reinhardt. It is situated in a small wood at the edge of a lake which over the years I have seen in all four seasons: the foliage turning colour in the first quiverings of autumn, the heavy snows of winter, the budding trees and the returning birds in spring, the full, raging heat of midsummer. From the schloss a mere twenty-minute walk along a narrow green path takes one across the Mönchsberg, just below the high white walls of the Festung, and down the many stairs on the other side, to the Herbert-von-Karajanplatz in the very heart of the town. If you happen to arrive on the hour, all the bells will be ringing, from the deep-throated boom of the cathedral to the glockenspiel in the tower of the Regierungsneugebäude. From there one can wander through the town, from one square to the next, from the throngs of the Getreidegasse with the house where Wolfgang Amadeus Mozart was born, across one of the graceful bridges to the floral excesses of the Mirabell Gardens; one can have a chocolate or a coffee with incomparable patisseries at Tomaselli's or a meal under the arches of the galleries in the town centre; or linger among the graves – among them the one where Mozart's sister Nannerl was laid to rest – or, on a sweltering summer's day, rest on a curved grass bank of the fast-flowing

Salzach. And everywhere, on every street corner and on every square, there will be music, mostly Mozart, a veritable Garden of Delight.

Then back to the schloss, for some of the most stimulating and challenging lectures or discussions or debates one might wish for. And retire, at the end of a hectic day, to the *Stube* in the basement, where the day's conversations can be continued. How I remember, from that first conference, the way in which the defences would go down and we would talk about where we all came from, the dangers and darkness of persecution and intrigue, of censorship and samizdat, of state control, and security police raids, and – at least for some of the participants – the memories of friends or parents or siblings or children tortured and murdered, just because they had dared to question or comment or criticise. And then the true miracle: how at the end of a long, exhausting day, we would huddle together to reminisce and reimagine, and how in a new-found brotherhood and sisterhood we would embrace, and tears would flow, and we would all yield to nostalgia and passionate longings – back to the good-bad old days of the very censorship and persecution that had kept us awake at night, and driven some to exile and some to their death.

What a weird business this was: for not a single one among us would for a moment really want to go back to those nightmare times. And yet, as we now remembered them, there was something in that past which we had known and would never know again, because it could exist only in dire circumstances when not only one's writing, but one's thoughts, one's life was at stake: a camaraderie, a closeness, a sharing and solidarity. Because we were all in it together, and in spite of the complications of our lives, there was a certain simplicity about them: we all had the same enemy, we shared the same fears, and the same hope kept us going.

Whether one came from South Africa, or Argentina, or the Balkans, from Nigeria or Chile or Bangladesh, from Cameroon or Egypt or China or East Germany: deep down we came from the same place, the same state of emergency, the same silences. And this discovery, renewed at least every night and often by day, in the improbable splendour of that schloss, brought us together as nothing else could. To some extent the theatricality of the setting created an unworldliness which prompted us to probe more deeply into ourselves, and into each other's lives. There were some spectacular explosions, among them the one on 'Literature and Politics', between the young Israeli and the magnificent Palestinian woman – prompted, we discovered only later, by a misunderstanding of the text the young man had read. Very soon almost everybody in the room was drawn into it. For a while it seemed as if the whole conference would collapse in chaos. But then the ever-diplomatic organiser, Tim Ryback, had the idea of proposing that we adjourn and take a walk around the lake, and we all set out in the falling dusk. The arguments and discussions in the small groups into which we'd splintered, had an intensity difficult to imagine and impossible to describe. But very gradually it became possible to reason and talk again; and by the time we'd completed the long, slow circle around the darkening lake which began to gleam almost eerily, as if illuminated from deep down, we could resume the evening's programme and grasp more profoundly, and with an all-encompassing sympathy, what divided us, and what in the end we truly shared.

Without fail each explosion led to a more rewarding communication. *This* was the true magic of the schloss. And the friendships we took away from those gatherings changed the tenor, and sometimes the direction, of our lives.

Not all the discussions were deadly serious or erudite. There were often refreshing interludes of humour. And there were breaks, often musical performances in the evenings. It came as no surprise – in fact, it seemed almost fitting – to learn that the young Mozart had most probably performed for the Archbishop of Salzburg in one of these ornate rooms. Sometimes there would be excursions, most memorably into the Salzkammergut, the region of lakes and mountains; or up the Wintersberg; or occasions to break away for a walk through the town, perhaps a visit to the St Peter restaurant shouldered in under the mountain where, it is alleged, Charlemagne had occasionally enjoyed a meal; or to a concert in the Mozarteum or the Festspielhaus or high up in the Festung.

The conferences at Leopoldskron began in the late forties when a few young Americans who had spent time in Austria during the war set in motion a project to establish a 'home from home' where academic discussions and cultural interaction could turn the war experience and its memories into something positive and lasting. Over the years, more and more of the conferences focused on education, economics, law, business, ethics . . . But there always used to be room for cultural matters too: drama, literature, philosophy.

Gradually, as the twenty-first century began to affirm its presence and press its demands, Schloss Leopoldskron appeared to follow the example of more and more 'educational facilities': turning them, no longer into institutions of intellectual, cultural and moral excellence as into well-run businesses which can show a profit. The face of America became more and more visible; and not always the face one likes to associate with its period of cultural excellence. For me, over the last few years, the schloss has, alarmingly, begun to lose its magic; and the loss was sealed by the departure of Tim Ryback and his charming family.

This has coincided with a slow but perceptible decline in what the name 'Salzburg' used to signify for me. Music has much to do with it.

Through the years, music has always been a major ingredient of my life. Not my early attempts at playing the piano, which had been mostly disappointing. But *living* with it. I find it difficult to write without music. I find it difficult to think without music. I find it difficult to live without it. This means, specifically, classical music. I have made some valiant efforts to extend my interest and my taste: there are moments when I can open the door and let in some jazz, a few phrases of Dylan or the Beatles, certainly Croatian *klapa*. But not much more. The *summum* remains Mozart. Hence my response to Salzburg. And certainly also Beethoven. Quite an array of others – Chopin, more and more since I met Karina. And certainly a wide range of baroque, from Vivaldi and Telemann and Scarlatti and Corelli to Bach. And then Brahms and some Wagner and Mahler and Richard Strauss, and yes, some Stravinsky. But that's about it. I'd like to hear Beethoven's Funeral March when my ashes are strewn at a cherished spot; or Chopin's. For the rest, I can rest peacefully and imagine, as George Eliot phrased it, to hear the grass grow and the squirrel's heart beat, and die of that roar which lies at the other side of silence.

Instruments, solo or in concerto: yes, the piano, or the flute, or the violin, sometimes the deep drone of the cello; often chamber music of many kinds and forms. And the great symphonies in turbulent or expansive mood. There, too, I would always be happy to slide back into Chopin, or Beethoven, and – ultimately and compulsively – Wolfgang Amadeus.

As a student I was fond of opera, but only because it seemed 'easy'. It took years before I cautiously returned to it and discovered, first through Gigli and Di Stefano, through Sutherland, soaringly through Callas, how sublime a form it could be. *Lucia di Lammermoor. Tosca. La Traviata.* And again Mozart, from *opera seria* to *opera buffa* – but who can think of *Così fan tutte* or *Le nozze di Figaro* as *opera buffa* after Mozart has been there? But it was only when, early in 2005, I was in Oudtshoorn with Gerrit and Marina and they made me listen to Anna Netrebko's now almost legenday first CD, *Sempre Libera*, that opera was irrevocably changed for me, into something comparable in scope and impact to Beethoven's Ninth, or Bach's *Das Wohltemperierte Klavier*, or one of Mozart's late piano concertos.

It was here in Salzburg that Netrebko made her phenomenal breakthrough on the world stage in 2002, after bewitching Russian audiences at the Mariinsky Theatre in St Petersburg and Americans in San Francisco as early as 1995, as Donna Anna in *Don Giovanni*. Since then, either on her own or with the inimitable Mexican tenor Rolando Villazón, she has become *the* name at the Met, or at La Scala, or Covent Garden, or of course at the Salzburger Festspiele – a too meteoric rise for some, an unforgivable veering from opera to show business, as a once-noted but now outdated singer like Christa Ludwig recently complained. Like Gigli and Galli-Curci, or Di Stefano and Callas, or Sutherland and Pavarotti, or more recently Alagna and Gheorghiu, these two, Netrebko and Villazón, have become the 'heavenly twins', a phenomenon which brought the whole world of gloss and promotion into overdrive. Regrettably, perhaps; because it can become difficult to see – or hear – through the hype. But in this case – and so far – their real greatness seems to have stayed a step or two ahead of the inventions of the media.

It took me one day with that early CD, *Sempre Libera*, and I was smitten. It was in the early days of my relationship with Karina, and before Gerrit and Marina and I had stopped listening, I sent Karina an SMS in Salzburg to tell her about the discovery. Within minutes she responded with a detailed write-up on Anna Netrebko. After that, there was no turning back for us.

2005 was the year of *La Traviata*, with Netrebko and Villazón. But many months beforehand there were no tickets to be had; on the black market, we learned, they went for 5,000 euros. Even so, undaunted and ever optimistic, we decided to travel to Salzburg and try our luck. But this was not to happen. On this occasion we were invited to spend a night in the schloss together, in the magnificent room I'd stayed in alone on two of my previous visits, overlooking the lake, a peerless view.

On the night we would have gone to the Festspielhaus to see *La Traviata*, we met Karina's brother Krystian in town and went for dinner in the restaurant Zirkelwirt. A good meal, but a sad and depressed evening. Because we knew that barely 200 metres or so away Anna was singing, while we were out here, literally in the cold.

After the main course we decided to go to Tomaselli's for dessert, a touch of sweetness on a bitter night. Along the way we passed several of the curious tall colourful cones the municipality had erected all over the city. There was a yellow one in the square near Tomaselli's too. In passing, Krystian heard music coming from it and bent over to listen. He motioned to us to come closer. I pressed my ear against the cold, wet, yellow thing and my heart missed a beat.

'It's *Traviata*,' I gasped. It had to be a direct broadcast from the Festspielhaus. It certainly was Netrebko. No doubt about it. In that spine-chilling farewell scene. As close to a live performance as we might ever be privileged to witness. We stood there in the rain, listening, transfixed. The next day I asked Karina to take a photograph while I embraced the yellow cone. I was convinced that this might well be the closest I could ever get to Anna Netrebko.

But a year later, in 2006, the impossible happened. There was no hope of getting tickets through the normal channels: every single performance of *Le nozze di Figaro* was sold out eight times on the day the bookings opened. We resigned ourselves to fate, resolved to make the pilgrimage. At least, we speculated, we might see it on the big screen erected during the festival on the Mozartplatz. And then, barely a month before the festival, one of the many pistes we had attempted, unexpectedly resulted in a hit. There were tickets waiting for us.

The performance was unbelievable, Anna breaking away from the old tradition of the *opera buffa* with Susanna as the coquettish *soubrette*. This was a performance in a new key, picking up on aspects of Beaumarchais usually left unexplored: a deeply disturbing unmasking of the *droit du seigneur* and the ruthless exploitation of women. This production was altogether darker and more disturbing, even though Anna managed with unbelievable deftness to do full justice to the deceptive lightness of the music as well.

We went back to the schloss, walking in the dark across the mountain, to our own private celebration.

Two days later there was an opportunity of meeting Anna at a signing in the Katholnigg music shop and for a few precious minutes we could talk to her.

In March 2007, a good friend, Jean Félix-Paganon, who used to be the French ambassador in South Africa and who had been instrumental in honouring me as an Officier de la Légion d'Honneur, succeeded in obtaining tickets for us to a recital of duets by Netrebko and Villazón in Paris. Only later did we learn about all the obstacles that had suddenly arisen, and how it took the personal intervention of the French prime minister to secure our seats.

This still didn't open any doors to Salzburg. Once again all tickets – this time for a *Domkonzert* with Anna Netrebko and Elina Garanča as the soloists in Pergolesi's *Stabat Mater* – were sold out even before the official opening of the bookings. But once more the impossible happened and through friends close to the Festspiele we managed to get tickets. Once again we set out on a pilgrimage of 12,000 kilometres to hear Anna.

But this time fate intervened in a new way. No fewer than five of the top performers at the festival withdrew at the last minute. Among them: Anna Netrebko and Elina Garanča and Rolando Villazón. We did not question the validity of their reasons. But what did seem unpardonable was that the festival office bluntly refused to refund the cost of the tickets. As for

399

travelling from South Africa to Salzburg to hear Anna, that was just too bad. It was advertised as a Pergolesi concert, insisted the woman at the ticket office, and it still is a Pergolesi concert, even if the venue had been changed and the main singers replaced. 'We are strongly against this new cult around "stars"', added the *intendant* of the festival in a television programme soon afterwards, in response to an outcry among festival-goers. Ignoring the fact that it was Salzburg that had first turned these musicians into stars.

This was comparable to setting up a tennis exhibition match at Wimbledon between Roger Federer and Rafael Nadal, and then informing fans, upon their arrival in London, that the match had been moved to a court in Kent, and that Federer and Nadal had been replaced by Tim Henman and Leyton Hewitt. Offering as an explanation, 'It's still a tennis match.'

The triumph of the bureaucrats. A blow for artistic integrity. The replacements found for Netrebko and Garanča in the *Domkonzert* were excellent. But like hundreds of other festival-goers, I had not gone to Salzburg to hear *them*. And the purely mercenary attitude of the organisers may yet bear some rather sour and shrivelled fruit in future. Karina and I will certainly not travel to Salzburg for another Festspiele. And we have heard from several others that they will also think twice about returning.

STILL BLACK AND WHITE

I HESITATE TO RETURN IN THIS FINAL CHAPTER TO THE THEME OF BLACK AND white. One would have liked to think that at the very heart of the shift in South Africa since the transition that began in the early nineties would have been a move *away* from race. And this appears to be borne out by the amazing reaction throughout the country to the two Springbok victories, in 1995 and 2007, in the Rugby World Cup. But the basic divisions in our society have not changed all that much. Over the last few years there may even have been a resurgence of racism. And the tragedy is that this is fuelled not only by stark white right-wing attitudes, but by actions and attitudes within the ANC itself.

What I find saddest about the country today is this: in the past, when I was driven by the urge to come to grips with Africa, there were some whites whose attitudes kept me at a distance: while they were there, Africa could not speak in its own voice. Today it has changed, and the ANC must bear the responsibility for this: because today I find that there are some blacks standing between Africa and me. People like Tony Yengeni, the poor man's Vladimir Putin; or our sick minister of health, Manto Tshabalala-Msimang; or our court-jester minister of safety and security, Charles Nqakula; or a number of other people who should have been proud symbols of Africa, but who are now betraying the continent and what it should stand for. And these names should not be read as refer-ring to individuals and exceptions, but as representatives of attitudes which obscure the history and the legacy of values that have been realised through much suffering, at a high price, and over many years. But how on earth did we get here?

The New South Africa was ushered in by an unforeseen event: early in 1990, the mad old emperor, P. W. Botha, whose apoplectic rages and intransigence had brought the country to the edge of the precipice during the eighties, was incapacitated by a stroke. Flanked by Foreign Minister Pik Botha, F. W. de Klerk lost no time stepping into the shoes of the unlamented leader. This did not necessarily herald significant change: de Klerk was still known as a dour right-winger who had launched some of the most odious apartheid legislation affecting education and social relations through parliament. And 1989 was a bad but fascinating year, wobbling along with two centres of power: P. W. Botha as state president, F. W. de Klerk as leader of the National Party. The outcome was predictable: assisted by the foreign minister, de Klerk outmanoeuvred P. W. Botha and took his place, leaving the old man vile and powerless in the background, trying dementedly to pull the strings of puppets that no longer danced to his tune.

The rest is, indeed, history. Even though everything inside him and every-thing in his past probably militated against it, de Klerk was a shrewd enough politician to read the signs of the times and the mood in the country and act accordingly. Behind him loomed and moved world events like the fall of the Berlin Wall, the liberation of Poland, Hungary, Czechoslovakia, rumblings in Latin America and Africa: with the Soviet Union suddenly no longer the pretext that had driven South African violent authoritarianism to the final excesses of apartheid. With a new worldwide surge towards national liber-ation, and the staggering increase of internal and external pressure in the country itself in the form of economic sanctions, demonstrations by trade unions, and agitation in the churches and the universities, the appearance of vigorous young black leaders within and around the United Democratic Front, de Klerk capitulated. But he had the skill and shrewdness to do it in style. Clearly still convinced that by initiating radical change he could continue to control it and define its parameters and its momentum, he catapulted the country into the future with the historic address to parliament on 2 February, 1990. The death penalty would be reconsidered and a moratorium placed on executions, all liberation movements would be unbanned, political prisoners, including Mandela, would be released.

We stared at the TV screen in stunned disbelief. Immediately afterwards we started telephoning friends, while outside in the streets a cavalcade of cars came past, with the clenched fists, black and white, of the Africa salute protruding from all the windows. It felt like a carnival; at the same time there was an element of irreality, a silence of awe and amazement. Surely this was not really true. It could not last.

11 February, 1990 became one of those days not only South Africans, but anyone who had lived through it, would ever forget. A day to be commemorated like the murder of Kennedy or the fall of the Berlin Wall, a day when, in Santayana's winged words, humanity started dreaming in a different key. The last-minute wrangling behind the scenes, the flaring tempers and frantic efforts to put a stop to it or push it in a different direction, only became known afterwards. What we, and the rest of the world, saw on our TV screens was a tall, greying, immaculately dressed man – he was already in his seventies – clutching the hand of his wife as he walked with long, slow strides through the green landscaped garden of Victor Verster prison outside Paarl, sixty kilometres from Cape Town, towards the massive crowd waiting outside. A moment in which, with incredible abruptness, a myth was transformed into a human being. A moment when an impossible dream became shockingly real. Nelson Rolihlahla Mandela was free.

I was in Grahamstown. In spite of all my efforts I could not break away and go to Cape Town for the occasion. For several years I had been working on my novel *An Act of Terror*, in which Mandela's walk to freedom formed a key episode. At the moment of writing, it was still an almost unbelievable vision of the dream that had kept the country going for so many years. Now it was actually, and unbelievably, happening in front of my eyes as I sat at the TV with my typewriter, writing the last few pages of that book. My vision was blurred. I was in tears. But in a way it was like seeing more clearly than ever before. It was like moving into another time frame, a different kind of reality. Suddenly anything and everything seemed within reach.

Later, I would write: *Now we have achieved the impossible. What remains is to manage the possible*. Which certainly turned out to be much more difficult than we could ever have expected.

But the threshold had been crossed. Nelson Mandela was free.

It is still hard to find words for the events of that searing summer's day and what followed. Yes, I was elated. But I also had lingering leaden doubts, as I still found it hard to trust de Klerk, having known the man since the time we were together at Potchefstroom University. We had never been close friends – he was always on the side of the establishment and took care to follow all the right channels to reach the top in student affairs; I was always, albeit cautiously, a heretic on the 'other' side – but at such a small university everybody knew everybody and we were bound together by a sense of family. Moreover, at that time I still supported the National Party, had a strong historical sense of Afrikaner identity.

Not very long after 11 February I wrote him a letter, congratulating him on his stance and expressing the hope that he would follow through on it. At the same time I mentioned that within a few weeks I would be leaving for Europe and I knew in advance that I was going to be approached by journalists and politicians in several countries for my view of the changing climate in South Africa. What, I asked FW in my letter, was I to tell them – given that at the time I was still under constant surveillance by the SB, that my mail was still being opened and my telephone calls intercepted? A few weeks later, just before I left for Europe, there was a short official letter from the presidency: Mr de Klerk would ask the police to investigate the matter.

From then on there was a rough ride to freedom. Well after negotiations had begun to take the country to a new dispensation, South Africa staggered under waves of violence, particularly fomented by the Zulu-dominated Inkatha Freedom Party in campaigns that largely had their origin in the province of Natal, but spreading to the Witwatersrand and elsewhere. The worst massacre took place at Boipathong, where there was strong evidence that the IFP had the full support of the police. The most obscene moment came when immediately after this outburst, de Klerk visited Boipathong escorted

404

by the very police believed to have been at the centre of the massacre. Not long afterwards, when the charismatic communist leader Chris Hani was gunned down in the driveway of his own home by right-wing activists and it seemed as if South Africa was going up in flames, de Klerk remained conspicuously invisible, while key figures of the ANC – notably Mandela and Tokyo Sexwale – took charge of the situation and displayed the clear vision and guidance one would expect of leaders.

When at Hani's funeral a white dove released as a symbol of hope in the cemetery, flew down into the grave, it really seemed like the worst possible omen for the future. But at the last moment a soldier of the armed wing of the ANC, Umkhonto we Sizwe – Spear of the Nation – in a gesture of both real and symbolic significance, clambered into the open grave to salvage the bewildered white dove and set it free. And the day, which could so easily have become mired in tragedy, soared above its dire possibilities and turned into an affirmation of hope. It demonstrated that, just as humanity had succeeded in triumphing over Auschwitz, or the murder of Gandhi, or that of Martin Luther King, we could also emerge from the shadow of apartheid and the death of Chris Hani. In a real moment of choice the country rejected the violent option and turned once again towards negotiation and peace. Which was, in retrospect, only fitting as a tribute to Hani, the committed soldier who always carried Shakespeare in his pocket.

There was still a long way to go, as the negotiations of CODESA, the Conference for a Democratic South Africa, stumbled from one hurdle to the next – including an invasion by 4x4 vehicles driven by members of the right-wing Afrikaner Resistance Movement, the AWB, of the International Trade Centre where the negotiations were taking place; a massacre of peaceful protesters by the police of the absurd little home-land of Ciskei; an attempt by the AWB to take over the bantustan of Boputhatswana; disgraceful manoeuvring by de Klerk to wreck the negotiations behind the scenes, which forced even the dignified and unflappable Mandela to lose his cool and fulminate against 'the leader of a disgraced, illegitimate regime'.

More than once it seemed as if everything would sink into despondency and despair and conflagrations of unmanageable violence. Even after a date for the first democratic elections in the country had finally been announced, it was difficult to believe that such a day would ever arrive. Until the last moment – the morning of 27 April, 1994, the very day of the elections – there were disquieting reports of violence in many parts of the country. But then, almost miraculously, it stopped. The day itself unfolded in unbelievable peace and quiet.

Over the previous month I had been in Montpellier in the south of France as a visiting professor, returning on the very eve of election day, just in time to vote. I have already written about that remarkable day; but it was such a watershed event, in my life and in the country's history, that I have to return to it here.

At eleven o'clock I go to the nearest poll station with Attwell Jongibandla Bontsa, who tends my garden once a week and who has chosen to wear a very natty outfit for this day, even though it is raining cats and dogs – to him, as a Xhosa, it is a very auspicious sign; to me less so. This is a unique experience for him: in his fifty years, this will be the first time he has ever voted. I have not voted all that many times either, but of course I'd always had the choice. Huddled closely together under a large black umbrella, the two of us set out for the sports centre where a long queue is already snaking along the main road; just before our arrival a few busloads of voters turned up from the black townships, to relieve the congestion in the voting stations there – so it is obvious that we are in for a long day. Fortunately a few enterprising individuals turn up with stacks of black rubbish bags that can be used as raincoats, and soon what seems to be a funeral procession is formed between the voting station and the freeway half a kilometre further on. But there is nothing funereal about the gathering. It is one of the happiest events I have ever experienced.

There are brief let-ups in the rain, but the earth is soggy, everybody is bedraggled and spattered with mud; yet there is an unrestrained exuberance in the crowd: we are representative of the whole rainbow of South Africa, all shades from shiny boot-polish black via various browns and ochres and beiges to the many shades of pale that pass for white; in the common predicament of bad weather and the shared experience of waiting through a seemingly interminable day, I remind myself that in Spanish the word for *waiting* also means *hoping*. Pools of conversation along the ever-growing line spill into each other to form one moving river of talk – bantering, encouraging, teasing, laughing, speculating, in Xhosa and English and Afrikaans and Sotho. Businessmen and street-sweepers, academics and domestics, society ladies and chars, the affluent and the jobless, all mingle easily, even exuberantly. From the badges some people are wearing, and the posters and flags on the minibuses that arrive with more and more people, it is clear that most of the nineteen parties contesting the election are also represented among us: yet no one, as far as I can make out, speaks a word of party politics. Instead, we talk about our lives, our jobs, our families, about the long wait. And the tone is mostly light-hearted, easy-going, with laughter constantly hovering just below the surface.

At one o'clock somebody arrives with coffee for a couple waiting behind Attwell and me; like the biblical loaves and fishes the two mugs multiply to be shared by seven, eight, ten, a dozen people; the last drops of sugar at the bottom are noisily slurped up by a cherubic black baby waiting on his mother's lap in a minibus.

There are many people with babies or small children: not a very wise idea, I think in the beginning – but as the day wears on I start wondering whether they were not more prescient than us. For by the time we reach the booth most of these children may well be old enough to vote.

More Samaritans appear with buns and sandwiches and fruit and soft drinks to dish out. And still there is no sign of the queue shortening. At one stage we are stuck in the same mudpool for an hour and a half; no one knows what has caused it, yet no one complains. There are no toilet facilities, so from time to time people drop out of the line and cross the broad street to a water tower which offers some protection on the far side.

At irregular intervals Attwell takes out his alarm clock to check the time. 'I think we shall still be here at three,' he confidently announces at one stage. It is the time he usually knocks off from work. Usually he starts getting fidgety about an hour before then; but today he seems unperturbed by the prospect. We have a long talk as we wait. About the twenty years or so he has been working in Cape Town. About the small plot he has in Transkei,

407

and his dream of going back – 'as soon as I have enough money' – to start cultivating it. Unfortunately, his earnings as a gardener just about cover the expenses of staying here, and all he can manage is a brief annual or biannual visit to his family. Still, that has not dampened his spirits, and today there is a new buoyancy in his attitude, as if the events in the country have enhanced his personal chances of a happy future.

Two o'clock. Half-past. Three o'clock. Half-past. Four o'clock. There is a new delivery of refreshments. This time there is enough for twenty or thirty members of the crowd. Black and white throng around the woman who has brought the food. 'Thank you, Mama. Thank you, Mama!' they call out after her.

Half-past. We are now at the periphery of the sports complex.

Occasionally the conversations falter and subside; people are really getting exhausted. But what the hell. Every inch one shuffles along is a step closer to consummation. Here I've been waiting for five hours. Some of these people, I remind myself once again, have been waiting for thirty, forty, fifty, sixty *years*. The country has been waiting for centuries.

Five o'clock. We are very close now. And each face emerging from those big doors ahead carries the radiant message of fulfilment, of a joy too great to express in words. New ripples of cheerfulness move through the crowd. We have all become members of one extended family. Black, brown, white: in the course of this one day a quiet miracle has been taking place. Only a week ago some white people in the country have begun to barricade themselves in their homes, expecting a wave of violence to swamp them today. What is happening here is the opposite. We are discovering, through the sharing of this experience, that we are all South Africans. It is as simple and as momentous as that. Tomorrow most of us will return to our separate existences. In the commotion of the coming days, months, years, much of this day may fade. But one thing we cannot, ever, forget: the knowledge of having been here together, black and white, the awareness of a life, a country, a humanity we share. By achieving what has seemed impossible, we have caught a glimpse of the possible.

Half-past five. Attwell and I have reached the threshold. Briefly, we look at each other. We put our hands on each other's shoulders. Then we go in, each towards his own voting booth, but sharing a small precious moment of history.

It takes only a minute. We return from the cubicles, Jongibandla Bontsa and I. It is over. But in so many ways it is just the beginning.

A few days later there was another momentous occasion when Mandela was sworn in as president in front of the Union Buildings, the stately crescent of the Herbert Baker edifice in Pretoria which had served as the seat of the executive wing of government ever since 1910. In front of the diplomatic corps and dignitaries from all over the world, the transition from the Old South Africa to the New was confirmed.

FW looked grim, his face like a skull on a Jolly Roger. His wife, Marike, never a warm or welcoming person and reputed still to be firmly entrenched in the mindset of apartheid, observed the events as if they all formed part of a funeral. And for people like her, of course, it was nothing less.

Shortly before the inauguration a number of artists were invited by Mandela's office to attend the ceremony and perform at the celebrations following it. These included a handful of writers – among them Nadine Gordimer, Antjie Krog, the poets Adam Small and Willie Kgositsile, the musician Johnny Clegg, and others. This was probably the first time writers were involved in such a celebration in South Africa. Under the previous regime, even at the inauguration of the Afrikaans Language Monument in the seventies, writers were studiously kept out of the way. Not that many of us would have been prepared to be seen in such company anyway. Now it was made clear that in the New South Africa there would officially be a place for us. Although it was obvious from the reaction of the vast audience that covered the sloping lawns of the Union Buildings that they were more tuned in to pop music than to literature, but at least our presence was acknowledged. Without ever discussing it between us, Nadine read the prophetic passage from *A Sport of Nature* in which an event from the future is depicted – the investiture of the first black president of an African country – while I read, from *An Act of Terror*, my own version of exactly the same event, now placed overtly in the New South Africa. Fact was indeed beginning to take over from fiction.

During the inauguration ceremony we were seated close to the podium with special guests from around the world: Fidel Castro was there, Father Trevor Huddleston, the Dalai Lama, Bill Clinton, Tony Blair, Jacques Chirac . . . My seat had been allocated somewhat to the right of the podium, in a position from where I would be able to see much of the stage, but not Mandela. But as the invited artists were shown to their places before anybody else, I took advantage of this and stealthily began to shift across to the centre, one seat at a time. When the diplomats arrived, I was prepared to beat a retreat, but as it happened I landed in the Hungarian delegation and they generously made room for me, affording me a prime position from where all the main role-players were fully visible and not a moment of the unfolding of this particular bit of history was allowed to pass me by.

After the momentous events that marked our transition to democracy, including also the first session of the new parliament, which I could not attend, thereby missing Mandela's reading of Ingrid's poem 'The Child', I was happy to fade into the background. At long last it was possible to focus only on my work: above all on my own writing, and on what remained of my career of teaching at UCT, focused more and more on students of creative writing.

There was only one occasion on which I agreed to get involved in the official process of transition, and that came when my good friend Kader Asmal asked me to compose a draft for the closing section of the new interim constitution, the 'reconciliation clause'. This I did, and it was indeed gratifying to see a final version of it incorporated in that document. It was, Kader told me later, the first time the term *ubuntu* was used in an official document. This was the clause which determined the parameters for the work of the Truth and Reconciliation Commission. To my regret, the clause was dropped from the definitive new constitution – mainly, I learned from 'informed sources', because of objections by F. W. de Klerk.

In its final form, the clause in the interim constitution reads as follows:

This Constitution provides a historic bridge between the past of a deeply divided society characterised by strife, conflict, untold suffering and injustice, and a future founded on the recognition of human rights, democracy and peaceful coexistence and development opportunities for all South Africans, irrespective of colour, race, class, belief or sex. The pursuit of national unity, the well-being of all South African citizens and peace require reconciliation between the people of South Africa and the reconstruction of society.

The adoption of this Constitution lays the secure foundation for the people of South Africa to transcend the divisions and strife of the past, which generated gross violations of human rights, the transgression of humanitarian principles in violent conflicts and a legacy of hatred, fear, guilt and revenge.

These can now be addressed on the basis that there is a need for understanding but not for vengeance, a need for reparation but not for retaliation, a need for *ubuntu* but not for victimisation.

Many events during our transition to democracy provided a context for what we experienced then, or could hope to experience in the near future. Some of these were very personal; and some even happened far away from South Africa. One of the most memorable involved a visit to the Caribbean island of Martinique, to which I'd been invited by a man from modern legend, Aimé Césaire.

It came at a time, in 2004, when I'd just planned a trip to two other islands in the region, the small paradise of Guadeloupe, and the tiny pimple of Carriacou, where H and I, temporarily reunited after decades of separate lives, spent a few blissful days with my son Danie.

For me, Martinique had first been evoked in a time beyond time by Mireille from the rue Saint-Denis in Paris, Mireille of the smooth amber-and-honey body and the flowing black hair and the dark-brown eyes flecked with gold and the musical voice, in which she told me about her family and her girlhood in a distant world of volcanoes and fairies and songs, which now, at last, became a geographical reality with its mountains and green valleys and its memory and deep scars of volcanic eruptions, marketplaces strung with festoons of brightly coloured drapes, palaces still startled by the haunting images of imperial, Napoleonic splendour, and in the heart of a palatial building, the tiny old man with the gleaming black shoes, Aimé Césaire, surrounded by chantings from his poetry.

It was of course Césaire who, with Senghor, introduced the world to *négritude*, that heady wave of black self-awareness that swept across the globe in the second half of the last century: the movement was largely misunderstood in the Third World, which came to view it as a sentimental philosophy of Uncle Toms appropriating the values of Western Europe in order to enhance their own status as black artists; equally misunderstood in the West that turned it into the very opposite, an early manifestation of Black Power as it expressed itself through a range of writers and activists ranging from the Black Panthers to Steve Biko. Behind all the hype, *négritude* boiled down to a space that offered the black artist a source of self-assurance and pride as an antidote to what had become known as 'colonial cringe'. Today it is difficult to appreciate just how much *négritude* contributed to changing our perception of the value of the individual in the years surrounding the Second World War: that is, no longer to base your definition of who and what you are on somebody else's perception of you; to see yourself as standing in the centre of your own world, and no longer on the periphery of somebody else's. A discovery as momentous, psychologically and philosophically, as Galileo's statement about the earth and the sun.

The most famous exponent of this philosophy was Senghor, and once he became president of Senegal, his position added weight to his poetic beliefs. After the ban on *Looking on Darkness* he invited me to Senegal, but it was not possible to accept at the time. When the new invitation came in 2004 to meet his great friend and colleague Aimé Césaire, I was resolved not to let another opportunity slip past. In a way it had become a personal appointment with history.

Hence our meeting in Martinique, late in April, when after the dry months in the Caribbean the weather was turning inclement. I was invited to visit him in his palace. In a manner of speaking. Because actually it is no more than the city hall of Fort-de-France, the capital of Martinique, where Césaire had by then been installed as president in all but name. In fact he was mayor, but in prestige and dignity he was the equal of any head of state. He had been mayor for fifty-six years, officially retiring at eighty. But only officially, because de facto he simply continued as before (in 2004 he was ninety-one): going to the office every morning to perform his duties in the imposing old *mairie* with its columns and decorated ceilings and stained-glass windows, surrounded by a contingent of devoted women.

The impression of the theatrical is heightened when the dapper little man makes his entrance: so small that when he takes his seat on the beautifully carved chaise longue those dainty black shoes do not even reach the plush carpet. Whenever emotion takes over, which constantly happens where the Caribbean and the French are in charge, his small feet start swinging and swirling excitedly, describing complicated pirouettes above the floral carpet. Behind him, through the large windows, something of the cityscape is visible, as well as vistas of luxuriant tropical vegetation. And far in the background, like a painted cloth, the Prussian blue sea. Inside, the walls are covered with paintings, including a few beautiful canvases from Haiti; there are also masks and carvings from Africa, and huge arrangements of massed flowers which on closer inspection turn out to be fake.

The tête-à-tête I had been led to expect is somewhat dampened by the presence of several other writers, from Martinique and Guadeloupe and Haiti and France, as well as a bustling press contingent. In addition, in spite of his brightness and alertness, Césaire is hard of hearing, which is not conducive to an easy conversation.

The Caribbean writers metaphorically wriggle and sail on their stomachs as they offer the gold, myrrh and incense of their adulation, and every utterance is repeated at least three times, each time more loudly than before, to ensure that His Excellency will not miss anything.

Césaire patiently listens to it all, his eyes gleaming with amusement behind the shiny gold frames of his spectacles. And his replies suggest that he is fully aware of the exaggerations and absurdities of the audience. When somebody asks what he thinks about entreaties for the West to write off the debt of the Third World, he quietly responds, 'That is *your* problem, not mine.'

Later in the morning I manage to draw Césaire aside as I have a small private homage to pay. It concerns something that goes back many years and has played a special role in my life: the long poem, *Cahier d'un retour au pays natal*, written as early as 1939, which I still regard as his greatest work, with its plethora of images and rhythms and surrealist inventions, celebrating his own rediscovery of the Caribbean, which many years later inspired much of *The First Life of Adamastor*. More specifically, it concerns my return to Paris for that year of 1968, and ultimately the decision to go back to South Africa. As I have said, many things contributed to this step that changed the course of my life: the discussions with Breyten, the ship-wreck of the relationship with H, the student revolt . . . But in the heart of it all was Césaire's *Cahier*, and the way in which it helped me realise the need to return to the land of my own birth. While we are alone, I can finally thank him for his role in that turning point.

Back with the others, there is, inevitably, much talk about Haiti, where the cause of freedom in the Caribbean is being betrayed, like so many times before – this time by the unscrupulous Aristide who, like Mugabe in Zimbabwe, arrived with messianic visions and promises, and turned into a monster.

There is talk about Césaire's *Tragédie du Roi Christophe*, which has become a fixed part of the repertoire of the Comédie Française: the early history of Haiti examined in the story of a runaway slave and cook, who becomes general of the revolutionaries in his country and has himself crowned as king – an astounding piece, somewhere between Shakespeare's *Henry IV* and Jarry's *Ubu Roi*, ranging from brutal satire to shocking seri-ousness, timeless in its understanding and portrayal of the political power game.

For some time Césaire entertains us with anecdotes from his long life, among them his first meeting with Senghor, on his very first day as a student in Paris: 'Senghor,' he declares, 'gave me the key to myself.' There are many snippets of wisdom, as in his Mandela-like response to a question about why there seems to be no hatred or bitterness in him. 'Hate?' he asks. 'That would make me dependent on someone else. I refused, once and forever, to be a slave like my ancestors. And so I will not allow hate to make me a slave again.'

When somebody ventures to ask how he sees himself – as a Frenchman? a Haiitian? a Martiniquais? – Aimé Césaire replies with the shadow of a smile, 'I am a human being.'

And that is probably my most lasting impression of that morning, framed in the comic theatricality of the long audience: the encounter with a human being.

In the New South Africa itself, I had met a few people of comparable stature. Among them, without doubt, two of the most unforgettable of our time.

I have shared less time with Archbishop Desmond Tutu than with Mandela. But in his case, too, there was, every time, a glow of happiness deep inside: the happiness of knowing that one is with one of those rare individuals in this world who has found his way through darkness and sorrow to understanding and joy. I don't think I have ever known a person who has packed so much joy into such a small body. Those, like Antjie Krog, who have been privileged to spend a long time with him during the Truth and Reconciliation Commission, who have seen him break into tears in his suffering with others, have experienced this much more profoundly than I ever could. But even in small shared moments I have seen – and felt – the joy he radiates, as if he himself is a source of warmth and light which is beamed to whoever is with him. One knows from many sources that when he faces dishonesty or injustice, his heat can also be scorching: on such occasions, however gracious and generous he may be in other situations, he does not mince his words when he is enraged, that in his totally fearless anger he will not allow anything to stop him. But what I have experienced of him, has always been joy: the joy of being alive, of being human; as if nothing in this world can match the miraculous rediscovery, every day, of what it means just *to be*.

And this is matched with his ever-bubbling sense of humour. On the very first occasion I met him, he told a story with himself cast as villain – he'd had a dream, he said, and in the dream he'd died and gone to hell, either because of some mistake or because he really deserved it. But he caused so much trouble in hell, he said, that after three days the devil couldn't stand it any more – causing him to flee to heaven and ask for political asylum. I've heard him tell this story the other way round as well: creating such chaos in heaven that God was driven out to seek asylum in hell. There is truth in both versions.

The first time we met was on the tarmac at the airport in Johannesburg.

We'd just boarded the plane when the flight was aborted and everybody was ordered out to spend an hour in the hot sun identifying their baggage because of some mix-up. Tempers flared. The only person on the plane who was not only unflappable but actually seemed to enjoy himself, was Desmond Tutu. That was where we started talking, a conversation that seems to have continued effortlessly on every subsequent occasion we met.

I can think of no other person quite so well equipped to head the Truth and Reconciliation Commission. There are critics who – justifiably perhaps – complain that the commission never went far enough in its work to arrive at some kind of closure; and that together with 'truth' and 'reconciliation' it could never fully succeed without including at least some sense of 'justice' in its brief as well. The consequences are there for all to see today, and they are corroborated by the little I have seen of the comparable process in Chile. But what I do know, is that, without the South African TRC, we could never have progressed to where we find ourselves today. It may not be nearly far enough; but without the TRC we would have been bogged down in a much, much greater mess and misery than the one we are in. And what measure of success the TRC has known, is overwhelmingly due to the presence of Desmond Tutu: his understanding, his empathy, his human warmth, his capacity to laugh, and his capacity to cry – for and with others. I am not a Christian. But of the very few true Christians I have met in my life who have made me feel that – maybe, just maybe – there is something to say for it, Tutu was one. I should add Beyers Naudé. And there was Rob Antonissen. But surely the first among them, for me, will remain this small package of unadulterated joy, Desmond Tutu.

Before the elections I'd met Mandela only once, at the home of Allan Boesak. This was before Allan was charged, and convicted, for the theft of monies contributed specifically for the alleviation of poverty among black children. This came as a heavy blow, because during the apartheid years he had been a beacon of light in the struggle against oppression, and had been particularly active as a leader of the United Democratic Front during the eighties. We were never close friends, but we had good relations, and I admired him for his unwavering dedication and his energy. Ever since the 1976 youth revolt, whenever I was abroad and people would ask me what they could do in the international campaigns against apartheid, I would suggest that, among other things, they could send money to Tutu and Boesak. I don't know how much of this ended up in Boesak's pocket; but I do know that when he was convicted, I felt that at least to some extent I had let down many ordinary people. Local reaction, particularly among coloured people to whom Boesak had been something of a saint, is illustrated by a small event in Cape Town, when a crowd gathered in front of Tuynhuys, an official residence of the president. While they were waiting for a particular dignitary to arrive at the gate, a cry went up that Boesak was on his way to join them. Previously, he would have received a hero's welcome. This time, the moment the news broke, a cry went up: 'Hold on to your handbags: Boesak is coming!'

But when Elna Boesak invited us for dinner to meet Mandela, all of this still lay, mercifully, in the future. There were only eight of us at the table, among them also Antjie Krog, all of us Afrikaans-speaking, as Mandela had a special wish to meet more Afrikaners. And we were all so much in awe that the conversation was not particularly glittering. Not that it mattered much. Wearing one of his trademark loose shirts in muted reds and blues, what most impressed us was his gentleness, his subdued wry humour. The most unexpected moment of the evening came when Mandela had to leave the table to take a telephone call from Elizabeth Taylor.

Afterwards, there were a few more occasions for meeting and talking, sometimes about the most ordinary things. In our most recent meeting, when he welcomed Karina and me to his house in Cape Town, he regaled us on the amusing and poignant story about an occasion when the queen had prevailed on him to spend the night in Buckingham Palace, and how he was unable to sleep a wink because of the oppressive presence of guards in the palace all night, which he found too disturbingly reminiscent of prison.

There were other meetings. Among them was an occasion for the handing over of a collection of essays on the first free elections which I'd edited, followed a year later by another, this time a series of reflections on the interim. Towards the end of his term as president, I approached him to write an introduction to my own volume of essays, *Reinventing a Continent*, which in the midst of an impossibly busy schedule he graciously accepted to do. And when the time came to present him with a copy, just before he handed over the reins to Thabo Mbeki, Mandela invited me to tea at his Cape Town residence, Genadendal. This time there were only the two of us, and the conversation flowed smoothly and happily. He was in an expansive mood, reminiscing freely about his last few years in prison and the negotiations between him, P. W. Botha, FW and others, to prepare for the transition; he spoke about efforts of many individuals in power to wreck the negotiations; about the struggle within himself to decide on entering into discussions with 'the enemy' without officially notifying the ANC or drawing them into the process. There were moments, he made clear, when being a leader meant taking the risk of making decisions on his own, relying only on his personal faith in the future and his conviction of doing the right thing – not for himself, but for the country and its people.

And this faith, he insisted, came not just from inside, but was fed by years of interacting with others; and years of reading. This was when the crucial moment came – the moment when he finally became, for me, not just the leader and statesman, but a human being. I remember him leaning over – he was sitting on a sofa, I on an easy chair right next to it – and placing his left hand on my wrist. And then he said:

'When I was in prison, you changed the way I saw the world.'

Each one of these words has been branded into my memory for ever.

I certainly do not believe that he was, at that moment, speaking to me as a specific and individual writer: he was thinking of 'you' as a collective, as the writers of the books he had read in prison. And so he may have spoken these very words to others – other writers, other individuals – on other occasions. He was paying homage to literature. To the written word. To the experience of reading.

But that did not alter the fact that, *at that moment*, he was addressing himself to *me*.

And what I felt at the time came to me in the words of the old man Simeon from the Bible, when he held the infant Jesus in his arms and raised his ancient eyes to the heavens: 'Lord, now lettest thou thy servant depart in peace, for mine eyes have seen thy salvation.' As a writer, nothing that could happen to me after this moment could ever go beyond this. So to die then would be to be most happy.

Just as well perhaps. For as it happened, things certainly started going downhill from there.

As early as 1996, in the Epilogue to the essays collected in *Reinventing a Continent*, I outlined the shift that was happening in South Africa, following the initial euphoria about 'the rainbow nation': a shift, first, towards what was called 'realism', followed by disillusionment, resentment, and rage tinged with despair.

This shift I saw as the ANC's 'turn for the worse' in its 'failure of integrity' and the weakness, indeed the rottenness, at the heart of what used to be its main strength: its commitment to transparency and democratic values, the premium it placed on morality, the tolerance it displayed toward a diversity of opinions, its regard for human dignity. What I found then was that the new government 'had become suspect, demonstrating all too often an arrogance, obtuseness, mendacity, and callousness dramatically at variance with its historical image.' And to illustrate the shift, I referred to eight specific examples. These deserve, I think, to be reiterated – amplified where necessary by remarks provoked by more recent events.

There was the debacle caused by the way in which the then minister of health, Nkosazana Zuma, flaunted all regulations and prescribed procedures in paying a preposterous amount to the playwright Mbongeni Ngema to write and produce an anti-Aids play. The venture came at vast expense at a time when many hospitals had to close down for lack of funds and doctors and nurses resigned in droves because of bad pay; but instead of investigating the matter the ANC closed ranks around the minister and arrogantly refused to acknowledge any hint of culpability. In due course the minister was moved into a more powerful position as minister of foreign affairs. In her first post she has been replaced by an even more grossly incompetent and more stupidly arrogant person, the infamous Dr Manto Tshabalala-Msimang, who has made South Africa the laughing stock of the world through her espousal of 'alternative' remedies for Aids, including beetroot and wild garlic. Which could be cause for mirth if it hadn't already caused the death of thousands.

Once again the ANC refused to take seriously accusations of incompetence – even including, in this case, allegations of alcohol abuse and theft – against a cabinet minister. On its front page the *Sunday Times* openly called Tshabalala-Msimang 'a thief and a drunk'. The response from the government was to block any discussion of the matter in parliament, and to threaten the editor of the *Sunday Times* and one of his journalists with arrest. And the president assured the nation that no stone would be left unturned in trying to find the person or persons responsible for the disappearance of the minister's medical files after her discharge from hospital where she had had a liver transplant. 'If people steal,' he said, 'they must expect the full power of the law, regardless of their status in society.' But no word was allowed to be said about the reports on Tshabalala-Msimang's alleged theft of patients' watches and other possessions while, a number of years ago, she had been in charge of a hospital in Botswana.

Another gripe was the way in which the boundaries of certain provinces, particularly Mpumalanga, were drawn, and promises of post-election referendums broken with impunity. That particular gripe is still festering, and remains only one instance among many of the way in which the government has been riding roughshod over the interests and the explicit demands of the electorate. The old Calvinist approach of the Nationalist regime has come back to robust life: that is, the attitude that the *vox populi* expressed through the ballot box turns immediately afterwards into the *vox dei*, ruling out any influence from the electorate.

This attitude was also demonstrated by the interference of the ANC in appointing leaders in top positions, against the expressed will of the electorates concerned. Thabo Mbeki's regime has made this even more apparent than before, and it is taken several steps further: it is not just the ANC as a body that bulldozes through demands and protests, but specifically the person of the president. In numerous instances Mbeki has been using state organs to silence opposition to his style of ruling. This extends particularly into the domain of jurisprudence, as in his vendetta against Jacob Zuma who, shady character as he may be, still deserves to be treated within the parameters of the constitution.

Another example is the provocative and frequently purely obtuse way in which 'affirmative action' was steamrollered through, allegedly to redress iniquitous imbalances in the past, in itself a praiseworthy ideal, but not when it is implemented at paralysing cost, in money and efficacy, throughout the Civil Service and in many companies. I gave the example of a publishing company which was 'restructured' by firing all the whites in top positions, replacing them with blacks, and then re-employing the dismissed staff, at double their previous salaries, as 'consultants'. Any criticism against such practices is invariably dismissed as 'racist' – the kind of reflex which has, unfortunately, come to characterise many of Thabo Mbeki's reactions. This has contributed to a serious lack of informed and intelligent debate among black and white intellectuals in the country.

It was imperative that the criminal white colonial and neocolonial exploitation of black labour had to be redressed as swiftly and efficiently as possible – among other measures, by eradicating the consequences of 'Bantu education' – but by handing inordinate power to the trade unions of COSATU, the Congress of South African Trade Unions, one of the key partners, with the Communist Party, in the government's tripartite alliance, there is a danger of constantly ceding to demands for wage increases without any commensurate increase in productivity, so that South Africa is being priced out of international competitiveness, and risks losing foreign investment. And at the time of writing this the ANC is being faced increasingly with the prospect of being defied by its own Frankenstein monster.

Yet another thorn in the flesh was the trial of Allan Boesak, in which leading members of the government, including key persons in the Ministry of Justice itself, openly supported the accused, making a mockery of judicial procedure. A few years later this was followed by the unedifying spectacle of members of government, including the Speaker of parliament, carrying the convicted criminal, the MP Tony Yengeni, to prison, where he was treated like a guest in a five-star hotel, until he was released well before the expiry of his sentence, when he was welcomed once more like a hero. Clearly, justice in the New South Africa threatens to become subservient to the machinations of power. To see Yengeni subsequently elected to the executive council of the ANC, is further cause for despondency and alarm.

There are also major concerns in other areas of public life. A radical overhaul of the education system has been long overdue. The breakdown of barriers between 'black education' and 'white education', between the education of the privileged and the underprivileged was a basic necessity. Certainly, the opening up of schools to all races has been one of the keystones of the New South Africa, and one of the measures that in the long run must go further than most others in eradicating old mindsets and introducing a new respect for a shared humanity. But some of the means employed to effect this have been, to say the least, ill-advised. These include the early decision to introduce a uniform ratio between teachers and learners in all schools. But instead of upgrading this ratio to the best available, thousands of teachers from 'privileged' schools, including, for obvious reasons, many of the best-qualified teachers in the country, were sacked at staggering expense in order to bring such schools down to the level of those with the worst ratios. The alternative was deemed too expensive, presumably because mismanagement, corruption, unrealistic extremes of affirmative action and the like, have so depleted the state coffers that there is nothing left when it comes to what really matters in the process of transformation. And of course this turns a blind eye to the billions available, in many countries abroad, to fund this kind of transition to a better future. And to the billions already contributed, by Scandinavian countries, the US, Canada and others, for the alleviation of poverty, the upgrading of education, housing and basic services, and which lie, unused, in the safekeeping of departments who seem to lack the will to use this money efficiently. That is, if there is anything left in the coffers after so much of it has been misappropriated or misspent by individuals in the top structures of such departments, to finance end-of-year parties for directors general or commissioners, trips abroad for ministers and their extended families and friends, and domestic expenses for the newly affluent.

After the interminable rule of the apartheid regime, when the Afrikaans language became the de facto language of the oppressor, it was good to see the language cut down to size as one of eleven official languages. But as the new rulers became more safely ensconced, and more arrogant, in their new-found positions of power, an alarming vindictiveness crept into their dealings with Afrikaans. This was highlighted when a cabinet minister revealed publicly that the Afrikaans language was the ultimate price the ANC would exact for their suffering under apartheid. One should now add to this the unseemly haste with which the changes of place names in the country has been approached. I can only applaud the elimination of historical names that were clearly offensive to the sensibilities of some culture, language, or race groups, most especially the black majority. But surely a certain measure of historical perspectivism should be welcomed. And by more or less 'inventing' black names for previously white towns, as in the case of Pretoria/Tshwane, simply to get rid of real or imagined connotations of 'Afrikaansness' in the old ones, suggests not only hypersensitivity, but cultural paranoia.

Today, there are other signs of derailing wherever one looks. This has become most obvious in moves to diminish the role and importance of parliament in the context of democracy, and replacing it by the party, the ANC. Not only does this set the stage for two centres of power in the future, but – even more importantly – it sidelines parliament as a decision-making body, elevating the party to the most crucial position in an undemocratic hierarchy. At the same time the change removes parliament from its position of overseeing the overall structuring and functioning of the state, a manoeuvre which makes it easier to ignore continuing abuses and generally to use state structures and apparatus for personal gain or to settle personal scores.

There are so many other forms of derailment that it becomes almost tedious to list them. Among the most important is the South African government's inability to do something decisive about Zimbabwe. Sometimes Thabo Mbeki's reluctance to take a firm stand, is understandable within the context of his hopeful if ineffectual 'quiet diplomacy'; more often than not it simply suggests wavering and weakness. And one knows exactly how members of the present government would have reacted if during the apartheid years our neighbour states had acted with the same pusillanimity. There is, also, the lack of decisive action against HIV/Aids, which makes one suspect that the president shares the health minister's dithering attitude. Among the many other criticisms one can raise is South Africa's unimpressive performance as a member of the Security Council after its admission to that body in 2007. One of the first opportunities of taking a firm stand in international affairs came when a decision about the inhuman excesses of the military junta in Myanmar had to be taken. South Africa sided with Russia and China in voting against action, even in the mild form of adopting a motion of censure. Anyone who has followed the events in that tragic country, and certainly anyone who has read Karen Connelly's devastating novel, *The Lizard Cage*, about the horrors of living there today, cannot but be outraged.

One might also cite the unacceptable manner in which the ANC has acted to undermine, vilify and paralyse the legally elected majority of the Democratic Party in Cape Town; the refusal to act against an ambassador accused and found guilty on several occasions of sexual harassment; the protection of ANC officials who have misbehaved – whether in financial transactions or through sexual abuse – in public positions but are not only blithely allowed to stay on in power, but are even amply rewarded for past or present loyalty to the cause, or whose future loyalty is timeously secured.

The malpractices promoted and/or permitted by the power elite are indeed staggering. The point is no longer the detail, but the basic fact that while in power the ANC has betrayed most of the principles and ideals it promoted before coming to power, and cast a shadow of deep doubt over the leaders who have placed their lives at stake to ensure that the long struggle for liberation led to an honourable victory – great names from Albert Luthuli to Oliver Tambo to Nelson Mandela. The present regime has become a disgrace to the party's history.

Most of the ills of government in South Africa today can be traced back, directly, to the scandalous arms deal which was imposed on the country in 1999 against the informed advice of the government's own experts. Ignoring most of the country's needs for job creation, the alleviation of poverty, addressing the skills shortage, priority was given to an exorbitant military enterprise which the country hardly needed and could certainly not afford – mainly because of the personal gain involved for ANC participants. Few members of government, from the top down, remained untainted by the corruption this raft of deals brought in its wake. Skilled and trustworthy minds in the legal and related fields, who were brought in to investigate the contracts and their consequences, were summarily dismissed when they came too close to the smells emanating from the smouldering centre, and lackeys were appointed who were sure not to rock the boat. It is sickening to discover, over and over again, how cabinet members and most of those in the concentric circles of power surrounding them, have been implicated in the deals for personal gain – and the increasing arrogance with which critics are dealt with. The entire process of choosing a successor to Mbeki has been stained by this unedifying spectacle as well – and it promises to get worse. The way in which the likely new president, Jacob Zuma, has been chosen reflects lamentably on all notions of democracy, morality and dignity. Zuma's supporters – particularly within the ANC Youth League – have shown little or no regard for the most basic forms of decency and respect. Sheer hooliganism has taken over, and democracy has become confused with demagoguery and populism.

Many, many misgivings about the 'state of the nation' can be aired, supported by the continuing brain drain, particularly among the youth, that afflicts the country and the lack of really adequate investment from abroad, and above all by the appalling statistics on crime in the country – however slyly these are doctored or however creatively they are interpreted by the Ministry of Safety and Security or the Bureau of Statistics.

In spite of the indignation I have been feeling over many years, I have tried, almost desperately, to give the ANC the benefit of the doubt. I have pointed at Russia and other countries in comparable situations, where liberation has been followed by waves of crime, corruption and inefficiency. And I still believe that in any country that undergoes the kind of massive and radical transformation we have been experiencing, it would be unrealistic *not* to expect some measure of turbulence of a socio-economic, psychological or cultural kind. But such arguments can become a reflex to bolster a comfort zone. Democracy in South Africa has now been in sway for well over a decade. Which – yes! – is a fleeting second in the history of a nation. And surely, as I have been arguing for a long time, if one stands back to survey the overall scene, and to compare where we are now with where we were less than two decades ago, only a fool can ignore the distance we have already travelled since that unforgettable day in February, 1990 when Nelson Mandela walked free from the Victor Verster prison. But this does not mean that *everything* can be condoned, or excused. One can get so used to making excuses that it becomes second nature. And of course it is always easier to pretend that the world is a better place than it is, because this may lessen the need for intervention or involvement. After all the years of apartheid, when I tried to remain committed to the urgencies of active opposition, it was almost a luxury to turn to 'other issues', to the many stories one had to leave unwritten during that age of darkness because there had always been more urgent tales to tell.

But one does reach a limit: where to remain silent becomes a culpable act. My time of silence is over. For me, the turning point came on a day in late June 2006.

After we'd attended a function at the French ambassador's *résidence* to welcome the visiting French rugby team – the then ambassador and I shared a passion for the game – my daughter Sonja and her husband Graham went to a restaurant in a quiet part of Somerset West for a late-night meal. They were ready to leave when five masked men came in and forced the patrons at gunpoint to hand over all their valuables. Anybody who resisted or protested, was manhandled; after the intruders had collected their loot, they moved from table to table assaulting all the women and the more vulnerable-looking men, before they were all herded into a small storeroom in the backyard. There, one of the captives took out his cellphone which he'd hidden in his shoe, and proceeded to call the police. But these guardians of the peace were otherwise occupied. The caller had to dial several more times and wait to be placed on hold every time before the call was passed on from one uninterested officer to another. It took a long time before there was any active response. In the end the police arrived together with employees of a security firm.

Nobody was killed. Nobody was raped. Which means that the incident was treated with such low priority that it received no more attention than a few lines on an inside page of a local newspaper. And why not? They were, as someone remarked, lucky to be alive. And that was what really enraged me. As if being alive should be deemed exceptional, not something that should in any way be regarded as 'normal'. The incident sank without trace amid the thousands of comparable, and much worse, crimes committed in South Africa every day, every night. Over 19,000 murders and 20,000 attempted murders in the past year. 52,600 rapes. Almost 14,000 hijackings. 127,000 cases of robbery with aggravating circumstances.

There was something worse than just the fact of the violent crime that outraged me, and that is the attitude of the authorities. At about the same time of the attack on the restaurant, the minister of safety and security, Charles Nqakula, launched a scathing attack on 'whingeing whites' who habitually complain about violence, and urged them to pack their bags and leave the country. Mr Nqakula, whose safety from criminal attack is presumably assured, perhaps by personal bodyguards provided by a private security agency, seems oblivious of the fact that many more black South Africans than whites are victims of violence in the country, and that calls for help from the black townships habitually go unheeded.

After having protested for a decade against the rising crime wave in the country, this attack was, for me, the last straw. Instead of broaching it, as I had done previously, in personal conversations with people in key positions, this time I turned to the media and aired my anger in newspapers and television programmes in many countries. The reaction of the South African authorities was illuminating. Instead of attacking me, or responding publicly, they appeared to have decided to 'buy' my loyalty by offering me awards – the Order of Ikhamanga (Silver) by the president, a Literary Lifetime Achievement Award by the Department of Arts and Culture. What made the latter particularly touching was that it bore the inscription: *Awarded posthumously*. Which I found at least as amusing as Mark Twain did the premature announcement of his death in the press.

But if the government hoped in this way to draw a curtain of silence over me, it has certainly had the opposite effect. I am firmly resolved not to stop giving them hell. Even from beyond the grave. In the changed circumstances of the New South Africa the ANC is playing exactly the same role as the Nationalist government under apartheid. What their actions over the past decade have in fact demonstrated is that apartheid as such was never the enemy of writers, artists and humanitarians: apartheid was only the mask worn, at a particular time and in a particular place, by the real enemy of whoever espouses the values of Albert Camus: freedom, justice, truth. And now that the ANC has moved into power, its regime sadly must be branded as the enemy of the people.

The crime tsunami is not an isolated phenomenon. Linked to the staggering refusal of the government to get involved in the tragic situation in Zimbabwe and its criminal denial of the full implications of the Aids pandemic it has become implicated in the death of thousands, if not millions.

For a considerable time after the political transition in South Africa I tried to comfort myself, and others in the same situation, with the argument that the many things that were going wrong in the country were just on the surface of a deep, unwavering stream that, down below, continued to run in the right direction. I am now tempted more and more to believe that the perpetrators of injustice in the country are not exceptions any longer. At the moment of writing this, there are judges of the Supreme Court under investigation for racism, for receiving hundreds of thousands of rands in private payments for 'services rendered', for drunken driving and malicious damage to property, for refusing to pay maintenance for a child after DNA tests have proved 'a 99.9 per cent probability that the judge in question is the father'. But unless it can be proved one hundred per cent, he argues, he cannot be held responsible.

A highly respected ex-judge of the Court of Appeal and the Constitutional Court, Johann Kriegler, who also has impeccable credentials from the Struggle era, was driven to attack the judge president of the Cape, John Hlope, as 'not a fit and proper person to be a judge. His retention of office constitutes a threat to the dignity and public acceptance of the integrity of the courts . . . By his greed he has betrayed us.'

It is revealing that black members of the legal fraternity declined to comment, arguing, most significantly, that 'it would be easier to discuss Hlope's conduct were he not black.' The refusal of the Black Lawyers' Association to join other law groups in the country in condemning the immoral behaviour of Chief Justice Hlope exacerbated the tensions between black and white. In this way the immemorial racial tension in South Africa continues to paralyse open democratic debate.

There is a growing suspicion in the country that the president is resorting to using state institutions to settle personal scores, to smother his critics and protect his allies. An atmosphere of uncertainty and suspicion has replaced the earlier optimism. And signs of malfunctioning proliferate. The country's chief of police is himself suspected of dealings with organised crime. Cabinet ministers, even the deputy president of the country, have been denounced for going abroad on shopping trips funded by taxpayers. Members of parliament have been found guilty of profiting from travel scams involving public funds. And when found out, especially if they are friends and/or supporters of the president, they are readily let off the hook. This can no longer be a matter of 'a few bad apples': such people have become the symptoms of an entire regime that has lost its way. And it is an open question for how much longer it can be expected to attract international investments. Or to organise a Soccer World Cup in 2010.

It may be argued that the *fact* of such malpractices still being investigated, and that a free press is openly reporting on them, is in itself proof that all is not yet lost. At the same time one should not – once again – be deluded by false optimism, as I have been for so long. South Africa *is* in a mess. And the old divisions between Black and White are still at the core of it. This was brought home quite sickeningly by an incident at the University of the Free State that came to light only recently, in February 2008. It concerned an 'initiation ceremony' arranged at the Reitz Residence on campus by white male students who made black cleaners, some of them elderly, eat a bowl of what seemed like dog food on which one of the students had urinated. Perhaps worse than the revolting event itself was the fact that the perpetrators subsequently attempted to shrug it off as 'a harmless student prank' – and that they were vociferously supported by parents and sympathisers. It is true that such practices have persisted among white students at several Afrikaans universities until recently and that there are indications that such 'traditions' may still survive clandestinely at some of them. But the overt racial context of this event, and the fact that it followed months of campaigning by a political party from the extreme right, the Freedom

Front Plus, against attempts by the university to open residences to all races, suggest that blatant racism still plays an active role in the country. It would seem that only a small minority of retrograde whites still cling to such expressions of a troglodyte past; but the support they continue to enjoy from their parents and a much wider community is both nauseating and very, very disturbing.

What is particularly depressing is the explanation of good intentions offered in all naïvety by the young R. C. Malherbe, the self-styled 'urinist'. The video had been made purely for entertainment, with no intention to humiliate anybody: 'It had to be somehing that the guys would find funny.' It is the measure of some people's 'fun' that is so appalling. And then the well-meaning prankster proceeds to place the event in the context of what he regards as good relations and cameraderie: 'We come from farms, so it's easy for us to bring meat and mealies, especially when we go on holiday. Everything that's left over, we give to them. It's a good relationship. Rather friendly.'

Everything that's left over, we give to them. This, it seems, is what 'a good relationship' between white and black in South Africa is still based on. After fourteen years of democracy.

The only heartening aspect of the whole sorry event is the near-unanimous outrage and condemnation with which it was received by South Africans of all races, all groupings, all ages.

And then the other side of the coin: one expected black students on the campus to react with rage and fury and protest. That at least a modicum of violence occurred in the protest marches and demonstrations was perhaps inevitable. What I cannot accept is that a group of black students marched to a residence for white female students and threatened them that they would all be raped in retaliation. Yes, it was done in the heat of the moment. But this goes beyond rage and revenge. This digs down into a level of barbarism that simmers on the other side of silence. Perhaps it is part of that *excess* of violence that has always marked black/white relations throughout the dark years of colonialism. But are we really still trapped in that stifling spiral? Are we still not able – even after Mandela, after all the suffering that has characterised our slow movement towards a new dispensation – to arrive at a level of human reason and tolerance? Rape. That is not just vengeance. That is an act which denies the basis on which humanity rests. We still have so very far to go.

As a country, it seems, we have come close to betraying the ideals of Mandela and of Tutu. And yet there may still be individuals and organisations in South Africa that care enough to get involved in order to ensure that something can be salvaged before the rot has gone too far. The response in the country to winning the latest Rugby World Cup revealed emphatically the potential for unity among the races and classes – but at the moment this huge potential is not allowed to develop naturally.

It may seem as if there is not much a writer – a mere writer – can do against the sordidness and the evil of the world. Yet writers have prevailed in the past, as that conference in Salzburg, and the legacy of writers over the centuries, have demonstrated. The word is an insignificant thing in itself, a little gasp of breath, no more. Yet it is in and through the word that we first reach awareness of our humanity. And as long as we have the word, we can reach out to others in a chain of voices that will never be silenced. That is our one, small, lasting guarantee in the world, and against the world.

As long as that is possible, I cannot, and will not, be silent. And for as long as there are forks in the road I shall be happy to join the heretic Don Quixote and take them.

POSTSCRIPT:
A LETTER TO KARINA

MY DEAREST KARINA,

This letter comes near the end, but it really concerns a beginning – the beginning of this memoir. It started with a train journey in December 2004, when you came to meet me at the airport in Vienna and escorted me to Salzburg for the conference on South African literature which you had helped to organise. By now that initial journey has grown out of all proportion, continuing in many different directions. And that is why what I have been writing here is taking this form.

I have persistently refused to yield to publishers and friends and strangers who asked me, over the years, to write an autobiography. I have always felt uncomfortable with the artificiality and the self-centredness of such a project. Besides, my life has been shaped by so many people who have shared parts of my itinerary, whose confidence I cannot betray. Their trust, or simply the privacy of those travels, sometimes short and simple, more often long and convoluted, should remain private. On the simplest level, I am not interested in kissing-and-telling. But it goes far beyond that.

I remember how, in the course of an exuberant night on the Danish island of Møn, a year before Günter Grass published *Beim Häuten der Zwiebel*, he regaled us with stories from his life and I pleaded with him to write his autobiography. 'Never!' he exclaimed through a cloud of pipe smoke. 'That is something I shall never do. I lie too much.' Fortunately for us, he relented and afterwards shared his magnificent stories with us after all. And taking a cue from René Magritte, I can now confirm: *This is not an autobiography.*

The endless conversation which began on that train between Vienna and Salzburg, and still continues, has made me acknowledge a need in myself to account for some things in my life I have not yet faced or probed sufficiently; many things I still do not understand; many things that have hurt or surprised me or given me joy and pleasure, and for which I have simply never had, or made, the time to explore, or even properly to savour. It has brought home very forcefully the awareness of the long and many journeys each of us had travelled *before* that meeting: journeys from and across different hemispheres, different time zones, different cultures and peoples, different mental spaces, different understandings of the world, and its past and present and possible futures. All of this has grown between us – like a drop of water in a tap, that grows and grows until it has acquired the weight it needs to fall – and has taken shape in the many letters we exchanged at the beginning of our relationship, and now in this book.

That first journey you and I took together was never even supposed to happen. It came at the end of an exceptionally busy year, filled with more travelling than I could really cope with. There was Mali in February, followed by Guadeloupe and Martinique in April and May, then Paris, in itself a return to origins. There was Glasgow in June, to celebrate South Africa's first ten years of democracy, a strange occasion haunted by elderly people from an anti-apartheid struggle already almost lost in history. There was the paradisiac island of Møn off the south-east coast of Denmark in August, in a small castle in a forest at the edge of a lake. There was, again, Scotland and England in October, wending my way down from Edinburgh, past Norwich and Cheltenham to London, with festivals and celebrations and lectures and discussions.

And so I was exhausted by December. But I had already accepted an invitation to Salzburg, for a joint conference on South African literature organised by the university and the seminar housed in Schloss Leopoldskron. I could hardly think straight by then. But Salzburg had already become a special place, a region of the mind, a *state* of mind. There had always been Mozart; then there was that conference following the fall of the Berlin Wall; and after that there had been the other visits to the schloss, most notably in 1998, that conference on drama with Arthur Miller, Ariel Dorfman and others. So how could I *not* accept the invitation to this conference in December 2004?

The obstacle to overcome was not only tiredness but the fact that the arrangements for travelling to Salzburg and back were mired in bungling and misunderstanding. At one stage I gave up and asked my hosts to cancel the trip, but the arrangements were too far advanced, and so I went. The only pinpoint of light in the whole murky business was when Dorothea Steiner of the Salzburg University, indefatigable in her efforts to salvage something out of the mess, assured me that someone on the organising committee had volunteered to meet me in Vienna to ease the last part of the way to Salzburg.

And when I stumbled out of the plane at Vienna airport, there you were, Karina, tall and beautiful and confidently smiling, your long dark hair in a thick braid behind your head, waiting.

'Now you can relax,' you said. 'You can sleep on the train if you want to. I'll get you to Salzburg safely.'

And you did.

On the way we tumbled headlong into that breathless conversation which has still not, as I'm writing this letter, subsided or paused.

There was a feeling, by the time you dropped me at the schloss in Salzburg, that something, somewhere, had shifted. There is a passage from the Black Panther Eldridge Cleaver's *Soul on Ice* (in the first edition, from the sixties; afterwards it was, sadly, omitted), which has returned to me at crucial moments in my life and which, every time, has marked a fork in the road. It comes from a letter written to Cleaver while he was in prison, by the lawyer who defended him, Beverley. For them the situation was impossible: he black, she white, at a time of racial madness in America. But they succeeded in transcending it.

Beverley writes:

What an awesome thing it is to feel oneself on the verge of the possibility of really knowing another person. Can it ever happen? I'm not
sure. I don't know that any two people can really strip themselves that
naked in front of each other. We're so filled with fears of rejection and
pretences that we scarcely know whether we're being fraudulent or real
ourselves.

To this he replies:

I seek a lasting relationship, something permanent in a world of change,
in which all is transitory, ephemeral, and full of pain. We humans, we
are too frail creatures to handle such titanic emotions and deep
magnetic yearnings, strivings and impulses.

The reason two people are reluctant to really strip themselves naked
in front of each other is because in doing so they make themselves
vulnerable and give enormous power over themselves to one another.
How awful, how deadly, how catastrophically they can hurt each other,
wreck and ruin each other forever! How often, indeed, they end by
inflicting pain and torment upon each other. Better to maintain
shallow, superficial affairs; that way the scars are not too deep, no
blood is hacked from the soul. You beautifully – O, how beautifully!!
– spoke, in your letter, of 'What an awesome thing it is to feel oneself
on the verge of the possibility of really knowing another person' and
'I feel as though I am on the edge of a new world.' Getting to know
someone, entering that new world, is an ultimate, irretrievable leap
into the unknown. The prospect is terrifying. The stakes are high. The
emotions are overwhelming. In human experience, only the perennial themes can move us to such an extent. Death. Birth. The Grave.
Love. Hate (. . .)

Then follows the passage I later used as a motto for *An Instant in the Wind*:

We live in a disoriented, deranged social structure, and we have transcended its barriers in our own ways and have stepped psychologically

435

outside its madness and repressions. It is lonely out here. We recognise each other. And, having recognised each other, is it any wonder that our souls hold hands and cling together even while our minds equivocate, hesitate, vacillate, and tremble?

For the moment, we did not, could not, acknowledge it. But the awareness was there. Even though we carefully, very carefully, managed to hide it even to ourselves, as the conference started and wore on, and we played our appointed roles: you, one of the organisers and facilitators, I one of the invited writers and critics. I remember how impressed I was by the paper you read on Nadine Gordimer: the lucidity of your thoughts, the depth of your understanding, the structured unfolding of your argument.

There was only one occasion when we came close to breaking through the barriers: I was exhausted at the end of one session and asked to be taken back to the schloss. You took my arm, and led me from the conference hall, around the cathedral, to a taxi rank from where I could make my escape. I thanked you, and gave you my hand. And then we both held on, and could not let go. As if that clasp was a lifeline.

But of course, in the end we did let go and you returned to the conference while I wended my way to the merciful asylum of the schloss.

Then came the final session. It was a long evening. But everybody had a feeling of satisfaction, even of elation, after a spell of impromptu readings recorded for the English Department by your brother Krystian. There was no way of prolonging it any more. I began to take my leave of the last departing visitors. Very formally and correctly I kissed each woman on both cheeks. Saving you for last. Left cheek, right cheek. And then I dragged myself upstairs, along that endless broad spiral.

When I finally drew the door to my suite shut behind me, I leaned back against it, reluctant to admit that I was alone again. After a while I turned back and grasped the handle. The urge was almost overwhelming to open the door, to go downstairs again. Perhaps you would still be there. But I did not. Leaning with my forehead against the cold painted wood of the door, I could not move. Only then did the thought – not even a thought, a mere intimation – rise to the surface that I might be turning my back on something that could have been vital to my life, could have changed the course of things. But still I made no move.

Only much later, you wrote to me about how, while I was standing pressed against the door from the inside, you were waiting downstairs, battling the urge to come up and knock on my door, without any idea of what you might say if I actually opened. Like me, you couldn't move. Like me, you didn't dare think about what *might* have happened.

I responded to your e-mail. You wrote again. Everything that had remained unsaid before – everything we might have sensed but had so scrupulously repressed – came tumbling out. Not long after that, we met again in Paris, where I had to lecture at the Sorbonne and the Bibliothèque Nationale. And then again in Egham outside London, and in Wales. Soon afterwards you came to Cape Town for my birthday. In due course we travelled together to your village of Geretsdorf in Austria and you introduced me to your parents, Roma and Jacek, who are now my parents too. Which is a delightful if most unusual situation, as I now happen to be older than both of my in-laws; and you are younger than all four of my children.

Today you are my wife. And still the journey continues. We have been to Scandinavia, on a boat trip along the fjords of Norway all the way to Kirkenes, and to Switzerland and France and Germany, and of course many times to Austria, and to Bosnia-Herzegovina, and to Croatia, and to Mexico, and you have taken me to Poland to show me all the places that had circumscribed your youth: the lovely Jelenia Góra, where you were born, and Kowary, near by, where your grandparents used to live and where your aunt Iwona now keeps the family hearth burning, where you visited in your childhood and where you played in the forest and made little houses under the trees and lived in a magic land beyond the reach of grown-ups; and Wroclaw with the reflections of its many-coloured houses in the river; and of course the beautiful city of Kraków where Copernicus sat in the carved wooden seats of the ancient university, and where horse-carriages ply the route between the town square and the castle with its battlements on the high hill and the cathedral with the huge bronze bell in its tall steeple, and the synagogue with its graves under leaves that never stop falling.

This is why what I am writing now – about the long road that lies behind, and all its many forks – is a mere continuation of what has gone before. To trace again some of the many highways and byways of the past. Perhaps to learn to see more clearly, to understand a bit more. But by no means everything.

There is so much more I could have written, and might have wished to write. But there is a certain sense of propriety in deciding where and when to stop.

So these notes are not answers. Attempts, at most. To explain some things, but not simply to settle scores. Perhaps a way of saying thank you. To so many people – women, men, children, lovers, friends, acquaintances – whom I have met along the way, exchanging a look or a mere glance, clasping a hand, touching a shoulder, sharing a gesture of encouragement, or a caress, or days, or nights: not all, but at least some of those who, for better or for worse, have made me what I am, and helped to bring me here. My father, and my mother. My children. My brother and my sisters. Music. Painting. The many beauties and joys of the world. The world itself, for offering us the space to be, and some time to do so.

And, above all, Karina, you, for bringing a roundness and a happiness and a meaning to it all.

With love,
André